Applications of Machine Learning and Artificial Intelligence in Modern Power and Energy Systems

Applications of Machine Learning and Artificial Intelligence in Modern Power and Energy Systems

Guest Editors

Valeri Mladenov
Panagiotis Sarigiannidis

Basel • Beijing • Wuhan • Barcelona • Belgrade • Novi Sad • Cluj • Manchester

Guest Editors
Valeri Mladenov
Department of Fundamentals of Electrical Engineering
Technical University of Sofia
Sofia
Bulgaria

Panagiotis Sarigiannidis
Department of Electrical and Computer Engineering
University of Western Macedonia
Kozani
Greece

Editorial Office
MDPI AG
Grosspeteranlage 5
4052 Basel, Switzerland

This is a reprint of the Special Issue, published open access by the journal *Electronics* (ISSN 2079-9292), freely accessible at: https://www.mdpi.com/journal/electronics/special_issues/90FO13KC60.

For citation purposes, cite each article independently as indicated on the article page online and as indicated below:

Lastname, A.A.; Lastname, B.B. Article Title. *Journal Name* **Year**, *Volume Number*, Page Range.

ISBN 978-3-7258-7182-7 (Hbk)
ISBN 978-3-7258-7183-4 (PDF)
https://doi.org/10.3390/books978-3-7258-7183-4

Contents

Preface

This Special Issue of *Electronics* on "Applications of Machine Learning and Artificial Intelligence in Modern Power and Energy Systems" addresses the intersection of electrical engineering and digital intelligence. Its scope spans eleven peer-reviewed works covering physics-based simulations, explainable AI, and proactive maintenance, as well as high-voltage diagnostics, renewable forecasting, and grid stability. The overarching goal is to provide a robust framework that helps improve energy reliability through hybrid modeling.

Motivated by the urgent need to ensure grid resilience, this collection is addressed to researchers, system operators, and engineers, seeking to bridge the gap between theoretical data science and practical infrastructure. By utilizing artificial intelligence and machine learning techniques, the contributions herein offer the technical insights necessary to meet the sustainability challenges of the evolving energy landscape.

Valeri Mladenov and Panagiotis Sarigiannidis
Guest Editors

electronics

MDPI

Editorial

Applications of Machine Learning and Artificial Intelligence in Modern Power and Energy Systems

Valeri Mladenov [1,*] and Panagiotis Sarigiannidis [2,3]

1 Neurocomputing Laboratory, Department of Fundamentals of Electrical Engineering, Technical University of Sofia, 8 Kliment Ohridski Blvd., 1000 Sofia, Bulgaria
2 Department of Electrical and Computer Engineering, University of Western Macedonia, 50100 Kozani, Greece; psarigiannidis@uowm.gr
3 R&D Department, MetaMind Innovations P.C., 50100 Kozani, Greece
* Correspondence: valerim@tu-sofia.bg

1. Introduction

The digital transformation of the energy sector has intensified the demand for intelligent, data-driven, and computationally efficient techniques to bolster the reliability, safety, and adaptability of modern electrical infrastructures. This Special Issue, entitled "Applications of Machine Learning and Artificial Intelligence in Modern Power and Energy Systems", presents a peer-reviewed collection of 11 high-quality papers. These developments cover the entire spectrum of modern energy—from physically based simulations and diagnostics of high-voltage systems to advanced machine learning for predicting the load and stability of the power grid. Collectively, the papers reflect an evolving research landscape where hybrid modeling, explainable AI (XAI), and proactive maintenance are becoming central to next-generation intelligent power systems.

2. Physics-Based and Hybrid Modeling

Contribution 1 investigated the data-driven dynamic behavior of SF_6 HVDC-GIS conical solid insulators. Using COMSOL Multiphysics 6.2 simulations, the authors analyzed ion-pair generation and dielectric performance under specific radioactive conditions, providing a robust framework for assessing insulation reliability.

Contribution 2 evaluated the impact of voltage-source converters (VSCs) on power systems by developing a refined P–Q capability curve. The work offers vital insights for renewable-integrated grid planning by accounting for the iterative nature of converter–grid interactions.

3. AI for State Estimation and Load Forecasting

Contribution 3 proposed an interpretable state estimation framework based on Kolmogorov–Arnold Networks (KANs), enhancing the transparency and accuracy of grid stability assessments compared with traditional neural network architectures.

Contribution 4 introduced a novel multi-scale wind power prediction model that accounts for temporal dependencies and cross-scale variable relationships, significantly reducing uncertainty in wind energy integration.

Contribution 5 examined the advancements in household load forecasting through a deep learning model optimized with meta-heuristic hyperparameter tuning, demonstrating robust performance across diverse energy consumption profiles.

4. Equipment Diagnostics and Proactive Maintenance

Contribution 6 developed an innovative methodology for the proactive maintenance of distribution transformers. By utilizing machine learning algorithms for predictive classification, the study identified transformers vulnerable to failure, enabling system operators to shift from reactive to cost-effective proactive maintenance strategies.

Contribution 7 proposed an LSTM-driven HVDC fault diagnosis framework enhanced with knowledge graphs. This hybrid approach leverages both historical data and domain-specific knowledge to increase the accuracy and explainability of fault localization.

Contribution 8 contributed to predictive maintenance by developing a deep convolutional neural network (CNN) for the automated detection and classification of rolling bearing defects in electrical machinery.

Contribution 9 explored fuel-consumption prediction models for electrified transportation, incorporating dynamic parameters such as vehicular "jerk" to achieve higher predictive fidelity.

5. Digital Twins and Reinforcement Learning

Contribution 10 improved parameter extraction in 3D grid information models (GIMs) using an enhanced CNN architecture, streamlining the creation of automated digital twins for power system analysis.

Contribution 11 conducted a comprehensive review of reinforcement learning (RL) applications in energy systems. Their survey covers the state of the art in optimization, control, and operational decision-making for both renewable and conventional resources.

6. Conclusions

This Special Issue highlights the transformative role of data mining techniques and computational intelligence in modern energy systems. The collected materials demonstrate the maturity of hybrid modeling approaches based on physics and machine learning, along with significant advances in renewable energy production forecasting and electricity load prediction. At the same time, the studies highlight the growing importance of the interpretability, reliability, and system-level integration of models, which are essential for the practical implementation of smart solutions in real-world energy systems.

Furthermore, the increasing adoption of predictive maintenance strategies and digital twin concepts illustrates the shift towards proactive asset management and increased grid resilience. The wider adoption of reinforcement learning methods for energy optimization further highlights the potential of smart control and decision-making frameworks in addressing the complexity of future energy infrastructures. Overall, the papers in this Special Issue point to a future characterized by smart, adaptive, and sustainable electrical systems capable of meeting the technical, economic, and sustainability challenges of the evolving energy landscape.

Funding: This research received no external funding.

Acknowledgments: The Guest Editors thank all contributing authors for their high-quality submissions and the reviewers for their expert evaluations. Appreciation is also extended to the *Electronics* Editorial Office for their professional support throughout the editorial and production processes.

Conflicts of Interest: Author Panagiotis Sarigiannidis was employed by the company R&D Department, MetaMind Innovations P.C. The remaining authors declare that the research was conducted in the absence of any commercial or financial relationships that could be construed as a potential conflict of interest.

https://doi.org/10.3390/electronics15051045

List of Contributions:

1. Urazaki Junior, K.; Lucchini, F.; Marconato, N. Data-Driven Dynamics Learning on Time Simulation of SF_6 HVDC-GIS Conical Solid Insulators. *Electronics* **2025**, *14*, 616. https://doi.org/10.3390/electronics14030616.
2. Brodzicki, M.; Kluczník, J.; Czapp, S. Evaluation of VSC Impact on Power System Using Adequate P-Q Capability Curve. *Electronics* **2023**, *12*, 2462. https://doi.org/10.3390/electronics12112462.
3. Wang, S.; Luo, W.; Yin, S.; Zhang, J.; Liang, Z.; Zhu, Y.; Li, S. Interpretable State Estimation in Power Systems Based on the Kolmogorov–Arnold Networks. *Electronics* **2025**, *14*, 320. https://doi.org/10.3390/electronics14020320.
4. Xu, Z.; Zhao, H.; Xu, C.; Shi, H.; Xu, J.; Wang, Z. A Novel Wind Power Prediction Model That Considers Multi-Scale Variable Relationships and Temporal Dependencies. *Electronics* **2024**, *13*, 3710. https://doi.org/10.3390/electronics13183710.
5. Al-Jamimi, H.A.; BinMakhashen, G.M.; Worku, M.Y.; Hassan, M.A. Advancements in Household Load Forecasting: Deep Learning Model with Hyperparameter Optimization. *Electronics* **2023**, *12*, 4909. https://doi.org/10.3390/electronics12244909.
6. Vita, V.; Fotis, G.; Chobanov, V.; Pavlatos, C.; Mladenov, V. Predictive Maintenance for Distribution System Operators in Increasing Transformers' Reliability. *Electronics* **2023**, *12*, 1356. https://doi.org/10.3390/electronics12061356.
7. Chen, Q.; Wu, J.; Li, Q.; Gao, X.; Yu, R.; Guo, J.; Peng, G.; Yang, B. Long Short-Term Memory Network-Based HVDC Systems Fault Diagnosis under Knowledge Graph. *Electronics* **2023**, *12*, 2242. https://doi.org/10.3390/electronics12102242.
8. Skowron, M.; Frankiewicz, O.; Jarosz, J.J.; Wolkiewicz, M.; Dybkowski, M.; Weisse, S.; Valire, J.; Wyłomańska, A.; Zimroz, R.; Szabat, K. Detection and Classification of Rolling Bearing Defects Using Direct Signal Processing with Deep Convolutional Neural Network. *Electronics* **2024**, *13*, 1722. https://doi.org/10.3390/electronics13091722.
9. Zhang, L.; Ya, J.; Xu, Z.; Easa, S.; Peng, K.; Xing, Y.; Yang, R. Novel Neural-Network-Based Fuel Consumption Prediction Models Considering Vehicular Jerk. *Electronics* **2023**, *12*, 3638. https://doi.org/10.3390/electronics12173638.
10. Li, X.; Liu, X. Optimizing Parameter Extraction in Grid Information Models Based on Improved Convolutional Neural Networks. *Electronics* **2024**, *13*, 2717. https://doi.org/10.3390/electronics13142717.
11. Stavrev, S.; Ginchev, D. Reinforcement Learning Techniques in Optimizing Energy Systems. *Electronics* **2024**, *13*, 1459. https://doi.org/10.3390/electronics13081459.

https://doi.org/10.3390/electronics15051045

electronics

MDPI

Article

Data-Driven Dynamics Learning on Time Simulation of SF_6 HVDC-GIS Conical Solid Insulators

Kenji Urazaki Junior [1], Francesco Lucchini [1,2] and Nicolò Marconato [1,2,*]

[1] Department of Industrial Engineering, University of Padova, Via Gradenigo 6/A, 35131 Padova, Italy; kenji.urazakijunior@unipd.it (K.U.J.); francesco.lucchini@unipd.it (F.L.)

[2] Consorzio RFX (CNR, ENEA, INFN, Università di Padova, Acciaierie Venete SpA), Corso Stati Uniti 4, 35127 Padova, Italy

* Correspondence: nicolo.marconato@unipd.it

Abstract: An HVDC-GIL system with a conical spacer in a radioactive environment is studied in this work using simulated data on COMSOL® Multiphysics. Electromagnetic simulations on a 2D model were performed with varying ion-pair generation rates and potential applied to the system. This article explores machine learning methods to derive time to steady state, dark current, gas conductivity, and surface charge density expressions. The focus was on constructing symbolic representations, which could be interpretable and less prone to overfitting, using the symbolic regression (SR) and sparse identification of nonlinear dynamics (SINDy) algorithms. The study successfully derived the intended expressions, demonstrating the power of symbolic regression. Predictions of dark currents in the gas–ground electrode interface reported an absolute error and mean absolute percentage error (MAPE) of 1.04×10^{-4} pA and 0.01%, respectively. The solid–ground electrode interface reported an error of 8.99×10^{-5} pA and MAPE of 0.04%, showing strong agreement with simulation data. Expressions for time to steady state had a test error of approximately 110 h with MAPE of around 3%. Steady-state gas conductivity expression achieved an absolute error of 0.55 log(S/m) and MAPE of 1%. An interpretable equation was created with SINDy to model the time evolution of surface charge density, achieving a root mean squared error of 1.12 $nC/m^2/s$ across time-series data. These results demonstrate the capability of SR and SINDy to provide interpretable and computationally efficient alternatives to time-consuming numerical simulations of HVDC systems under radiation conditions. While the model provides useful insights, performance and practical applications of the expressions can improve with more diverse datasets, which might include experimental data in the future.

Keywords: HVDC; gas insulated transmission lines; solid-gas surface charging; SF_6; physics-informed machine learning; SINDy; SR

1. Introduction

High-voltage direct current (HVDC) gas-insulated lines (GILs) enable the transmission of power over long distances with high system stability, with advantages such as ecological aspect and economic benefits and are increasingly attractive due to the energy turnaround that requires the transport of energy in some cases for hundreds of kilometers [1,2].

Positive and negative ion pairs are responsible for the gas conductivity. Under normal circumstances, natural background radiation generates these ion pairs. SF_6 gas insulation systems have a big issue when operating in the presence of radiation, such as near a tokamak, which emits neutrons, X-rays, and gamma rays. Radiation increases the ion-pair generation of the gas by ionization and dissociation, consequently increasing the conductivity of the gas [3–6].

The increase in conductivity affects the system's electric field distribution and the insulators' surface charge accumulation, resulting in a modification of the time to a steady state and the breakdown voltage, for example. It gives rise to dark currents, i.e., leakage current through the insulating system flowing out of the ground electrode, which can cause power losses, heating, and breakdowns [6,7]. Therefore, the design and operation of HVDC-GIS systems must consider radiation-induced effects. In modeling and simulation, a source parameter denoted as S accounts for the ionization process, representing the volumetric rate of ion-pair generation [3].

Many scenarios of radiation fields are possible. For example, in the ITER Tokamak, there are two orders of magnitude uncertainties in the radiation to which the gas insulator will be subjected, from 0.02 Gy/s to 2 Gy/s [4]. A. De Lorenzi et al. (2009) [8] suggested that more detailed modeling of the RIC (Radiation Induced Conductivity) phenomenon is needed.

Besides the ionization of the gas, the main issue that affects HVDC-GIS systems is the accumulation of electric charges on the interface between the gas and solid insulators, which may lead to a decrease in the flashover voltage and breakdowns [1]. The dynamics of the surface charge accumulation is a critical factor in the design of the systems, and the enhanced SF_6 conductivity caused by radiation modifies the dynamics and increases the hetero-charge distribution in the insulator surface [8].

The investigations in this work use data-driven methods to learn the dynamics and relations in HVDC-GIS using SF_6 as gas insulation in different radiation conditions. The data were collected through simulations in COMSOL Multiphysics® using the electric currents and transport diffusion of diluted species physics, as described in [9]. Migration of charges in the solid insulator and gas models the surface charge accumulation; the models did not implement surface conductivity for simplicity but can be easily implemented.

The systems studied were at 500 kV DC, the operating voltage of the Neutral Beam Injector of the Divertor Tokamak Test (DTT) facility [3,10]. The parameters that varied in the simulations were the ion-pair generation rate and the potential applied.

The ML (machine learning) models were trained and validated with simulation data. The SR [11] and SINDy [12–15] algorithms were evaluated for learning the dynamics of surface charge and predicting time to steady state, conductivity, and dark current at steady state. The SR algorithm aimed to find the best functional form to predict the target variable, while the SINDy one sought to find the best sparse regression of the dynamics of the target variable. The present work employed both methods and evaluated the results.

Previous works in obtaining an analytical solution for the steady-state time for the system demonstrated that the expression computed fails when the conductivity of the gas is affected by radiation, i.e., the ion-pair generation parameter S is high. The difference between the analysis time and the time computed by the analytical expression was in one order of magnitude [8].

Building an analytical expression for the steady-state conditions aims to provide important information in advance without performing simulations. Further works can use dynamic models built with SINDy, such as optimizing the design of HVDC structures in RIC conditions. The optimization of electromagnetic problems is a very demanding task, as the computational cost is high and the function to be optimized is unknown [8]. Simulation and optimization using surrogate models built with ML, such as the surface charge density dynamics, can reduce the time needed to obtain a feasible solution.

Data-driven strategies for modeling physical and engineering systems have often proven successful. Machine learning and artificial intelligence can tackle complex, large datasets that normally appear in engineering and physical problems, as it is the case of the system evaluated in this work. The data-driven framework can help discover missing physics [16], improve control [17], find reduced models [18,19], and model discrepancies between the real systems and simulation results that use first-principle laws [16].

A practical example of how analytical expressions might accelerate simulations in HVDC RIC systems was presented in the paper [9]. The authors demonstrated the feasibility of simplifying the drift diffusion reaction (DDR) equations of ions in the gas using a conductivity analytical expression. The analytical expression is a compromise between the most detailed simulation using DDR equations and the simplest one using a constant gas conductivity, which does not work when RIC conditions occur in the system.

Although many works on HVDC using machine learning exist, they mainly focus on monitoring [20], control [21,22], partial discharges [23–25], and fault detection and prediction [26–29] in the systems. One previous work in the literature involves directly predicting the flashover voltage of an AC gas-insulated system, but it uses experimental data for learning [30]. New forms of applying machine learning to the HVDC-GIL system, such as the present work, might bring new paths for optimizations using surrogate models, fast assessments with analytical expressions, and learning and understanding more of the systems with the derived interpretable representations, especially in high-radiation environments.

The main contributions of this work are summarized as follows:

- Symbolic expressions for key variables: Developed interpretable symbolic models for dark currents, gas conductivity, and time to steady state using symbolic regression.
- Symbolic dynamic expression: Applied SINDy to derive a sparse surface charge density model, resulting in an interpretable expression that models a complicated phenomenon evolution in time.
- Method's applicability: Demonstrated how machine learning-derived models can be obtained from simulated data, showcasing their capability in high-complexity HVDC systems. Extensions for experimental data are trivial.

2. Electromagnetic Modeling

This section recalls the approach for electromagnetic (EM) modeling of HVDC gas-insulated equipment, such as HVDC-GIS and HVDC-GIL. The capacitive to the resistive transition of the electric field following the application of DC voltage is described by the electro-quasistatic (EQS) approximation of Maxwell equations. Particularly, during the time evolution, the surface charge density ϱ_s accumulates along the interface between dielectric gas and solid insulator according to the law [31]:

$$\frac{d\varrho_s}{dt} = \hat{\mathbf{n}} \cdot (\mathbf{J}_i - \mathbf{J}_g) - \nabla \cdot (\sigma_s E_t), \tag{1}$$

where $\hat{\mathbf{n}}$ is the normal vector pointing out from the solid insulator, $\mathbf{J}_i$ and $\mathbf{J}_g$ the current densities within the insulator and the gas, σ_s is the interface electric conductivity, and E_t the electric field tangent to the interface. It is well recognized that the accumulation of ϱ_s is related to the main fault phenomena within HVDC gas-insulated systems [32].

A complete description of the electric field in the dielectric gas ($\mathbf{E}_G$) requires the solution of a self-consistent model, described by the following set of Partial Differential Equations (PDEs) [1,33]:

$$\frac{\partial n^+}{\partial t} = S - Rn^+n^- - \nabla \cdot (n^+\mu^+\mathbf{E}_G) + D^+\Delta n^+ \quad (2)$$

$$\frac{\partial n^-}{\partial t} = S - Rn^+n^- + \nabla \cdot (n^-\mu^-\mathbf{E}_G) + D^-\Delta n^- \quad (3)$$

$$\nabla \cdot \mathbf{E}_G = \frac{e(n^+ - n^-)}{\varepsilon_G}. \quad (4)$$

Equations (2) and (3) describe the generation, drift, diffusion, and recombination of positive (n^+) and negative (n^-) ion number densities through a set of transport parameters: the mobility (μ), diffusion coefficient (D), and the recombination ratio R. The source of ion pairs is driven by the parameter S, e is the elementary charge and ε_G is the permittivity of the gas. A detailed description of the boundary and initial conditions for the solution of the model, as well as the coupling with the model for the conduction in the solid insulator, is out of the scope of the paper; however, the interested reader can find details, e.g., in [34,35].

Combining Equations (2) and (3), the expression of the current density in the gas $\mathbf{J}_G$ is inferred:

$$\mathbf{J}_G = e[\mathbf{E}_G(\mu^+n^+ + \mu^-n^-) - \nabla(D^+n^+ - D^-n^-)]. \quad (5)$$

3. Machine Learning Methods

This section briefly describes the machine learning methods. Sparse Identification of Nonlinear Dynamics and symbolic regression search for a symbolic representation to fit the target variable. This learning process uses data that might be generated by simulations or collected in experiments and operations. This work uses only simulated data from a physical model. The methods permit the search for parsimonious models, either by promoting the sparseness of the fitted coefficients or evaluating the expression's complexity. The learning tasks are supervised, i.e., the target is known and provided to the algorithm. The model space comprises analytic expressions that use predictive variables collected or generated simultaneously with the target.

3.1. SINDy

The SINDy (Sparse Identification of Nonlinear Dynamics) used in this work was proposed by [13] to find the governing equations from measurement data of nonlinear dynamical systems. The method uses machine learning and promotes the sparsity of the parameters, determining the fewest terms sufficient to describe the observed data accurately. It might be classified as a symbolic regression method, focusing on fitting polynomial expressions to describe derivative data, as presented in Equation (6), assuming that only a few terms are essential for the regression to build low-order models that tend to generalize and avoid overfitting [14,36].

Later, robust dynamics learning with rational polynomial candidates was proposed and developed by [36], increasing the robustness of the algorithm to noise, and constrained SINDy was proposed and developed by [14], which enables the constrain on the coefficients given a prior knowledge, for example, from physics. The SINDy method was successfully applied for fluid dynamics combined with model order reduction (POD) [14], complex mechanical problems [13,36], and reaction kinetics [36]. The identified models are parsimonious, accurately equilibrating complexity, and remain interpretable as a symbolic representation [14].

$$\frac{d}{dt}\mathbf{x}(t) = \mathbf{f}(\mathbf{x}(t)). \quad (6)$$

The sparsity-promoting characteristics of the method make it a good algorithm for finding simplified or reduced models of apparently complicated/complex systems [13,14].

Equation (7) presents the general regression of the nonlinear dynamical system, and an example of a sparse, regularized, regression problem to find Ξ, using LASSO, is presented in Equation (8) [13].

$$\dot{X} = \Theta(X)\Xi, \tag{7}$$

where $\Theta \in \mathbb{R}^{m\times p}$ represents the feature library, which is the candidate functions to describe the evolution in time of the system; $X \in \mathbb{R}^{m\times n}$ is the matrix with the row vector of state $x(t) \in \mathbb{R}^n$ at each $t = [t_1, t_2, \ldots, t_m]$; $\Xi = [\xi_1\ \xi_2\ \ldots\ \xi_n]$ are the vector coefficients $\xi \in \mathbb{R}^p$

$$\xi = \arg\min_{\xi'}(\|\Theta\xi' - y\|_2 + \lambda\|\xi'\|_1), \tag{8}$$

where λ weights the sparsity constraint of the optimization. Each column of $\dot{X}$ is learned separately to find a sparse vector of coefficients for each variable of interest.

The state vector $x(t) \in \mathbb{R}^n$ can be collected during the simulation or from measurement data, sampled at different times $t_1, t_2, \ldots, t_m$. The derivative of the interested dynamic state comes from the time-series data collected, and the values of the state of the system at the time t build the feature library [13]. An example of a feature library is presented in matrix (9), where each column in $\Theta(X)$ represents a candidate function for the right-hand side on Equation (6).

$$\Theta(X) = \begin{bmatrix} | & | & | & | & | & | & | & | & | \\ 1 & X & X^{P_2} & X^{P_3} & \cdots & \sin(X) & \cos(X) & \sin(2X) & \cos(2X)\cdots \\ | & | & | & | & | & | & | & | & | \end{bmatrix}, \tag{9}$$

where X^{P_α} represents all candidate polynomial functions of order α. For example, matrix (10) presents the library when $\alpha = 2$.

$$\mathbf{X}^{P_2} = \begin{bmatrix} x_1^2(t_1) & x_1(t_1)x_2(t_1) & \cdots & x_2^2(t_1) & x_2(t_1)x_3(t_1) & \cdots & x_n^2(t_1) \\ x_1^2(t_2) & x_1(t_2)x_2(t_2) & \cdots & x_2^2(t_2) & x_2(t_2)x_3(t_2) & \cdots & x_n^2(t_2) \\ \vdots & \vdots & \ddots & \vdots & \vdots & \ddots & \vdots \\ x_1^2(t_m) & x_1(t_m)x_2(t_m) & \cdots & x_2^2(t_m) & x_2(t_m)x_3(t_m) & \cdots & x_n^2(t_m) \end{bmatrix}. \tag{10}$$

The feature library can be a nonlinear function built and chosen before optimization. No assumptions or priors are needed to obtain a sparse system representation. During the fitting of Ξ, the optimization algorithm promotes the system's sparseness. The algorithm for learning the coefficients is the sequential thresholded least-squares (STLSs) [13]. If the feature library consists only of linear terms and the optimization is not penalized, the SINDy algorithm reduces to the dynamic mode decomposition one [14].

The sequential thresholded least-squares (STLSs) algorithm begins with a least-squares solution for Ξ, where all coefficients smaller than a cutoff value λ are thresholded. This thresholding process repeats iteratively until the non-zero coefficients converge. The method is computationally efficient, rapidly achieving a sparse solution in only a few iterations. Furthermore, it is remarkably robust to noise, performing well even when the derivatives come from noisy data [13,14]. The best λ and the model selection should be chosen by varying the parameter and searching at the Pareto front [14].

As evident from the algorithm, the λ cutoff threshold controls the number of predictive variables in the model, bringing a tradeoff between complexity and accuracy in the learned model. Generally, the higher the λ, the lower the complexity and accuracy; it might be underfitting the data in this case. Choosing simpler models with a sparse matrix of coefficients and good accuracy is advisable. Physical systems generally have only a few relevant terms in the governing Equations [13], and this enables the bypassing of the intractable brute force search to sweep through all possible model structures [14] by promoting the sparseness in the solution.

This work uses the PySINDy library, which implements different SINDy methods readily available in Python [37,38].

3.2. Symbolic Regression

Discovering equations from observed data is one of the pillars of science. Symbolic regression, a machine learning algorithm that discovers generalizable and interpretable symbolic models, can automate this process.

The software used in this article is the package described in [11], the library PySR that implements an efficient and distributed symbolic regression. PySR is a generalizable and open-source algorithm that can be passed custom losses and operators to the optimization process by default, aimed at "accelerating the discovery of interpretable symbolic models from data" [11].

In [11], implementation, a genetic algorithm searches for potential equations with a multi-population evolution in a loop of evolve–simplify–optimize. Although real-value coefficients appear in the expressions, they are optimized using classical methods. The genetic algorithm is used to optimize the presence of operations, represented by integers. This way, symbolic regression is optimized, as discovering equations from data is complicated and time-consuming [11]. Figure 1 presents a tree-based representation of the expression $1.15y + 0.86$, where '+' and '*' nodes are the binary operators of addition and multiplication, respectively. A "node" in a tree represents each operation and operand of an analytical expression. The default complexity used for the fittings in this article in PySR is the total number of nodes in the expression independently of its content [11].

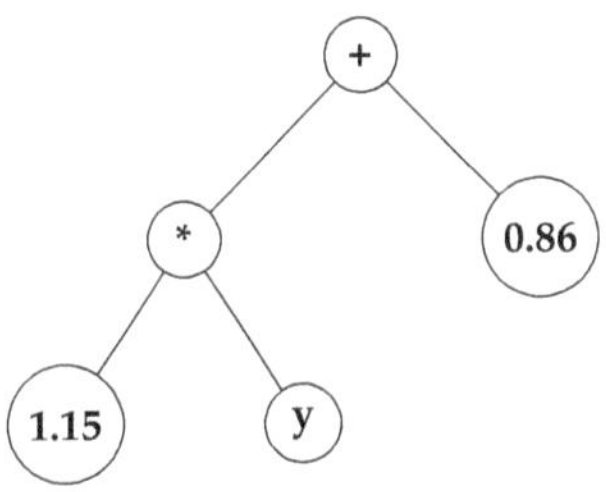

Figure 1. Expression tree for $1.15y + 0.86$.

The generalization and interpretability of the models are promoted by jointly minimizing the prediction error and the model complexity. A penalization term on the loss function related to the frecency of the complexity of the expression promotes parsimony in the learning. Frecency measures the frequency and recency of a given complexity in the population [11].

The analysis of the best model in the fitting considers a score value as presented in Equation (11). This score combines the reduced loss of the discovered equation and its increased complexity related to the precedent candidate.

$$\text{Score} = -\frac{\log\left(\frac{\text{loss}_i}{\text{loss}_{i-1}}\right)}{\text{complexity}_i - \text{complexity}_{i-1}}. \tag{11}$$

The optimization process of PySR is the classical genetic algorithm based on the tournament for individual selection and mutations and crossovers to generate new ones. The software has some adaptations of the algorithms, mainly due to the nature of the model being optimized [11].

A simple evolutionary algorithm starts with a population of individuals, a fitness function, and a set of mutation operators. The algorithm evaluates each individual's fitness in a randomly chosen subset of individuals (e.g., ns-sized, where ns = 2 for standard tournament selection), and the fittest one is selected with a probability p. If it is not selected, the process repeats until only one remains. A copy of the designated winner individual undergoes a randomly chosen mutation. Finally, the mutated individual replaces the weakest member of the population. PySR, at this last step, replaces the eldest member, known as "age-regularized" evolution. Simulated annealing algorithm selects individuals, controlling individuals' increase and narrowing diversity by setting a high or low temperature, respectively, [11].

The second modification of PySR from the classical evolution algorithm is adapting for the mathematical expressions, introducing the loop of evolve–simplify–optimize. The evolve step is the evolution selection as previously described; simplify is the simplification phase of reducing equations to an equivalent, simpler form using algebraic transformations, Finally, the optimization step uses a classical optimization algorithm to fine-tune constants within the equations.

The third and last modification is the adaptative parsimony metric already described previously, i.e., using frecency instead of the complexity of the expression in the loss function, which gives the adaptability and results in the number of expressions at different complexities being roughly the same.

4. Methodology

This section describes the steps performed in this work and details some important aspects of the methodology. The work can be split into three macro steps: data generation, transformation, and modeling. The flowchart in Figure 2 presents the steps and subtasks performed.

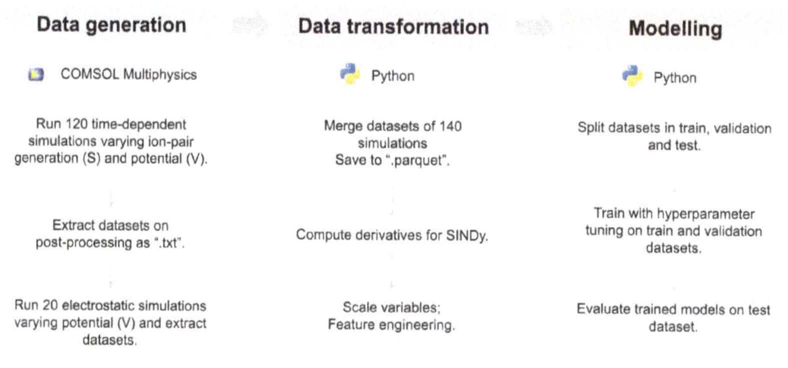

Figure 2. Workflow: steps and subtasks performed.

4.1. Data Generation

The data generation was performed in the commercial Finite Element Software (FEM) COMSOL® Multiphysics 6.2, which can be used to simulate many engineering problems, from heat transfer to electromagnetic, by modeling the physical phenomena. The physics used was the *electric current (ec)* interface in the whole domain, setting the suitable boundary conditions in the electrodes. The drift diffusion reaction model, which implements Equations (2) and (3) in the gas domain, was set up using the *Transport of Diluted Species (tds)* interface. The *ec* and *tds* interfaces are coupled to solve for electric field and charge concentration. The current density in the gas, contributing to the surface charge accumulation and described by Equation (5), was implemented as a variable in the physics, using the solutions of *ec* and *tds*. Further details of implementation can be consulted in [9]. All simulations are time-dependent studies, i.e., the solution of the system's evolution in time. The java code of the time-dependent simulations can be accessed in the repository [39].

The model described in Section 2, whose geometry depicted in Figure 3 inspired by [40], was run 120 times on COMSOL®, varying the ion-pair generation rate and the potential applied. The results from the time-dependent simulations compose the final datasets in the learning tasks, from which the target and predictive variables values were extracted. The total simulation time was 8000 h for each pair of varied parameters, with 1000 time sampling points uniformly distributed.

Additional electrostatic simulations, which solve the Poisson PDE for potential without the DDR formulation and surface charging, were performed with varying potential applied in the same geometry of Figure 3 and the same material properties used in the previous 120 simulation runs described. The results from the electrostatic simulations were only used as predictive variables in the learning tasks, not being used as targets.

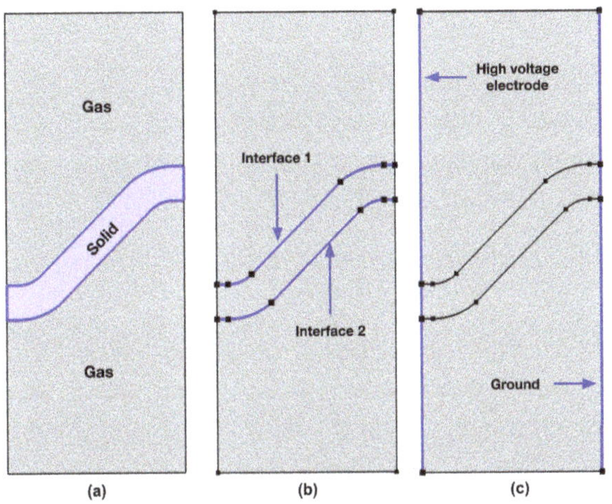

Figure 3. Axisymmetric geometry with conical insulator used in simulations. (**a**) Domains, (**b**) interfaces, (**c**) electrodes.

4.2. Data Transformation

This work involved learning tasks focused on different targets to predict. Three were related to the system's steady-state conditions, and one focused on modeling the dynamics. In the latter one, the surface charge density derivative in time was the target variable, specifically, the derivative of the time series. The targets for the steady-state condition were the time to steady state, the value of dark currents, and the equivalent gas conductivity. The predictive variables used were the simulations' input conditions, the system's time-dependent solutions using the model described in Section 2, and the system's electrostatic solutions.

The steady state in the time series data was identified by comparing the standard deviation of the time series in an analyzed rolling window and the whole collected time. It is important to note that the timestep in the simulations was roughly 10 h, so the steady-state time was inferred by this method, and the data had up to this precision.

The number of data points used for each rolling window in steady-state identification was 20, and the step was 1, so sequential rolling windows overlapped. A threshold $\epsilon = 10^{-3}$ was applied to identify the reach of the steady state based on a relative deviation for each window. All simulations reached a steady state, so there was no problem with unidentified cases. Therefore, the value considered for the steady state was the one at the last step for all variables.

The analyzed dataset for dynamics was surface charge densities, so each sampled coordinate in the arc length of the gas–solid insulator interface had a computed time to reach the steady state. The maximum value calculated on the arc was used as the time to reach the steady state for each simulation.

There was some scaling of variables to make predictive and target close in order of magnitude. This was important as the algorithms used were sensitive to large differences. Feature engineering was performed as well, specifically for dynamics learning. The list below presents the scaling and feature engineering that was performed.

- Conductivity and currents: transformed units to pico multiplying by 10^{12} or nano multiplying by 10^9;
- Time to steady state: converted to hours divided by 3600;
- Feature engineering: the reciprocal of exponential of time divided by 300, i.e., $e^{-t/300}$; the reciprocal of variables such as potential and surface electric field.

4.3. Modelling

The SR was used to learn the variables' values at steady state, and SINDy was used to predict the derivative of surface charge density over time. The learning algorithms were applied to 80% of the data collected in the simulations, called the training set, 15% was used as the validation dataset, and the test error was computed in the 5% not used in training and validation, called the test set. Random sampling without replacement of all collected data split the sets.

Each algorithm, SR and SINDy, had hyperparameters to be tuned to perform the learning task better. The validation dataset was used in this tuning procedure. The process involved try-and-error evaluating the final validation error in each iteration and using a grid search to find the optimal combination of parameters. It is important to highlight that the test dataset was never used in this process; it was only evaluated at the end when all hyperparameters were already chosen.

The hyperparameters tuned in each learning case for SR are presented in the list below. Descriptions of all other parameters can be consulted in the doc strings of the code in the repository indicated on [11]. Other available input parameters in the software were not tuned, and their default value was used.

- niterations: maximum number of iterations of the learning algorithm;
- unary_operators: allowed unary operators;
- binary_operators: allowed binary operators;
- maxsize: maximum complexity, related to the number of operations allowed;
- model_selection: model selection criteria;
- parsimony: punishes complexity;
- constraints: set constraints for the equations.

The hyperparameters tuned in the learning for SINDy, mostly related to the STLSQ optimizer and library, are presented in the list below. Descriptions of all other parameters can be consulted in the doc strings of the code in the repository indicated on [37,38]. Other available input parameters in the software were not tuned, and their default value was used.

- threshold: minimum coefficient value to not be set to zero;
- alpha: weight on the L_2 regularization;
- max_iter: maximum iterations of the optimization algorithm;
- polynomial_degree: polynomial degree of the feature library;

- include_bias: include the 1s column in the feature library.

The SR implementation in Python used the library PySR described in the paper [11], version 0.19.4; and the SINDy implementation, used the library PySINDy described in the papers [37,38], version 1.7.5.

5. Results

This section presents the results from the simulations and the learning tasks. The focus is on fittings' performance, i.e., root mean squared error, and the complexity of the final learned equation. The ideal symbolic equation is the one with the lowest complexity to good accuracy, i.e., the point where increasing complexity brings a diminishing rate of increase in accuracy.

Table 1 presents the values for each variable used in the grid. The other parameters used in the simulation are presented in Table 2. The summary statistic of the target of each learning task is presented in Table 3.

Table 1. Varied parameters S and potential in the simulations.

Parameter	Values
S [IP/(m^3·s)]	$10^7, 4 \cdot 10^7, 5 \cdot 10^7, 8 \cdot 10^7, 10^8, 2 \cdot 10^8$
Potential applied [kV]	$15 \div 500$, uniform 20 data points

Table 2. List of parameters fixed in the simulations.

Parameter	Value
Gas pressure (P) [MPa]	0.4
Recombination coefficient (R) [m^3/s]	$6 \cdot 10^{-13}$
Positive mobility (μ_p) [m^2/(V·s)]	$4.8 \cdot 10^{-6}$
Negative mobility (μ_n) [m^2/(V·s)]	$4.8 \cdot 10^{-6}$
Positive diffusion (D_p) [m^2/s]	$1.2 \cdot 10^{-7}$
Negative diffusion (D_n) [m^2/s]	$1.2 \cdot 10^{-7}$
Relative permittivity of epoxy [-]	5
Electric conductivity of epoxy (k) [S/m]	$4.2 \cdot 10^{-17}$
Relative permittivity of SF_6 [-]	1.002

Table 3. Summary statistics of the targets.

Variable	Mean	std	Min/Max
Dark current gas–ground [pA]	0.68	0.52	0.09/1.74
Dark current solid–ground [pA]	1.67	0.93	0.09/3.18
Time to steady-state [h]	3458	171	3067/4484
Surface charge dynamics [nC/m^2/s]	−0.51	2.25	−40.75/9.43
Conductivity log [log(S/m)]	−40.29	1.28	−45.69/−37.27

5.1. Generated Datasets

This section briefly explores the datasets generated in the simulations so the learning tasks can be better understood. The data extracted in the simulations were related to the current, electric field, charge, and ion concentration. The values in the sampling times can be statistics from the gas volume, i.e., maximum, minimum, and average; sampled values from surfaces; and integrals over surfaces. Table 4 presents the variables extracted from the time-dependent simulations.

Table 4. Datasets extracted from time-dependent simulations.

Dataset	Description
Dark current	Integral of $\mathbf{J}_G$ in the ground electrode.
Electric field	Volume integral on the gas, computing maximum, minimum, and average on time of field in r and z directions.
Surface charge density	Sampled charge density values, in the arc and in time, of both solid-gas interfaces.
Surface electric field	Minimum, maximum, and average of the electric field in the surfaces of the solid-gas interface and electrodes in time.
Ion concentration	Volume integral on the gas, computing total ion concentration on time.

The electric and surface electric field datasets, presented in Table 4, were also extracted from the simulations' electrostatic solutions to be used as predictive variables. The electrostatic solution is 10 times faster to finish than the simulations of electric currents coupled with DDR equations, taking around 8 s. Therefore, an analytical expression that uses electrostatic solutions as predictive variables can be helpful.

Figure 4 presents the dark current variation on the ground electrode by potential and ion-pair generation rate. The results are presented considering two sets of boundaries; Figure 4a is the current only in the gas interface with the electrode; and Figure 4b, the total current considering the solid and gas interfaces. It is possible to see that the gas–ground electrode current at steady state is inversely proportional to potential and directly proportional to ion-pair generation. The total current increase with potential is related to the linear current increase in the solid–ground electrode interface.

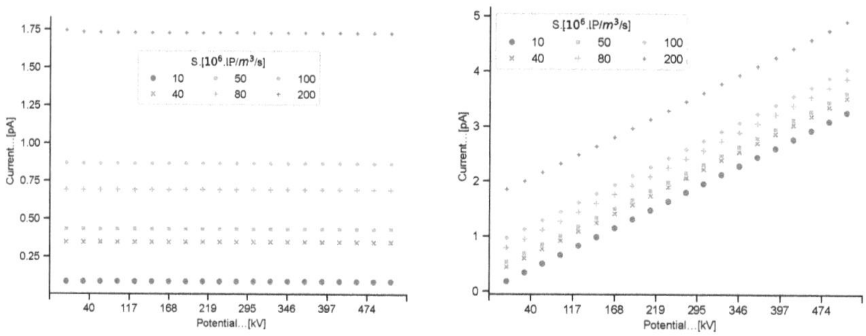

(a) (b)

Figure 4. Dark currents in the ground electrode as a function of potential and ion-pair generation rate. (**a**) Dark current through the gas–electrode interface. (**b**) Dark current through the ground electrode.

Figure 5 presents the surface charge density and the time to steady state by normalized arc length on interface 1, as defined in Figure 3. It is possible to observe that the boundary conditions of zero concentration are satisfied in the electrodes and that the curved part of the solid insulator is an important factor in the shape of the surface charge density.

The time to steady state presents a narrow variation between voltages and ion-pair generation, and the crucial parts are close to the electrodes, where the maximum times occur. The curve near the ground electrode presents some numerical oscillation. This part was removed from the learning task as the variation of the surface charge density in this region is two orders of magnitude lower than the rest of the curve.

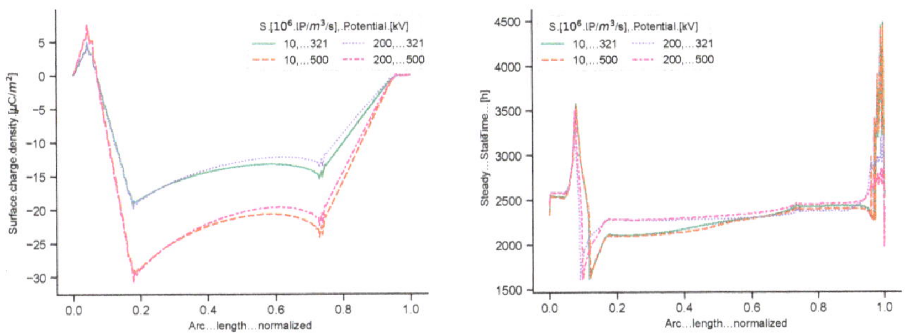

(**a**) (**b**)

Figure 5. Steady-state time and surface charge density by normalized arc length on interface 1, as identified in Figure 3. (**a**) Surface charge density variation along solid insulator boundary; (**b**) time to steady-state variation along solid insulator boundary.

Figure 6 presents the evolution of the surface charge density in two arc length positions on interface 1, on condition of $S = 8 \cdot 10^7$ $\mathrm{IP/m^3/s}$ and $V = 346$ kV. It is possible to observe that interface 1 has positive and negative charging and is monotonic, i.e., there is no switch on the first derivative signal.

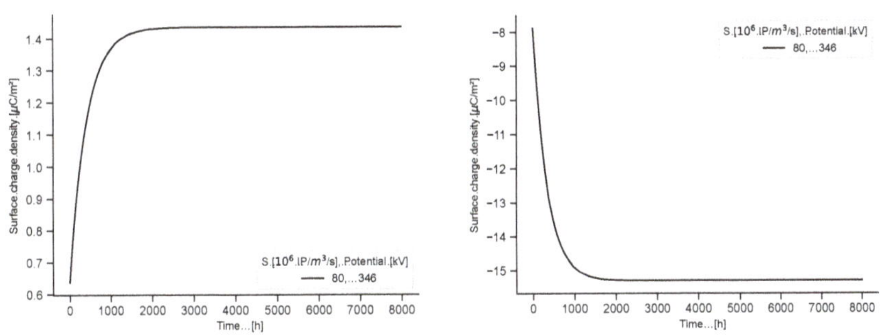

(**a**) (**b**)

Figure 6. Evolution in time of surface charge density in two arc positions on interface 1, as identified in Figure 3. (**a**) Increase in positive surface charge density until saturation on normalized arc length = 0.13; (**b**) Increase in negative surface charge density until saturation on normalized arc length = 0.4.

5.2. Dark Currents in Steady State

This learning problem aimed to find an expression that relates the ion-pair generation rate and voltage to the dark current in the system at steady state. The symbolic regression was performed using PySR and Table 5 presents the hyperparameters tuned. In the table, +, −, *, /, and ^ are the binary operators of addition, subtraction, multiplication, division and exponentiation, respectively.

Table 5. Hyperparameters tuned for SR on dark currents in gas–ground electrode.

Hyperparameter	Value
niterations	500
unary_operators	exp, log
binary_operators	+, −, *, /,^
maxsize	15
model_selection	accuracy
parsimony	0.002
constraints	^:(−1, 3)

Equation (12) presents the final best fit obtained in terms of accuracy to predict the current in the gas–ground electrode interface, where V is in kV and S in IP/m^3/s.

$$current\ [\text{pA}] = 8.64 \cdot 10^{-9}S + 6.71 \cdot 10^{-18}\frac{S^2}{V}, \tag{12}$$

Table 6 presents the set of four equations with the highest complexity found by the symbolic regression fitting of current in the gas–ground electrode interface. Column $RMSE_{val}$ presents the mean of error and standard deviation for eight validation groups.

Table 6. Expressions for dark currents in gas–ground electrode fitted by symbolic regression.

$\mathcal{O}$ *	Equation	Loss **	Score ***	RMSE_{val}
10	$8.64 \cdot 10^{-9}S + \left(1.02 \cdot 10^{-9}S\right)^{\log(V)}$	$1.88 \cdot 10^{-7}$	0.47	$(7.94 \pm 3.86) \cdot 10^{-4}$
12	$8.64 \cdot 10^{-9}S + \left(2.67 \cdot 10^{-9}S^{0.954}\right)^{\log(V)}$	$7.33 \cdot 10^{-8}$	0.47	$(5.77 \pm 2.33) \cdot 10^{-4}$
14	$8.64 \cdot 10^{-9}(S - V) + \left(2.67 \cdot 10^{-9}S^{0.954}\right)^{\log(V)}$	$7.22 \cdot 10^{-8}$	$7.08 \cdot 10^{-3}$	$(5.75 \pm 2.33) \cdot 10^{-4}$
15	$8.64 \cdot 10^{-9}S + 6.715 \cdot 10^{-18}\frac{S^2}{V}$	$1.35 \cdot 10^{-8}$	1.68	$(1.72 \pm 0.17) \cdot 10^{-4}$

* As computed by PySR: the final expressions reported are simplified, ** MSE [pA^2], *** As defined in Equation (11).

The root mean squared error for the test set of Equation (12) is $1.04 \cdot 10^{-4}$ pA and Figure 7 presents the true vs. predicted value for the target using the learned model for the training and test datasets.

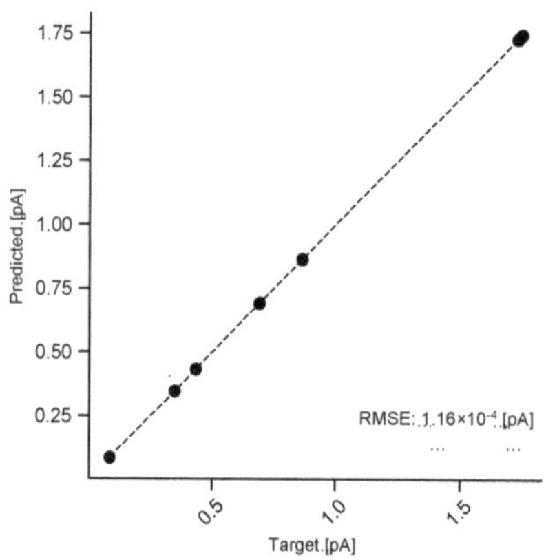

(a) Training set.

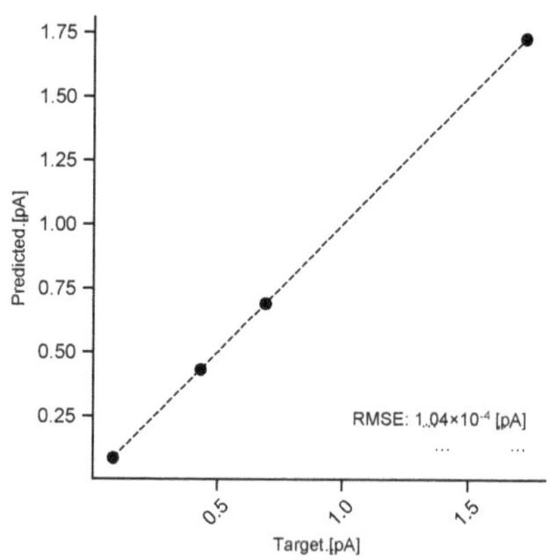

(b) Test set.

Figure 7. Dark currents in gas–ground interface symbolic regression target vs. predicted for the best equation in the training and test set.

Equation (13) presents the final best fit obtained in terms of accuracy to predict the current in the solid–ground electrode interface, where V is in kV and S in IP/m^3/s. The *niterations* hyperparameter's value used was 250, the other ones had same the values as reported in Table 5. It is important to note that the final dark current through the ground electrode will be a sum between the current in the gas and the solid interfaced with the ground electrode, i.e., summing Equations (12) and (13).

$$current\ [\text{pA}] = 6.35 \cdot 10^{-3} V + 4.23 \cdot 10^{-11} e^{\frac{2.69}{V}} S. \tag{13}$$

Table 7 presents the four equations with the highest complexity found by the symbolic regression fitting of current in the solid–ground electrode interface.

Table 7. Expressions for dark currents in solid–ground electrode fitted by symbolic regression.

$\mathcal{C}$ *	Equation	Loss **	Score ***	RMSE$_{\text{val}}$
9	$6.35 \cdot 10^{-3} V + 4.34 \cdot 10^{-11} S$	$5.19 \cdot 10^{-8}$	$4.17 \cdot 10^{-2}$	$(3.31 \pm 1.69) \cdot 10^{-4}$
11	$6.35 \cdot 10^{-3} V + 4.23 \cdot 10^{-11} \left(S + \frac{S}{V}\right)$	$3.22 \cdot 10^{-8}$	0.24	$(3.07 \pm 1.82) \cdot 10^{-4}$
12	$6.35 \cdot 10^{-3} V + 4.23 \cdot 10^{-11} e^{\frac{1.65}{V}} S$	$2.04 \cdot 10^{-8}$	0.45	$(2.59 \pm 1.61) \cdot 10^{-4}$
13	$6.35 \cdot 10^{-3} V + 4.23 \cdot 10^{-11} e^{\frac{2.69}{V}} S$	$1.26 \cdot 10^{-8}$	0.49	$(2.01 \pm 1.24) \cdot 10^{-4}$

* As computed by PySR: the final expression reported are simplified, ** MSE [pA^2], *** As defined in Equation (11).

The root mean squared error for the test set of Equation (13) is $8.99 \cdot 10^{-5}$ pA and Figure 8 presents the true vs. predicted value for the target using the learned model for the training and test datasets.

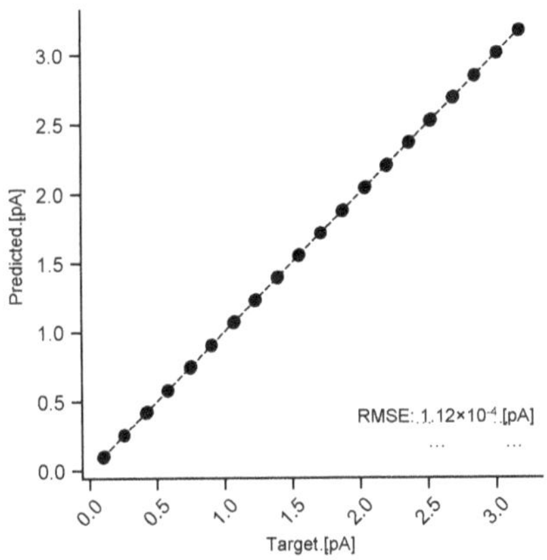

(**a**) Training set.

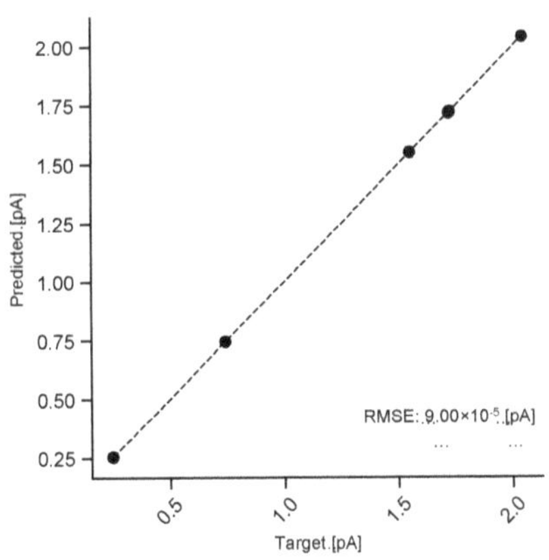

(**b**) Test set.

Figure 8. Dark currents in solid–ground interface symbolic regression target vs. predicted for the best equation in the training and test set.

5.3. Time to Steady State

For each simulation, the steady-state time was defined as the maximum time it took for the surface charge density to stabilize across the entire arc of interface 1, as described in Figure 3. The symbolic regression was performed using PySR and Table 8 presents the hyperparameters tuned. In the table, +, -, *, /, and ^ are the binary operators of addition, subtraction, multiplication, division and exponentiation, respectively

Table 8. Hyperparameters tuned for SR on time to steady state.

Hyperparameter	Value
niterations	10,000
unary_operators	exp, log
binary_operators	+, −, *, /,^
maxsize	20
model_selection	accuracy
parsimony	0.0005
constraints	^:(−1, 3)

The final best equation for accuracy, untying by score, obtained is presented in Equation (14).

$$Time_{sst} = 1.52 \cdot 10^4 \tilde{E}r_{i2}^{ES}(S - 547\tilde{E}r_{i2}^{ES} - 4.72 \cdot 10^6)^{-1} - 3.40 \cdot 10^3 \max(Ez_{i2}^{ES}), \quad (14)$$

where time is in hours; Ej_{ik}^{ES} is the electric field in V/m in the surface of interface k in the j-direction from the electrostatic solution; $j = r, z$ and $k = 1, 2$. The tilde over the E letter represents the median operator.

Table 9 presents the four equations with the highest complexity found by the symbolic regression fitting of the time to reach a steady state in surface charge density. The variable $\overline{||E^{ES}||}$ in Table 9 is the electric field's mean norm in the gas volume from the electrostatic solution.

Table 9. Expressions for time to reach steady state fitted by symbolic regression.

$\mathcal{O}$ *	Equation	Loss ** ($\times 10^4$)	Score *** ($\times 10^{-4}$)	RMSE$_{\text{val}}$
16	$\max(Ez_{i2}^{ES})(8.47 \cdot 10^{-5}S - 4.08 \cdot 10^{-2}\overline{\|\|E^{ES}\|\|} - 342)^{-1} + \log(\tilde{E}r_{i2}^{ES}) + 3.48 \cdot 10^3$	1.80	18.2	(90 ± 8)
17	$1.52 \cdot 10^4 \tilde{E}r_{i2}^{ES}(S - 547\tilde{E}r_{i2}^{ES} - 4.72 \cdot 10^6)^{-1} - 3.40 \cdot 10^3 \max(Ez_{i2}^{ES})$	1.63	988	(85 ± 25)
19	$2.12 \cdot 10^{-4} \max(Ez_{i2}^{ES}) + 1.52 \cdot 10^4 \tilde{E}r_{i2}^{ES} - 5.3 \cdot 10^7(S - 547\tilde{E}r_{i2}^{ES} - 4.83 \cdot 10^6)^{-1} + 3.40 \cdot 10^3$	1.63	4.15	(85 ± 25)
20	$(6.53 \cdot 10^{-5} + (6.43 \cdot 10^{-5}S - 3.51 \cdot 10^{-2}\tilde{E}r_{i2}^{ES} - 311)^{-1}) \cdot \tilde{E}r_{i1}^{ES} - \log(S) + 3.41 \cdot 10^3$	1.63	27.0	(85 ± 25)

* As computed by PySR: the final expression reported are simplified, ** MSE $[h^2]$, *** As defined in Equation (11).

The root mean squared test error of Equation (14) is 110 h, and Figure 9 presents the true vs. predicted value for the target using the learned model.

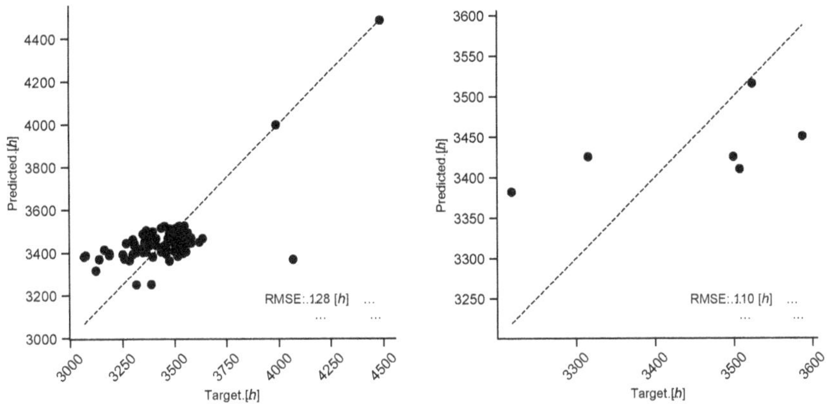

(a) Training set. (b) Test set.

Figure 9. Time to steady-state symbolic regression target vs. predicted for the selected equation in the training and test sets.

5.4. Gas Conductivity in Steady State

This learning problem aimed to find an expression that relates the ion-pair generation rate and electric field in the r-direction to the conductivity of gas at steady state from the time-dependent simulations of the model described in Section 2. The log value of conductivity was modeled, which is better for the search as it conditions the loss during the learning. The symbolic regression was performed using PySR and Table 10 presents the hyperparameters tuned. In the table, +, −, *, /, and ^ are the binary operators of addition, subtraction, multiplication, division and exponentiation, respectively.

Table 10. Hyperparameters tuned for SR on conductivity.

Hyperparameter	Value
niterations	250
unary_operators	exp, log
binary_operators	+, −, *, /, ^
maxsize	15
model_selection	accuracy
parsimony	0.002
constraints	^:(−1, 3)

Equation (15) presents the final best fit obtained in terms of accuracy and complexity to predict the conductivity of the gas at a steady state. The equation was chosen based on the score computed to untie the choices, as all highest complexity expressions had the same validation error.

$$log(\sigma_{gas}) = 4.63 \cdot 10^{-8} Er + \log\left(\frac{S}{Er}\right) - 45.4, \quad (15)$$

where σ_{gas} is the gas electric conductivity in S/m, S is in IP/m^3/s, and Er is the electric field in r-direction in V/m.

Table 11 presents the four equations with the highest complexity found by the symbolic regression fittings of conductivity.

Table 11. Expressions for conductivity fitted by symbolic regression.

$\mathcal{O}$ *	Equation	Loss **	Score ***	$RMSE_{val}$
8	$\log\left(0.538 + \frac{S}{Er}\right) - 45.4$	0.276	$2.19 \cdot 10^{-4}$	0.53 ± 0.01
10	$4.63 \cdot 10^{-8} Er + \log\left(\frac{S}{Er}\right) - 45.4$	0.275	$2.18 \cdot 10^{-3}$	0.53 ± 0.01
12	$4.63 \cdot 10^{-8} Er + \log\left(\frac{S}{Er} - 0.205\right) - 45.4$	0.275	$4.70 \cdot 10^{-5}$	0.53 ± 0.01
14	$4.63 \cdot 10^{-8} Er + \log\left(4.63 \cdot 10^{-8} Er + \frac{S}{Er}\right) - 45.4$	0.275	$8.29 \cdot 10^{-5}$	0.53 ± 0.01

* As computed by PySR: the final expressions reported are simplified, ** MSE [pA^2], *** As defined in Equation (11).

The root mean squared error for the test set of Equation (15) is 0.55 log(S/m), and Figure 10 presents the true vs. predicted value for the target using the learned model for the training and test datasets.

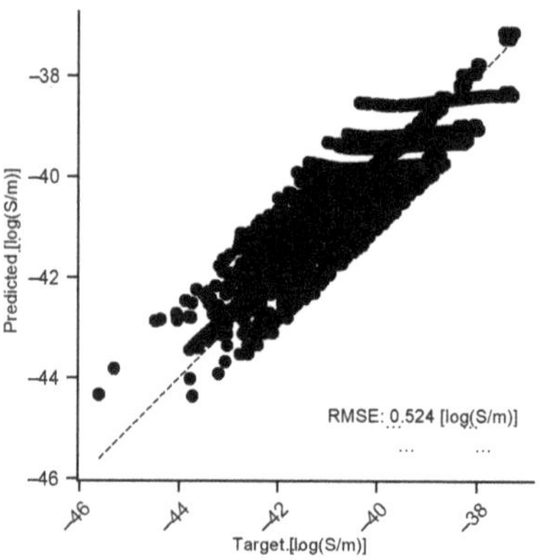

(**a**) Training set.

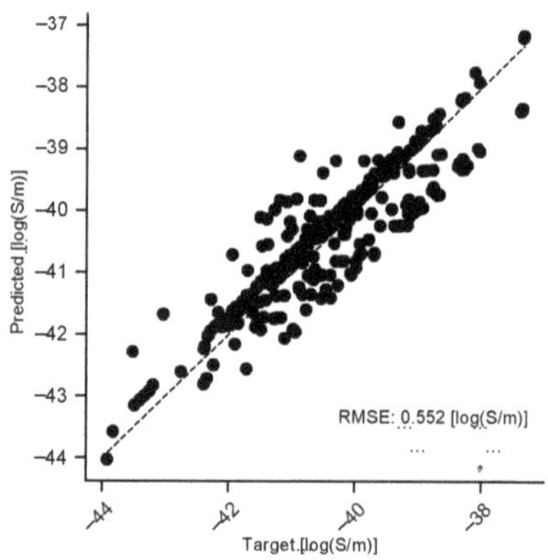

(**b**) Test set.

Figure 10. Conductivity symbolic regression target vs. predicted for the best equation in the training and test set.

5.5. Surface Charge Density Dynamics

The objective of modeling the surface charge density is to obtain an analytical expression as Equation (16). The derivative is computed using simulation data and is the target of this task's learning. The SINDy algorithm is applied to fit the function f and obtain a sparse symbolic representation.

$$\frac{\partial \sigma}{\partial t} = f(X). \tag{16}$$

The candidate library of equations used in SINDy included second-degree polynomials with bias (exponent = 0) excluded. As the magnitude of the predictive variables was low, the optimization process threshold was 0.005. Table 12 presents all hyperparameters selected in the tuning and used in the fitting.

Table 12. Hyperparameters tuned for SINDy on surface charge density dynamics.

Hyperparameter	Value
threshold	0.005
alpha	0.1
max_iter	20
polynomial_degree	2
include_bias	False

The final equation obtained is presented in Equation (17), where t is in hours, V is potential applied in kV, and Ej_{i1} is the electric field in V/m in the surface of interface 1 in the j-direction at time t; $j = r, z$. The model's root mean squared test error is 1.12 nC/m^2/s, and Figure 11 presents the true vs. predicted value for the target using the learned modeling in the training and test sets.

$$\frac{\partial \sigma}{\partial t} = (0.010Er_{i1} - 1.108 - 0.076V - 0.032Ez_{i1})e^{-t/300} + 2.765e^{-t/150}. \quad (17)$$

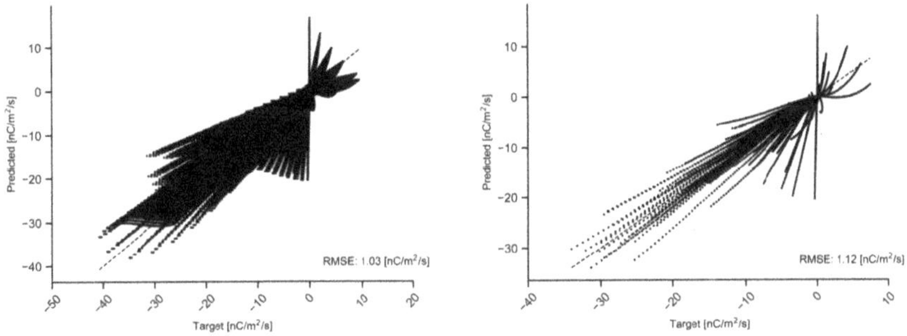

(a) Training set. (b) Test set.

Figure 11. Derivative target vs. predicted of the learned equation in training and test sets.

6. Discussion

The learning tasks were successfully performed using the symbolic regression and SINDy algorithms, yielding relatively good results based on the validation and test errors. Dark currents and conductivity required low-complexity symbolic equations to fit the data, while time to steady state, even with highly complex equations, could not reach very good results.

The final Equation (12) for dark current in the gas is plausible and has the same behavior related to radiation as observed in the literature [3], i.e., the dark current increases linearly with ion-pair generation rate in the saturation condition reached in steady state. In the lower voltage conditions, the dark current through the gas–electrode is higher in the steady state as there is a higher concentration of ions in the gas that generate the current, which is caused by the lower flux in the interface of the gas–solid insulator. The higher the voltage, the higher the current in the solid insulator and the flux in the gas–solid insulator boundary.

The results derived in [6] disagree with Equation (12) as the dark current increases with the increase in potential applied. Still, it is important to note that the model constructed by the authors is for air and for a different geometry, which does not incorporate the intricate dynamics of the flux in the boundary gas–solid insulator. The authors also observe the linear relation of radiation dosage related to the ion-pair generation rate and the dark current.

The time to steady state does not vary much between the conditions simulated, demonstrating it is not strongly dependent on ion-pair generation rate and voltage. Further analysis, including simulations with varying conductivities and permittivities in the gas and solid, might improve the model with more significant variations in the time to steady state, as different conductivities will influence the system time constant. The relatively high test error indicates that the model will perform even worse for other simulation conditions not present in the training dataset.

Conductivity on the steady state was fitted and has a relatively low test error. Still, it can significantly impact time-dependent simulations as the errors might add up over time. Furthermore, the values of the electric field and ion concentrations might differ considerably in the initial times of the simulation compared to the steady-state ones in which the model was fitted, so it is not currently advisable to use it as a surrogate model. Further investigations are needed to compare simulations using DDR and the analytical expression. The DDR shows that the conductivity of the gas cannot be modeled as constant (see [9] for further reference), so the current analytical expression is a better alternative.

Good model performance is observed in SINDy surface charge density dynamics fitting. This learning task was more demanding, as it had more data points—it is a time series that varies in space, and the surface charging couples gas dynamics and electric field solutions. However, work is needed to improve the expressions for use as a surrogate model in the simulations. The current one demonstrated the power of the algorithm in discovering dynamics from data; even for large amounts of data and a big library, it efficiently fitted a sparse representation.

The dynamic of saturation of the surface charge density observed in Figure 6 is called capacitive-resistive transition, described in many previous papers [1,9] and expected. The charging of positive or negative particles is influenced by the geometry of the solid insulator interface and its proximity to the electrodes, as seen in Figure 5. The fast saturation behavior, observed in the curves on Figure 6, is related to neglecting the interface conductivity of the boundary, so all current from the gas that cannot be dissipated by the current in the solid insulator accumulates at the interface, as can be seen in Equation (1) excluding the last term. The geometry and distance from the electrode create specific points of accumulation on the boundary; the same preferred accumulation near the positive electrode of negative particles is observed in [9]. The varying time to steady state observed in Figure 5b is discussed and derived by [40] as well, although with a different method. As discussed previously, the linear increase in current in the solid with potential is expected and can be seen in Figure 4b.

The physical units of the learned Equations (12) and (14) can be used to infer the physical units of the learned coefficients using dimensional analysis. These units and values can be coupled with prior knowledge about the system to develop its symbolic representation further, for example, by combining system conditions that were not varied in the study to compute the learned coefficients. This further step is out of the scope of this work, but it might be an interesting path to explore with combinatorics and symbolic programming.

One of the challenges in the learning tasks was the considerable discrepancy in the variables' order of dimension. It interferes mainly with applying the STLS in SINDy, which depends on the absolute value of the coefficients in the pruning based on the threshold step. The discrepancy was overcome by normalizing the variables or transforming the units, for example, in kilo, nano, and pico.

It is important to point out that the system's physics is simplified, and other phenomena might be important in the simulated conditions, such as the anode's emittance of electrons, the surface conductivity of the gas–solid insulator interface, and spatial and temporal variation in temperature. The conditions simulated are restricted to the same geometry and material properties. Further enrichment of the dataset with variations of these properties is interesting for building more generally applicable analytical expressions for the HVDC-GIS in RIC conditions.

7. Conclusions

This work explored machine learning methods to derive time to steady state, dark current, gas conductivity, and surface charge density expressions. The learning tasks were completed successfully using simulated data, bringing new analytical expressions useful for analyzing HVDC systems in RIC conditions and further developing machine learning predictions. The absolute error and MAPE reported for predicting dark currents in the gas–ground electrode are $1.04 \cdot 10^{-4}$ pA and 0.01%, respectively, and $8.99 \cdot 10^{-5}$ pA and 0.04% in the solid–ground electrode. The model's predictions of time to steady state did not perform so well in the test set, reaching around 110 h in error with a MAPE of around 3%. The gas conductivity prediction model performed well in the test set with error of 0.55 log(S/m) and MAPE of 1%. The test error on the dynamics estimation was 1.12 nC/m^2/s. Further works with varying gas and solid properties and geometries might improve the performance of the models and make the expressions more useful for more general contexts. All algorithms used in this work might also be applied to experimental data, which might unveil discoveries about the systems' behaviors.

Author Contributions: Conceptualization, K.U.J., F.L. and N.M.; methodology, K.U.J. and F.L.; software, K.U.J.; formal analysis, K.U.J. and F.L.; data curation, K.U.J.; writing—original draft preparation, K.U.J. and F.L.; writing—review and editing, K.U.J., F.L. and N.M. All authors have read and agreed to the published version of the manuscript.

Funding: Project financially supported by BIRD 2023 Research Program of University of Padova (prot. BIRD235204).

Data Availability Statement: The original contributions presented in the study are included in the article, further inquiries can be directed to the corresponding author.

Conflicts of Interest: The authors declare no conflicts of interest.

Abbreviations

The following abbreviations are used in this manuscript:

RMSE	Root Mean Squared Error
MSE	Mean Squared Error
DDR	Drif-Diffusion-Reation
SR	Symbolic Regression
SINDy	Sparse Identification of Nonlinear Dynamics
STLS	Sequentially Thresholded Least Squares
HVDC	High Voltage Direct Current
GIL	Gas Insulated Line
GIS	Gas Insulated System
AC	Alternating Current
DC	Direct Current
RIC	Radiation-induced conductivity

References

1. Lucchini, F.; Marconato, N.; Bettini, P. Automatic optimization of gas insulated components based on the streamer inception criterion. *Electronics* **2021**, *10*, 2280. [CrossRef]
2. Volpov, E. Electric field modeling and field formation mechanism in HVDC SF/sub 6/gas insulated systems. *IEEE Trans. Dielectr. Electr. Insul.* **2003**, *10*, 204–215. [CrossRef]
3. Lucchini, F.; Marconato, N. Development of HVDC Gas-Insulated Components for the Power Supply of Neutral Beam Injectors. *IEEE Access* **2023**, *11*, 9731–9741. [CrossRef]
4. Fujiwara, Y.; Hanada, M.; Inoue, T.; Miyamoto, K.; Miyamoto, N.; Ohara, Y.; Okumura, Y.; Watanabe, K. Radiation induced conductivity and voltage holding characteristics of insulation gas for the ITER NBI. *AIP Conf. Proc.* **1998**, *439*, 205–216. [CrossRef]
5. Fujiwara, Y.; Inoue, T.; Miyamoto, K.; Miyamoto, N.; Ohara, Y.; Okumura, Y.; Watanabe, K. Influence of radiation on insulation gas at the ITER–NBI system. *Fusion Eng. Des.* **2001**, *55*, 1–8. [CrossRef]
6. Hodgson, E.; Moroño, A. A model for radiation induced conductivity in neutral beam injector insulator gases. *J. Nucl. Mater.* **2002**, *307*, 1660–1663. [CrossRef]
7. Hodgson, E.; Moroño, A. Radiation effects on insulating gases for the ITER NBI system. *J. Nucl. Mater.* **1998**, *258*, 1827–1830. [CrossRef]

8. De Lorenzi, A.; Grando, L.; Pesce, A.; Bettini, P.; Specogna, R. Modeling of epoxy resin spacers for the 1 MV DC gas insulated line of ITER neutral beam injector system. *IEEE Trans. Dielectr. Electr. Insul.* **2009**, *16*, 77–87. [CrossRef]
9. Lucchini, F.; Frescura, A.; Urazaki Junior, K.; Marconato, N.; Bettini, P. Modeling Approaches for Accounting Radiation-Induced Effect in HVDC-GIS Design for Nuclear Fusion Applications. *Appl. Sci.* **2024**, *14*, 11666. [CrossRef]
10. Romanelli, F. Divertor Tokamak Test facility Project: Status of Design and Implementation. *Nucl. Fusion* **2024**, *64*, 112015. [CrossRef]
11. Cranmer, M. Interpretable machine learning for science with PySR and SymbolicRegression.jl. *arXiv* **2023**. [CrossRef]
12. Champion, K.; Lusch, B.; Kutz, J.N.; Brunton, S.L. Data-driven discovery of coordinates and governing equations. *Proc. Natl. Acad. Sci. USA* **2019**, *116*, 22445–22451. [CrossRef] [PubMed]
13. Brunton, S.L.; Proctor, J.L.; Kutz, J.N. Discovering governing equations from data by sparse identification of nonlinear dynamical systems. *Proc. Natl. Acad. Sci. USA* **2016**, *113*, 3932–3937. [CrossRef] [PubMed]
14. Loiseau, J.C.; Brunton, S.L. Constrained sparse Galerkin regression. *J. Fluid Mech.* **2018**, *838*, 42–67. [CrossRef]
15. Pecile, A.; Demo, N.; Tezzele, M.; Rozza, G.; Breda, D. Data-driven Discovery of Delay Differential Equations with Discrete Delays. *arXiv* **2024**. [CrossRef]
16. Ebers, M.R.; Steele, K.M.; Kutz, J.N. Discrepancy Modeling Framework: Learning Missing Physics, Modeling Systematic Residuals, and Disambiguating between Deterministic and Random Effects. *SIAM J. Appl. Dyn. Syst.* **2024**, *23*, 440–469. [CrossRef]
17. Lore, J.; De Pascuale, S.; Laiu, P.; Russo, B.; Park, J.S.; Park, J.; Brunton, S.; Kutz, J.; Kaptanoglu, A. Time-dependent SOLPS-ITER simulations of the tokamak plasma boundary for model predictive control using SINDy. *Nucl. Fusion* **2023**, *63*, 4. [CrossRef]
18. Lucchini, F.; Frescura, A.; Torchio, R.; Alotto, P.; Bettini, P. Reduced order modeling for real-time monitoring of structural displacements due to electromagnetic forces in large scale tokamaks. *Plasma Phys. Control. Fusion* **2024**, *66*, 11. [CrossRef]
19. Alves, E.P.; Fiuza, F. Data-driven discovery of reduced plasma physics models from fully kinetic simulations. *Phys. Rev. Res.* **2022**, *4*, 033192. [CrossRef]
20. Matteri, A.; Palo, M.; Ogliari, E.; Schubert, B.; Wei, J.; Gu, K.; Liu, W. Separation of radio-frequency signals triggered by valve switching in a HVDC converter by supervised machine learning methods. In Proceedings of the 2021 IEEE International Conference on Environment and Electrical Engineering and 2021 IEEE Industrial and Commercial Power Systems Europe (EEEIC / I&CPS Europe), Bari, Italy, 7–10 September 2021; pp. 1–6. [CrossRef]
21. Narendra, K.; Sood, V.; Khorasani, K.; Patel, R. Investigation into an artificial neural network based on-line current controller for an HVDC transmission link. *IEEE Trans. Power Syst.* **1997**, *12*, 1425–1431. [CrossRef]
22. Dash, P.; Routray, A.; Mishra, S. A neural network based feedback linearising controller for HVDC links. *Electr. Power Syst. Res.* **1999**, *50*, 125–132. [CrossRef]
23. Beura, C.P.; Wenger, P.; Tozan, E.; Beltle, M.; Tenbohlen, S. Classification of Partial Discharge Sources in HVDC Gas Insulated Switchgear using Neural Networks. In Proceedings of the VDE High Voltage Technology; 4. ETG-Symposium, Berlin, Germany, 8–10 November 2022; VDE: Berlin, Germany, 2022; pp. 1–6.
24. Tuyet-Doan, V.N.; Do, T.D.; Tran-Thi, N.D.; Youn, Y.W.; Kim, Y.H. One-Shot Learning for Partial Discharge Diagnosis Using Ultra-High-Frequency Sensor in Gas-Insulated Switchgear. *Sensors* **2020**, *20*, 5562. [CrossRef]
25. Seitz, S.; Götz, T.; Lindenberg, C.; Tetzlaff, R.; Schlegel, S. Towards Generalizable Classification of Partial Discharges in Gas-Insulated HVDC Systems Using Neural Networks: Protrusions and Particles. *IEEE Trans. Power Deliv.* **2024**, *39*, 1491–1499. [CrossRef]
26. Chen, Q.; Wu, J.; Li, Q.; Gao, X.; Yu, R.; Guo, J.; Peng, G.; Yang, B. Long Short-Term Memory Network-Based HVDC Systems Fault Diagnosis under Knowledge Graph. *Electronics* **2023**, *12*, 2242. [CrossRef]
27. Patil, M.; Paramane, A.; Das, S.; Rao, U.M.; Rozga, P. Hybrid Algorithm for Dynamic Fault Prediction of HVDC Converter Transformer Using DGA Data. *IEEE Trans. Dielectr. Electr. Insul.* **2024**, *31*, 2128–2135. [CrossRef]
28. Yousaf, M.Z.; Singh, A.R.; Khalid, S.; Bajaj, M.; Kumar, B.H.; Zaitsev, I. Enhancing HVDC transmission line fault detection using disjoint bagging and bayesian optimization with artificial neural networks and scientometric insights. *Sci. Rep.* **2024**, *14*, 23610. [CrossRef] [PubMed]
29. Zhou, R.; Gao, W.; Liu, W.; Ding, D.; Zhang, B. Statistical Feature Extraction Combined with Generalized Discriminant Component Analysis Driven SVM for Fault Diagnosis of HVDC GIS. *Energies* **2021**, *14*, 7674. [CrossRef]
30. Lin, C.; Zhu, L.; Lin, X.; Chen, Y.; Chen, H.; Chen, H.; Zheng, Y. AC Surface Flashover Voltage Prediction of Epoxy Resin by Tree-Based Model. In *Proceedings of the 5th International Symposium on Plasma and Energy Conversion, Nanjing, China, 27–29 October* 2023; Springer Nature: Singapore, 2024; pp. 399–412. [CrossRef]
31. Luo, Y.; Tang, J.; Pan, C.; Yin, J.; Zhang, Y.; Zhang, B.; Zhu, Q. The Transition of Surface Charge Accumulation Dominating Way in HVDC GIS. In Proceedings of the 2018 IEEE International Conference on High Voltage Engineering and Application (ICHVE), Athens, Greece, 10–13 September 2018; pp. 1–4. [CrossRef]

32. Wu, S.; Xu, H.; Zhang, X.; Liang, Y.; Shao, Y.; Wang, C.; Tu, Y.; Xu, Y. Towards the surface flashover in DC GIL/GIS: The electric field distribution and the surface charge accumulation. *Phys. Scr.* **2022**, *97*, 072001. [CrossRef]
33. Zhong, J.; Zhang, B.; Guo, Y.; Wang, Z.; Yao, Y.; Zhang, H.; Liu, Y. Gas and solid insulation in HVDC gas insulated switchgear. In Proceedings of the 2017 IEEE Conference on Energy Internet and Energy System Integration (EI2), Beijing, China, 26–28 November 2017; pp. 1–5. [CrossRef]
34. Ma, G.m.; Zhou, H.y.; Li, C.r.; Jiang, J.; Chen, X.w. Designing epoxy insulators in SF 6-filled DC-GIL with simulations of ionic conduction and surface charging. *IEEE Trans. Dielectr. Electr. Insul.* **2015**, *22*, 3312–3320. [CrossRef]
35. Qin, S.c.; Tu, Y.p.; Wang, C.; Zhou, F.w.; Ma, G.m.; Zhou, H.y. The influence of the insulator volume conductivity on charge accumulation in HVDC-GIL. In Proceedings of the 2016 IEEE Electrical Insulation Conference (EIC), Montreal, QC, Canada, 19–22 June 2016; pp. 325–328. [CrossRef]
36. Kaheman, K.; Kutz, J.N.; Brunton, S.L. SINDy-PI: A robust algorithm for parallel implicit sparse identification of nonlinear dynamics. *Proc. R. Soc. A Math. Phys. Eng. Sci.* **2020**, *476*, 20200279. [CrossRef]
37. de Silva, B.; Champion, K.; Quade, M.; Loiseau, J.C.; Kutz, J.; Brunton, S. PySINDy: A Python package for the sparse identification of nonlinear dynamical systems from data. *J. Open Source Softw.* **2020**, *5*, 2104. [CrossRef]
38. Kaptanoglu, A.A.; de Silva, B.M.; Fasel, U.; Kaheman, K.; Goldschmidt, A.J.; Callaham, J.; Delahunt, C.B.; Nicolaou, Z.G.; Champion, K.; Loiseau, J.C.; et al. PySINDy: A comprehensive Python package for robust sparse system identification. *J. Open Source Softw.* **2022**, *7*, 3994. [CrossRef]
39. Urazaki Junior, K. 2024. Available online: https://github.com/kjurazaki/HVDC-GIL-physics-informed-ML (accessed on 23 January 2025).
40. Winter, A.; Kindersberger, J. Transient field distribution in gas-solid insulation systems under DC voltages. *IEEE Trans. Dielectr. Electr. Insul.* **2014**, *21*, 116–128. [CrossRef]

electronics

MDPI

Article

Evaluation of VSC Impact on Power System Using Adequate P-Q Capability Curve

Michal Brodzicki [1], Jacek Klucznik [2] and Stanislaw Czapp [2,*]

1 Faculty of Mechanical and Electrical Engineering, Polish Naval Academy, Smidowicza 69, 81-127 Gdynia, Poland; m.brodzicki@amw.gdynia.pl
2 Faculty of Electrical and Control Engineering, Gdansk University of Technology, Narutowicza 11/12, 80-233 Gdansk, Poland; jacek.klucznik@pg.edu.pl
* Correspondence: stanislaw.czapp@pg.edu.pl

Abstract: Renewable energy sources, which are becoming increasingly popular, often use a voltage source converter (VSC) for connection to the power system. Assessing the effects of connecting such a source to the power system is essential to ensure the proper operation of the power system and the connected source. For this purpose, it is necessary to know the range of active and reactive power generation by the converter. The authors indicate that the interaction between the power system and the converter affects its range of available active and reactive power. Therefore, a strictly defined range of the converter's generating capability should not be assumed as invariant, but its capability for a given operating condition of the power system should be determined iteratively. In order to confirm this thesis, the authors analyzed the operation of the VSC-based energy source in an example power system using the PowerFactory software. Extending the calculation procedure to include iterative determination of the converter's available power range showed a significant influence of the system's operating state on the converter's generating capabilities. The results obtained in this work extend the knowledge, and thanks to them, the operation of VSC systems can be modelled more accurately.

Keywords: load flow calculation; reactive power; renewable energy sources; voltage control; voltage source converter

1. Introduction

Recent years have brought a major change in terms of electrical energy generation, which is the turn towards renewable energy sources (RES). Climate change, along with new legal directives, forced an increase in participation in RES, so-called green sources in power systems [1–4]. One of the very popular groups among these devices are photovoltaic (PV) systems [5–7]. The second very important group is energy generation systems utilizing wind turbines [8,9] as well as hybrid PV–wind systems [10]. Wind turbines can be located both onshore and offshore, and they are very important elements in the context of transition to green energy production [11–13].

Nowadays, a very popular method of connecting offshore wind farms with onshore power grids is to use direct current (DC) links, which cannot operate without converters [14,15]. This leads to an unequivocal conclusion that the increase in the number of offshore wind farms connected to power systems entails an increase in the number of converters, especially voltage source converters (VSCs). As it is known, VSCs have the unique ability to exchange active and reactive power independently. This ability could possibly be used to influence the alternating current (AC) grid's voltage levels using a specific VSC's operation mode [16–18].

Many studies were conducted throughout the years, whose goals were to analyse VSC impact on the power system in different manners. In [19], a three-phase VSC model is used to determine the steady-state operating characteristics of a VSC, taking into account the harmonic interactions. Steady-state operating conditions are also considered in [20]. A detailed computer model of a VSC is presented in [21]. Direct and vector control have been implemented to control the degrees of freedom related to the VSC transmission system. The author of the paper in [22] describes a predictive-corrective control method of the VSC system. Two variants of space vector pulse width modulation (PWM) methods for VSC systems are investigated. The operation of VSC is analyzed for the model of VSC with a three-value transistor branch state function. Power system state estimation with the use of the generalized steady state multi-terminal VSC model is performed in paper [23]. The effectiveness of the proposed state estimation algorithm is demonstrated. The authors of paper [24] consider the high-voltage DC link's converter substation for a reactive power regulator in the power system. It has been shown that there is a possibility of specific activation of the converter to both limit and increase the amount of consumed reactive power. In [25], a sequential AC/DC power flow algorithm is implemented to solve networks containing multi-terminal VSC high-voltage DC system. In the analyses, the authors also took the converter losses into account using a generalized converter loss model. They underlined that this problem is often neglected or not taken into account in a proper way in VSC high-voltage DC power flows. Detailed analysis of the VSC high-voltage DC power system with the use of the model including reactor and converter losses is conducted in [26]. Various control modes of converters and losses reduction have been investigated. The paper [27] estimates the conversion power losses in the VSC converters as well as power losses occurring in DC cables, coupling transformer and filters. Taking these factors into account enables researchers to calculate the efficiency of the VSC high-voltage DC transmission links. A complete and unified DC power grid steady-state model is proposed in [28]. This model includes a VSC inverter, DC bus, DC line, DC/DC converters. An AC/DC power flow algorithm is developed and validated by application to the CIGRE B4-58 DC power test system. The authors of the paper in [29] discuss a nonlinear dynamic model for VSC-based high-voltage DC links. This model is composed of the main physical elements and is controlled by proportional integral (PI) controllers with antiwindup.

Generally, the published papers are focused on the operating area of the VSC converter in separation from the influence of the power system to which it is connected, which has some disadvantages. The active power–reactive power (P-Q) area constraints are then derived from the limits of currents, voltages, and modulation factor, and a 'textbook', symmetrical, idealised operating area is obtained. Using only a fixed theoretical P-Q area/curve can lead to an incorrect assessment of the impact of the converter on the power system. Consideration of the properties of the power system and its demand for active and reactive power indicates that the converter's operating area may change depending on the current operating state of the system. Therefore, procedures for calculating load flow in the power grid should take into account not a rigidly defined converter operating area dependent on active power, reactive power, and voltage level, but the actual equations defining these constraints. This can be realised iteratively, as presented in the paper. The purpose of this work is to present a consistent VSC model, that fulfils its actual P-Q capability curve. The second goal is the analysis and evaluation of VSCs' capabilities to impact the AC power system. The conducted analysis focuses on the whole VSC capability curve and the different operation points' influence on AC grid behaviour. The results obtained in this work contribute to the knowledge and, thanks to them, the operation of VSC systems can be modelled more accurately, which is important as the number of converters connected to the power systems is growing rapidly. The DIgSILENT PowerFactory software was used to model the VSC systems [30]. In the simulation studies, the guidelines contained in [31–33] have been taken into account.

The paper is organized as follows. Section 2 comments on the P-Q capability curve. Section 3 describes the proposed VSC model. In Section 4, the structure of the grid model for simulation tests, along with the research procedure, is presented. Results of the simulations and discussion are provided in Section 5. Final conclusions are presented in Section 6.

2. VSC P-Q Capability Curve

The VSC active and reactive power exchanged with the power grid depends on the voltage and phase difference between the converter and the power system. A simplified diagram of VSC connection to the grid is presented in Figure 1.

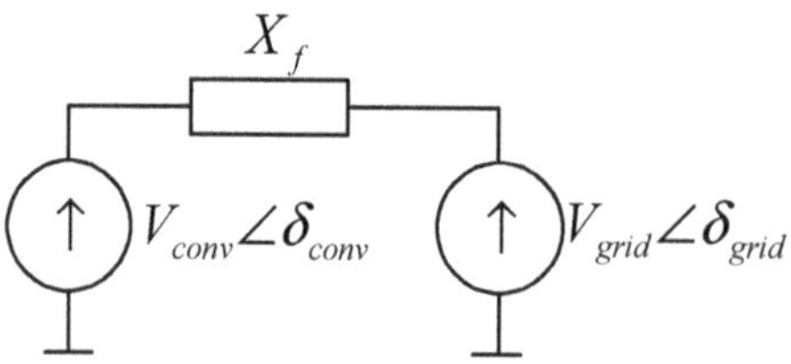

Figure 1. Simplified diagram presenting the connection of the voltage source converter (VSC) to the power system. V_{grid}—AC grid voltage, δ_{grid}—AC grid voltage angle, V_{conv}—VSC output AC voltage, δ_{conv}—AC converter voltage angle, and X_f—coupling reactance.

The exchanged power is described using Equations (1) and (2), as follows:

$$P_{VSC} = -\frac{V_{grid} \cdot V_{conv}}{X_f} sin\delta \tag{1}$$

$$Q_{VSC} = \frac{V_{grid}^2}{X_f} - \frac{V_{grid} \cdot V_{conv}}{X_f} cos\delta \tag{2}$$

where P_{VSC} is the VSC active power, Q_{VSC} is the VSC reactive power, V_{grid} is the AC grid voltage, V_{conv} is the VSC output AC voltage, δ is the phase difference between V_{grid} and V_{conv}, ($\delta = \delta_{conv}$—δ_{grid}), and X_f is the coupling reactance.

Equations (1) and (2) indicate that the VSC's active power mainly depends on the phase shift between the grid and VSC's voltages, whereas the converter's reactive power mainly depends on the differences between mentioned voltages. However, the values of the power exchanged with the grid cannot be arbitrary, as they are limited by the design parameters of the converter.

The first limitation, related to VSC power generation capabilities, derives from the IGBT maximum current capacity. The maximum power value is limited by the permissible transistor's current capacity, but it also depends on the voltage level. Therefore, a shrinking of the operating area is observed at reduced voltage (V_{conv} = 0.9 in Figure 2), and an area expansion at increased voltage (V_{conv} = 1.1 in Figure 2) can be observed.

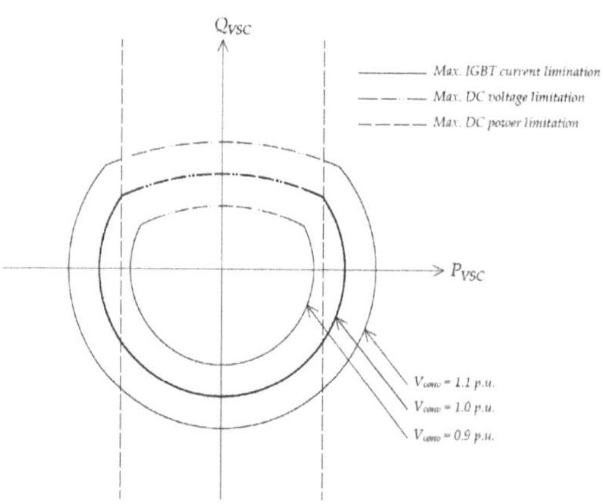

Figure 2. Voltage source converter (VSC) active power–reactive power (P-Q) capability curve, based on [16].

The second limitation derives from DC-side voltage. The DC voltage level is crucial for VSC capabilities in terms of reactive power generation. Higher levels of capacitive reactive power require higher DC voltage levels, which may exceed admissible levels. The third and final limitation is a consequence of maximum DC-side power, which is often lower than the VSC rated apparent power.

Active and reactive power ranges of the VSC are typically described by its P-Q capability curve, for which a classic example [16] is presented in Figure 2.

3. VSC Model

The model used for all analyses was designed in the DIgSILENT PowerFactory software. It was based on a VSC model with singular DC and AC connections, which was improved with several parameters, e.g., conducting losses. Figure 3 illustrates the structure of the PowerFactory library-based VSC model, while Table 1 presents crucial parameters of the whole converter substation (VSC along with the converter transformer).

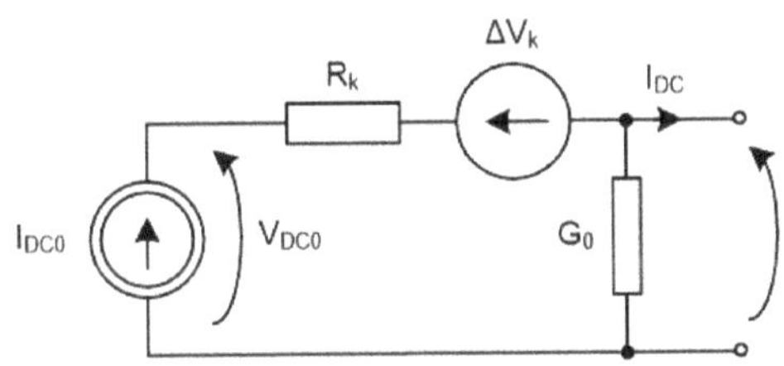

Figure 3. VSC model implemented in PowerFactory, based on [30]. I_{DC0}—model of converter's internal current, R_k—model of converter's conducting losses, ΔV_k—conductive voltage droop, G_0—model of converter's no-load losses.

Table 1. Converter substation model parameters.

Parameter Name	Symbol	Value	Unit
VSC rated apparent power	S_{rCv}	400	MVA
VSC DC rated power	P_{CvDC}	400	MW
VSC AC rated voltage	V_{CvAC}	145	kV
VSC DC rated voltage	V_{CvDC}	320	kV
VSC series reactor short circuit impedance	x_{kr}	0.1	p.u.
VSC series reactor load losses	ΔP_{Cv}	360	kW
VSC no-load losses	ΔP_{Cv0}	291.28	kW
Converter transformer rated apparent power	S_{rCvT}	440	MVA
Converter transformer rated HV-side voltage	U_{rCvTHV}	400	kV
Converter transformer rated LV-side voltage	U_{rCvTLV}	145	kV
Converter transformer short-circuit voltage	u_{kr}	0.132	p.u.
Converter transformer load losses	ΔP_{CuBT}	440	kW
Converter transformer no-load current	i_{0BT}	0.011	p.u.
Converter transformer no-load losses	ΔP_{FeBT}	115	kW

The VSC P-Q capability curve control was implemented to the model using a scripting tool, which is built in PowerFactory. It is based on the DIgSILENT programming language (DPL), an original programming language used for automating calculations and analysis conducted with PowerFactory. Implementing VSC P-Q capability curve to the model was a phased process, which improved control and "on-line" verification of the limitations' implementation.

The first and basic stage of modelling was to calculate the VSC P-Q curve based on the rated apparent power with no additional limitations included, as follows:

$$S_{rCv} \geq \sqrt{P_{VSC}^2 + Q_{VSC}^2} \tag{3}$$

where S_{rCv} is VSC's rated apparent power (Table 1).

Given that (3) is in fact a transformed circle equation, the resulting P-Q curve is a circle with a radius deriving from the VSC rated apparent power (S_{rCv}), assuming that both the active and reactive power maximum values are equal to S_{rCv}. The achieved P-Q capability curve fulfils these assumption, which can be observed in Figure 4.

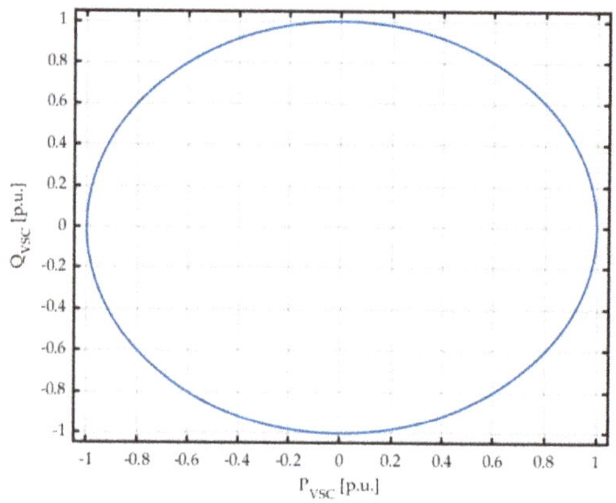

Figure 4. VSC P-Q basic capability curve with no additional limitations.

In this paper, the authors use relative units (per units) commonly used in electrical power engineering. The base value to which the presented results refer is the apparent rated power of the converter (S_{rCv}). The relative units allow us to easily assess how much the operating area of the converter changes.

The resultant curve was obtained as a result of iterative calculations, which fulfilled the condition based on (3). At each step, the VSCs' active power was set, and adequate reactive power was calculated, both generated and consumed. Initial DC- and AC-side voltage levels were set to rated values.

The next step was implementing maximum DC power limitation P_{CvDC} (Table 1) to the model. It was completed by adding a converter maximum DC current control loop, because the DC power limitation, at certain voltage levels, depends on the converter current. When a DC current transgression was detected, the model began a loop of reducing the converter's active power to an acceptable level. The achieved P-Q capability curve with DC power (current) limitation is presented in Figure 5.

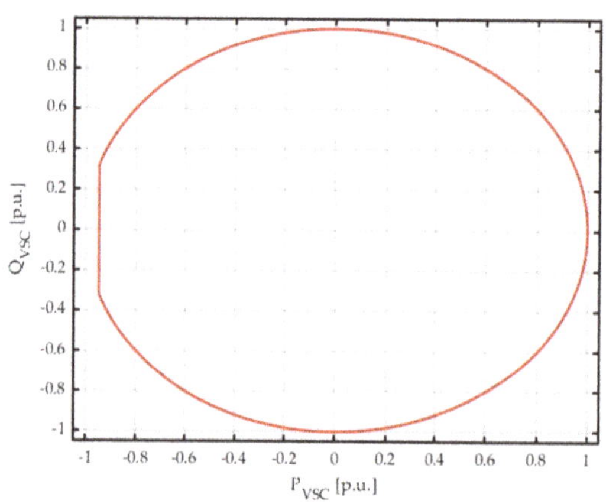

Figure 5. VSC P-Q capability curve with DC power (current) limitation.

As can be seen, the included limitations affected only the inverter side of the P-Q curve (flattening on the left side of the curve). This comes from the fact that the inverter-type operation of the converter results in decreasing DC-side voltage, which implicates an increase in current which is limited by the VSC transistor's thermal capabilities. Rectifier-type operation of the converter results in increasing DC-side voltage, which implicates a reduction in current, and the power level is not limited.

The third step consisted of adding an AC current limitation along with a DC current limitation. The updated P-Q curve is illustrated in Figure 6. The AC current limitation value results from the apparent power rating and AC voltage rating are given in Table 1.

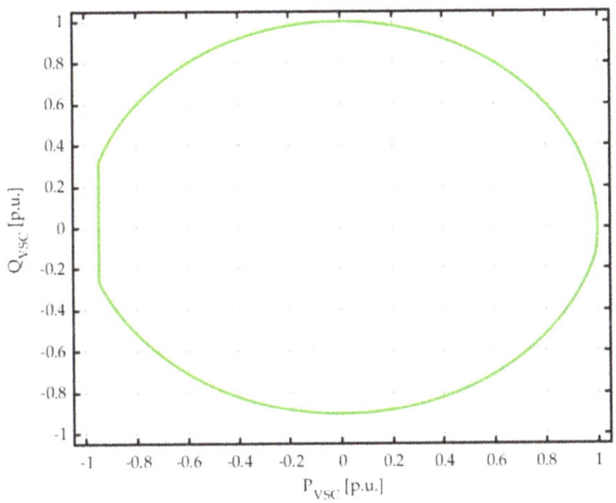

Figure 6. VSC P-Q capability curve with AC and DC current limitations.

This limitation implementation was achieved similarly to the former addition of the DC current control loop (the curve at the bottom does not reach the value −1; reactive power consumption is limited). When AC current transgression was detected, a loop of reducing the converter's reactive power began. When the measured AC current value dropped below rated level, the admissible operation point was noted.

The final stage was implementing the control of DC-side voltage. This improvement needed a bit more workload, as the link between the reactive power and DC voltage is not directly stated. Firstly, there is a relationship between AC- and DC-side voltages, described by Equation (4), as follows:

$$V_{AC} = k_0 \cdot m \cdot V_{DC} \tag{4}$$

where V_{AC} is the AC-side voltage, V_{DC} is the DC-side voltage, m is the modulation index (max permissible value 0.8), and k_0 is the modulation type-dependent coefficient.

AC-side voltage stated as V_{AC} in (4) is in fact the value of V_{conv} present in (1) and (2). Using this along with assuming sinusoidal-type modulation, (4) can be rewritten into (5), as follows:

$$V_{conv} = \frac{\sqrt{3}}{2\sqrt{2}} \cdot m \cdot V_{DC} \tag{5}$$

While (2) can be transformed into (6), as follows:

$$V_{conv} = \frac{V_{grid}}{cos\delta} \left(1 - \frac{Q_{VSC} \cdot X_f}{V_{grid}^2} \right) \tag{6}$$

A comparison of Equations (5) and (6) leads to the conclusion that the VSC's reactive power limitation seen in Figure 2 not only derives from the DC voltage level, but also from the modulation index. Thus, implementation of the VSC's P-Q curve to the model comes down to controlling several parameters' values, namely the AC- and DC-side voltages and currents and the modulation index.

The modulation index control loop was included similarly as in former steps—when a transgression of the modulation index maximum value had been detected, the model entered the loop of additional reactive power reduction. This loop overlapped the former condition of keeping the AC current in a proper range. At first, reactive power is reduced until the AC current meets admissible value, and after that the reduction is continued if the modulation index exceeds the limitation. Figure 7 shows the final shape of the VSC P-Q capability curve with all limitations included.

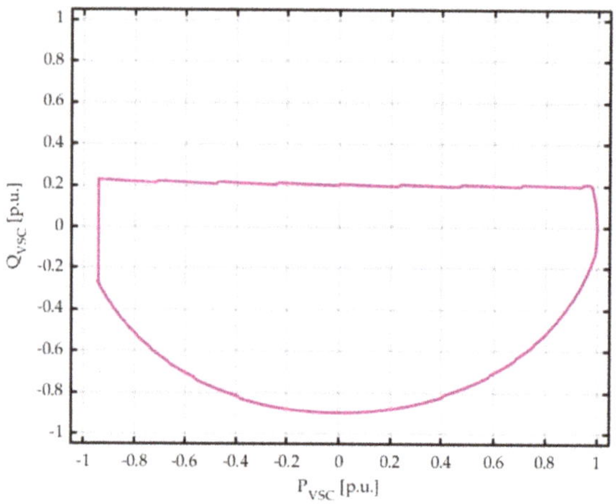

Figure 7. VSC P-Q capability curve with the modulation index and AC and DC current limitations.

A general flowchart of the VSC P-Q capability curve implementation into the load–flow procedure is presented in Figure 8.

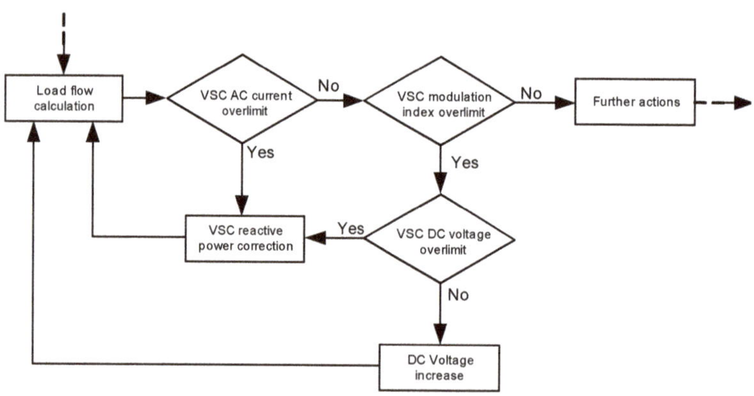

Figure 8. Flowchart of P-Q capability curve implementation into the load–flow procedure.

The iteration loop shown in Figure 8 is a part of larger script that controls the whole load flow calculations performed using the model. The steps concerning DC current limitation was omitted in the chart, as it is a part of an active power control loop. The first step after load flow calculation (followed by preliminary checking and eliminating possible transgressions except those concerning voltage levels) is the control of VSC's AC current. If it exceeds the limit, then the VSC's reactive power is immediately corrected by decreasing its absolute value. If the AC current is within the admissible range, the loop goes on to check the VSC's modulation index value. If it exceeds designated value, then the correction process is taken. First, the value of the VSC's DC voltage is checked. If it is not over the limit, then its value is increased. If the DC voltage reaches its limitation and the modulation index is still over the limit, then the VSC's reactive power is decreased. After setting the VSC's operation point, the script moves on to execute further actions.

4. Research Procedure

All studies were conducted using a test grid model designed in PowerFactory. The structure of the grid is presented in Figure 9.

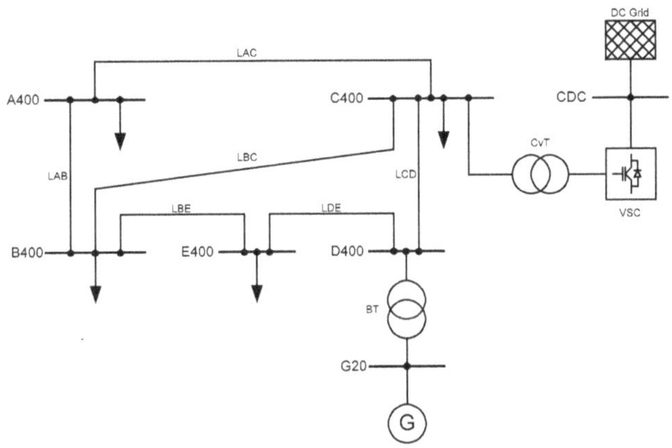

Figure 9. Test grid model structure. The symbols are explained in the text.

The VSC model previously described is supplied by an equivalent DC subsystem (DC grid). The DC grid is modelled using a single DC voltage source with specified internal resistance enabling its voltage level deviation. The VSC converter is connected to one of the power system terminals (C400) via a converter transformer (CvT). This allows sufficient representation of the VSC-type converter substation. The model consists of four PQ-type terminals feeding the loads' models (A400, B400, C400, E400). All loads are constant impedance type models. The thermal power plant model consists of two elements—a synchronous generator (G) and unit step-up transformer (BT). All overhead lines' (LAC, LBC, LAB, LBE, LDE, LCD) model parameters are calculated for aluminum conductor steel-reinforced (ACSR) with a nominal cross-section area 525 mm^2.

The aim of the studies was to verify the possible VSC power capabilities based on its P-Q capability curve. This should have led to achieving extreme points in a power system operation including different VSC operating conditions. All analysis were iterative, including different power system loading and different levels of VSC active power. The range of examined power system loadings was 40%, 50%, 60%, 70%, 80%, 90%, which refers to the rated power plant loading. At each power system loading, the whole load-flow analysis was conducted. Firstly, the VSC active power level was set and the adequate reactive power was calculated, using Equation (3). After that, the control of all designated parameters took place. Both active and reactive power were reduced when needed if any transgression was detected.

5. Results and Discussion

Taking into account the above-presented assumptions, various P-Q capability curves have been obtained (Figure 10).

The curves presented in Figure 10 indicate that the VSC's admissible operation area in terms of reactive power strongly depends on power system loading level. Although the shape of the curve for individual percentage load 40–90% does not significantly change, it becomes moved upwards along with the AC grid loading increase. Thus, VSC capabilities in terms of generating additional reactive power are wider for higher power system loadings (the highest for 90%). At higher loadings, the VSC is capable of operating more like an additional reactive power source, whereas at lower loadings it is capable of acting more like a reactive power receiver. Reactive power generation capabilities are also less dependent on the VSC's active power. As far as reactive power consuming is concerned, VSC has more to offer within lower power system loadings. This is a major advantage, as low loadings often cause problems with reactive power surplus (due to lines' charging power) when high loadings result in its deficiency (due to increased reactive power losses caused by heavier loading). Having that, VSC seems to act as a perfect compensator both in terms of inductive and capacitive reactive power.

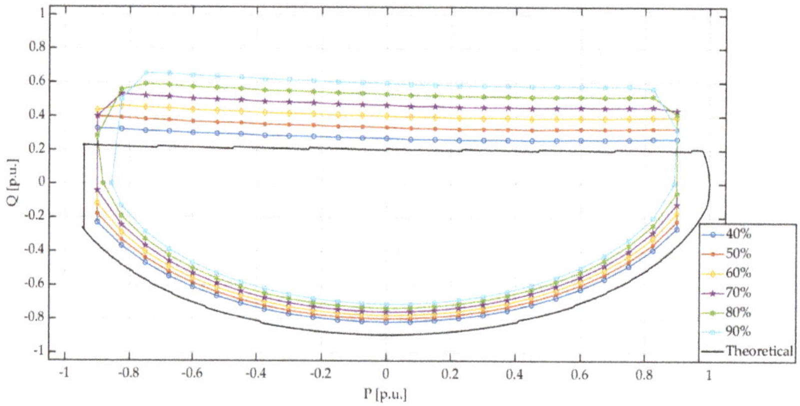

Figure 10. VSC P-Q capability theoretical curve ("Theoretical"—solid black curve) and P-Q curves at different power system loadings. Loadings 40–90% refers to the power plant loading range.

It should also be mentioned that generating reactive power allows the VSC to operate with a slightly larger active power export, as the voltage on the converter substation's terminal increases. As far as active power import is concerned, neither reactive power generation nor drain have any impact on the VSC active power level (apart from at the highest analyzed loading level of 90%).

According to the fact that the VSC is able to affect the power system both in terms of active and reactive power, the grid's response may differ and depends on the power exchange level provided by the VSC. Taking into account that both aforementioned powers exchanged at the same time can influence one another, a more accurate way of analysing data should consider the VSC P-Q capability area as a combined parameter, rather than as separate variables (P or Q).

The theoretical P-Q capability curve, calculated earlier from converter parameters (Table 1) and presented in Figure 7, has also been included in Figure 10. As can be seen, the theoretical capabilities of the VSC differ from real cases. The shape of the curves remains the same, but the operating area is different. VSC operation is inseparable from the power grid it is connected to. Thus, the power grid properties affect the capabilities provided by the VSC device. Figure 10 indicates that different power systems' loading significantly enlarge VSC's capabilities in terms of reactive power generation, whereas the reactive power consumption capabilities are slightly narrowed. This comparison illustrates the effect and importance of the presented work. Using only a fixed theoretical P-Q curve can lead to an incorrect assessment of the impact of the converter on the power system. The actual operating capability of the converter may be overestimated or underestimated.

Figures 11 and 12 present voltage levels in two chosen grids' terminals, respectively, as a function of the converter's P-Q capability curve. Terminal B400 is the farthest from the converter substation coupling point, whereas terminal C400 is at this point itself. The results are also presented with connected point curves (area/surface boundaries) as they show the limitations of the VSC's P-Q capability curve at each power system's loading. Thus, all the operating points within the designated areas are admissible.

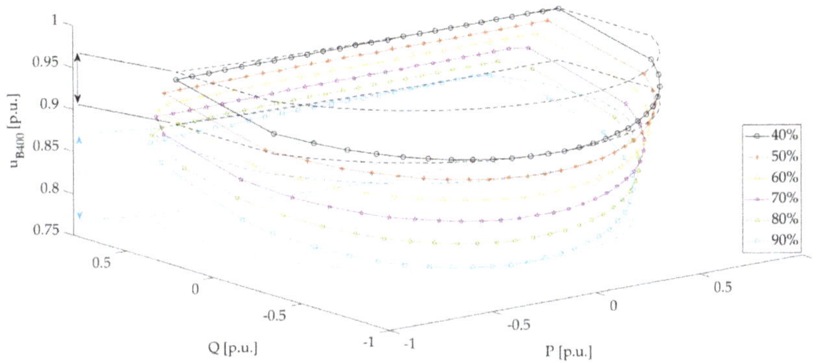

Figure 11. Voltage level in terminal B400 as a function of the converter's P-Q capability curve.

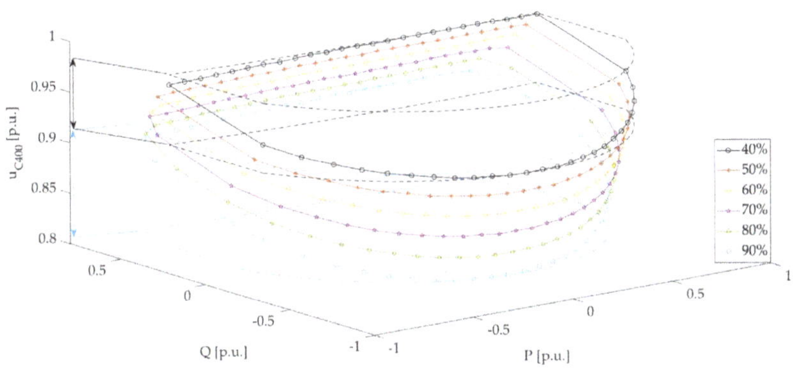

Figure 12. Voltage level in terminal C400 as a function of the converter's P-Q capability curve.

Figures 11 and 12 indicate that the converter's active and reactive power generation/consumption strongly influences the voltage in the grid. The voltage range at terminals B400 and C400 shows a significantly stronger sensitivity to the converter's reactive power (Q) change than to the active power (P) change. This is an expected result, as voltage and reactive power form a pair of interrelated parameters. However, when both powers (active and reactive) are taken into consideration, there is a wide range of voltage levels variability to be obtained.

A strong connection with global power system loading can also be observed. Operating within a low loadings range result in a narrower range of voltage levels, which extends along with the global loading increase. The lowest and highest voltage levels for the extreme power system loadings are marked with dotted lines in Figures 11 and 12, and voltage levels' variability are indicated with arrows. At the 40% loading level, the potential voltage level variability range reaches about 5% (black line with arrows), whereas at the 90% loading level this range was about 10% wide (blue line with arrows). Another thing worth mentioning is that the shape of the curves in different terminals does not change, which means that the converter affects all of them the same way. They only change in position with respect to the voltage level axis, which is a natural effect of voltage drops occurring within transmission lines.

Another issue that must be taken under consideration is the potential influence of reactive power variability on other VSC crucial parameters, in terms of AC current, DC current, and modulation index. These values, as a function of the converter's reactive power, are illustrated in Figures 13–15. Figures 13–15 indicate that limitations included in the proposed VSC model are adequate and fill initially stated assumptions. As can be seen in Figure 13, the converter's AC current values limit its capabilities of reactive power exchange at each designated active power set-point (−1P, ... , 0P, ... , 1P). What is also worth mentioning is that the direction of active power flow through the converter (generation and consumption) does not significantly change its compensative capabilities.

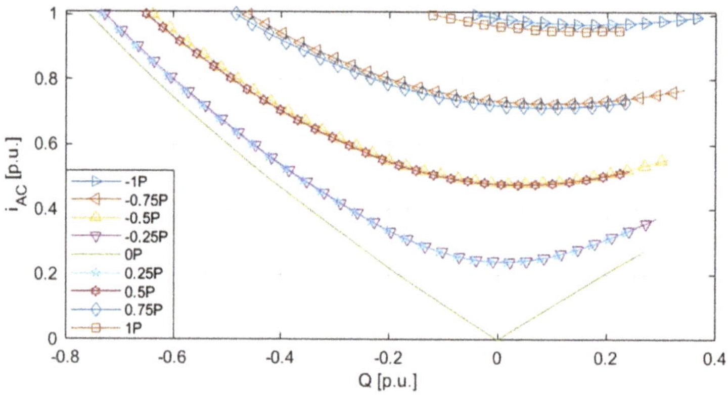

Figure 13. Converter's AC current (i_{AC}) as a function of reactive power. (−1P, ... , 0P, ... , 1P-values of constant VSC active power generation/consumption.

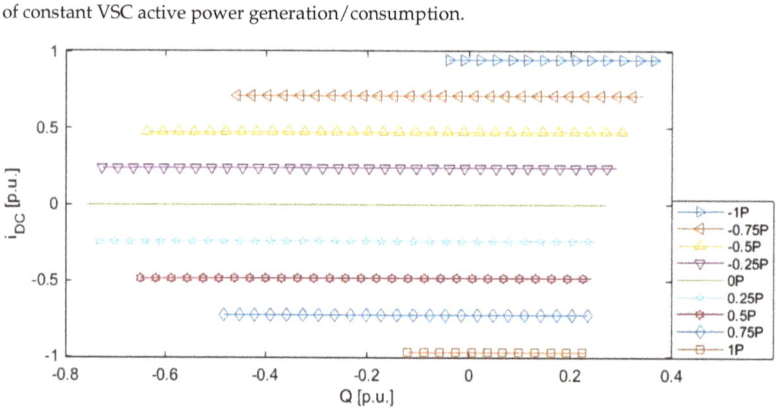

Figure 14. Converter's DC current (i_{DC}) as a function of reactive power. (−1P, ... , 0P, ... , 1P-values of constant VSC active power generation/consumption.

The converter's DC current shows no dependence on its reactive power (Figure 14), which means that the active power exchange realised by the converter remains undisturbed. In other words, the reactive power control provided by the converter can be performed with no negative impact on other operation conditions.

The converter's modulation index curves also indicate (Figure 15) that the value of this index does not exceed 0.8, which is the maximum permissible value as stated in Equation (4). Its value was kept within designated range for all obtained points of operation. It can be seen that the reactive power generation results in AC voltage increase, corresponding with Equation (6). Such operation forces the converter to operate with higher

DC voltage or at higher values of the modulation index, corresponding with Equation (4). Table 2 present a summary of the converter's parameters and power system nodes' voltage levels for extreme reactive power values.

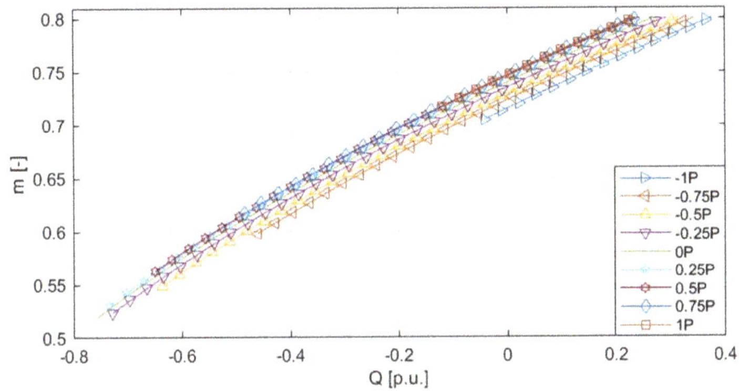

Figure 15. Converter's modulation index (m) as a function of reactive power. (−1P, ..., 0P, ..., 1P-values of constant VSC active power generation/consumption.

Table 2. Load flow calculation results for extreme reactive power values. Limit values: 1 p.u. for the AC current; 0.8 p.u. for the modulation index.

Active Power [p.u.]	Reactive Power [p.u.]	AC Current [p.u.]	DC Current [p.u.]	Modulation Index [p.u]	B400 Voltage [p.u.]	C400 Voltage [p.u.]
			Inverter-type operation			
−1	−0.041	1	0.95	0.705	0.865	0.896
	0.375	0.994	0.949	0.8	0.889	0.922
−0.75	−0.459	1	0.714	0.598	0.841	0.87
	0.343	0.769	0.713	0.8	0.893	0.926
−0.5	−0.636	1	0.476	0.549	0.832	0.861
	0.315	0.557	0.476	0.8	0.896	0.929
−0.25	−0.728	1	0.238	0.524	0.829	0.858
	0.291	0.373	0.238	0.8	0.898	0.931
			No active power exchange			
0	−0.758	1	−0.002	0.519	0.83	0.858
	0.27	0.274	0.001	0.8	0.9	0.933
			Rectifier-type operation			
0.25	−0.734	1	0.242	0.531	0.835	0.863
	0.254	0.344	0.241	0.8	0.901	0.934
0.5	−0.65	1	0.484	0.563	0.843	0.871
	0.243	0.52	0.483	0.8	0.901	0.934
0.75	−0.484	1	0.726	0.617	0.855	0.885
	0.235	0.729	0.725	0.8	0.901	0.934
1	−0.12	1	0.97	0.717	0.879	0.91
	0.233	0.952	0.969	0.8	0.9	0.932

The main conclusion coming from the Table 2 analysis is that the VSC's reactive power exchange capabilities depend on two parameters: the AC current "i_{AC}" and modulation index "m", and their max permissible values are reached. The maximum reactive power that can be drained from the power system by the VSC is limited by its AC current (the AC current reached a value of 1 p.u.), whereas the maximum reactive power generation is limited by the modulation index (the modulation index reached a value of 0.8 p.u.). The fact that these capabilities do not interfere with active power exchange is a major advantage. Obviously, the widest possible reactive power exchange range (from −0.758 p.u. to 0.27 p.u.) occurred for no active power exchange.

6. Conclusions

The achieved outcomes indicate that the presented VSC model is adequate and operates properly. All included limitations fulfil the assumptions and make the model's operation closer to reality, along with being simple and flexible in terms of the implementation.

This model provides the possibility to test and analyse different VSC operation points and their influence on the power system. It has been shown that the actual active and reactive power generation capability of the converter, with all the constraints on converter operation, can deviate from the initial (ideal) characteristics of the converter. This is due to the interaction between the converter and the power system. Therefore, an ideal, fixed P-Q characteristic determined in isolation from the real operating conditions of the converter should not be used for power system planning and development.

As has been presented, the converter provides a wide range of possible influence on voltage levels within the AC grid. As the VSC's active and reactive power can be set independently, they both, however, influence the interaction with the power system. Thus, it seems advisable to analyse the crucial grid's parameters as a function of the VSC P-Q capability curve, rather than its active and reactive power separately.

From the power system managing point of view, VSCs should be considered as elements of voltage and reactive power control within the grids. Considering lower power system loadings, the VSC is able to drain more reactive power that can be used, e.g., to eliminate its surpluses caused by lines operating with lower loadings. When power system loading increases, VSCs' P-Q capability curve moves upwards relative to the Q axis, meaning that its generative capabilities increase. What is more, the noted possible voltage regulation range for 90% power system loading was about 10%, being significantly wider in comparison to the approximately 5% noted for 40% power system loading. This proves that VSC, in terms of its compensative capabilities, becomes more flexible and useful within higher power system loadings.

Further presented results indicate (Figure 14, Table 2) that the described process of reactive power control has no impact on the active power transmitted by the VSC. The VSC's compensative capabilities (range of reactive power exchange) are obviously limited along with the active power transmission increase.

The approach presented by the authors can be used in any power flow calculation software that allows the calculation to be automated on the basis of a user script. Most of today's power system analysis tools have the ability to implement this method.

The authors intend to conduct further analyses of the use of the proposed method on more complex multi-node power system models. The authors also want to assess what differences there will be when using the classical approach with fixed converter characteristics against the proposed method in a large-scale power system model.

The increasing number of converters connected to the power system (wind turbines, photovoltaic sources, HVDC systems) requires certainty of results as a basis for the development and operation of the power grid, and the approach presented by the authors increases this certainty.

Author Contributions: Conceptualization, J.K. and M.B.; methodology, J.K.; software, M.B.; validation, J.K. and M.B.; formal analysis, M.B.; investigation, J.K. and M.B.; resources, S.C. and J.K.; data curation, M.B.; writing—original draft preparation, M.B.; writing—review and editing, S.C. and J.K.; visualization, M.B.; supervision, S.C. All authors have read and agreed to the published version of the manuscript.

Funding: This research received no external funding.

Data Availability Statement: Data are contained within the article.

Conflicts of Interest: The authors declare no conflict of interest.

References

1. Moriarty, P.; Honnery, D. Renewable Energy and Energy Reductions or Solar Geoengineering for Climate Change Mitigation? *Energies* **2022**, *15*, 7315. [CrossRef]
2. Chudy-Laskowska, K.; Pisula, T. An Analysis of the Use of Energy from Conventional Fossil Fuels and Green Renewable Energy in the Context of the European Union's Planned Energy Transformation. *Energies* **2022**, *15*, 7369. [CrossRef]
3. Riyaz, A.; Sadhu, P.K.; Iqbal, A.; Alamri, B. Comprehensive Survey of Various Energy Storage Technology Used in Hybrid Energy. *Electronics* **2021**, *10*, 2037. [CrossRef]
4. Mladenov, V.; Chobanov, V.; Georgiev, A. Impact of Renewable Energy Sources on Power System Flexibility Requirements. *Energies* **2021**, *14*, 2813. [CrossRef]
5. Jo, K.-Y.; Go, S.-I. Operation Method of PV–Battery Hybrid Systems for Peak Shaving and Estimation of PV Generation. *Electronics* **2023**, *12*, 1608. [CrossRef]
6. Abdel-Rahim, O.; Chub, A.; Vinnikov, D.; Blinov, A. DC Integration of Residential Photovoltaic Systems: A Survey. *IEEE Access* **2022**, *10*, 66974–66991. [CrossRef]
7. Zhou, D. A Review of Applied Research on Household Photovoltaic Power Generation Systems. In Proceedings of the 2nd International Conference on Electronic Materials and Information Engineering, Hangzhou, China, 15–17 April 2022.
8. Astolfi, D. Wind Turbine Operation Curves Modelling Techniques. *Electronics* **2021**, *10*, 269. [CrossRef]
9. Khodabux, K.; Bhujun, B.S.; Dhawankar, P.; Busawon, K. A review of offshore wind turbines and their various classifications. In Proceedings of the 7th International Conference on Environment Friendly Energies and Applications (EFEA), Bagatelle Moka MU, Mauritius, 14–16 December 2022.
10. Nabipour-Afrouzi, H.; Yii, S.H.W.; Ahmad, J.; Tabassum, M. Comprehensive Review on Appropriate Sizing and Optimization Technique of Hybrid PV-Wind System. In Proceedings of the IEEE PES Asia-Pacific Power and Energy Engineering Conference (APPEEC), Kota Kinabalu, Malaysia, 7–10 October 2018.
11. Shi, G.; Cai, X.; Chen, Z. Design and control of multi-terminal VSC-HVDC for large offshore wind farms. *Prz. Elektrotechniczny* **2012**, *88*, 264–268.
12. Liang, J.; Ekanayake, J.; Bellmunt, O.G.; Jenkins, N. Operation and control of multi-terminal HVDC transmission for offshore wind farms. *IEEE Trans. Power Deliv.* **2011**, *26*, 2596–2604. [CrossRef]
13. Kłosowski, Z.; Cieślik, S. The Use of a Real-Time Simulator for Analysis of Power Grid Operation States with a Wind Turbine. *Energies* **2021**, *14*, 2327. [CrossRef]
14. Rafin, S.M.S.H.; Islam, R.; Mohammed, O.A. Power Electronic Converters for Wind Power Generation. In Proceedings of the Fourth International Symposium on 3D Power Electronics Integration and Manufacturing (3D-PEIM), Miami, FL, USA, 1–3 February 2023.
15. Kirakosyan, A.; Ameli, A.; EL-Fouly, T.H.M.; El Moursi, M.S.; Salama, M.M.A.; El-Saadany, E.F. A Novel Control Technique for Enhancing the Operation of MTDC Grids. *IEEE Trans. Power Syst.* **2023**, *38*, 559–571. [CrossRef]
16. Oni, O.E.; Davidson, I.E.; Mbangula, K.N.I. A review of LCC-HVDC and VSC-HVDC technologies and applications. In Proceedings of the 16th International Conference on Environment and Electrical Engineering (EEEIC), Florence, Italy, 7–10 June 2016.
17. Xu, L.; Yao, L.; Bazargan, M.; Williams, B.W. Control and operation of multi-terminal DC systems for integrating large offshore wind farms. In Proceedings of the 7th International Workshop on Large-Scale Integration of Wind Power and Transmission Networks for Offshore Wind Farms, Madrid, Spain, 26–27 May 2008; pp. 339–344.
18. Xu, L.; Yao, L.; Bazargan, M. DC grid management of a multi-terminal HVDC transmission system for a large offshore wind farm. In Proceedings of the International Conference on Sustainable Power Generation and Supply, Nanjing, China, 6–7 April 2009.
19. Lehn, P.W. Exact Modelling of the Voltage Source Converter. *IEEE Trans. Power Deliv.* **2002**, *17*, 217–222. [CrossRef]
20. Chai, R.Z.; Zhang, B.H.; Bo, Z.Q.; Dou, J.M. A generalized unified power flow algorithm for AC/DC networks containing VSC-based multi-terminal DC grid. In Proceedings of the International Conference on Power System Technology, Chengdu, China, 20–22 October 2014; pp. 2361–2366.
21. Zakaria Moustafa, M.M.; Filizadeh, S. Simulation of a VSC transmission scheme supplying a passive load. In Proceedings of the 34th Annual Conference of IEEE Industrial Electronics, Orlando, FL, USA, 10–13 November 2008; pp. 942–946.
22. Radomski, G. Control and modulation methods of Voltage Source Converter. *Bull. Pol. Acad. Sci. Tech. Sci.* **2009**, *57*, 323–336. [CrossRef]
23. Cao, J.; Du, W.; Wang, H.F. The incorporation of generalized VSC MTDC model in AC/DC power system state estimation. In Proceedings of the International Conference on Sustainable Power Generation and Supply (SUPERGEN 2012), Hangzhou, China, 8–9 September 2012.
24. Brodzicki, M.; Kowalak, R. DC link converter station as var control element in power network. *Sci. Pap. Fac. Electr. Control. Eng. GdaŃSk Univ. Technol.* **2018**, *61*, 19–22.
25. Beerten, J.; Cole, S.; Belmans, R. A sequential AC/DC power flow algorithm for networks containing Multi-terminal VSC HVDC systems. In Proceedings of the IEEE PES General Meeting, Minneapolis, MN, USA, 25–29 July 2010; pp. 1–7.
26. Agrawal, S.; Kundu, P. A unified power flow analysis for VSC-MTDC system with distributed generation. In Proceedings of the 7th International Conference on Power Systems (ICPS), Pune, India, 21–23 December 2017; pp. 659–664.
27. Kalcon, G.; Adam, G.P.; Anaya-Lara, O.; Burt, G.; Lo, K.L. Analytical efficiency evaluation of two and three level VSC-HVDC transmission link. *Int. J. Electr. Power Energy Syst.* **2013**, *44*, 1–6. [CrossRef]

28. Chen, X.L.; Zhao, Z.; Zi, P.; Zhou, X.X. VSC based DC grid power flow algorithm and AC/DC power flow algorithm. In Proceedings of the International Conference on Power System Technology, Chengdu, China, 20–22 October 2014; pp. 2109–2114.
29. Imhof, M.; Andersson, G. Dynamic Modeling of a VSC-HVDC Converter. In Proceedings of the 48th International Universities' Power Engineering Conference (UPEC), Dublin, Ireland, 2–5 September 2013.
30. *Technical Reference PWM Converter*; DIgSILENT GmbH: Gomaringen, Germany, 2022.
31. Gu, M.; Meegahapola, L.; Wong, K.L. Coordinated voltage and frequency control in hybrid AC/MT-HVDC power grids for stability improvement. *IEEE Trans. Power Syst.* **2021**, *36*, 635–647. [CrossRef]
32. Kabiri, R.; Holmes, D.G.; McGrath, B.P. *DIgSILENT Modelling of Power Electronic Converters for Distributed Generation Networks*; DIgSILENT GmbH: Gomaringen, Germany, 2017.
33. Liu, Y.; Yao, L.; Zhao, D.W.; Qian, M.; Jiang, D. Steady-State Modelling of VSC MTDC for Power System Analysis in DIgSILENT Power Factory. In Proceedings of the China International Conference on Electricity Distribution (CICED), Tianjin, China, 17–19 September 2018; pp. 1765–1768.

electronics

MDPI

Article

Interpretable State Estimation in Power Systems Based on the Kolmogorov–Arnold Networks

Shuaibo Wang [1], Wenhao Luo [1], Sixing Yin [1,*], Jie Zhang [2,3], Zhuohang Liang [2,3], Yihua Zhu [2,3,4] and Shufang Li [1]

1 School of Information and Communication Engineering, Beijing University of Posts and Telecommunications, Beijing 100876, China; wangshuaibo@bupt.edu.cn (S.W.); rome1453a@bupt.edu.cn (W.L.); lisf@bupt.edu.cn (S.L.)
2 National Energy Power Grid Technology R&D Centre, Guangzhou 510663, China; zhangjie5@csg.cn (J.Z.); liangzh2@csg.cn (Z.L.); zhuyih@csg.cn (Y.Z.)
3 Guangdong Provincial Key Laboratory of Intelligent Operation and Control for New Energy Power System, Guangzhou 510663, China
4 State Key Laboratory of HVDC, Electric Power Research Institute, China Southern Power Grid, Guangzhou 510663, China
* Correspondence: yinsixing@bupt.edu.cn; Tel.:+86-1369-361-2055

Abstract: Power system state estimation is a critical task for ensuring stable grid operation and serves as the foundation of grid control and analysis. Conventional approaches largely involve field measurements, network topology, and manual anomaly detection, which present significant limitations, particularly while dealing with dynamic and complex power systems. In recent years, deep learning techniques have been progressively applied in this field to overcome the shortcomings of conventional approaches, which are based on mathematical models and static analysis. However, existing deep learning techniques primarily focus on power system security analysis and computational resource management. In spite of the powerful capabilities in supervised learning tasks, the lack of interpretability still makes deep learning models less convincing, and thus might hinder their practical applications. In response to this issue, we apply a computational model for power system state estimation based on the Kolmogorov–Arnold network (KAN) model with learnable activation functions, visualization capabilities, and pruning features. From the perspective of feature interpretability, we find the influence of bus features on the model output, such as bus voltage magnitude. Moreover, through analysis of the internal structure of the model, we uncover a possibility of potential mechanisms of power system state estimation. Experimental results show that our study not only enhances the interpretability of power system state estimation but also effectively ensures grid security and stability through state estimation.

Keywords: power system; state estimation; KAN; interpretability

1. Introduction

Due to the ever-increasing size and complexity of power systems, the demand for ensuring stability and security keeps growing as a critical challenge. To ensure the safety and stability of power systems, accurately estimating key state variables and potential anomalous events becomes essential, which makes state estimation involving effectively analyzing and processing large volumes of operational data imperative, so as to ensure the stable operation of power grids.

In response, Fred C. Schweppe initially introduced mathematical models and static analysis in power system state estimation, employing weighted least squares for state estimation [1–3]. As related technologies develop, more advancing tools such as phasor measurement units (PMUs) have been incorporated to improve estimation accuracy. However, these methods primarily rely on linearization techniques, which struggle in dealing with the nonlinear, time-variant, and uncertain characteristics of power systems, especially when handling complex dynamic processes and variable operating conditions. Furthermore, the expanding scale of power systems has increased computational complexity, posing great challenges to real-time performance and accuracy.

To overcome these limitations, deep learning has been considered as a helpful aid to be integrated into power system state estimation. With their robust learning capabilities on massive dataset, deep learning models are more adaptive to the growing scale and complexity of power systems. Applications of deep learning include computational scheduling, state estimation, and security monitoring in order to improve computational efficiency, estimation accuracy, and anomaly detection performance. However, existing deep learning models often work as "black boxes", which fail to interpret how the input features contribute to the output results and obscure the internal decision-making processes. Such lack of interpretability makes the credibility of deep learning models questionable and thus limits their practical applications due to potential risks.

To address this issue, we focus on the interpretability of state estimation models in power systems. By employing the Kolmogorov–Arnold network (KAN) model [4], we aim at enhancing internal model interpretability with feature importance analysis. The KAN model utilizes learnable activation functions, pruning, and visualization techniques to effectively reduce overfitting risks and improve the explainability of feature contributions. Compared to conventional neural networks, KAN models are capable of effectively learning the input-to-output mapping functions with visualizable feature impacts [5], excelling in handling stable state data and offering a more transparent and interpretable solution for complex data scenarios, thereby making the internal mechanism of models more understandable.

With help of the KAN models for power system state estimation, the complex multi-dimensional input can be decomposed into multiple one-dimensional features and each is fed to a univariant function. Therefore, how the model works internally for state estimation can be transparentized, and more insights on important factors relevant to the power system states can be gained. Moreover, the KAN model enables computational visualization, thereby facilitating interpretability elaboration for illustrative purposes. KAN replaces traditional matrix operations with learnable activation functions, which improves model transparency. This allows research to visualize the impact of different features on the output. The transparent structure of KAN enables us to more easily observe which input features significantly impact the nodes in the subsequent layers and ultimately the model's output. This visualization capability allows us to gain insights into the importance of different features in a way that MLP cannot, as the matrix is difficult to explain.

Notably, due to the necessity of maintaining stable grid operations, data samples for unstable events are relatively rare to collect, which leads to inherent data imbalance between stable and unstable samples. We tackle such datasets with skewed distribution by modifying the model loss (such as shrinkage loss [6]).

The experimental results show that the KAN network can successfully visualize the network structure, clearly presenting the influence between different nodes, and effectively estimate the contribution of different features to the output through the pruning function. The KAN model not only intuitively reveals the interpretability of the model, but also extends this interpretability to the entire model, which is difficult to traditional networks.

In this paper, our contribution is proposing an approach to power system state estimation using the Kolmogorov–Arnold network model, with a primary focus on improving interpretability, which is a key challenge in deep learning applications. The analytical approach includes analyzing feature importance, addressing the issues of data imbalance and model overfitting. Additionally, we highlight the practical implications of the proposed method for power system, emphasizing its scalability and adaptability for future research.

2. Related Works

For power system state estimation, many studies have explored neural network-based approaches, such as reinforcement learning techniques in optimizing systems by Stefan et al. [7], and random forest classification by Cheng et al. [8]. However, these studies have primarily focused on computational scheduling, fault classification, and security analysis, but relatively lack research on interpretability.

In terms of interpretability, researchers have proposed various methods from different perspectives: Tree regularization [9] enhances model interpretability by embedding a tree structure and has been applied in power system transient stability assessment. However, it primarily focuses on internal model interpretation, making it difficult to directly assess the impact of input features on state estimation. Optimization-based machine learning [10] extracts physically interpretable rules, but in complex and dynamic power systems these rules often lack generalizability and real-time applicability. Interpretable neighborhood deep models [11] improve prediction accuracy and interpretability in total transfer capability (TTC) assessments by partitioning the state space. However, the division of complex state spaces may increase model complexity, negatively impacting the efficiency of practical applications.

While the aforementioned studies offer various methods to achieve interpretability, aiding in understanding the decision logic and feature influence in power systems from different perspectives, they still exhibit certain limitations. For instance, the tree regularization method, while beneficial for internal model interpretability, has limitations in feature interpretability. Optimization-based machine learning can struggle with rule generation in complex scenarios, and interpretable neighborhood deep models face difficulties in managing large-scale complex environments due to the need for multiple neighborhood partitions. Therefore, a more generalizable method is required—one that can handle complex scenarios without significantly increasing training costs while efficiently realizing both model and feature interpretability.

In this paper, we introduce the KAN model to achieve interpretability. Compared to the interpretability methods discussed above, KAN exhibits significant advantages in its architecture for interpretability. KAN leverages its learnable activation functions and visualization features to achieve a tighter integration of model interpretability and feature interpretability. Additionally, KAN has a certain level of generality, making it well suited for complex scenarios. Section 3.1 provides a detailed discussion of the advantages of KAN compared to traditional multi-layer perceptrons (MLPs).

3. Preliminaries

In this section, we introduce the necessary preliminary knowledge to facilitate the understanding of the following technical parts. In Section 3.1, the computational model of KAN is explained in detail and its advantages over traditional multi-layer perceptrons (MLPs) are discussed. In Section 3.2, methodologies with shrinkage loss as part of the model training objective for handling imbalanced samples are introduced. In Section 3.3, we elaborate on how the experiments in this paper were conducted, including data processing, model training, and interpretability analysis.

3.1. Kolmogorov–Arnold Networks (KANs)

The Kolmogorov–Arnold network was proposed as a novel neural-network-like computational model, which is inspired by the Kolmogorov–Arnold theorem [12,13]. The Kolmogorov–Arnold theorem states that any continuous n-dimensional function can be expressed as a finite sum and composite of one-dimensional continuous functions. This provides the theoretical foundation for KANs, allowing them to approximate a complex high-dimensional function with a combination of multiple one-dimensional ones, thereby reducing the model complexity and transparentizing the importance of each dimension to the function output.

The decomposition of a multi-dimensional function as described by the Kolmogorov–Arnold theorem is as follows:

$$f(x_1, x_2, \ldots, x_n) = \sum_{q=1}^{2n+1} \phi_q \left(\sum_{p=1}^{n} \psi_{pq}(x_p) \right), \tag{1}$$

where f is a continuous n-dimensional function, and ϕ_q and ψ_{pq} are continuous one-dimensional functions.

In KAN models, the combination of L layers is expressed as follows:

$$\text{KAN}(x) = (\Phi_{L-1} \circ \Phi_{L-2} \circ \cdots \circ \Phi_1 \circ \Phi_0)x, \tag{2}$$

where Φ_l are learnable (parameterized) activation functions. In contrast, the affine transformation structure of a MLP is expressed as follows:

$$\text{MLP}(x) = (W_{L-1} \circ \sigma \circ W_{L-2} \circ \sigma \circ \cdots \circ W_1 \circ \sigma \circ W_0)x, \tag{3}$$

where σ is a fixed activation function, and W are trainable weights. Comparison between KANs and MLPs reveals notable structural differences. In MLPs, linear and nonlinear transformations are handled separately, where the former is represented by weight matrices W while the latter is implemented through nonlinear activation functions σ. In contrast, the KAN model integrates both linear and nonlinear transformations within Φ, allowing for a more compact combination in the processing stages. Such computational structure enables the KAN models to facilitate more convenient layer-by-layer stacking, thereby providing greater flexibility in organizing and adjusting the neural network structures.

Compared to traditional MLPs, KAN exhibits significant advantages in its architecture. First, regarding activation function configuration, traditional MLPs typically incorporate non-adjustable activation functions at each node, which limits the model's flexibility for better training performance. Consequently, while MLPs perform well across various tasks, the fixed nature of these activation functions limits the model's flexibility and adaptability in different scenarios. In contrast, KAN is equipped with learnable activation functions at its edges, which can be dynamically adjusted during model training to better meet the specific needs of tasks. Additionally, only simple operations like addition and subtraction are performed at each node in KANs, which reduces computational complexity and makes the computation process more streamlined. Importantly, each activation function in KAN is by default represented by B-spline functions, which not only provide numerical flexibility but also offer intuitional and visualizable results. With such visualization capability, deeper insights into the internal mechanisms of the model can be readily gained, thereby demonstrating high interpretability along with superior accuracy compared to traditional MLPs. The KANs show significant structural advantages over MLPs in terms of both internal model interpretability and feature-level interpretability. Such flexibility and adaptability make KANs a competent computational structure for interpretable and trustful state estimation in power systems.

In contrast to traditional MLPs, which lack transparency due to the difficulty of intuitively interpreting the weight matrix, the KAN offers a distinct advantage. KAN replaces the matrix-based weight operations with changeable activation functions, allowing nodes to retain only simple additive and subtractive operations. This characteristic enhances the model's interpretability.

It is noteworthy to mention that, in the subsequent experiments, we will adjust the hyperparameters of the KAN model. In the paper on KANs, the authors improved the loss function by introducing an L_1 regularization term and made the following two modifications: First, yjr calculation of the weight matrix in MLPs was replaced by the average magnitude Φ of each activation function in KANs, which helps favor sparsity. Second, due to the fact that L_1 regularization alone was insufficient to achieve adequate sparsity in KANs, an additional entropy regularization term was introduced. λ, as overall penalty strength, is designed to effectively control the sparsity, and many redundant functions that we do not want might arise without the entropy regularization term. The total model loss is formulated as follows:

$$\ell_{\text{total}} = \ell_{\text{pred}} + \lambda \left(\mu_1 \sum_{l=0}^{L-1} \|\Phi_l\|_1 + \mu_2 \sum_{l=0}^{L-1} S(\Phi_l) \right), \tag{4}$$

where μ_1 and μ_2 are relative scaling factors, typically set as $\mu_1 = \mu_2 = 1$, and λ controls the overall level of regularization, typically set as $\lambda = 0$. When trying to adjust regularization, λ is recommended to be set between 0 and 1, usually as 1×10^{-2}, and if λ is set too large, the model will be overly sparse while the activation functions will be compressed severely. As for the regularization term, the first part represents the average magnitude of all activation functions, while the second part represents the entropy of Φ. The second part of the regularization term is defined as

$$S(\Phi) \equiv -\sum_{i=1}^{n_{\text{in}}} \sum_{j=1}^{n_{\text{out}}} \frac{|\phi_{i,j}|_1}{|\Phi|_1} \log\left(\frac{|\phi_{i,j}|_1}{|\Phi|_1} \right), \tag{5}$$

3.2. Handling Class Imbalance

As for power system state estimation with data-driven approaches, class imbalance is a prominent issue. Specifically, stable state samples usually dominate the dataset while unstable state samples are relatively rare, which is unsurprising since normal operation of power systems must be ensured with top priority. Such class imbalance inevitably compromises the model's training performance in supervised learning tasks. To address this issue, a variety of solutions have been proposed with specialized loss functions [14–17], such as the focal loss proposed for logistic regression [18]. In this paper, we introduce shrinkage loss [6] in the loss function, which compensates for samples with the rare class (i.e., the unstable state in this paper) so as to improve the model's performance on datasets with imbalanced classes.

The rationale of the shrinkage loss is to assign higher weight to samples with less chance of happening, thereby making the model focus more on those samples that are more challenging to accurately classify. This approach alleviates the class imbalance issue and encourages the model to learn more from a minority of samples.

The shrinkage loss is formulated as follows:

$$L_{\text{shrink}} = \frac{1}{N} \sum_{i=1}^{N} w_i \cdot \text{Loss}(y_i, \hat{y}_i), \tag{6}$$

where N is the total number of samples, y_i is the true label of the i-th sample, $\hat{y}_i$ is the predicted value for the i-th sample, $\text{Loss}(y_i, \hat{y}_i)$ is the standard loss function (such as cross-entropy loss), and w_i is the weight for the i-th sample, adjusted according to the rareness of the sample. Specifically, the weight w_i is calculated as follows:

$$w_i = \frac{1}{1 + \exp(-\alpha(y_i - \hat{y}_i))}, \tag{7}$$

where α is a hyperparameter used to control the magnitude of the weight adjustment. It is obvious to find that if α becomes larger, the curve of function (7) becomes steeper. It helps to add penalties to simple samples and decrease loss of simple samples without affecting hard samples. Hyperparameter α is recommended to be set as 10 in [6], as it can accelerate convergence efficiently in this situation. Evidently, the introduction of shrinkage loss can significantly enhance the model's ability to estimate minority class samples while mitigating the negative impact of class imbalance during the training process.

3.3. State Estimation Pipeline

In this subsection, we introduce the pipeline of power system state estimation, a three-step procedure that includes sample processing, KAN model training, and interpretability analysis, as illustrated in Figure 1. Each step is detailed as follows:

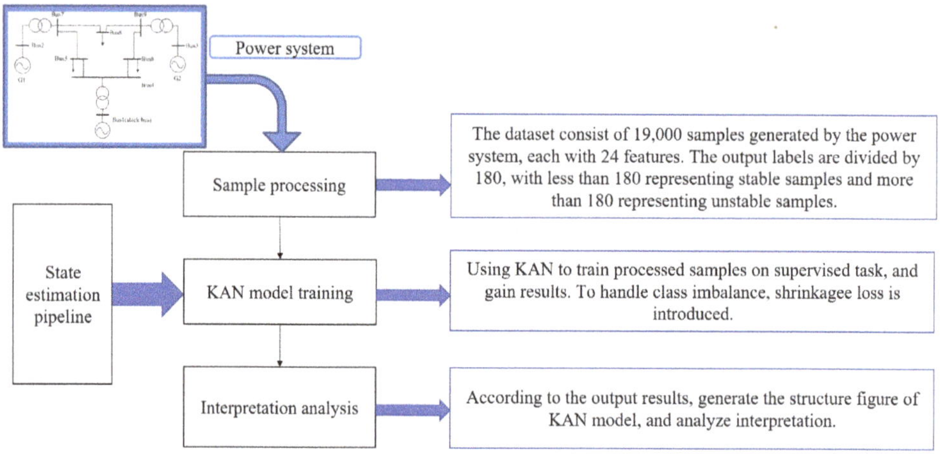

Figure 1. This figure illustrates the overall procedure of power system state estimation, including sample processing, KAN model training, and interpretation analysis of power system state estimation. The figure details the flow of each step.

1. Sample processing: As previously discussed, class imbalance between stable and unstable samples is a significant issue in power system state estimation. Our dataset consists of 19,000 samples generated from the power system, each of which contains 24 features. These features are sequentially divided into six groups, with each group representing an individual bus: Bus C, Bus A, Bus 1, Bus 3, Bus B, and Bus 2. The four features of each group correspond to bus voltage magnitude, bus voltage phase angle, bus reactive power, and bus active power of the respective bus pairs.
   The output label is defined as the maximum relative power angle, with 180 as the threshold, i.e., values less than 180 indicate stability; otherwise, they signify instability. The total 19,000 samples comprise 2,658 unstable samples and 16,342 stable ones, resulting in a highly imbalanced ratio of approximately 6.14:1. (In our design, the state estimation is based on the classification of alert and secure states, which are determined specifically by three-phase short-circuit faults.)
   Additionally, we would like to clarify that the threshold of 180 in our study is not intended to represent the steady-state stability, but rather the transient stability. For transient stability, when a system loses stability, the relative power angle typically continues to increase beyond 90 degrees, and 180 degrees is often used as a practical criterion to indicate the loss of transient stability.
   To address the class imbalance issue, we employed the shrinkage loss function (as discussed in Section 3.2) to attach greater importance to samples with unstable labels in order to mitigate the impact caused by class imbalance. (It is still noteworthy that there have been other technical approaches to dealing with imperfect training data, such as robust regression, semi-supervised learning, and progressive training. For example, robust regression techniques are often used to handle noisy labels or outliers in data, and semi-supervised learning can take advantage of both labeled and unlabeled data to improve model performance when labels are scarce or noisy. Also, progressive training allows the model to start with simpler, less noisy data before

gradually incorporating more complex, potentially noisy data, enabling it to better handle imperfections in real-world datasets.

In this paper, in order to achieve interpretability, we introduced focal loss to deal with samples.) The distribution of samples is illustrated in Figure 2, where the histogram displays the occurrence frequency of the output values, with the upper half showing stable samples and the lower half showing unstable ones. This histogram provides an intuitive understanding of the data distribution through statistics, serving as a basis for the subsequent processing.

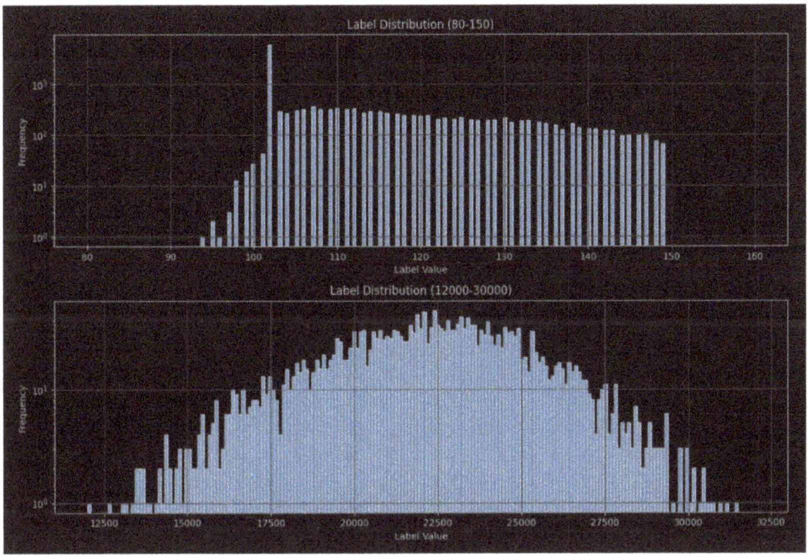

Figure 2. Distribution of 19,000 samples generated by the power system. Outputs with values less than 180 represent stable samples, and those with values greater than 180 represent unstable samples. Almost all the labels fall into one of two ranges: either [80, 150] or [12,000, 30,000]. As shown above, a huge gap lies between the two portions.

2. KAN Model training: The processed samples are then fed to the training algorithm. Unlike traditional neural networks, KAN retains learnable activation functions on its edges while performing only addition and subtraction operations at the nodes. Such a computational process simplifies the model structure, avoiding the complex weight and bias parameter settings in training traditional neural networks, thereby enhancing the model's fitting performance and predictive accuracy. The training process involves tuning hyperparameters (e.g., learning rate) to optimize the loss function.
3. Interpretation analysis: After training the KAN model as a regression task, we proceed to the interpretation step. The model's interpretability is analyzed from both the structural and feature-wise perspectives. Using the generated network structure, we visualize the well-trained mode to understand how different features influence the output, i.e., the maximum relative power angle. Furthermore, pruning within KAN helps simplify the network structure by removing nodes and connections that contribute less to the final prediction. This not only enhances the model's interpretability but also provides insights into the critical factors that lead to power system stability/instability.

According to the sample distribution shown in Figure 2, there exists a noticeable gap between stable and unstable samples, particularly in the range from 180 to 12,000. This gap may negatively impact the model's regression performance in this interval. Additionally, the size of stable samples is approximately six times that of unstable samples, highlighting a significant class imbalance issue. Consequently, the experiments are conducted through two main steps: first, training the model on the entire dataset, and second, training the model on the two subsets of the data separately.

In training, the model's performance on the full dataset will help us understand the relationships between different distributions and assess the impact of incorporating shrinkage loss to address class imbalance issues. For the localized training, samples with output labels less than 180 will be used to train the model. By employing the KAN network structure, we aim to capture the influence of each feature on the prediction results more accurately. Furthermore, unstable samples with output labels greater than 180 will be trained independently and compared to the results from stable samples, which helps determine whether the model's interpretability can be generalized from stable to unstable states and to the whole system. Finally, a comprehensive analysis of feature interpretability and model interpretability will be conducted based on the results of all experiments.

4. Experiment

In this section, we provide a detailed description of the experimental design and result analysis based on the procedures outlined in Section 3.3. In Section 4.1, the generation of our dataset along with its specification is given. In Section 4.2, we describe experiment and attempt to improve the results through shrinkage loss. In Section 4.3, we explore feature interpretability by leveraging the pruning of the KAN model. In Section 4.4, we further analyze the interpretability of the KAN model trained with the entire dataset.

Throughout the experiment, we employed the KAN for training for two main reasons. Initially, KAN can be viewed as a specialized form of MLP, where MLP requires both linear and nonlinear adjustments in each layer, as KAN requires only a single processing step. By using KAN in the experiment, we can avoid errors due to structural differences between KAN and MLP, and highlight the interpretability advantages of KAN. Secondly, the focus of this experiment is on exploring KAN's performance in interpretability. Thus, the comparison with MLP's performance is beyond the scope of this study.

4.1. Dataset

The dataset came from a power system simulation platform. The simulation platform used was a laptop equipped with an Intel(R) Core(TM) i7-11800H 2.30 GHz CPU and 32 GB of memory (The manufacturer is Lenovo, and the equipment was sourced from Beijing, China). Data simulation was conducted in the dynamic simulation program (DSP) using the international IEEE-9 standard test case [19]. The simulation parameters were set as follows: six scenarios for generator output ranging from 0% to 100% in 20% increments, and five scenarios for bus load ranging from 80% to 120% in 20% increments, with random load disturbances applied. All faults were three-phase short-circuit faults, with a duration of 0.1 s and fault locations set at 10%, 30%, 50%, 70%, and 90% of the transmission line. The simulation lasted for 30 s, generating 19,000 simulation samples after data cleaning. The output data included bus voltage magnitude, bus voltage phase angle, bus active power, and bus reactive power.

Sample generation and simulation calculation were based on the simulation platform, and the workflow is as follows. Firstly, the simulation platform is configured, and the number of threads and related files is calculated (power flow data, stable data, fault sets, sample signature files, etc.). Then, the fault type is selected, the load level and sample number are set, and stable data files are generated based on the fault set. Then, the load level list is traversed, the corresponding power flow data file is generated, and the convergence of power flow calculation is verified. If the power flow calculation converges, the transient stability calculation is carried out, the simulation results are analyzed, and information such as voltage and frequency is extracted to generate sample labels. Finally, the power flow result data are written to the sample file according to the partition, checking whether the number of samples reaches the set value, and finally the sample generation and fault statistics are completed.

4.2. Results with Entire Samples

We conducted the experiment on the whole dataset (including both stable and unstable samples) using the pipeline described in Section 3.3, and 15,000 and 4000 samples were shuffled out as the training set and testing set, respectively. Four structures were taken into account for KAN model design: [24, 1], [24, 12, 1], [24, 12, 6, 1], and [24, 12, 6, 2, 1], where the numbers in each layer's structure are the number of neurons. In this expression, the number represents neurons in different layers, with the comma separating consecutive layers. For example, [24, 12, 1] indicates that there are 24 neurons in the input layer, i.e., 24 dimensions for the input features. The hidden layer has 12 neurons and the output layer has 1 neuron.

Taking the 4-layer model [24, 12, 6, 2, 1] as an example, the model structure and the loss function value as training proceeds for 1000 iterations are shown in Figure 3. From Figure 3, it can be observed that due to significant class imbalance in the samples (i.e., the lack of samples with labels between 180 and 12,000 means that this portion of output values can barely be attained) and outputs for unstable samples being excessively large, KAN model training exhibits severe overfitting in Figure 3b, i.e., the loss function continuously decreases for the training set as training proceeds while the case is totally different for the testing set.

In order to alleviate overfitting, we introduced shrinkage loss to replace the original root mean squared error (RMSE) in the loss function. The results with shrinkage loss are presented in Figure 4. However, Figure 4 indicates that introducing shrinkage loss did not effectively solve the overfitting issue.

Additionally, we explore adjustments to hyperparameters in (4). The default regularization parameter was set as $\lambda = 0$, and the results with different settings of λ are shown in Figure 5. The experiment reveals that neither the introduction of shrinkage loss nor tuning the regularization parameter is able to effectively solve the overfitting issue. In particular, Figure 3 suggests that the influence of nodes on the model is different, which guides us to simplify the KAN structure for further experiments.

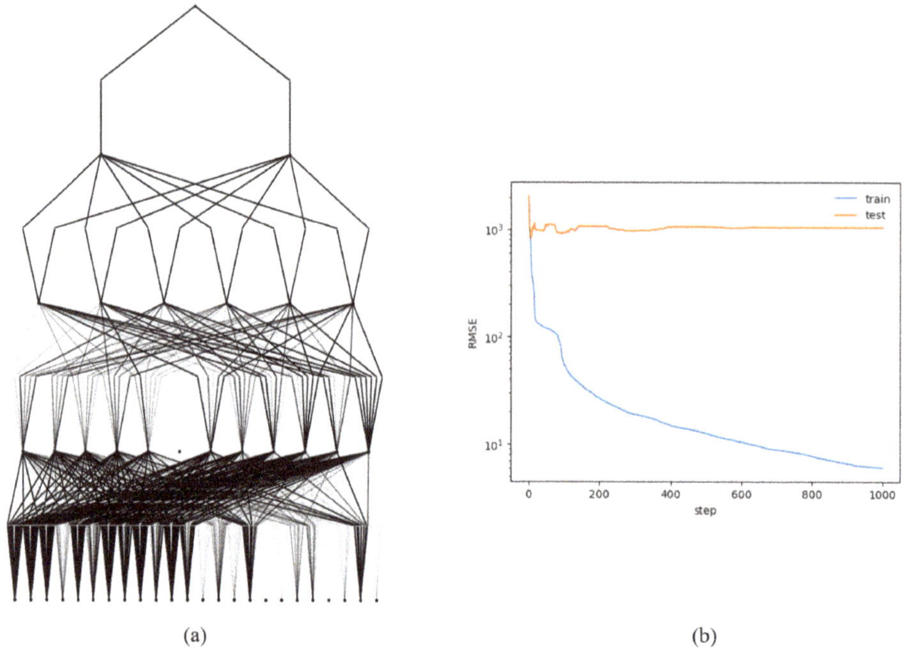

Figure 3. (**a**) The figure represents the fitting of all samples after 1000 iterations in the 4-layer model [24, 12, 6, 2, 1]. Here, the line break means activation function (to avoid shelter, we set pictures of activation function small), and the convergence nodes of lines mean a neuron. The lowest nodes mean the input layer, while the highest nodes mean the output layer. For edges between two nodes, as the edge is more obvious, the output of the lower node has a greater impact on the next node through this edge. It can be viewed by edge transparency that the inputs of the right half make less contributions, as does the sixth node in the first hidden layer. (**b**) This figure represents the change in the loss function in model training. The blue curve represents the change in the loss function in the training set and the yellow curve represents the change in the loss function in the test set.

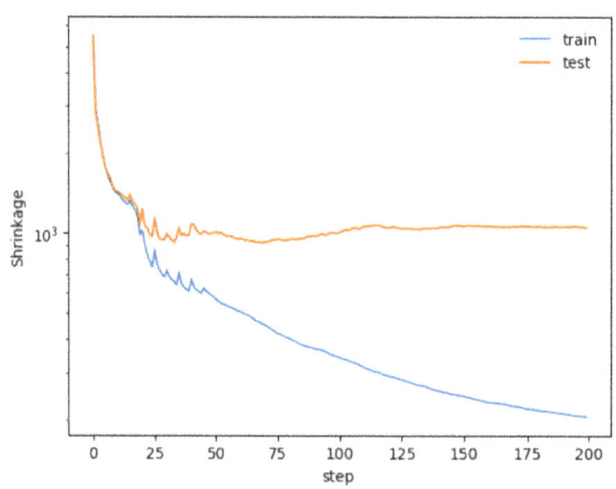

Figure 4. The loss function of model training after introducing shrinkage loss. Compared with (b) in Figure 3, the curve for the test loss still stays at a high level, which means severe overfitting issues that have not been solved.

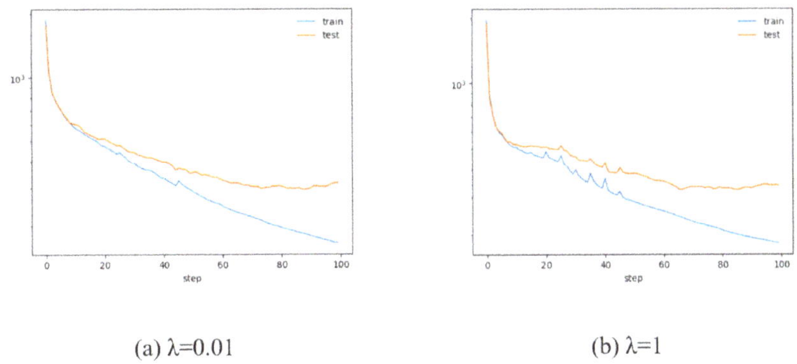

Figure 5. (**a**) Loss function with λ = 0.01. (**b**) Loss function with λ = 1. Tuning hyperparameters improves performance while the gain is still limited.

Taking the 3-layer model [24, 12, 6, 1] as an example, the model structure after 1000 iterations, the results from using the RMSE loss function and shrinkage loss function, and the impact of adjusting λ are depicted in Figure 6. Although simplifying the structure alleviates overfitting to some extent, such improvement might be gained at the cost of information loss due to the structural simplification, which may not lead to effective performance enhancement. This observation suggests that simply modifying the loss function may have limited effectiveness when the distribution imbalance is as severe as it is in our dataset. The imbalance between the stable and unstable samples profoundly impacts the training of the model. The experiments in Section 4.3 will investigate this issue further.

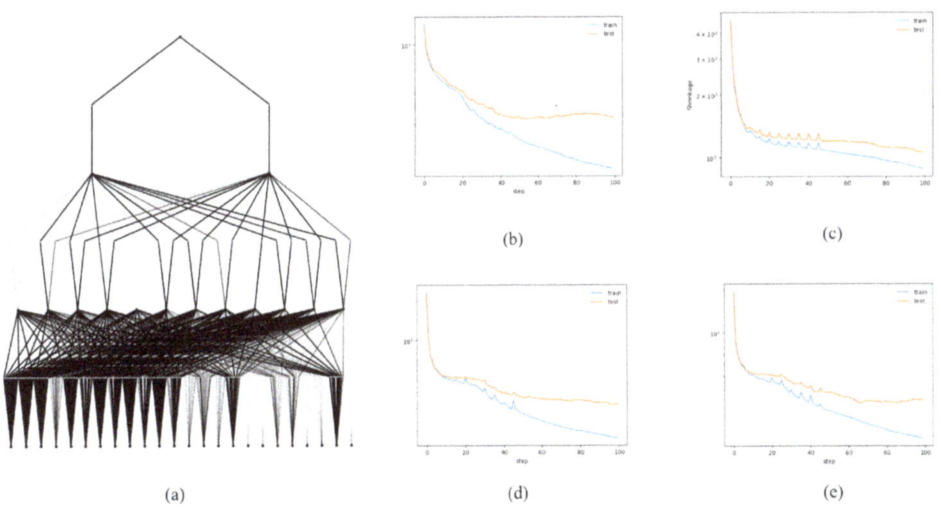

Figure 6. (**a**) This figure shows the fitting of samples in the 3-layer model. Compared with the 4-layer model in (a) of Figure 3, the inputs of right half part still make less contributions. Simplifying the model shows little benefit. (**b**) This figure represents the loss curve with the RMSE loss function. Default λ is set to 0. (**c**) The loss function of model training after introducing the shrinkage loss function instead of the RMSE loss function. Default λ is set to 0. Results might be better than (**b**), but still have obvious limits. (**d**) Loss function of λ = 0.01 with RMSE loss function. (**e**) Loss function of λ = 1 with RMSE loss function.

From the global perspective, the imbalanced distribution of the dataset has led to poor fitting performance and significant overfitting. This provides the need for in-class analysis, suggesting that handling the data separately for stable and unstable samples may help achieve favorable performance on the dataset with stable labels.

4.3. Results with In-Class Samples and Interpretability of Features

In the KAN, unlike the global explanations based on the experiment in Section 4.2, in-class explanations focus on handling stable samples within samples and training the model accordingly. Local analysis aims to dive into the model's performance on the dataset with stable labels, qualitatively assessing the correlation between feature inputs and output predictions to evaluate impact from features. We prepare the experiment following the pipeline.

In terms of sample processing, for samples with the same distribution, we divide the dataset into two subsets: stable samples and unstable samples. The stable samples are named as dataset A in our experiment, including 16,342 samples with output labels lower than 180, while the unstable samples are named as dataset B, including 2658 samples with output labels greater than 180. We reallocated the training and testing sets for datasets A and B. For dataset A, the training set for the new model was set to 13,000 samples, and the testing set included 3342 samples. For dataset B, the training set was set to 2100 samples, with 558 samples for the test set. The experiment maintains a ratio of approximately 3.8:1, including both dataset A and dataset B.

Initially, we conducted an experiment on the [24, 12, 6, 2, 1] model, training it with 1000 iterations on datasets A and B separately. The loss function results for datasets A and B are shown in Figure 7. The results indicate that, under the same distribution, the KAN model can effectively fit the stable samples but performs poorly on the unstable samples. This might be caused by the situation that stable samples keep outputs lower than 180, which are easy to fit, while there are huge variations in unstable samples, making them hard to fit. The result also highlights the significant impact of the gap (180–12,000) between stable and unstable samples, as the results of the experiment in Section 4.2 cannot fit well. Considering the better fitting performance of dataset A, it was selected as the focus for local analysis.

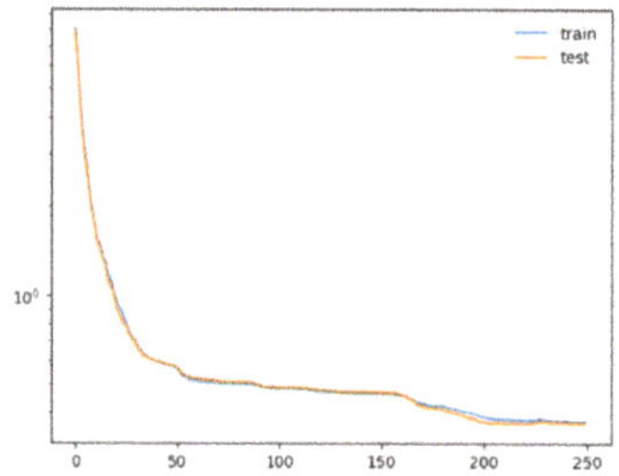

(a)

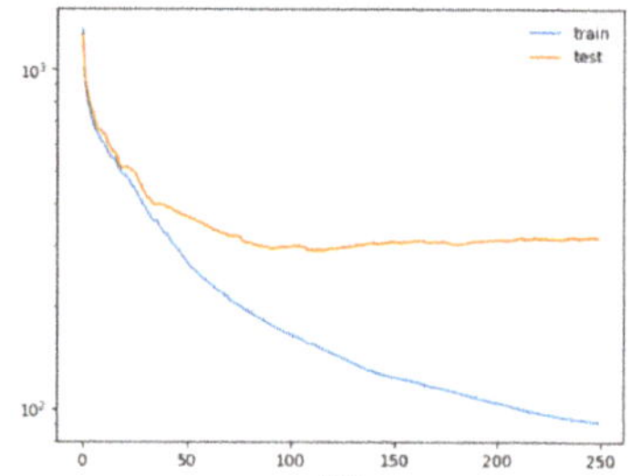

(b)

Figure 7. (**a**) Loss function of dataset A. Loss function is set as RMSE. λ follows default 0. In this figure, we can nearly obtain an overlap between the train loss curve and test loss curve, which means effective fitting. (**b**) Loss function of dataset B. Loss function is set as RMSE. λ follows default 0. Compared with (a), the results are similar to the results of the entire dataset in Figure 3. This can indicate that dataset B is also hard to fit.

Figure 8 illustrates the KAN structure for dataset A. Compared to Figure 3, Figure 8 shows that many nodes and activation functions on edges have lower transparency levels, which aids in distinguishing the effects of different features on the output and enhancing feature interpretability. Through KAN's visualization structure, we can more clearly check features with higher or lower contributions. Additionally, by using KAN's pruning tool to remove nodes and activation functions below a preset threshold, we can simplify the structure, reduce computational costs by reducing nodes, and highlight features with higher contributions.

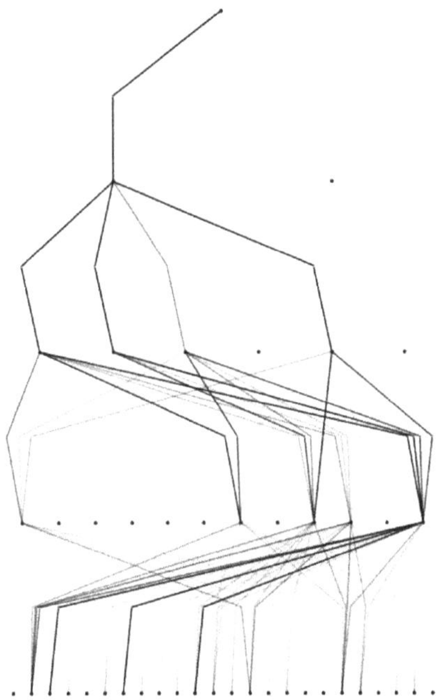

Figure 8. KAN structure of dataset A. Compared with the structure in Figure 3, it has less obvious edges between nodes. This indicates that it reduces a lot computation and focus on less edges. It is easier to view which node can make more contributions to the next node, and which input is more important.

The analysis of the experimental results indicates that feature interpretability for the stable samples is well represented in the 4-layer KAN (see Figure 8). For example, the bus active power and bus reactive power of the third bus pairs (features 17 and 18) have minimal impact on the output phase angle, with low transparency in the next nodes, suggesting these features contribute less to the output. Conversely, the bus voltage magnitude of the first bus pairs and the bus voltage phase angles of the second, fourth, and sixth bus pairs have a significant impact on the output, with higher transparency.

We also attempted to simplify the KAN network's layers and observed the performance of the simplified model. Figure 9 presents the KAN structures [24, 12, 2, 1] and [24, 12, 1] and their respective loss functions. The simplified model retains good feature interpretability on the stable samples, consistent with the results in Figure 8. This result demonstrates that the simplified KAN model can consistently represent feature interpretability without losing information. Also, this suggests that simplifying the KAN structure helps maintain feature interpretability and extends the application of pruning in structural simplification. In addition, it can indicate that local analysis of stable sample contributions can generalize to the whole dataset, which will be demonstrated below.

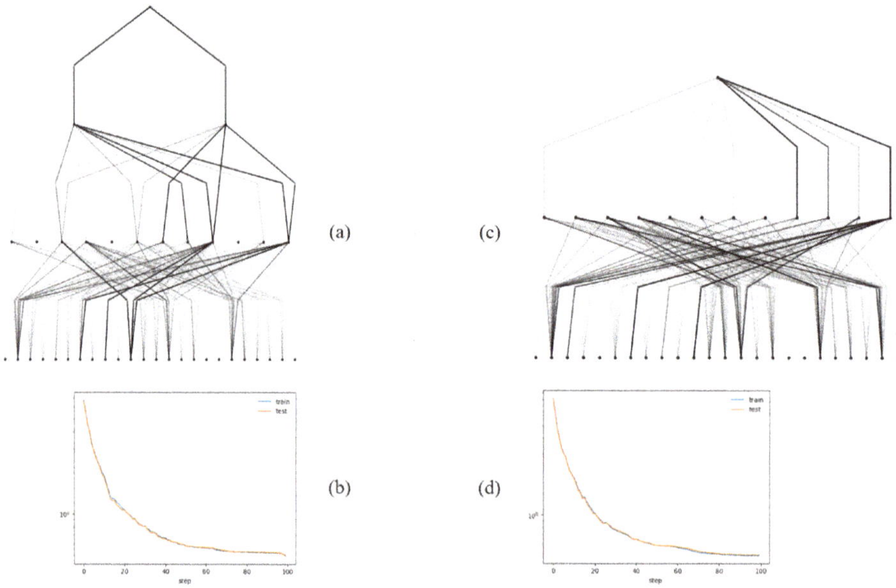

Figure 9. (**a**) Three-layer KAN structure of dataset A. Experiment sets are as above. (**b**) Loss function of 3-layer KAN. (**c**) Two-layer KAN structure of dataset A. (**d**) Loss function of 2-layer KAN. It can be viewed that simplifying the KAN model does not affect the fitting results, as the test curve shows good results and the nodes of the KAN structure are similar to Figure 8.

Furthermore, we manually modified the KAN structure to improve the fitting of the whole dataset. Local analysis revealed that features with higher contributions in the stable samples could enhance the fitting of the whole dataset. Nodes with lower contributions in the stable samples were removed and used to form a new structure for the whole dataset for training (for results, see Figure 10). The results show that the new structure, after removing these nodes, performed similarly to the model with the original structure, suggesting that these nodes had minimal impact on the output, which can reduce computational costs and emphasize nodes that are more important.

Similarly to removing unimportant nodes, we attempted to remove input features with lower contributions to improve the whole dataset's fitting (see Figure 11). The results demonstrate that, after removing features with lower contributions, the modified KAN model's performance on the complete dataset improved through the loss curve. This further confirms that feature interpretability from the stable samples can be partially generalized to the whole dataset, as some nodes and inputs are relatively representative, providing valuable insights for further analysis of feature interpretability.

Our experiments in Section 4.3 demonstrate that pruning, whether applied to certain nodes in the layers or input features, significantly outperforms simply introducing shrinkage loss (as shown in Figure 4). While the prediction of entire samples, especially unstable ones, remains challenging, we observe that pruning helps reduce the influence of irrelevant nodes, which improves the model's ability to predict. Thus, although the KAN does not directly achieve perfect predictions for unstable samples, its pruning provides a valuable tool to improve performance, particularly when compared to MLP.

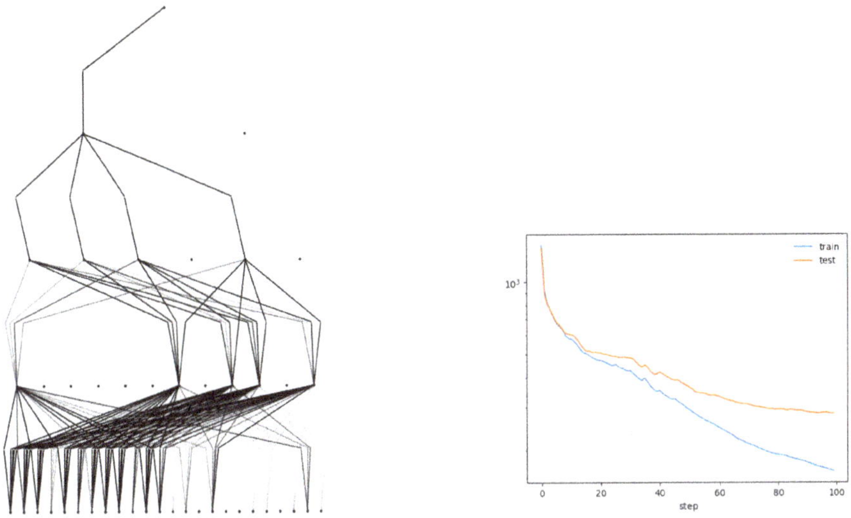

(a) (b)

Figure 10. (**a**) The structure of the complete dataset on the pruned KAN. We pruned some of the nodes in the hidden layer, which we modified with reference to Figure 8, cutting inputs and outputs. It is found that the complete dataset can also show good results on the KAN network pruned as dataset A, which indicates that the feature interpretation can be generalized from the local scale to the whole. (**b**) The figure shows changes in the loss function. Compared with Figure 3b, the overfitting has been significantly improved.

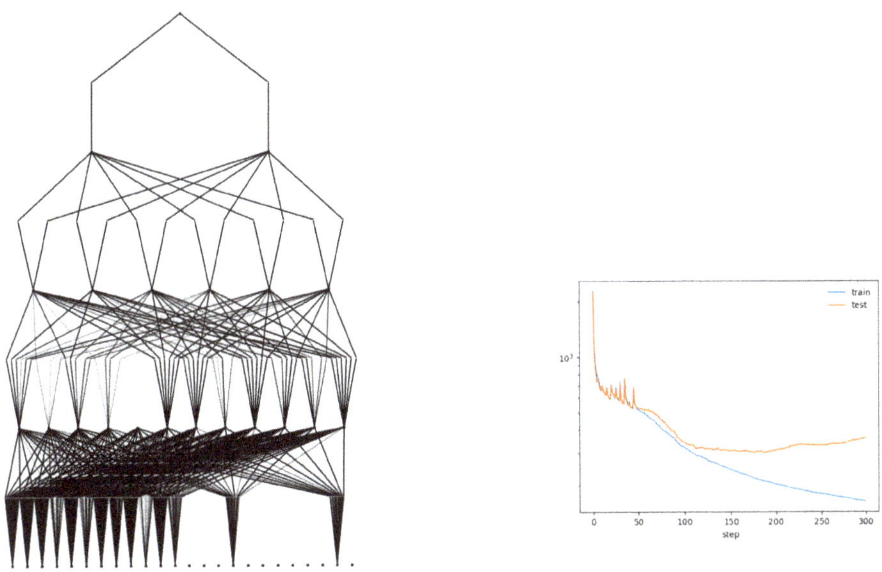

(a) (b)

Figure 11. (**a**) The structure of the complete dataset on the pruned KAN. We pruned some of the inputs, which we modified with reference to Figure 8. Results show that overfitting has been improved. (**b**) The figure shows changes in the loss function.

4.4. Interpretability of Model

In the experiment conducted in Section 4.3, we observed that the KAN model not only provides intuitive interpretability through its structure but also effectively extends feature interpretability to the entire model. Although further subdividing the unstable samples, similarly to the partitioning of stable and unstable samples, might reveal more nuanced fitting details, this approach would be considerably labor-intensive. Overall, by leveraging the KAN model's capability to generalize feature interpretability, we can achieve explanations with a sufficiently representative subset of data and extrapolate these findings to the entire model. This method significantly reduces the need for comprehensive feature analysis, allowing for a more efficient description and understanding of the interpretability of the model.

Additionally, to help readers better understand our experiments, we would like to conclude our experiments as three pipelines: improving overfitting using the full samples in Figure 12, analyzing the stable and unstable samples in Figure 13, and using KAN pruning to mitigate overfitting in Figure 14.

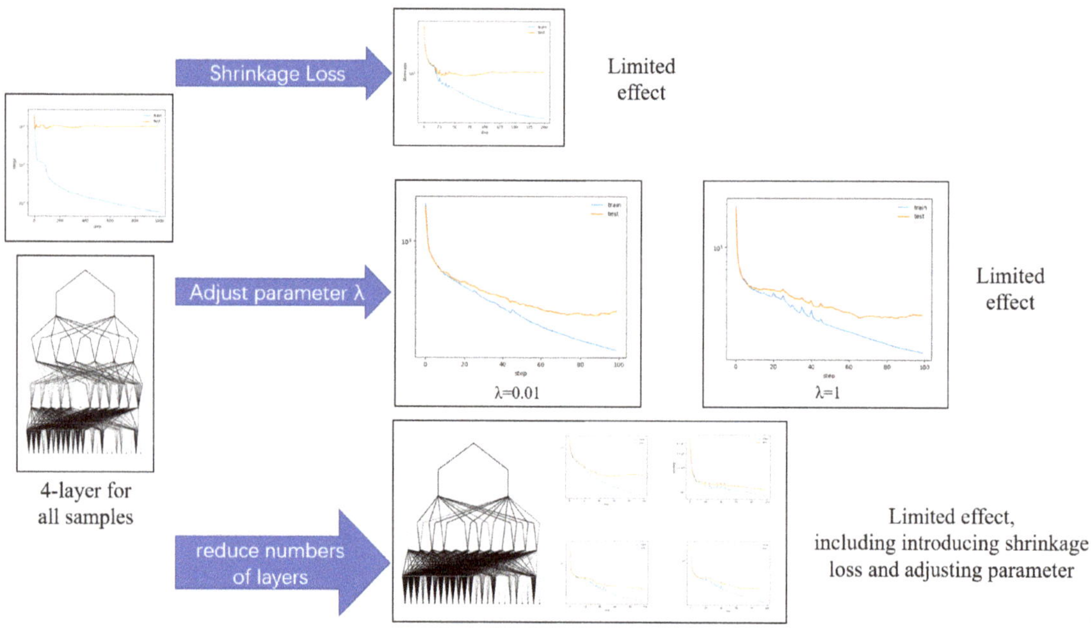

Figure 12. In Section 4.2, we found severe overfitting with entire samples. To improve fitting, we introduced shrinkage loss, adjusted parameters, and modified model structure by reducing the number of layers. But none of them worked well to improve overfitting.

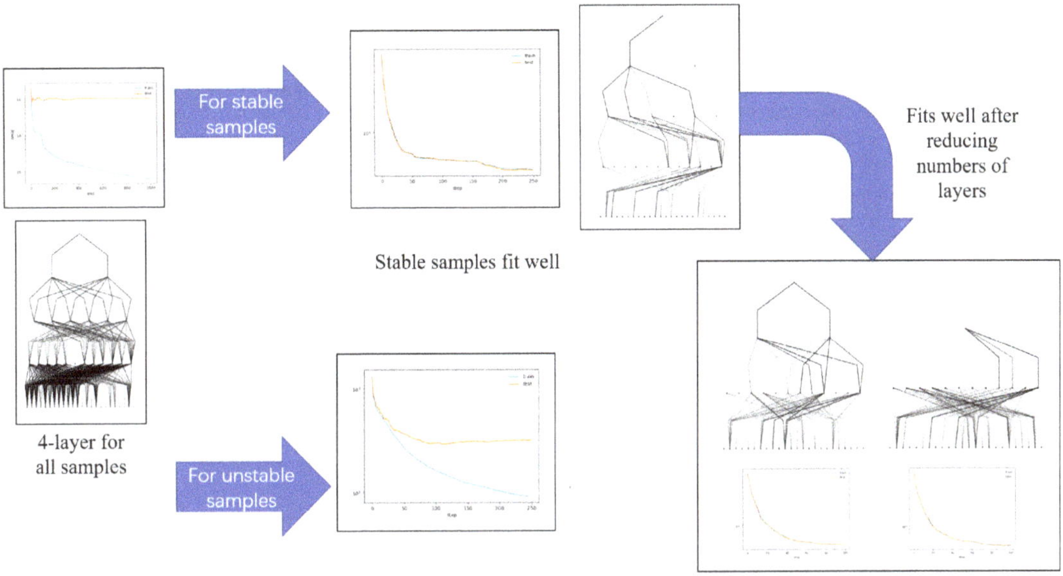

Figure 13. We found it useful to divide the entire samples into stable samples and unstable samples, as stable samples can fit well. After reducing the number of layers, the model still fits well.

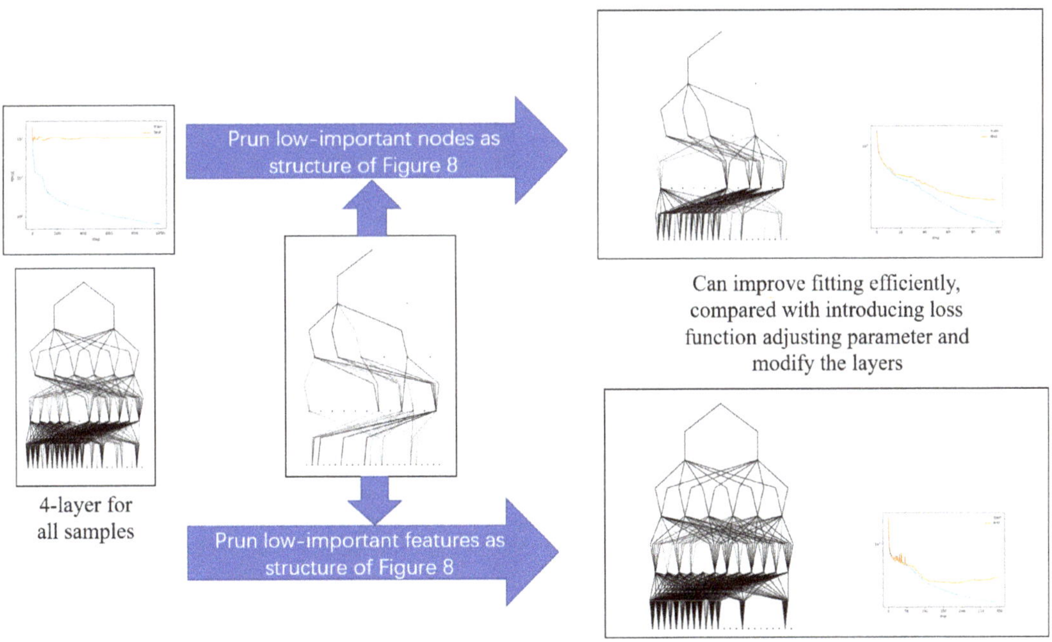

Figure 14. Using pruning in KAN can efficiently improve overfitting, including nodes and features. Compared with the results of introducing the loss function and adjusting the parameters, it can be more useful.

5. Discussion

In this study, we explore the use of the KAN model for power system state estimation with imbalanced datasets, with a particular focus on model interpretability. The experimental results demonstrate that the KAN model not only provides an intuitive analysis of in-class feature interpretability but can also be well generalized through its characteristics. Traditional methods for handling imbalanced data, such as oversampling or undersampling, often struggle to maintain data representativeness in high-dimensional feature spaces. In contrast, the KAN model, through its structure and pruning operations, allows for a more effective interpretation of the model's performance on imbalanced datasets without incurring additional computational cost.

Imbalanced datasets are not uncommon in practical machine learning tasks, particularly in regressions, such as phase angle prediction in power systems. In these cases, the imbalanced data distribution is usually multi-mode, which makes it difficult to fit the data with one single model. A similar example can be found in the distribution of urban populations. Small cities typically have populations in the tens of thousands, while large cities, due to the siphon effect, have populations exceeding millions, with almost no medium-sized cities in between. This distribution pattern resembles the bathtub curve in engineering: a scarcity of data points in the middle and a concentration at both ends, with significant differences in the data space. Traditional regression models are prone to overfitting in denser regions while neglecting the sparse regions in such cases. The KAN model, through feature interpretability analysis, helps estimate these differences, thereby effectively handling regression problems in imbalanced datasets. This finding can have broad applicability to other regression problems involving imbalanced datasets.

While the KAN model shows promise for power system state estimation, it is not without limitations. One key challenge is its scalability when applied to large-scale power systems with millions of nodes. Although the model's pruning operations help reduce complexity, the inherent structure of the KAN model can still lead to increased computational demands. Furthermore, while the interpretability of the KAN model is a significant strength, the trade-off between model complexity and interpretability should be carefully considered. In real-world applications, where model efficiency is critical, the increased complexity of the KAN model may not always be justified. Future research could explore techniques for simplifying the model's architecture without compromising its interpretability, such as leveraging hybrid models or incorporating domain-specific knowledge into the network design.

Also, it is effective to conduct experiments on parameter sensitivity, but further sensitivity analysis on hyperparameters, such as pruning thresholds or relative scaling factors, is necessary to better understand the model's behavior across different configurations. Specially, the method proposed in our paper could potentially be adapted to estimate the states of the converter layer by analyzing key system parameters, or addressing potential nonlinearities and transient behaviors typical in power conversion processes [20]. A more detailed exploration of how these parameters influence the model's accuracy and interpretability would contribute to the fine-tuning of the approach for practical use cases, especially in the context of highly imbalanced and noisy datasets.

Additionally, we propose several promising research directions. In our experiments, we divided the samples into stable and unstable categories. However, unstable samples may arise from various distinct instability states. If we can estimate a subset of part-unstable samples with a high degree of fit, this would facilitate the estimation of specific instability patterns to help find new ideas in this area. Through feature interpretability analysis, we could further deduce which features are likely contributing to these instability phenomena, providing deeper insights into their underlying causes.

6. Conclusions

In this paper, we introduce a method based on the KAN model to address regression problems in imbalanced datasets, with a focus on model interpretability. The experimental results demonstrate that the KAN model can not only intuitively reveal the interpretability of the model but also extend interpretability to the entire model. This explains that the KAN model exhibits feature interpretability and related model interpretability. By utilizing the pruning and visualization tools of the KAN model, we can effectively estimate and distinguish the contributions of features to the output, thereby tackling the regression challenges posed by imbalanced datasets.

The approach proposed in this paper performs well in phase angle prediction within power systems. Moreover, the KAN model also presents great potential for datasets with imbalanced distribution, such as urban population distribution. By leveraging representative in-class samples, the KAN model reduces the complexity of overall feature analysis, providing a straightforward and effective approach to understanding how the model works. This approach offers an innovative solution to regression tasks within imbalanced datasets.

The results of this study suggest that the integration of the KAN model into power system state estimation holds great promise for enhancing grid security and stability. Future work could explore the application of this method to broader fields and more complex situations, further refining the interpretability of deep learning models.

Author Contributions: Conceptualization, S.Y.; Methodology, S.W.; Software, W.L.; Validation, J.Z., Z.L. and Y.Z.; Funding acquisition, S.L. All authors have read and agreed to the published version of the manuscript.

Funding: This work was financially supported by the Science and Technology Project of China Southern Power Grid (No. GZKJXM20232014).

Data Availability Statement: Data are contained within the article.

Conflicts of Interest: Author Yihua Zhu was employed by the company China Southern Power Grid. The remaining authors declare that the research was conducted in the absence of any commercial or financial relationships that could be construed as a potential conflict of interest.

Abbreviations

The following abbreviations are used in this manuscript:

KAN	Kolmogorov–Arnold network
MLP	Multi-layer perceptron

References

1. Schweppe, F.C.; Wildes, J. Power system static-state estimation, Part I: Exact model. *IEEE Trans. Power Appar. Syst.* **1970**, *1*, 120–125. [CrossRef]
2. Schweppe, F.C.; Rom, D.B. Power system static-state estimation, Part II: Approximate model. *IEEE Trans. Power Appar. Syst.* **1970**, *1*, 125–130. [CrossRef]
3. Schweppe, F.C. Power System Static-State Estimation, Part III: Implementation. *IEEE Trans. Power Appar. Syst.* **1970**, *1*, 130–135. [CrossRef]
4. Liu, Z.; Wang, Y.; Vaidya, S.; Ruehle, F.; Halverson, J.; Soljačić, M.; Hou, T.Y.; Tegmark, M. Kan: Kolmogorov-arnold networks. *arXiv* **2024**, arXiv:2404.19756.
5. Cheon, M. Demonstrating the efficacy of kolmogorov-arnold networks in vision tasks. *arXiv* **2024**, arXiv:2406.14916.
6. Lu, X.; Ma, C.; Ni, B.; Yang, X.; Reid, I.; Yang, M.H. Deep regression tracking with shrinkage loss. In Proceedings of the European Conference on Computer Vision (ECCV), Munich, Germany, 8–14 September 2018; pp. 353–369.
7. Stavrev, S.; Ginchev, D. Reinforcement Learning Techniques in Optimizing Energy Systems. *Electronics* **2024**, *13*, 1459. [CrossRef]
8. Li, C.; Wang, B. A Knowledge Graph Method towards Power System Fault Diagnosis and Classification. *Electronics* **2023**, *12*, 4808. [CrossRef]
9. Ren, C.; Xu, Y.; Zhang, R. An interpretable deep learning method for power system transient stability assessment via tree regularization. *IEEE Trans. Power Syst.* **2021**, *37*, 3359–3369. [CrossRef]
10. Cremer, J.L.; Konstantelos, I.; Strbac, G. From optimization-based machine learning to interpretable security rules for operation. *IEEE Trans. Power Syst.* **2019**, *34*, 3826–3836. [CrossRef]
11. Wang, Z.; Zhou, Y.; Guo, Q.; Sun, H. Interpretable neighborhood deep models for online total transfer capability evaluation of power systems. *IEEE Trans. Power Syst.* **2021**, *37*, 260–271. [CrossRef]

12. Kolmogorov, A.N. On the representation of continuous functions of several variables as superpositions of continuous functions of a smaller number of variables. *Dokl. Akad. Nauk.* **1956**, *108*, 953–956.
13. Braun, J.; Griebel, M. On a constructive proof of Kolmogorov's superposition theorem. *Constr. Approx.* **2009**, *30*, 653–675. [CrossRef]
14. Cui, Y.; Jia, M.; Lin, T.Y.; Song, Y.; Belongie, S. Class-balanced loss based on effective number of samples. In Proceedings of the IEEE/CVF Conference on Computer Vision and Pattern Recognition, Long Beach, CA, USA, 15–20 June 2019; pp. 9268–9277.
15. Shwartz-Ziv, R.; Goldblum, M.; Li, Y.; Bruss, C.B.; Wilson, A.G. Simplifying neural network training under class imbalance. *Adv. Neural Inf. Process. Syst.* **2023**, *36*, 35218–35245.
16. Guo, H.; Viktor, H.L. Learning from imbalanced data sets with boosting and data generation: The databoost-im approach. *ACM Sigkdd Explor. Newslett.* **2004**, *6*, 30–39. [CrossRef]
17. Han, H.; Wang, W.Y.; Mao, B.H. Borderline-SMOTE: A new over-sampling method in imbalanced data sets learning. In Proceedings of the International Conference on Intelligent Computing, Tianjin, China, 5–8 August 2005; Springer: Berlin/Heidelberg, Germany, 2005; pp. 878–887.
18. Lin, T. Focal Loss for Dense Object Detection. *arXiv* **2017**, arXiv:1708.02002.
19. Anderson, P.M.; Fouad, A.A. *Power System Control and Stability*, 2nd ed.; IEEE Press: Piscataway, NJ, USA; Wiley-Interscience: Hoboken, NJ, USA, 2003.
20. Lin, H.; Cai, C.; Chen, J.; Gao, Y.; Vazquez, S.; Li, Y. Modulation and control independent dead-zone compensation for H-bridge converters: A simplified digital logic scheme. *IEEE Trans. Ind. Electron.* **2024**, *71*, 15239–15244. [CrossRef]

electronics

Article

A Novel Wind Power Prediction Model That Considers Multi-Scale Variable Relationships and Temporal Dependencies

Zhanyang Xu [1], Hong Zhao [1,*], Chengxi Xu [2], Hongyan Shi [1], Jian Xu [1] and Zhe Wang [1]

1 School of Software, Nanjing University of Information Science and Technology, Nanjing 210044, China
2 Halıcıoğlu Data Science Institute, University of California San Diego, La Jolla, CA 92092, USA
* Correspondence: zhaohong@nuist.edu.cn

Abstract: Wind power forecasting is a critical technology for promoting the effective integration of wind energy. To enhance the accuracy of wind power predictions, this paper introduces a novel wind power prediction model that considers the evolving relationships of multi-scale variables and temporal dependencies. In this paper, a multi-scale frequency decomposition module is designed to split the raw data into high-frequency and low-frequency parts. Subsequently, features are extracted from the high-frequency information using a multi-scale temporal graph neural network combined with an adaptive graph learning module and from the low-frequency data using an improved bidirectional temporal network. Finally, the features are integrated through a cross-attention mechanism. To validate the effectiveness of the proposed model, extensive comprehensive experiments were conducted using a wind power dataset provided by the State Grid. The experimental results indicate that the MSE of the model proposed in this paper has decreased by an average of 7.1% compared to the state-of-the-art model and by 48.9% compared to the conventional model. Moreover, the improvement in model performance becomes more pronounced as the prediction horizon increases.

Keywords: wind power forecasting; multi-scale modeling; graph neural network; temporal convolutional network

1. Introduction

As global warming intensifies and energy crises escalate, the need to seek clean and sustainable energy solutions has become an international consensus. Wind power generation, as a green energy technology, is becoming key to the global energy transition due to its renewable nature and low carbon emissions [1]. Figure 1 provides a detailed depiction of the workflow of a modern wind turbine, from the capture of wind energy to the output of electricity. The left side of the image illustrates the main components of a wind turbine. Wind is captured by the turbine blades and converted into mechanical energy through transmission gears, which drive the generator to produce electricity. The right side of the image then describes the further processing and distribution of electricity. Power is first transmitted to a charge controller, then flows to a battery bank for storage or directly to an inverter, which supplies power to the grid or directly to the load. According to data released by the Global Wind Energy Council (GWEC) [2], global cumulative installed wind power capacity grew from 433 GW in 2015 to 906 GW in 2022, with an annual compound growth rate of 11.12%. Accurate wind power prediction is crucial for realizing precise scheduling and efficient power supply, thus making wind power prediction technology essential. However, the variability and intermittency of wind power present significant challenges to the planning, operation, and control of power systems [3].

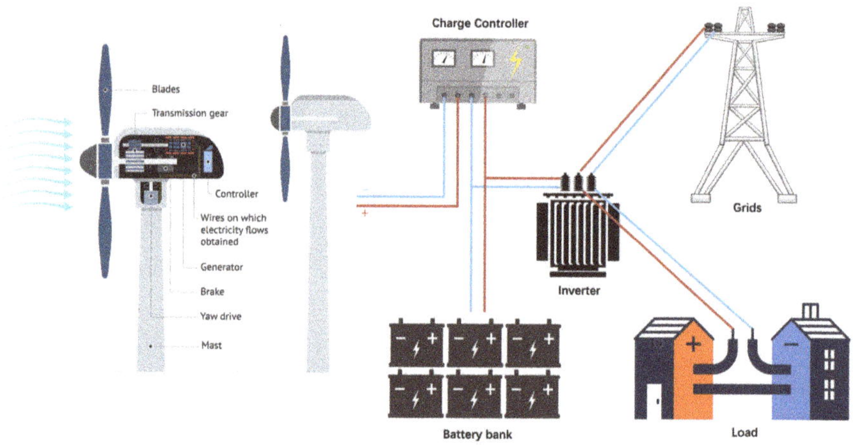

Figure 1. Wind turbine workflow.

Wind power prediction methods are primarily divided into physical models, statistical models, and machine learning algorithms. Physical models depend on numerical weather predictions (NWP), utilizing meteorological data and surface information to solve equations of fluid dynamics and thermodynamics for predicting wind speed and direction, and subsequently calculating the power output of wind farms [4]. However, these models are computationally complex and sensitive to initial conditions, which limits their application in short-term high-precision forecasting. Statistical methods predict by establishing a relationship between input and output based on historical data [5]. Despite being computationally efficient, statistical models have drawbacks such as difficulty in model order selection and sensitivity to climate changes, which limit their effectiveness in long-term applications and environments with severe climate variability.

With the development of artificial intelligence technology, potential applications in energy forecasting have emerged. Traditional machine learning methods such as Artificial Neural Networks (ANN), Support Vector Machines (SVM), Extreme Gradient Boosting (XGBoost), and Multi-Layer Perceptrons (MLPs) have been widely utilized. The literature [6–8] proposes hybrid neural network architectures combining modal decomposition, optimization algorithms, and Extreme Learning Machines (ELM) to further improve prediction accuracy. The literature [9] introduces a novel wind power curve model integrating Isolation Forest anomaly detection, Asymmetric Fuzzy Mean Radial Basis Function Neural Network modeling, and meta-heuristic algorithm optimization. Although these traditional machine learning methods have high training efficiency, they still require extensive feature engineering and have limitations in handling long-term dependency relationships. Deep learning, as a branch of machine learning, has shown significant advancements in the field of sequence data prediction. The literature [10–12] proposes models integrating Recurrent Neural Networks (RNN) and Long Short Term Memory (LSTM) based on reinforcement learning, a wind power prediction method based on Gated Recurrent Units (GRU), and a model combining Self-Attention Temporal Convolutional Networks (SATCN) with LSTM for wind power prediction, respectively. These models aim to enhance prediction accuracy and reduce computational costs. Despite their strong fitting capabilities, they face issues like vanishing gradients, exploding gradients, and sensitivity to noise, which can lead to poor prediction outcomes.

In recent years, due to the ability of Graph Neural Networks (GNNs) to effectively model interactions between nodes through weighted edges, their application in wind power forecasting has gradually increased. The literature [13] proposed a Multi-dimensional Spatio-Temporal Graph Neural Network, which combines Wind Transformer for single-point wind speed prediction and utilizes GNNs to integrate wind speed information from multiple points in the spatial dimension, thereby improving wind speed prediction accuracy. Additionally, another study [14] combined Graph Convolutional Networks (GCN) with multiresolution convolution neural networks to dynamically extract spatial and temporal features among input variables, thus enhancing prediction accuracy. The literature [15] combined GNN with an improved Bootstrap technique to model the spatio-temporal characteristics between wind farms and meteorological factors, improving the precision and reliability of ultra-short-term predictions. The literature [16] integrated GNN with a Gated Dilated Inception Network, specifically considering the blockage effects between wind turbines, which further improved prediction accuracy.

With the introduction of the Vanilla Transformer [17], the attention mechanism it employs has greatly enhanced the model's ability to handle long-distance sequence dependencies, heralding a new era in time series prediction. Models that integrate attention mechanisms and Transformer-based variants have become the focus of current research. The literature [18–21] demonstrates that integrating attention mechanisms with models such as CNN, LSTM, and GRU has enhanced the accuracy of wind power prediction to varying degrees. The Vanilla Transformer, due to its need to compute the relevance of every position in the input sequence to all others, exhibits high complexity. In contrast, the Informer [22] utilizes the Kullback–Leibler divergence distribution measure to filter out dominant queries on the order of $O(N \log N)$, reducing complexity and designing a generative decoder to directly produce results, avoiding cumulative errors associated with one forward-step predictions. However, its reliance on single-step time calculations may result in the loss of crucial information under highly volatile wind power data. The Autoformer [23] attempts to decompose seasonal-trend features and auto-correlation attention for patch-level connections, but its essentially manual design may fail to capture all semantic information within the patch. The FEDformer [24], by transforming time series into the frequency domain to compute attention, achieves linear computational complexity, though this method may overlook detailed temporal dependencies, affecting prediction accuracy. The iTransformer [25] applies attention mechanisms and feed-forward networks in inverted dimensions, effectively capturing multivariate correlations and learning nonlinear representations.

Through in-depth observation of wind power sequence data, we found that power data present diverse time patterns at different sampling scales. For instance, wind power data recorded hourly reveal intra-day variations in wind speed, while data sampled daily highlight seasonal fluctuations. From a macro perspective, quarterly climate trends dominate the patterns of annual average power. These observations suggest that understanding complex temporal variations requires a multi-scale analysis approach, which can capture both short-term changes and long-term climate patterns, thereby offering a more comprehensive perspective for wind power prediction. Regarding references [13–16], most of the GNNs primarily focus on modeling the interactions between wind turbines within wind farms from a spatial dimension. These methods typically adopt a data-driven approach for constructing the graph structure; while capturing correlations between time series to some extent, they exhibit limited flexibility as they often only learn a specific type of dependency between variables. Consequently, they struggle to effectively handle complex temporal features across different time scales. This paper, from the perspective of capturing dependencies at various scales, combines a multi-scale temporal graph neural network with an adaptive graph learning module and optimizes the synergistic effects of features across different time scales through a fusion module. Furthermore, we introduce an improved temporal convolutional network, which enhances prediction capability by aggregating information from different scales and leveraging the complementarity of multi-scale observations.

The contributions of this paper are as follows:

(1) We developed a multi-scale frequency decomposition (MSF-Decomp) module that effectively extracts seasonal and trend changes from data of different sampling sizes, transforming them into high and low-frequency components for independent modeling.

(2) The Multi-Scale Temporal Graph Convolutional Network (MST-GCN) was designed to use low-frequency components as inputs, capturing correlations across multi-scale sequences.
(3) A Bidirectional Temporal Gated Convolution Network (Bi-TGCN) was introduced, utilizing high-frequency components to effectively handle dependencies within multi-scale sequences.
(4) By using a multi-head cross-attention mechanism to fuse the prediction results of two models and comparing them with several benchmark models, the advantages of our method in terms of robustness and accuracy were validated.

The remainder of this paper is organized as follows: Section 2 provides a detailed explanation of the proposed model's construction and key techniques. Section 3 introduces the data sources and preprocessing steps. Section 4 covers the experimental design, result analysis, and performance comparison of the model. Finally, Section 5 summarizes the research findings and limitations and discusses future research directions.

2. Proposed Methodology

We propose a novel method for processing and predicting multi-scale time series data, whose overall framework is displayed in Figure 2. This method begins by decomposing the original series into low and high-frequency components using the MSF-Decomp module. The high-frequency component, which contains rapid change information, reflects local fluctuations and is processed through the designed Bi-TGCN to capture internal sequence dependencies. The low-frequency component, which reflects overall trends, is handled by the MST-GCN, utilizing graph node propagation to reveal deep trends and temporal patterns. Finally, the outputs of the two modules are integrated through a multi-head cross-attention mechanism to form a comprehensive prediction result.

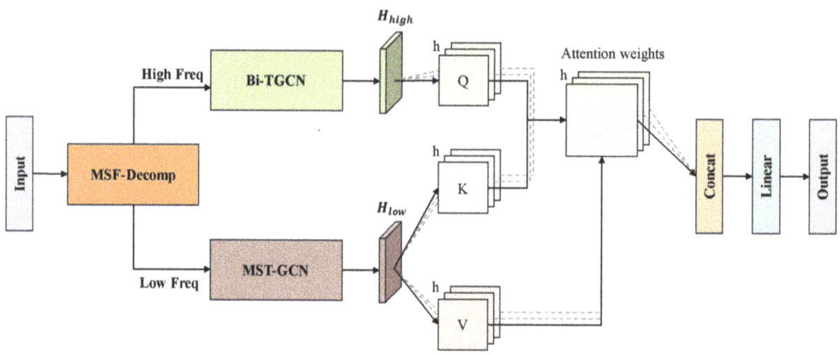

Figure 2. The overall framework of the proposed model.

2.1. Multi-Scale Decomposition Module

When analyzing the original wind power data, we observed that even at the finest granularity of sampling, the data exhibited mixed temporal patterns containing both seasonal and trend changes. The superposition and coupling of these patterns increase the complexity and variability of the sequence. Inspired by seasonal and trend decomposition methods [26], we propose a multi-scale frequency decomposition strategy. This strategy separates high-frequency signals, which include abrupt changes and noise, from low-frequency signals, modeling them separately. This approach enhances the model's ability to capture long-term trends and improves prediction stability.

Previous time series decomposition methods primarily used a moving average strategy to smooth the original data. Specifically, given an input sequence $X \in \mathbb{R}^{L \times d}$, where L represents the total length of the sequence and d represents the dimensions, the decomposition steps are as follows:

$$X_t = AvgPool(P(X))_{kernel} \tag{1}$$

$$X_s = X - X_t \tag{2}$$

where $X_t, X_s \in \mathbb{R}^{L \times d}$ represent the trend component and seasonal component, respectively. $AvgPool\ (\cdot)$ denotes the average pooling operation, and $P\ (\cdot)$ represents the padding operation. However, the fixed pool size in this method may not be adequate for adapting to the dynamic mixed modes in wind power sequences. Moreover, using the difference to extract the seasonal component X_s overlooks the nonlinear coupling relationship between trend and seasonal components.

Based on the aforementioned method, we designed the MSF-Decomp module shown in Figure 3. This module uses average and max pooling to process data, where average pooling captures general trends, and max pooling highlights peaks or extreme values. It also incorporates various-sized pooling kernels, enhancing the separation of high-frequency and low-frequency components. Specifically, the module concatenates components from different-sized pooling operations. To maintain the original temporal data, it expands the data by one dimension, transforming it into a vector X_L, with the last dimension being 3. Integration of various components is achieved through a weighted sum operation. For the input sequence $X \in \mathbb{R}^{L \times d}$, the expression is as follows:

$$X_{low} = sum(AvgPool(P(X))_{k_1}, \ldots, AvgPool(P(X))_{k_n} X_L) \tag{3}$$

$$X_{high} = sum(MaxPool(P(X))_{k_1}, \ldots, MaxPool(P(X))_{k_n} X_L) \tag{4}$$

where $X_{low}, X_{high} \in \mathbb{R}^{L \times d}$ respectively represent the low-frequency and high-frequency components, and $MaxPool(\cdot)$ denotes the max pooling operation. Through this design, the MSF-Decomp module provides a basis for subsequent modeling by extracting high and low-frequency features.

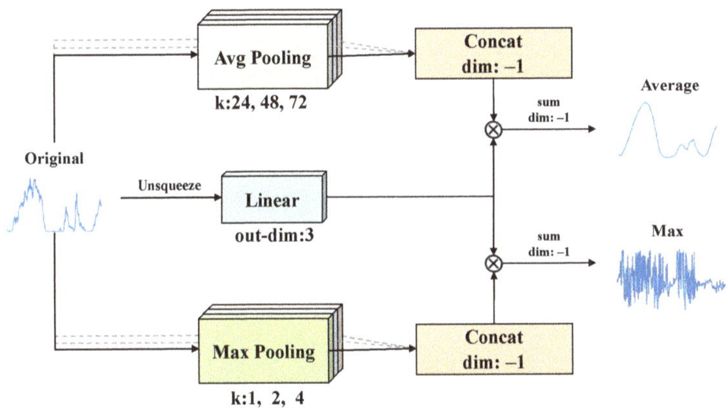

Figure 3. Framework diagram of MSF-Decomp module.

2.2. *Multi-Scale Graph Neural Network Modeling*

2.2.1. Dynamic Graph Learning

Wind power data are considered a unique form of graph-structured data, with nodes representing different variables connected by an adjacency matrix that depicts their correlations. Traditional methods [27–29] typically learn a single adjacency matrix, capturing only significant shared temporal patterns and often overlooking the diversity of time scales.

In response, this paper adopts a Dynamic Graph Learning strategy with M scale layers [30]. In this strategy, continuous values at different time granularities are used to quantify the associations between variables. Specifically, the parameter $E_{\text{nodes}} \in \mathbb{R}^{L \times d}$ is shared across all scales, while $E_{\text{scale}} \in \mathbb{R}^{M \times d}$ represents the embeddings within each scale. Ultimately, embeddings from both spaces are fused using the Hadamard product to generate scale-specific weight information E_{space}. The formula is as follows:

$$E^m_{\text{space}} = E_{\text{nodes}} \odot E^m_{\text{scale}} \tag{5}$$

where $E^m_{\text{scale}} \in \mathbb{R}^{1\times d}$, and $m \in \{0, \ldots, M\}$, represents the embedding at scale m. Then, the proximity similarity between nodes a and b is computed as follows:

$$D^m_a = \tanh\left(E^m_{\text{space}}\varphi^m_1\right) \tag{6}$$

$$D^m_b = \tanh\left(E^m_{\text{space}}\varphi^m_2\right) \tag{7}$$

$$A^m = \sigma\left((D^m_a)^T D^m_b - D^m_a (D^m_b)^T\right) \tag{8}$$

where $\varphi^m_1, \varphi^m_2 \in \mathbb{R}^{1\times 1}$ are learnable parameters used to capture the features between nodes D^m_a and D^m_b. $A^m \in \mathbb{R}^{N\times N}$ is normalized by the activation function σ into the range $[0, 1]$, indicating node connection weights. To generate a continuous sparse adjacency matrix, we introduce the Smoothed Sparse Unit (SSU), which is defined by the following formula:

$$A'_m = \text{Softmax}(\alpha \tanh(\beta(A^m))) \tag{9}$$

where α and β are learnable parameters. The SSU balances reconstruction error and sparsity by adjusting the regularization coefficient λ, aiming to align the actual sparsity ρ' of the adjacency matrix with the target sparsity ρ [31]. The formula is as follows:

$$\min_{A^m,\alpha,\beta}\left(\|A^m - A'_m\|^2_F + \lambda KL(\rho\|\rho')\right) \tag{10}$$

where $\|A^m - A'_m\|^2_F$ is the Frobenius norm of the reconstruction error, $\text{KL}(\cdot)$ calculates the Kullback–Leibler divergence, and ρ' is the actual sparsity of A^m, defined as $\rho' = \frac{1}{N^2}\sum_{ij} A^m_{ij}$. Ultimately, this yields a specific scale of sparse adjacency matrices $\{A^1, \ldots, A^m, \ldots, A^M\}$.

2.2.2. Multi-Scale Temporal Graph Convolution Network

Based on the Dynamic Graph Learning strategy, we have proposed MST-GCN to generate and process multi-scale adjacency matrices. Figure 4 illustrates the overall framework of the network.

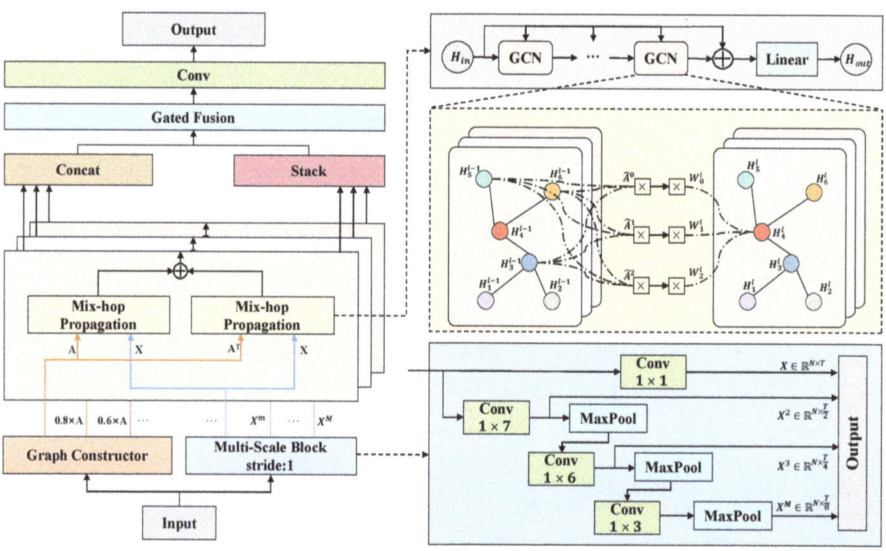

Figure 4. The primary structure of MST-GCN.

In this framework, low-frequency components enter the Multi-Scale Block and are processed through multi-layer convolution operations for scale division. Specifically, given the initial input data $X_{\text{low}} \in \mathbb{R}^{N \times T}$, where N represents the feature dimensions and T represents the time steps, undergoes a 1×1 Conv operation that preserves sequence information. It then proceeds through m Conv layers, with the output results being $\{X_{\text{low}}, \ldots, X_{\text{low}}^{m}, \ldots, X_{\text{low}}^{M}\}$, where $X_{\text{low}}^{m} \in \mathbb{R}^{N \times \frac{T}{2^{m-1}}}$, and each Conv layer halves the time dimension. The lower right of Figure 4 shows the processing flow in the Multi-Scale Block, with kernel sizes 1×1, 1×7, 1×6, and 1×3 for the convolution layers.

In the graph constructor, the original information of nodes and edges is encoded into graph representations, and an activated sparse adjacency matrix is generated using Formulas (5)–(10).

GCNs effectively utilize the topological structure of graphs to propagate features and capture local connectivity patterns between nodes. The mathematical formula is as follows:

$$H^{l} = \sigma\left(\widetilde{D}^{-\frac{1}{2}} \hat{A} \widetilde{D}^{-\frac{1}{2}} H^{l-1} W^{l}\right) \tag{11}$$

where $H^{l}, H^{l-1} \in \mathbb{R}^{N \times d}$ are the feature results of the lth and $(l-1)^{th}$ layers respectively, $\hat{A} = A + I$ includes self-connections, $\widetilde{D}$ is the degree matrix of $\hat{A}$, and W^{l} is the learnable weight matrix. As the number of GCN layers increases, node representations often converge, leading to an over-smoothing phenomenon. To address this, we introduce the Mix-hop Propagation mechanism [32], which integrates neighbor information from multiple hop counts, thoroughly considering both the direct connections of nearby nodes and the indirect influences of more distant neighboring relationships. Its structure is shown in the upper right of Figure 4, where $\hat{A}^{i}$ represents the ith power of $\hat{A}$ with $i = 0, 1, 2$, and the operator $\times$ has a fixed relative position. Specifically, given input features X and the normalized adjacency matrix $\hat{A}$, node features are updated through g layers of depth propagation. In each layer i, node features H are updated as follows:

$$H^{i+1} = \alpha X + (1 - \alpha) \cdot (\hat{A} H^{i} W^{i}) \tag{12}$$

where H^{i} is the feature after i iterations, α is the mixing factor controlling the proportion of input information retained.

After g iterations, features across all scales are concatenated along the feature dimension, and an output feature matrix h is generated through an MLP:

$$h = MLP(\text{Concat}[H^{0}, H^{1}, \ldots, H^{g}]) \tag{13}$$

Finally, in Gated Fusion, importance weights of different scales are learned to fuse feature representations across multiple scales.

2.3. Multi-Scale Temporal Convolution modeling

In wind power prediction, we often have access to covariates for the upcoming period, such as weather forecast data and time indicators. To better utilize this forward-looking information, we have designed the Bi-TGCN based on the TCN architecture. We aim for the current state to be related not only to past observations but also to integrate a perspective on the upcoming period, accurately predicting rapid fluctuations in high-frequency components and quickly identifying key power change points [33]. For this, we perform forward and backward dilated convolutions on the data in the temporal dimension, concatenate them, and then pass the result through a linear projection to achieve a specific size. This is added to the vector X_r after Residual Conv, and finally, the output is obtained after linear processing and Dropout. The left side of Figure 5 shows the overall framework of the Bi-TGCN, which is expressed as follows:

$$X_{\text{output}} = \text{Dropout}(\text{Linear}(\text{Concat}(FTC, BTC)) + X_r) \tag{14}$$

where FTC and BTC represent Forward Temporal Convolution and Backward Temporal Convolution, respectively.

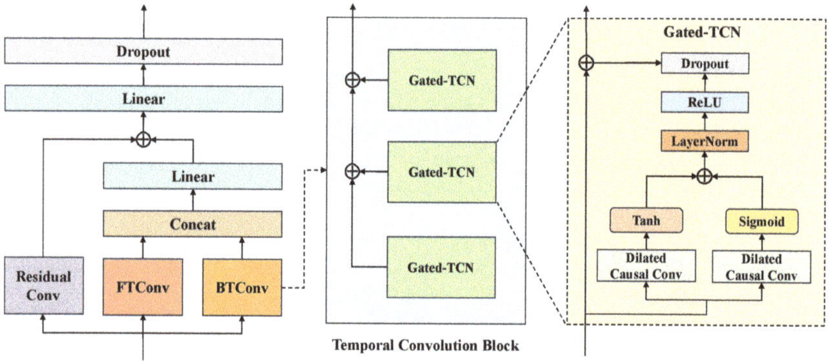

Figure 5. Overall architecture diagram of Bi-TGCN.

We introduce a gating mechanism in TCN, designing the Gated-TCN component to enhance the model's control over information flow and optimize attention to key temporal points. The process is divided into two branches. First, the input data are initialized using two dilated causal convolution layers, then processed through the tanh and Sigmoid functions for activation, and their outputs are merged. This is followed by layer normalization, activation via the ReLU function, and Dropout processing to produce the final output. The core formula is expressed as follows:

$$h(x) = \tanh(x * \theta_1 + b) + \text{Sigmoid}(x * \theta_2 + c) \tag{15}$$

where b and c are bias terms for the different convolution kernels θ_1 and θ_2, respectively; $\tanh(\cdot)$ and $\text{sigmoid}(\cdot)$ control the speed of information flow and the proportion of information retained. The right side of Figure 5 displays the structure of the Temporal Convolution Block and Gated-TCN, where the Temporal Convolution Block consists of the outputs from three Gated-TCNs with different dilation factors added together.

Figure 6 depicts the bidirectional architecture of a three-layer TCN, which utilizes forward and backward dilated convolutions to extend its coverage across a broader time span without compromising resolution. As indicated, dilation factors of 1, 2, and 4 are employed to effectively capture seasonal fluctuations in wind power data over multiple time scales. The outputs from these dilated convolutions are concatenated and then subjected to a linear projection to generate the forecast. To enhance the model's robustness, a skip connection is implemented that reintroduces the linear projection results back to the original input, countering potential vanishing gradient issues caused by layer accumulation.

2.4. Fusion Mechanism

In multi-scale time series forecasting, various scale patterns play distinct roles in influencing prediction outcomes. To effectively merge feature representations from MST-GCN and Bi-TGCN, a multi-head cross-attention mechanism is employed instead of simpler methods such as concatenation or global pooling. This approach effectively integrates and balances high and low-frequency information from different scales for the final prediction. As depicted on the right side of Figure 2, MST-GCN processes the low-frequency component X_{low} to produce $H_{\text{low}} \in \mathbb{R}^{N \times d_1}$, while Bi-TGCN processes the high-frequency component X_{high} to generate $H_{\text{high}} \in \mathbb{R}^{N \times d_2}$. In this setup, the high-frequency features act as the query, with the low-frequency features forming the key-value set. Through the multi-head cross-attention mechanism, the final multi-scale fused feature representation $H_{\text{fuse}} \in \mathbb{R}^{N \times d}$ is computed as follows:

$$H_{\text{fuse}} = \text{Concat}(head_1, head_2, \ldots, head_i)W^O \tag{16}$$

$$head_i = \text{CrossAttention}(H_{\text{high}}Q_i, H_{\text{low}}K_i, H_{\text{low}}V_i) \tag{17}$$

$$\text{CrossAttention}(H_{\text{high}}, H_{\text{low}}) = \text{Softmax}\left(\frac{QK^T}{\sqrt{d_k}}\right)V \tag{18}$$

$$Q = H_{\text{high}}W^Q, \quad K_i = H_{\text{low}}W_i^K, \quad V_i = H_{\text{low}}W_i^V \tag{19}$$

where $W^O \in \mathbb{R}^{hd \times d}$, $W^Q \in \mathbb{R}^{d_1 \times d_k}$, $W^K \in \mathbb{R}^{d_2 \times d_k}$, and $W^V \in \mathbb{R}^{d_2 \times d_k}$ are learned projection matrices. i is the number of attention heads, and d_k is the dimension of the key-value set.

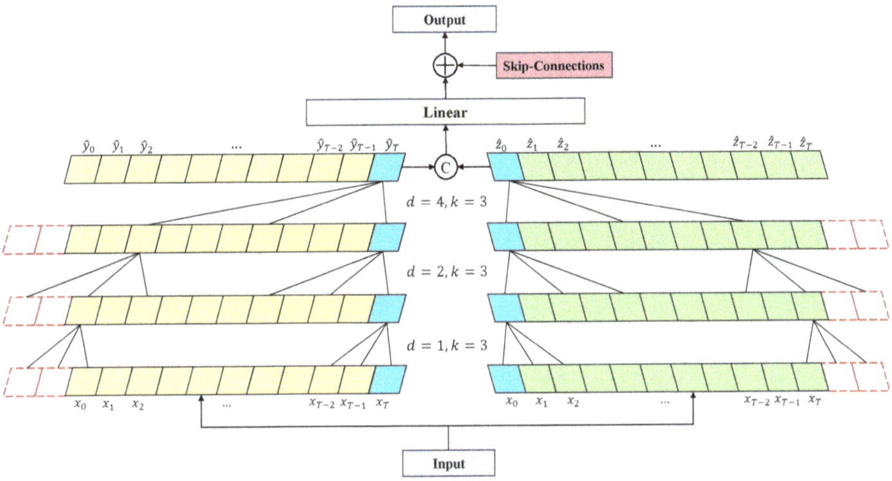

Figure 6. Bidirectional architecture diagram of three-layer TCN.

3. Data Collection and Analysis

3.1. Data Collection

The dataset used in this study comes from the Chinese State Grid (CSG) [34], including actual power output and corresponding weather data for wind energy generation from 2019 to 2020. The dataset comprises over seventy thousand data points, with a time interval of 15 min. These data were collected via Supervisory Control and Data Acquisition (SCADA) systems and involved wind farms located in various terrains across North, Central, and Northwest China. A detailed description of all feature variables can be found in Table 1.

Table 1. Description of the feature variables for CSG.

Heading Name	Shortened Name
Wind speed at height of x meters (m/s)	WS_x
Wind direction at height of x meters (°)	WD_x
Air temperature (°C)	Air_T
Atmosphere (hpa)	Air_P
Relative humidity (%)	Air_H
Power output(MW)	Power (MW)

3.2. Data Preprocessing and Analysis

For the collected raw dataset, we first used linear interpolation to fill in missing values, then applied box plot methods to identify and analyze outliers. The trends in wind power generation and the fluctuations in wind speed at hub height in wind farm site 1 for the year 2019 are respectively shown in Figure 7. These trends indicate that the power series is influenced by various environmental factors, displaying non-stationarity and high volatility, while the wind speed is higher in the summer and lower in the winter, demonstrating clear seasonal variations. Figure 8a illustrates the close relationship between wind speed and power output, showing that once the wind speed reaches a certain critical point, the power output no longer increases, which is associated with the turbine's rated power and cut-out wind speed. Additionally, Figure 8b reveals significant differences in wind speeds from different directions. When the angle difference between the wind direction and the turbine orientation is minimized, the turbine's rotational speed significantly increases, thereby effectively enhancing the efficiency of wind power output.

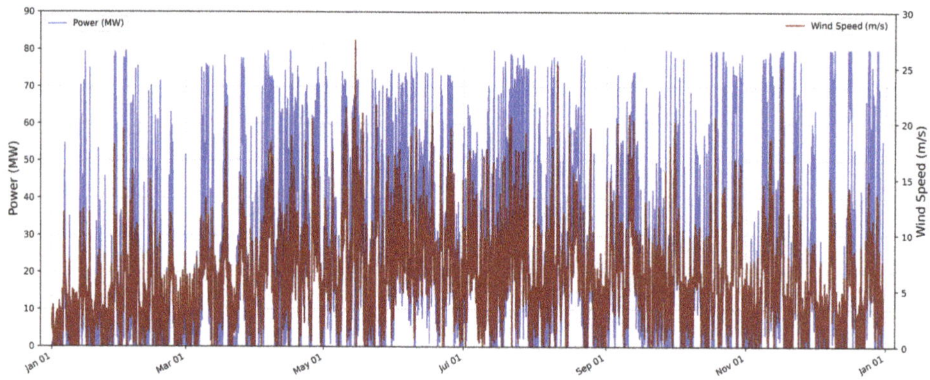

Figure 7. Data distribution of power and wind speed.

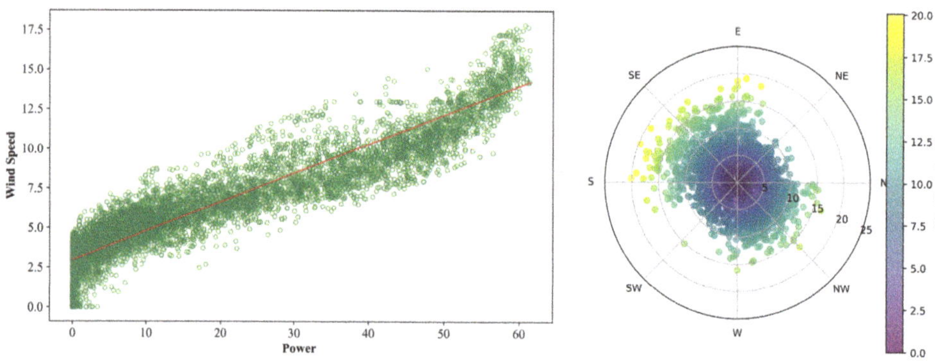

(**a**) Power VS Wind speed (**b**) Power VS Wind direction

Figure 8. Scatter plot of power versus wind speed and direction.

To further reveal the dependencies between power output and various variables, we evaluate these relationships using Pearson correlation coefficients (PCC) and Maximum Information Coefficients (MIC). The mathematical formulas are as follows:

$$f_{\mathrm{PCC}}(x,y) = \frac{\sum x_i y_i - n\overline{xy}}{(n-1)s_x s_y} \tag{20}$$

$$I(x,y) = \int p(x,y) \log_2 \frac{p(x,y)}{p(x)p(y)} dxdy \tag{21}$$

$$f_{\mathrm{MIC}}(x,y) = \max_{a*b<B} \frac{I(x,y)}{\log_2 \min(a,b)} \tag{22}$$

where x, y represent different variables, s_x and s_y are the variances of the variables, $p(x, y)$ is the joint probability between variables x and y, a and b are the number of grid distributions, and B is set to the 0.6 power of the total data count. Based on the analysis results, we created heatmaps in Figure 9. The results indicate that wind speed is highly correlated with power output, while wind direction and environmental factors have weaker correlations with power. However, their correlation with wind speed is moderate. Relative humidity has the lowest correlation with both wind speed and power output and, therefore, is not considered in the analysis.

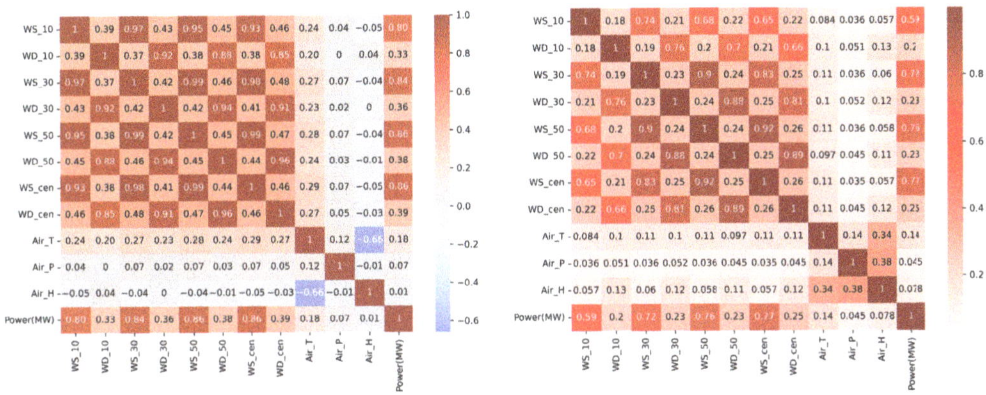

(a) PCC (b) MCI

Figure 9. Correlation analysis results.

4. Experimental Case Studies

4.1. Evaluation Metrics

To comprehensively assess the performance of the wind power prediction model, this study has chosen Mean Squared Error (MSE), Mean Absolute Error (MAE), and the coefficient of determination R^2 as key evaluation metrics [35]. The specific formulas for these metrics are as follows:

$$MSE = \frac{1}{n}\sum_{i=1}^{n}(Y_i - \hat{Y}_i)^2 \tag{23}$$

where the Y_i are the actual values, the $\hat{Y}_i$ are the predicted values, and n is the number of observations.

$$MAE = \frac{1}{n}\sum_{i=1}^{n}|Y_i - \hat{Y}_i| \tag{24}$$

$$R^2 = 1 - \frac{\sum_{i=1}^{n}(Y_i - \hat{Y}_i)^2}{\sum_{i=1}^{n}(Y_i - \overline{Y})^2} \tag{25}$$

where $\overline{Y}$ is the mean of the actual values. The model's predictive results are normalized to facilitate direct comparison and evaluation with actual wind power generation values.

Additionally, to compare the performance of two time series forecasting models, we employed the Diebold-Mariano (DM) test [36], which is used to detect whether there is a significant difference in the forecasting errors between the two models. If the forecasting errors of models A and B are e_t^A and e_t^B, respectively, the difference sequence is defined as $d_t = e_t^A - e_t^B$. The average of the difference sequence is then calculated as $\bar{d} = \frac{1}{L}\sum_{t=1}^{L} d_t$, and the autocovariance estimate at lag $h = 0$ is computed as $\hat{\gamma}(h=0) = \frac{1}{L}\sum_{t=1}^{L} d_t^2$.

The DM test statistic is given by the following:

$$\mathrm{DM} = \frac{\bar{d}}{\sqrt{\frac{\hat{\gamma}(h=0)}{L}}} \tag{26}$$

where L is the length of the time series. The null hypothesis H_0 of the DM test is that there is no significant difference in the forecasting errors between the two models, while the alternative hypothesis H_1 suggests a significant difference. By comparing the DM statistic to the standard normal distribution, the resulting p-value determines the outcome: if the p-value is greater than 0.05, we accept the null hypothesis, indicating that the two models perform similarly; if the p-value is less than 0.05, we reject the null hypothesis, indicating that the two models perform differently. Typically, a positive DM test value indicates that model B outperforms model A, while a negative value suggests that model A outperforms model B.

4.2. Experiment Parameter

The system environment used in this study is Ubuntu 22.04, with 64GB of memory and a GeForce RTX 4090 D graphics card (NVIDIA, Santa Clara, CA, USA). The deep learning framework employed is PyTorch 1.9.0, and the software used for the experimental simulation and graphing is Pycharm 2024.1.4. The dataset is divided into training, validation, and test sets with a ratio of 7:1:2. In this study, we systematically explored the parameter space using grid search and Bayesian optimization as quantitative optimization techniques and combining with trial and error to determine the optimal parameters for multi-step ahead forecasting. Specific parameters are provided in Table 2.

Table 2. Parameter list.

Parameter	Value
GCN depth	2
Bi-TGCN scale	[12,12,12]
Dimensions of embedding	256
Number of heads of attention	6
Batch size	32
Optimizer	Adam
Dropout	0.2
Initial learning rate	1×10^{-5}

4.3. Case 1: Wind Farm Site 1

To validate the effectiveness of the proposed model, we designed two types of comparative experiments. In the first category, we selected five popular baseline models: RF, BiLSTM, CNN-LSTM, GRU, and TCN. The second category includes time series prediction models based on improvements to the Transformer architecture, which encompasses the Informer, Autoformer, FEDformer, and iTransformer. Among them, iTransformer is the current state-of-the-art (SOTA) model in the field of long-term time series forecasting. The short-term forecasting results can be observed in Table 3, where the prediction steps for both Case 1 and Case 2 are set to 2 steps (half an hour ahead). Our proposed model outperformed others across all evaluation metrics, with an MSE of 11.231, MAE of 2.445, and an R^2 of 0.981. This showcases the model's robustness and accuracy in wind power prediction tasks.

We plotted the indicator radar charts by equal scaling in Figure 10, which clearly demonstrates the outstanding performance of the proposed model on the metrics. The results of the first category of experiments show that in the context of short-term wind power prediction, RF performed the worst in terms of MSE and MAE, with scores 61.07% and 60.70% higher, respectively, than those of the proposed model, due to its limited capability to handle highly volatile time series. Although the other four models featured improvements in feature extraction, they failed to fully capture the impact of wind speed at different scales on wind power output. In the second category of experiments, the performance was generally far superior to that of the common baseline models used in the first category. Notably, the performance of Autoformer and FEDformer was significantly worse than their performance on general datasets, mainly because their full-sequence self-attention mechanisms overly focus on internal dependencies of variables, leading to high computational costs and excessive sensitivity to local noise. This makes them poorly suited to the high volatility of wind power data. The iTransformer showed performance similar to the proposed model, but the proposed model, by integrating MST-GCN and Bi-TGCN, optimized the capture of dependencies both between and within variables, making it more effective in handling real wind power data.

Table 3. Models prediction error results in wind farm site 1.

Model	MSE	MAE	R^2
RF	28.856	5.221	0.785
BiLSTM	25.371	4.873	0.812
CNN-LSTM	23.790	4.210	0.819
GRU	23.182	3.789	0.931
TCN	20.530	3.940	0.940
Informer	16.458	2.991	0.968
Autoformer	18.131	3.514	0.963
FEDformer	19.415	3.661	0.941
iTransformer	11.743	2.532	0.980
Proposed	11.231	2.445	0.981

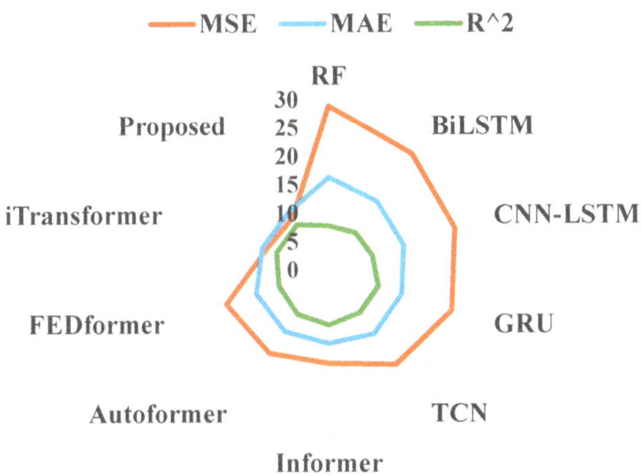

Figure 10. Prediction accuracy comparison.

Figure 11 displays the visualized prediction results of the top five performing models. Specifically, Figure 11a shows the prediction curves of each model, while Figure 11b provides a magnified view of the prediction curves to facilitate the observation of details. The results show that the proposed model excels in capturing the fluctuation trends of wind power, validating its effectiveness. Interestingly, the proposed model predicts up and down fluctuations when the true value is 0, indicating difficulty for the model to predict 0 directly. Additionally, in cases where the power consumption of SCADA leads to negative power values, the predicted values show significant errors. These issues will be addressed and further optimized in future research.

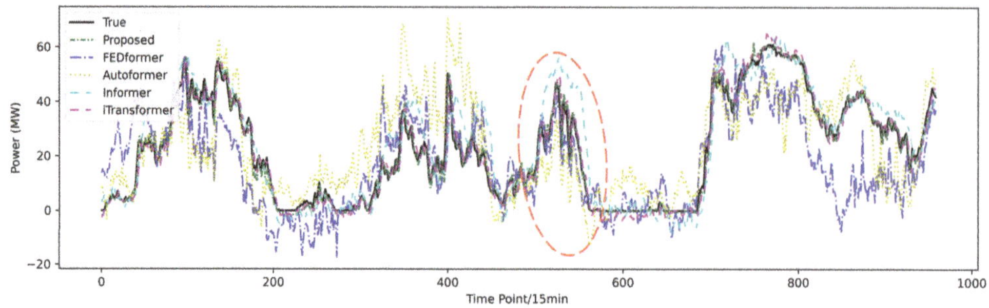

(**a**) Comparison of short-term forecast results

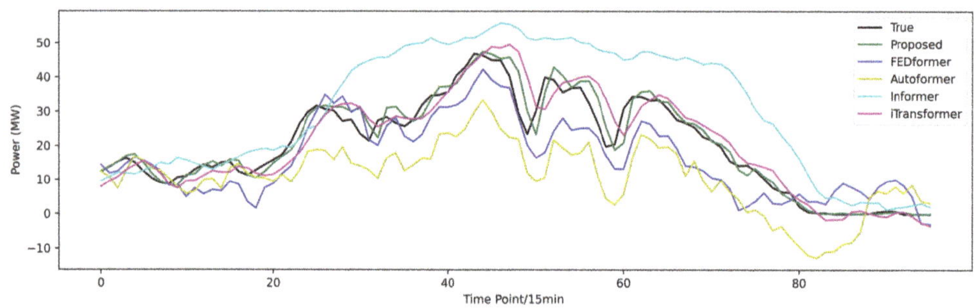

(**b**) Zoom view of curve tracing

Figure 11. Visualization of forecast results in wind farm site 1. The section within the red circle in Figure 11a is magnified and displayed in Figure 11b.

In short-term wind power prediction, model stability and robustness are crucial. In Figure 12, we present the PCC between each model and the actual wind power, along with the corresponding scatter plots. The proposed model achieves the highest PCC value, indicating the strongest linear correlation between its predictions and the actual power output. Notably, it demonstrates high stability and accuracy in the low-value regions (bottom right of the figure), as well as a high degree of fit with the actual values in the peak regions (top right of the figure). Combining the DM detection values in Table 4 to observe and compare the stability of other models, we found that the proposed model is better than other models, and the DM statistical value with the largest difference reaches −37.23, further verifying the excellent performance of the proposed model.

Table 4. DM detection results of the proposed method and the comparison model.

Methods	DM Statistic	*p* Value
Proposed vs. RF	−37.23	1.26×10^{-168}
Proposed vs. BiLSTM	−25.00	3.15×10^{-67}
Proposed vs. CNN-LSTM	−18.89	9.25×10^{-120}
Proposed vs. GRU	−19.97	2.14×10^{-148}
Proposed vs. TCN	−21.23	7.25×10^{-122}
Proposed vs. Informer	−14.90	1.67×10^{-40}
Proposed vs. Autoformer	−16.23	6.78×10^{-48}
Proposed vs. FEDformer	−17.29	1.27×10^{-54}
Proposed vs. iTransformer	−8.91	4.73×10^{-19}

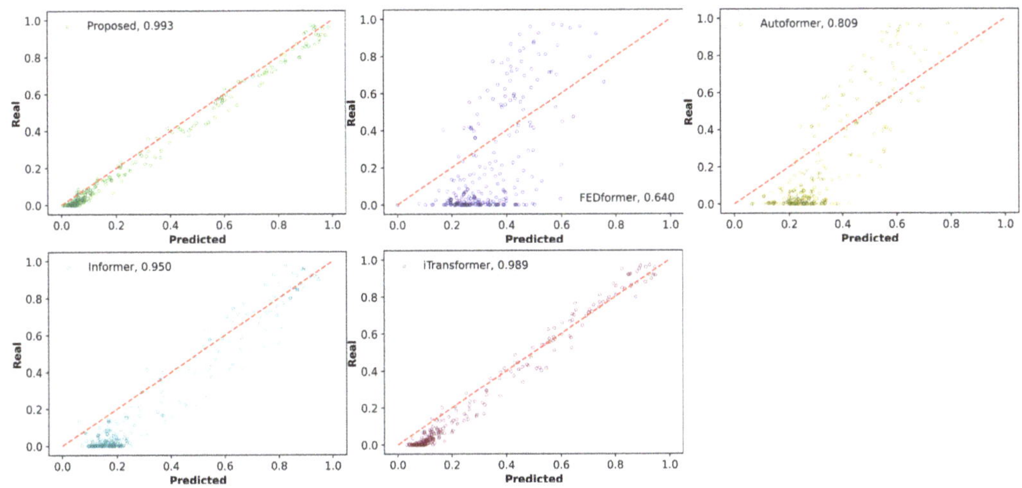

Figure 12. PCC scatter plot of predicted and true values in wind farm site 1.

4.4. *Case 2: Wind Farm Site 4*

In this subsection, we evaluate the proposed model using the dataset of wind farm site 4. The evaluation results are presented in Table 5, focusing on two key performance indicators: MSE and MAE. The proposed model achieved the lowest prediction errors among all models evaluated, with an MSE of 13.730 and an MAE of 2.511. The iTransformer's metrics were slightly higher than those of the proposed model, ranking second in performance, while traditional popular baseline models exhibited higher MSE and MAE values. These results show that the proposed model has good generalization performance in the field of wind power prediction.

Table 5. Models prediction error results in wind farm site 4.

Model	MSE	MAE	R^2
RF	30.043	5.034	0.783
BiLSTM	25.991	4.427	0.833
CNN-LSTM	25.774	4.029	0.845
GRU	24.101	4.384	0.883
TCN	22.451	3.848	0.937
Informer	18.119	2.907	0.951
Autoformer	19.857	3.582	0.952
FEDformer	21.534	3.661	0.939
iTransformer	14.005	2.540	0.975
Proposed	13.730	2.511	0.978

In the analysis for Case 2, we selected the five best-performing models for visualization. Figure 13 clearly shows that the proposed model continues to maintain the best performance, which demonstrates its strong fitting capabilities. We plotted violin plots in Figure 14 to compare the probability densities and distributions of the predicted values against the actual values across different models. In Figure 14, the central part is a boxplot, with the white dot representing the median. The violin plot and kernel density plot of the proposed model more closely match the actual data distribution, exhibiting the least volatility and the best stability, further validating the high robustness of the proposed model.

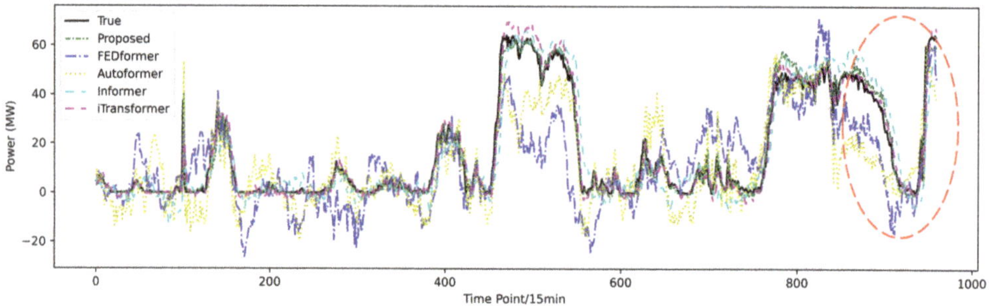

(a) Comparison of short-term forecast results

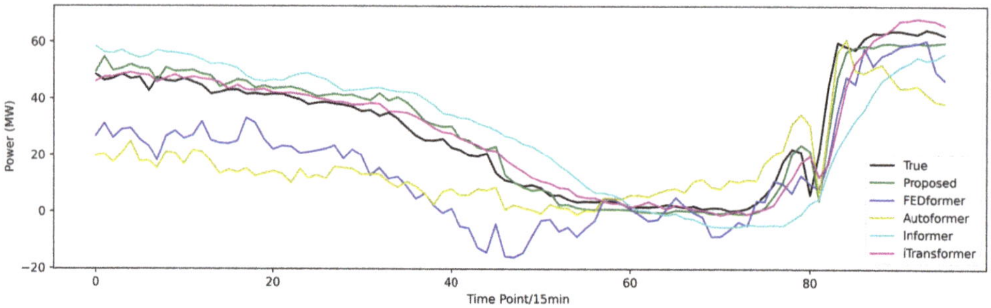

(b) Zoom view of curve tracing

Figure 13. Visualization of forecast results in wind farm site 4. The section within the red circle in Figure 13a is magnified and displayed in Figure 13b.

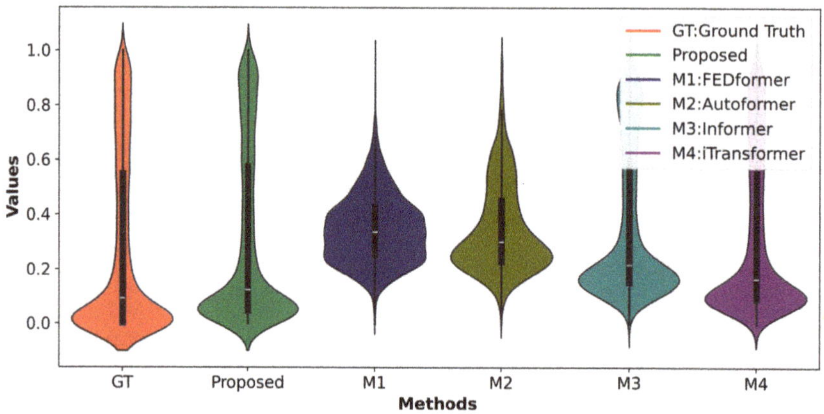

Figure 14. Voilin plots of predicted and true values in wind farm site 4.

4.5. Model Analysis

To further validate the effectiveness of the proposed model, this subsection conducts an ablation study to analyze the importance and contributions of each component, with specific results detailed in Table 6.

Initially, the MSF-Decomp module (Proposed-D) was removed, and raw data were directly inputted into the Bi-TGCN and MST-GCN for feature extraction. The absence of the MSF-Decomp module prevents the model from effectively separating complex modalities, thereby reducing model performance. Further, removing Bi-TGCN (Proposed-DT) and MST-GCN (Proposed-DG) from the Proposed-D configuration resulted in performance degradation. The absence of the Bi-TGCN prevents the model from effectively capturing the periodicity and abrupt changes in high-frequency sequences. Meanwhile, without MST-GCN, the model struggled to thoroughly analyze the correlations and evolutionary patterns among nodes (variables) across various time scales.

Table 6. Results of ablation study.

Model	MSE	MAE	R^2
Proposed-D	14.868	2.896	0.961
Proposed-DT	21.501	4.080	0.937
Proposed-DG	17.543	3.767	0.949
Proposed	11.231	2.445	0.981

In summary, the effective integration of the above three modules significantly enhances the model's capability to handle complex dependencies in wind power data, thereby effectively improving prediction accuracy and robustness.

4.6. *Seasonal Variation Analysis*

To assess the impact of seasonal changes, we extracted data from 2020 and divided them into four seasonal segments: Spring (March to May), Summer (June to August), Autumn (September to November), and Winter (December to February). We then re-evaluated the proposed model and selected baseline models for each segment.

The results of Table 7 clearly demonstrate the significant advantages of the proposed model in adapting to seasonal changes, especially in the transitional seasons of Spring and Autumn. In these seasons, the proposed model recorded the lowest MSE and MAE values at 12.563 and 2.547 for Spring, and 11.564 and 2.45 for Autumn, respectively. These performance metrics were slightly better than those of the iTransformer model and significantly surpassed other baseline models. Moving into Summer, as the climate and wind patterns become relatively stable, all models generally showed improved performance. The iTransformer's capability to learn nonlinear representations for each variable individually allowed it to exhibit higher predictive efficiency and accuracy in the relatively stable summer, slightly leading the proposed model with lower MSE and MAE values by 0.204 and 0.08, respectively. As for Winter, characterized by high wind speeds and variable wind directions, which increase prediction difficulties, all models saw a rise in errors. However, the proposed model still demonstrated superior performance, with MSE and MAE values of 14.115 and 2.842, respectively, and an R^2 value close to 1, indicating that its predictions closely matched the actual wind power outputs, showcasing its exceptional robustness and adaptability.

Overall, the seasonal analysis highlights the effectiveness of the proposed model's MST-GCN and Bi-TGCN networks in capturing and adapting to the nonlinear dynamics of seasonal wind changes, further demonstrating the model's potential value and superior performance in practical wind power forecasting applications.

Table 7. Seasonal Variation in Model Performance.

Season	Model	MSE	MAE	R^2
Spring	Informer	18.512	3.42	0.948
	Autoformer	16.12	3.581	0.957
	FEDformer	17.638	3.593	0.951
	iTransformer	13.107	2.551	0.978
	Proposed	12.563	2.547	0.978

Table 7. *Cont.*

Season	Model	MSE	MAE	R^2
Summer	Informer	16.018	2.589	0.971
	Autoformer	17.416	2.471	0.977
	FEDformer	16.555	2.4	0.975
	iTransformer	10.75	2.139	0.989
	Proposed	10.954	2.219	0.988
Autumn	Informer	16.589	3.41	0.971
	Autoformer	18.964	3.471	0.96
	FEDformer	19.564	3.51	0.947
	iTransformer	11.69	2.578	0.981
	Proposed	11.564	2.45	0.982
Winter	Informer	21.04	4.224	0.937
	Autoformer	20.417	4.346	0.931
	FEDformer	22.471	4.851	0.935
	iTransformer	14.864	2.799	0.969
	Proposed	14.115	2.842	0.972

4.7. Discussion of Multi-Step Ahead Forecasting

In wind power forecasting and grid scheduling, short-term predictions are insufficient to support mid-to-long-term decisions such as grid load balancing and energy storage scheduling. Therefore, this subsection focuses on evaluating the performance of the proposed model in mid-to-long-term forecasting scenarios.

The error of all prediction methods increases with the number of forecasting steps, reflecting the challenges of mid-to-long-term forecasting. We chose a second category baseline model with better performance for comparative experiments. The mid-to-long-term prediction results are displayed in Table 8. The results show that although the proposed model's MSE and MAE reached 47.752 and 4.265 for mid-term forecasting and 89.818 and 5.847 for long-term forecasting, it still performed better than the comparison models. The iTransformer showed similar metrics to those of the proposed model in short-term forecasts but had significantly higher errors in mid-to-long-term forecasts. In summary, the proposed model demonstrates significant competitive advantages in the mid-to-long-term wind power forecasting domain, providing a precise and reliable forecasting tool for wind farm management and grid scheduling.

Table 8. Medium and long-term forecast results.

Model	12-Step (3 h Ahead)			24-Step (6 h Ahead)		
	MSE	MAE	R^2	MSE	MAE	R^2
Informer	58.531	4.976	0.787	126.458	7.457	0.688
Autoformer	66.544	5.446	0.731	145.581	7.575	0.649
FEDformer	62.998	5.22	0.743	131.912	7.22	0.653
iTransformer	55.184	4.492	0.827	100.31	6.656	0.71
Proposed	47.752	4.265	0.833	89.818	5.847	0.737

5. Conclusions

Due to the uncertainty and high volatility of wind power, the accuracy of wind power prediction is often unsatisfactory. To address this issue, this paper proposes a new prediction model. First, the MSF-Decomp module is used to decompose the wind power data into high- and low-frequency components, mitigating the impact of wind power uncertainty. Then, feature extraction is performed using the Bi-TGCN and MST-GCN networks, and the results are fused to obtain the final prediction. Thanks to its excellent multi-scale processing capabilities, the proposed model, in comparison experiments, reduced the MSE error by an average of 7.1% compared to state-of-the-art models and by an average of 48.9% compared to traditional models. The results demonstrate that the proposed model can effectively capture and integrate data dynamics across different time scales, showing significant practical value in short-term data analysis and mid-to-long-term decision support and proving its advantages in handling complex forecasting tasks.

Although the wind power prediction model proposed in this paper performs excellently in handling multi-scale data and capturing temporal dependencies, it still has some limitations. Firstly, the model's ability to predict zero or negative wind power values has not been fully optimized, which is crucial for ensuring reliability in practical applications as these values can represent critical operational scenarios. Secondly, due to the integration of MSF-Decomp, Bi-TGCN, and MST-GCN, the complexity of the model might pose challenges in real-time processing, particularly when deployed in online systems that require quick decision-making. Finally, although the model shows higher accuracy and stability compared with the baseline model, different application scenarios in actual operation still need to be considered.

Future research will focus on optimizing the model's accuracy in predicting zero values and negative power and exploring methods to enhance the precision of mid-to-long-term forecasts. Additionally, we plan to develop an online wind power prediction system for integration into actual power scheduling systems, thus further advancing the practicality of wind power technology.

Author Contributions: Conceptualization, Z.X. and H.Z.; methodology, H.Z.; software, C.X.; validation, H.S., J.X. and Z.W.; investigation, H.Z., Z.X. and H.S.; resources, C.X.; data curation, H.S.; writing—original draft preparation, H.Z.; writing—review and editing, Z.X. and H.Z.; visualization, H.S. and J.X.; supervision, Z.W.; project administration, Z.W.; funding acquisition, Z.X. All authors have read and agreed to the published version of the manuscript.

Funding: This work was supported by Science and Technology Project of State Grid of China, grant number 5108-202218280A-2-289-XG.

Data Availability Statement: The original contributions presented in the study are included in the article, further inquiries can be directed to the corresponding author.

Conflicts of Interest: The authors declare no conflicts of interest.

Abbreviations

The following abbreviations are used in this manuscript:

MLP	Multi-Layer Perceptron
RF	Random Forest
LSTM	Long Short Term Memory
GRU	Gated Recurrent Units
MSF-Decomp	Multi-Scale Frequency Decomposition
MST-GCN	Multi-Scale Temporal Graph Convolutional Network
Bi-TGCN	Bidirectional Temporal Gated Convolution Network
CSG	Chinese State Grid
SCADA	Supervisory Control and Data Acquisition
PCC	Pearson correlation coefficients
MIC	Maximum Information Coefficients
MSE	Mean Squared Error
MAE	Mean Absolute Error

References

1. Li, N.; Dong, J.; Liu, L.; Li, H.; Yan, J. A novel EMD and causal convolutional network integrated with Transformer for ultra short-term wind power forecasting. *Int. J. Electr. Power Energy Syst.* **2023**, *154*, 109470. [CrossRef]
2. Zhen, Z.; Qiu, G.; Mei, S.; Wang, F.; Zhang, X.; Yin, R.; Li, Y.; Osório, G.J.; Shafie-khah, M.; Catalão, J.P. An ultra-short-term wind speed forecasting model based on time scale recognition and dynamic adaptive modeling. *Int. J. Electr. Power Energy Syst.* **2022**, *135*, 107502. [CrossRef]

3. Yang, T.; Yang, Z.; Li, F.; Wang, H. A short-term wind power forecasting method based on multivariate signal decomposition and variable selection. *Appl. Energy* **2024**, *360*, 122759. [CrossRef]
4. Ouarda, T.B.; Charron, C. Non-stationary statistical modelling of wind speed: A case study in eastern Canada. *Energy Convers. Manag.* **2021**, *236*, 114028. [CrossRef]
5. Ding, Y.; Ye, X.W.; Guo, Y.; Zhang, R.; Ma, Z. Probabilistic method for wind speed prediction and statistics distribution inference based on SHM data-driven. *Probabilistic Eng. Mech.* **2023**, *73*, 103475. [CrossRef]
6. Fu, W.; Fu, Y.; Li, B.; Zhang, H.; Zhang, X.; Liu, J. A compound framework incorporating improved outlier detection and correction, VMD, weight-based stacked generalization with enhanced DESMA for multi-step short-term wind speed forecasting. *Appl. Energy* **2023**, *348*, 121587. [CrossRef]
7. Xiong, J.; Peng, T.; Tao, Z.; Zhang, C.; Song, S.; Nazir, M.S. A dual-scale deep learning model based on ELM-BiLSTM and improved reptile search algorithm for wind power prediction. *Energy* **2023**, *266*, 126419. [CrossRef]
8. Hua, L.; Zhang, C.; Peng, T.; Ji, C.; Shahzad Nazir, M. Integrated framework of extreme learning machine (ELM) based on improved atom search optimization for short-term wind speed prediction. *Energy Convers. Manag.* **2022**, *252*, 115102. [CrossRef]
9. Li, T.; Liu, X.; Lin, Z.; Morrison, R. Ensemble offshore Wind Turbine Power Curve modelling—An integration of Isolation Forest, fast Radial Basis Function Neural Network, and metaheuristic algorithm. *Energy* **2022**, *239*, 122340. [CrossRef]
10. Lin, L.; Li, M.; Ma, L.; Baziar, A.; Ali, Z.M. Hybrid RNN-LSTM deep learning model applied to a fuzzy based wind turbine data uncertainty quantization method. *Ad Hoc Netw.* **2021**, *123*, 102658. [CrossRef]
11. Kisvari, A.; Lin, Z.; Liu, X. Wind power forecasting—A data-driven method along with gated recurrent neural network. *Renew. Energy* **2021**, *163*, 1895–1909. [CrossRef]
12. Xiang, L.; Liu, J.; Yang, X.; Hu, A.; Su, H. Ultra-short term wind power prediction applying a novel model named SATCN-LSTM. *Energy Convers. Manag.* **2022**, *252*, 115036. [CrossRef]
13. Wu, Q.; Zheng, H.; Guo, X.; Liu, G. Promoting wind energy for sustainable development by precise wind speed prediction based on graph neural networks. *Renew. Energy* **2022**, *199*, 977–992. [CrossRef]
14. Song, Y.; Tang, D.; Yu, J.; Yu, Z.; Li, X. Short-Term Forecasting Based on Graph Convolution Networks and Multiresolution Convolution Neural Networks for Wind Power. *IEEE Trans. Ind. Inform.* **2023**, *19*, 1691–1702. [CrossRef]
15. Liao, W.; Wang, S.; Bak-Jensen, B.; Pillai, J.R.; Yang, Z.; Liu, K. Ultra-short-term Interval Prediction of Wind Power Based on Graph Neural Network and Improved Bootstrap Technique. *J. Mod. Power Syst. Clean Energy* **2023**, *11*, 1100–1114. [CrossRef]
16. Qiu, H.; Shi, K.; Wang, R.; Zhang, L.; Liu, X.; Cheng, X. A novel temporal–spatial graph neural network for wind power forecasting considering blockage effects. *Renew. Energy* **2024**, *227*, 120499. [CrossRef]
17. Vaswani, A.; Shazeer, N.; Parmar, N.; Uszkoreit, J.; Jones, L.; Gomez, A.N.; Kaiser, L.; Polosukhin, I. Attention is all you need. In Proceedings of the 31st International Conference on Neural Information Processing Systems, Red Hook, NY, USA, 4–9 December 2017; NIPS'17; pp. 6000–6010.
18. Xiong, B.; Lou, L.; Meng, X.; Wang, X.; Ma, H.; Wang, Z. Short-term wind power forecasting based on Attention Mechanism and Deep Learning. *Electr. Power Syst. Res.* **2022**, *206*, 107776. [CrossRef]
19. Niu, Z.; Yu, Z.; Tang, W.; Wu, Q.; Reformat, M. Wind power forecasting using attention-based gated recurrent unit network. *Energy* **2020**, *196*, 117081. [CrossRef]
20. Huang, B.; Liang, Y.; Qiu, X. Wind Power Forecasting Using Attention-Based Recurrent Neural Networks: A Comparative Study. *IEEE Access* **2021**, *9*, 40432–40444. [CrossRef]
21. Ma, Z.; Mei, G. A hybrid attention-based deep learning approach for wind power prediction. *Appl. Energy* **2022**, *323*, 119608. [CrossRef]
22. Zhou, H.; Zhang, S.; Peng, J.; Zhang, S.; Li, J.; Xiong, H.; Zhang, W. Informer: Beyond Efficient Transformer for Long Sequence Time-Series Forecasting. In Proceedings of the AAAI Conference on Artificial Intelligence, San Francisco, CA, USA, 7–11 August 2021; Volume 35, pp. 11106–11115. [CrossRef]
23. Wu, H.; Xu, J.; Wang, J.; Long, M. Autoformer: Decomposition Transformers with Auto-Correlation for Long-Term Series Forecasting. In Proceedings of the Advances in Neural Information Processing Systems, Online, 6–14 December 2021; Ranzato, M., Beygelzimer, A., Dauphin, Y., Liang, P., Vaughan, J.W., Eds.; Curran Associates, Inc.: Red Hook, NY, USA, 2021; Volume 34, pp. 22419–22430.
24. Zhou, T.; Ma, Z.; Wen, Q.; Wang, X.; Sun, L.; Jin, R. FEDformer: Frequency Enhanced Decomposed Transformer for Long-term Series Forecasting. In Proceedings of the 39th International Conference on Machine Learning, Baltimore, MA, USA, 17–23 July 2022; Proceedings of Machine Learning Research; Chaudhuri, K., Jegelka, S., Song, L., Szepesvari, C., Niu, G., Sabato, S., Eds.; PMLR: Westminster, UK, 2022; Volume 162, pp. 27268–27286.
25. Liu, Y.; Hu, T.; Zhang, H.; Wu, H.; Wang, S.; Ma, L.; Long, M. iTransformer: Inverted Transformers Are Effective for Time Series Forecasting. *arXiv* **2024**, arXiv:2310.06625. Available online: http://arxiv.org/abs/2310.06625 (accessed on 26 May 2024).
26. Wang, H.; Peng, J.; Huang, F.; Wang, J.; Chen, J.; Xiao, Y. MICN: Multi-scale Local and Global Context Modeling for Long-term Series Forecasting. In Proceedings of the International Conference on Learning Representations, Kigali, Rwanda, 1–5 May 2023.
27. Wu, Z.; Pan, S.; Chen, F.; Long, G.; Zhang, C.; Yu, P.S. A Comprehensive Survey on Graph Neural Networks. *arXiv* **2019**, arXiv:1901.00596. Available online: http://arxiv.org/abs/1901.00596 (accessed on 26 May 2024).
28. Veličković, P. Everything is connected: Graph neural networks. *Curr. Opin. Struct. Biol.* **2023**, *79*, 102538. [CrossRef] [PubMed]

29. Gao, C.; Zheng, Y.; Li, N.; Li, Y.; Qin, Y.; Piao, J.; Quan, Y.; Chang, J.; Jin, D.; He, X.; et al. A Survey of Graph Neural Networks for Recommender Systems: Challenges, Methods, and Directions. *ACM Trans. Recomm. Syst.* **2023**, *1*, 1–51. [CrossRef]
30. Chen, L.; Chen, D.; Shang, Z.; Zhang, Y.; Wen, B.; Yang, C. Multi-Scale Adaptive Graph Neural Network for Multivariate Time Series Forecasting. *arXiv* **2022**, arXiv:2201.04828. Available online: http://arxiv.org/abs/2201.04828 (accessed on 26 May 2024).
31. Peters, B.; Martins, A.F.T. Smoothing and Shrinking the Sparse Seq2Seq Search Space. In Proceedings of the 2021 Conference of the North American Chapter of the Association for Computational Linguistics: Human Language Technologies, Online, 6–11 June 2021; Toutanova, K., Rumshisky, A., Zettlemoyer, L., Hakkani-Tur, D., Beltagy, I.;, Bethard, S., Cotterell, R., Chakraborty, T., Zhou, Y., Eds.; ACL Anthology: Melbourne, Australia, 2021; pp. 2642–2654. [CrossRef]
32. Abu-El-Haija, S.; Perozzi, B.; Kapoor, A.; Alipourfard, N.; Lerman, K.; Harutyunyan, H.; Steeg, G.V.; Galstyan, A. MixHop: Higher-Order Graph Convolutional Architectures via Sparsified Neighborhood Mixing. In Proceedings of the 36th International Conference on Machine Learning, Long Beach, CA, USA, 9–15 June 2019; Chaudhuri, K., Salakhutdinov, R., Eds.; Proceedings of Machine Learning Research; PMLR: Westminster, UK, 2019; Volume 97, pp. 21–29.
33. Sprangers, O.; Schelter, S.; de Rijke, M. Parameter-efficient deep probabilistic forecasting. *Int. J. Forecast.* **2023**, *39*, 332–345. [CrossRef]
34. Chen, Y.; Xu, J. Solar and wind power data from the Chinese State Grid Renewable Energy Generation Forecasting Competition. *Sci. Data* **2022**, *9*, 577. [CrossRef]
35. González-Sopeña, J.; Pakrashi, V.; Ghosh, B. An overview of performance evaluation metrics for short-term statistical wind power forecasting. *Renew. Sustain. Energy Rev.* **2021**, *138*, 110515. [CrossRef]
36. Diebold, F.X.; Mariano, R.S. Comparing Predictive Accuracy. *J. Bus. Econ. Stat.* **2002**, *20*, 134–144. [CrossRef]

electronics

MDPI

Article

Advancements in Household Load Forecasting: Deep Learning Model with Hyperparameter Optimization

Hamdi A. Al-Jamimi [1,2,*], Galal M. BinMakhashen [1,2], Muhammed Y. Worku [3,4] and Mohamed A. Hassan [3,*]

[1] Computer Science and Engineering, King Fahd University of Petroleum and Minerals, Dhahran 31216, Saudi Arabia; binmakhashen@kfupm.edu.sa
[2] Research Excellence, King Fahd University of Petroleum & Minerals, Dhahran 31261, Saudi Arabia
[3] Interdisciplinary Research Center for Renewable Energy and Power Systems (IRC-REPS), Research Institute, King Fahd University of Petroleum and Minerals, Dhahran 31261, Saudi Arabia; muhammedw@kfupm.edu.sa
[4] Electrical Engineering Department, King Fahd University of Petroleum and Minerals, Dhahran 31261, Saudi Arabia
* Correspondence: aljamimi@kfupm.edu.sa (H.A.A.-J.); mhassan@kfupm.edu.sa (M.A.H.)

Abstract: Accurate load forecasting is of utmost importance for modern power generation facilities to effectively meet the ever-changing electricity demand. Predicting electricity consumption is a complex task due to the numerous factors that influence energy usage. Consequently, electricity utilities and government agencies are constantly in search of advanced machine learning solutions to improve load forecasting. Recently, deep learning (DL) has gained prominence as a significant area of interest in prediction efforts. This paper introduces an innovative approach to electric load forecasting, leveraging advanced DL techniques and making significant contributions to the field of energy management. The hybrid predictive model has been specifically designed to enhance the accuracy of multivariate time series forecasting for electricity consumption within the energy sector. In our comparative analysis, we evaluated the performance of our proposed model against ML-based and state-of-the-art DL models, using a dataset obtained from the Distribution Network Station located in Tetouan City, Morocco. Notably, the proposed model surpassed its counterparts, demonstrating the lowest error in terms of the Root-Mean-Square Error (RMSE). This outcome underscores its superior predictive capability and underscores its potential to advance the accuracy of electricity consumption forecasting.

Keywords: load forecasting; artificial intelligence; deep learning; hyperparameter optimization

1. Introduction

Modern power generation facilities require a consistent and uninterrupted supply of electricity to effectively meet load demands [1]. This necessitates precise predictions of both current and future load requirements, minimizing errors. To achieve this, researchers and scientists have focused on developing an efficient method known as load forecasting [2,3]. This technique involves forecasting future electricity consumption demands and playing a vital role in decision-making processes like unit commitment, network management, dispatch strategies, fuel allocation, and other operational aspects [4–6]. The increasing integration of renewable energy resources (RES) into the energy mix and the transformation of the traditional electric grid into a more intelligent, flexible, and interactive system have elevated the importance of electrical load forecasting in smart grid planning and operation [7–11]. The multi-stage real-time stochastic operation of grid-tied multi-energy microgrids (MEMGs) via the hybrid model predictive control (MPC) and approximate dynamic programming (ADP) approach was studied [10]. Accurate multi-node load forecasting is the key to the safe, reliable, and economical operation of the power system [11].

Since power generated from RES fluctuates based on factors such as weather conditions like irradiation and wind speed, maintaining a careful balance between power demand and supply through accurate load forecasting becomes crucial [10–13].

Electric load consumption data are a time series that comprise a sequence of observations at regular time intervals, encompassing both linear and nonlinear components [9]. Overestimating load requirements can result in excess power generation and market trading, while underestimation can lead to a mismatch between demand and supply, causing grid instability. Predicting electric load is a challenging task due to its high volatility and uncertainty, whether in the distribution system or within individual households [14,15]. Load forecasting (LF) serves as a methodology for predicting future load demands by analyzing historical data and identifying dependency patterns within its time-step observations. Its applications in power system operation and planning are extensive, encompassing demand response, scheduling, unit commitment, energy trading, system planning, and energy policy [14]. Precise LF is essential for power companies and decision makers to strike a balance between supply and demand, prevent power interruptions due to load shedding, and avoid an excess reserve of power generation [14]. Accurate forecasting enables utilities to plan demand response management, unit commitment, load dispatch, contingency planning, and optimal load flow with minimal resource wastage and cost overruns. The complexity, uncertainty, and the multitude of factors influencing predictions make LF a challenging task, categorized as a type of time-series problem necessitating specialized solutions [15]. Depending on the time horizon, forecasting can be short-term (hours to a week), medium-term (a week to a year), or long-term (over a year) [8]. Forecasting outputs can be pointing forecasts, providing a single estimated value of the future load, or density forecasts, offering estimates of the future load probability distribution, either pointwise or interval-wise. Various techniques are employed based on the forecast horizon. Although there is not a universally agreed-upon classification determined by the predictive horizon, it is crucial to acknowledge that diverse forecasting scenarios come with distinct challenges and advantages, requiring varied modeling strategies [9,10,16].

Currently, the prevailing approach involves utilizing classical and deep machine learning algorithms, genetic algorithms, wavelet analysis, singular spectral analysis, and similar methodologies [2]. Nevertheless, the selection of methods is contingent upon the specific problem under consideration and the inherent structure of the initial data. Recent studies have extensively reviewed state-of-the-art techniques in LF [17–26], categorizing them into two main groups: statistical and machine learning (ML) methods. Statistical methods, including autoregressive integrated moving average (ARIMA), linear regression, and exponential smoothing, map input data to output. These methods function by adhering to pre-established rules and assumptions, crafting a prediction model that delineates the relationship between variables [27]. It entails fitting project-specific probabilities to historical data and generating load predictions through statistical inference. These techniques are frequently characterized by their speed, simplicity, interpretability, and computational efficiency. However, they suffer from uncertainty and low accuracy, particularly in high nonlinear systems. ML techniques, such as artificial neural networks (ANN), deep learning (DL), and recurrent neural networks, have more complex setups and longer training times but offer higher accuracy and performance. As a branch of AI, the methodology of ML empowers computers to learn and adjust automatically through experience [28,29]. The process includes training a model on a dataset and employing the trained model to predict outcomes on new data. While these techniques can capture intricate relationships and patterns, they demand meticulous feature selection and parameter tuning [29]. DL represents an advanced iteration of ML, utilizing layered algorithms and neural networks with multiple hidden layers to acquire knowledge and formulate predictions [28,29]. DL architectures usually comprise intricately layered networks with multiple hidden layers, enabling them to grasp intricate data representations and generate precise predictions, especially when handling extensive and intricate datasets. However, it is important to note that they can be computationally demanding and necessitate substantial amounts of data for effective training [28,29].

This paper introduces a novel approach to electric LF, employing advanced DL techniques. The key contributions of this study are as follows: Firstly, the presentation of a hybrid predictive model that integrates DL methods to enhance the accuracy of multivariate-to-multivariate time series forecasting in the energy domain. Secondly, the use of a Keras Regressor wrapper and Randomized Search cross-validation (CV) technique to optimize the DL model's hyperparameters, improving its overall performance. Additionally, an innovative early stopping algorithm is developed to efficiently monitor and terminate the training process, conserving computational resources. The research also delves into feature significance and provides a comprehensive analysis of how varying the number of features influences training performance, shedding light on feature selection's impact. Through extensive simulations and experiments, the proposed model consistently outperforms existing approaches, demonstrating the lowest Root-Mean-Square Error (RMSE) in comparisons. Lastly, the study encompasses a thorough literature review of recent deep-learning models used for power consumption prediction, offering insights into the field's advancements and trends.

The aspects of novelty of this work can be summarized as follows:

- Hybrid predictive model—this paper introduces a novel hybrid predictive model that integrates DL methods for electric LF. While DL is a well-explored area, the unique contribution lies in the hybrid nature of our model, combining different DL techniques to enhance the accuracy of multivariate time series forecasting in the energy domain. The specific combination and integration of these techniques represent a novel approach.
- Hyperparameter optimization and early stopping algorithm—we employ a Keras Regressor wrapper and Randomized Search cross-validation technique for hyperparameter optimization, enhancing the overall performance of the DL model. Additionally, we introduce an innovative early-stopping algorithm designed to efficiently monitor and terminate the training process, conserving computational resources. These elements contribute to the novelty of our proposed methodology for training DL models in the context of electric LF.
- Comparative analysis and superior predictive capability—the comparative analysis evaluates the performance of our proposed model against other state-of-the-art DL models, using a real-world dataset from the Distribution Network Station in Tetouan City, Morocco. Our proposed model consistently outperforms existing approaches, achieving the lowest RMSE. This outcome underscores its superior predictive capability, representing a significant advancement in accuracy compared to the current state of the art.

The remainder of this paper is structured as follows: Section 2 summarizes the related work. Section 3 provides an in-depth examination of the dataset, conducts relevant data analysis, and introduces both DL and ML models. In Section 4, we delve into the details of our proposed hybrid model. Section 5 is dedicated to presenting the results of our experiments, including comprehensive comparisons between our model and previous approaches. Finally, Section 6 serves as the conclusion of this paper, summarizing key findings and outlining potential future research directions.

2. Related Work

Anticipating electricity consumption holds a pivotal role in the effective management and strategic planning of the energy usage. The electric load profile in metropolitan areas exhibits complex cyclic and seasonal patterns influenced by industrial production, weather, and human activities. Contemporary research in this field is focused on exploring aspects such as smart grid technologies, the integration of renewable energy sources, and the establishment of local energy communities [30]. Numerous LF methods have been developed over the years, categorized into statistical models and modern ML and artificial intelligence (AI) models [10]. Statistical models include linear models like autoregressive (AR), moving average (MA), autoregressive moving average (ARMA), and ARIMA, seasonal ARIMA

(SARIMA), as well as Kalman filtering algorithms, grey models, and exponential smoothing [11]. These models assume stationary and linear time series data following known statistical distributions [8]. They effectively capture the historical trends and seasonality inherent in consumption data [31,32]. However, they may struggle with big data and nonlinear relationships between load values and external factors. Modern techniques based on ML and AI offer an alternative to statistical models by autonomously extracting patterns and trends from data [5]. Commonly used ML models for time series forecasting include support vector regression (SVR), and ANNs [4,5,31].

DL approaches, such as recurrent neural networks (RNN), gated recurrent networks, and (LSTM), have also gained attention for their ability to model complex non-linear patterns [10,32,33]. DL methods have been applied to LF with promising results. DL, a specialized domain within the broader field of ML, harnesses the power of ANNs with multiple layers to comprehend and represent intricate mappings between input and output data [34,35]. The momentum behind DL surged notably with the introduction of Multi-Layer Perceptrons (MLP) and the refinement of back-propagation algorithms during the 1980s and 1990s [35]. One of the distinguishing features of DL techniques is their effective handling of the vanishing gradient problem, setting them apart from shallower models. Consequently, models based on DL exhibit superior capabilities in dealing with complex functions, achieving higher accuracy in their predictions [36]. The perspective on DL has gained substantial traction, especially in recent times, driven by the unprecedented availability of extensive datasets and the advancement of sophisticated algorithms [34,36]. DL methods employ multi-layer network models to construct linear or non-linear functions that aim to minimize the correlation between input data and output response. This evolution is such that the ML techniques discussed in preceding sections have undergone a transformative process, evolving into DL models through the incorporation of additional mapping layers. In the specific context of LF, DL approaches necessitate the construction of intricate networks, offering distinct advantages over classical techniques, particularly in multi-point scenarios within the load profile. However, it is crucial to acknowledge certain drawbacks, notably in terms of computational complexity and limitations in deterministic point forecasting [37]. Despite these challenges, the appeal of DL approaches for LF remains strong due to their remarkable ability to capture short- and long-term dependencies within input data. Moreover, DL models provide viable solutions to computational challenges, making them more preferable than shallower learning models. A review of DL methods applied to LF revealed that DL-based approaches are more accurate and stable than traditional statistical techniques and time series analysis [16]. DL models such as Long Short-Term Memory (LSTM) are effective in electric LF [38,39]. Therefore, DL would be an important candidate among other methods for electric-LF.

The recent surge in ML and DL models has brought forth sophisticated tools capable of unraveling complex patterns and dependencies in electricity consumption. The advanced ML and DL models showcased excellence in handling non-linear relationships and long-term dependencies, making them particularly suitable for precise energy forecasting within building contexts [40]. The hybrid models, amalgamating multiple forecasting techniques, present a promising avenue by leveraging the unique strengths of different algorithms to enhance the accuracy of predictions [41,42]. The effectiveness of ML and DL models crucially relies on feature engineering techniques. These techniques involve extracting relevant information from data to ensure that the models can discern and capture the key factors influencing electricity consumption. The application of such techniques not only facilitates improved energy management decisions but also contributes to grid stability and supports the integration of distributed generation [43,44]. The continuous evolution and progress in this field contribute to the generation of precise and timely forecasts, thereby aiding in effective energy planning and optimization. In a specific study [45], a novel approach is proposed, utilizing generative adversarial networks (GAN) to generate parallel energy consumption data. These generated data are then combined with the original dataset to enhance the performance of energy consumption prediction. The evaluation of the proposed method involves metrics such as the mean absolute error (MAE), mean absolute percentage error (MAPE), and Pearson correlation coefficient. Another study [22] puts forth a method that integrates convolutional neural network (CNN) and long short-term memory (LSTM) for the prediction of electric charges. The performance of this approach is compared with other models, including LSTM, XGBoost, and radial basis functional network (RBFN), using metrics such as RMSE, MAPE, MAE, and goodness of fit (R2). Taking a different approach [46], a non-parametric regression model is introduced, utilizing Gaussian process (GP) for the selection of input data to predict electricity consumption in buildings. The study evaluates the effectiveness of support vector regression (SVR), LSTM, and random forest (RF) through metrics such as symmetric mean absolute percentage error (sMAPE), MAE, and RMSE. Various models and metrics have conducted extensive analyses to predict energy consumption [47–50]. These studies involve evaluating the performance of models like random forest (RF), support vector regression (SVR), multilayer perceptron (MLP), and others. The metrics employed in these evaluations include the mean absolute percentage error (MAPE), R2, RMSE, and more. A comprehensive summary of the most recent related work is presented in Table 1.

Table 1. Summary of the most recent related work.

Proposed Technique(s)	Main Objective	Ref.	Year
Trilinear deep residual network with self-adaptive dropout method based on hierarchical clustering and Gaussian noise.	To put forth a resilient model that addresses challenges related to vanishing and exploding gradients, tackles overfitting concerns, and concurrently enhances forecasting accuracy.	[51]	2021
Hybrid interval forecasting model combining *k*-NN optimized by genetic algorithm (GA), DBN and self-adaptive kernel density estimation techniques	To showcase the effectiveness of the proposed interval forecasting model in terms of precision and adaptability, all while maintaining the simplicity of the forecasting procedures.	[52]	2021
Online adaptive RNN	To achieve higher accuracy than the stand-alone offline LSTM network	[53]	2021
The algorithms of concrete dropouts, deep ensembles, Bayesian NNs, deep Gaussian processes, and functional neural processes	To delve into the probabilistic extensions and performance capabilities of DL algorithms.	[54]	2021
Non-linear fully connected feed-forward ANN by autoencoder with localized stochastic sensitivity	To suggest a DL model with the primary goal of improving prediction accuracy and reliability by minimizing errors, which are characterized by the training error and stochastic sensitivity.	[55]	2021
k-means CNN-LSTM forecast model with clustering approach	To acquire dependable energy consumption data for an academic building, specifically for Demand Response (DR) application purposes.	[56]	2021
Asynchronous deep reinforcement learning (RL) based model with deterministic policy gradient	To tackle the challenges of high temporal correlation and convergence instability in STLF by employing a deep RL model.	[57]	2021
Bidirectional LSTM based sequence to sequence regression approach	To assess the effectiveness of the proposed model by comparing it with other competitive techniques on both public holidays and regular days, considering factors such as accuracy and its performance under conditions of limited data availability.	[58]	2021
Ensemble learning model using multi-modal multi-objective evolutionary algorithm and random vector functional link network-based ensemble learning	To uncover additional trade-off multimodal solutions by leveraging the mapping capabilities of the proposed ensemble learning approach within the context of STLF problems.	[59]	2021
CNN	To improve the model's capability to capture non-linear relationships, a proposed feature selection process is introduced.	[60]	2021

Table 1. *Cont.*

Proposed Technique(s)	Main Objective	Ref.	Year
Deep RNN	To enhance forecasting accuracy and performance, especially in the presence of uncertain model dynamics.	[61]	2021
Deep RL	To contemplate the utilization of a pre-trained dataset, as opposed to a random one, when presenting LF results with the aim of optimizing DR applications.	[62]	2021
RNN, vanilla LSTM, stacked LSTM, bidirectional LSTM and GRU	To assess the performance of LF, a comparative analysis is conducted involving RNN, three different variants of the LSTM model, and GRU.	[63]	2021
A prioritized experience replay automated RL	To provide a coupled approach with multi period forecasting and DR program.	[64]	2021
Hybrid network consisted the layers of autoencoder LSTM, bidirectional LSTM, and stack of LSTM	To showcase the superior performance of the proposed hybrid model when tested with a dataset collected from a residential home, in comparison to previous studies with similar objectives.	[65]	2021
Comparative analysis with linear regression, tree-based regression, linear support vector machine (SVM), quadratic SVM, cubic SVM and RNN	To evaluate the performance of various ML and DL-based residential LF models.	[66]	2021
CNN with squeeze-and-excitation modules	To depict the robust relationship between climate variables and the volatile load demand in residential settings through the proposed model.	[67]	2021
Past vector similarity	To predict the load at a finer granularity by extracting precise load patterns associated with the occupants' routines and socio-economic values.	[68]	2021
RNN with LSTM	To evaluate the predictive performance of the proposed model in comparison to other models utilizing the same dataset.	[69]	2021
Separate use of LSTM and GRU	To show that the accuracy performance of STLF better than the longer focused forecasting models.	[70]	2021
Residential LF framework combined by *k*-means clustering algorithm and federated learning	To institute a collaborative training procedure by leveraging fine-grained monitored consumption data.	[71]	2021
CNN sequence to sequence model with an attention mechanism based on a multi-task learning method	To demonstrate the superior accuracy performance of the proposed model.	[72]	2021
Deep forward NN by automated selecting the best Box–Jenkins models	To obtain higher accuracy than the shallow networks.	[73]	2021
LSTM by mix-up and transfer learning techniques	To suggest a dependable model by considering the shortage of sufficient historical data on consumption, a factor that diminishes accuracy.	[74]	2022
Backward-eliminated exhaustive ensemble model for future selection method, and the LF techniques of *k*-NN, CNN, RNN and SVR.	To achieve higher accuracy, the proposal includes a backward-eliminated exhaustive approach for the feature selection technique.	[75]	2022
Ensemble model with LSTM, GRU, and TCN	To illustrate that the ensemble models proposed exhibit superior performance compared to traditional individual models.	[76]	2022
LSTM, federated stochastic gradient descent and federated averaging.	To train a single federated learning-based model when dealing with multiple smart meters, thereby eliminating the necessity of sharing local data.	[77]	2022
Federated learning model with ANN architecture	To meet the privacy and security requirements for residential LF by considering the dynamic power demand data from smart meters.	[78]	2022

Table 1. *Cont.*

Proposed Technique(s)	Main Objective	Ref.	Year
CNN based on wavelet and varying mode decomposition	To extract more detailed spectral and temporal information to improve forecasting performance, particularly in situations where exogenous data are unavailable.	[79]	2022
Hybrid model including the CNN and an attention-based sequence to sequence network.	To enhance the forecasting performance by capturing the long-term spatial and temporal features inherent in the data.	[80]	2022
Consecutive applications of STLF network with a layer of GRUs and STLF network constructed by stacking several TCNs	To improve the DL-based elastic model, ensuring robust performance under diverse conditions, such as variations in accommodation, temperature, humidity, and wind speed.	[81]	2022
Ensemble structure based on LSTM and XGBoost	To suggest a more accurate and scalable model, aimed at alleviating some of the limitations present in current approaches.	[82]	2022
Two stage encoder-decoder architecture based on receptive field-based dilated causal convolutional and bidirectional LSTM networks.	To increase the STLF performance by encoder–decoder configuration.	[83]	2022
A dynamic ANN model motivated by meta-learning	To introduce a fine-tuning approach for predicting highly non-stationary points, aiming to implement a robust forecasting procedure.	[84]	2022
LSTM with back propagation NN and XGBoost	To seek a balanced solution to the trade-off between forecasting accuracy and computational speed.	[85]	2022
Ensemble model with XGBoost and light-gradient boosting machine (GBM), RF regression and stacking regressor	To analyze the correlation between various variables in the dataset and assess the model performance with a focus on the most influential variables.	[86]	2022
Bidirectional LSTM	To suggest seasonal segmentation as a strategy to achieve relatively higher accuracy in the forecasting procedure. This approach considers the seasonal factors specific to the dataset of the geographical territory, enhancing the precision of predictions.	[87]	2022
A multi-channel bidirectional nested LSTM framework	To improve the prediction accuracy by following multiple sub-signal processing approach.	[88]	2022
XGBoost	To determine the occurrence range of peak load considering the load, weather and time factors.	[89]	2022
Hybrid model called as variational autoencoder bidirectional LSTM	To demonstrate the effectiveness of the proposed method compared to classical models.	[90]	2022
Autoencoder based LSTM	To introduce a dual-channel structure in the encoder section to extract various levels of time series data. Furthermore, a three-channel output structure in the decoder part is recommended to augment the model's representation ability.	[91]	2022
ML models of SVR, RF, XGBoost, light-GBM, adaptive boosting, bidirectional LSTM, GRU, and a DL regression model.	To specify best features and searching for nest ML model for predicting the hourly demand.	[92]	2022
Hybrid model with integrated GA bidirectional GRU	To introduce a more stable and reliable model compared to models developed using classical methods.	[93]	2022
ML approach with deep ANN and decision tree-based prediction	To show that the ML algorithms and regression analysis have adequate accuracy for LF.	[94]	2022
Hybrid structure with empirical mode decomposition, one-dimensional CNN, TCN, a self-attention mechanism, and a LSTM	To propose hybrid model having more stable and accurate prediction for STLF problem.	[95]	2022

Table 1. *Cont.*

Proposed Technique(s)	Main Objective	Ref.	Year
Joint structure with multi-feature fusion, self-attention mechanism, convolutional graph network	To obtain better prediction performance than some of the benchmark models.	[96]	2022
Hybrid structure with CNN, LSTM and MLP	To propose a solution that offers both adequate accuracy and robustness for LF problems.	[97]	2022
A self-adaptive DL model with particle swarm optimization (PSO)	To enhance the accuracy, robustness, repeatability, and self-adaptive capability in load prediction.	[98]	2022

On the one hand, predicting short-term load is challenging due to its high correlation with residents' stochastic behavior, which makes it difficult to predict [20]. On the other hand, short- and very short-term loading predictions favor ML methods that are capable of modeling building and occupancy characteristics, as well as environmental data. In this study, we aim to study the performance of ML modeling using a hybrid technique that integrates DL methods to enhance electricity LF.

3. Materials and Methods

3.1. Dataset Description

The Tetouan power consumption dataset, publicly available and used in this study, spans a one-year time series from 1 January 2017, to 31 December 2017. The dataset captured power consumption measurements at regular 10 min intervals, ensuring a complete and continuous set of data without any missing values. The dataset was collected from three different distribution substations located in the Quads, Boussafou, and Smir zones of Tetouan City, situated in northern Morocco. In addition to power consumption readings, the dataset includes various weather-related information such as temperature and humidity. These weather data provide additional context for analyzing and understanding the relationship between power consumption and environmental conditions. Each data entry in the dataset provides power consumption information at 10 min intervals. Additionally, complementary data about the calendar and weather conditions are included, enhancing the dataset's richness and potential for deeper analysis. By leveraging the comprehensive Tetouan power consumption dataset, researchers can gain insights into the dynamics of power consumption in different districts of the city. This dataset, with its detailed power consumption measurements, calendar information, and weather conditions, offers valuable opportunities to study load patterns, forecast power demands, and develop advanced prediction models for short-term LF.

This paper conducts a statistical analysis of the dataset to explore the relationships among the different variables, as shown in Table 2. The statistical analysis conducted on the dataset involves computing various descriptive statistics for each variable. The rationale behind this analysis is to gain insights into the distribution, central tendency, variability, skewness, and kurtosis of the data. By calculating these statistics for each variable in the dataset, we can gain a better understanding of the data's characteristics. These statistics can help identify patterns, outliers, and the overall shape of the distributions. They provide a summary of the dataset's properties and serve as a foundation for further analysis and decision making.

Table 2. Statistical analysis of the descriptors and target.

	Mean	STD	Maximum	Minimum	Skewness	Kurtosis
Temperature (°C)	18.81	5.82	40.01	3.247	0.197	−0.303
Humidity (g·m^{-3})	68.26	15.56	94.8	11.34	−0.625	−0.122
Wind Speed (m/s)	1.96	2.35	6.48	0.05	0.462	−1.783
General Diffuse Flows (°C)	182.7	264.4	1163.0	0.004	1.307	0.403
Diffuse Flows (°C)	75.03	124.21	936.0	0.01	2.457	7.003
PowerConsumption_Zone1 (KW)	32,344.97	7130.56	52,204.4	13,895.7	0.229	−0.754
PowerConsumption_Zone2 (KW)	21,042.51	5201.47	37,408.87	8560.08	0.329	−0.437
PowerConsumption_Zone3 (KW)	17,835.41	6622.17	47,598.33	5935.17	1.024	1.086

Figure 1 depicts the distribution of each data factor namely the temperature, humidity, wind speed, general diffusion flows, and diffusion flows. As observed from Table 2 both the general diffusion flows and diffusion flows are suffering a positive tail, Figure 1 shows how severely the diffusion flows are skewed. The wind factor has two clear modes, while the temperature factor has two close modes.

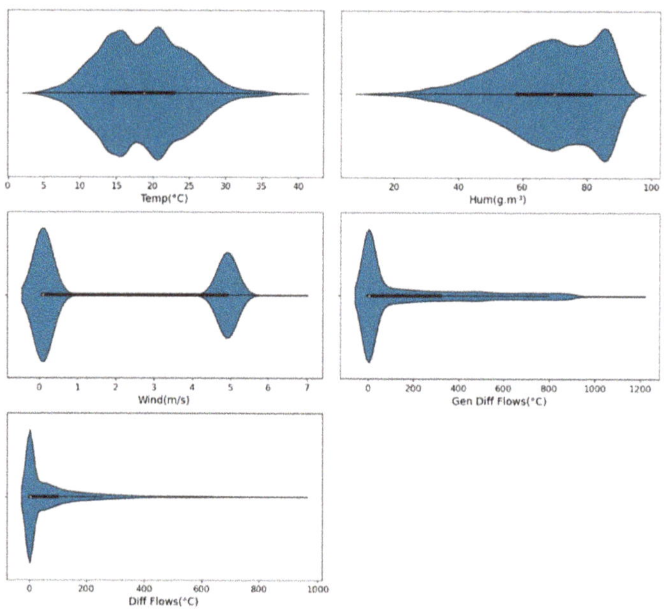

Figure 1. Data feature distribution analysis using violin plot.

Figure 2 illustrates the power consumption of the three zones by looking at the month and day of a week. For Zone 1 and 2, the power consumption is at its peak in August, while Zone 3 July is the month of power's highest demand. Also, the month boxplot of Zone 3 showed many outliers with high power consumption in February, March, April, May, July, August, September, October, and November. Such abnormal power consumption is also reflected in the Day boxplot subfigure. In general, the power consumption during the weekdays is almost similar. However, in Zone 1 and 2, the power consumption is a little less during Sundays.

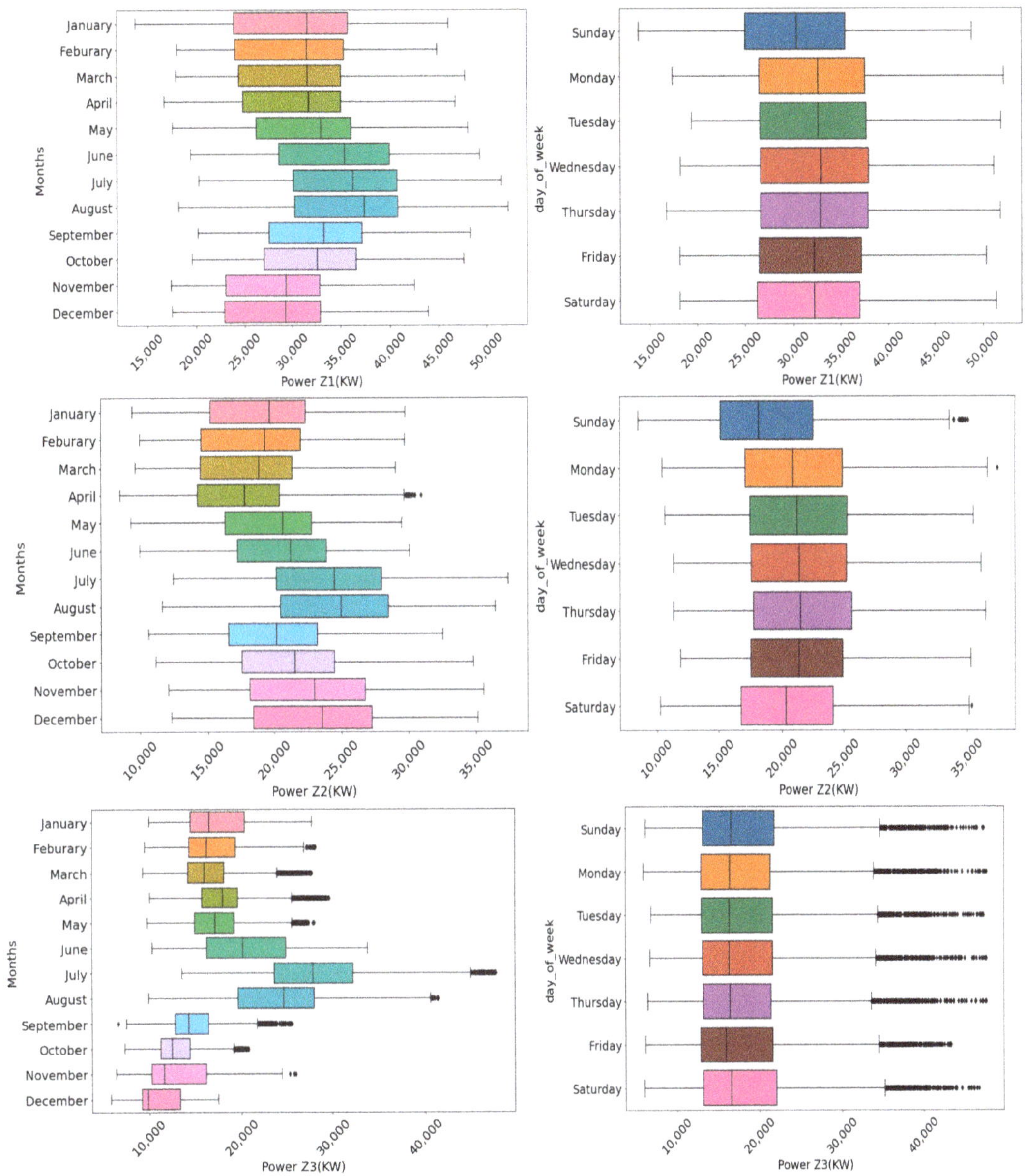

Figure 2. Box plot analysis of the power consumption of the three zones.

Pearson's correlation coefficient, denoted as RHO, measures the strength and direction of linear relationships between two variables. It ranges from −1 (perfect negative correlation) to +1 (perfect positive correlation), with 0 indicating no linear relationship. When applied to evaluate relationships between independent and dependent variables, RHO helps identify which independent variables are more strongly associated with the dependent variables in a linear manner. The analysis conducted in our study is illustrated in Figure 3. The Temperature variable exhibited the highest correlation when compared to other independent variables, with correlation coefficient values of 0.44, 0.39, and 0.49

in relation to the three target variables (Power Consumption_Zone1, Power Consumption_Zone2, and Power Consumption_Zone3). On the other hand, the Humidity variable showed comparable correlation coefficient values to the three targets, ranging from −0.23 to −0.29, suggesting a moderate negative linear relationship. In contrast, the Wind Speed and General Diffuse Flows variables demonstrated low correlation coefficient values, with the Diffuse Flows variable exhibiting nearly no correlation with the three target variables. These findings provide valuable insights into which independent variables have the most substantial linear impact on the dependent variables, aiding in model selection and interpretation.

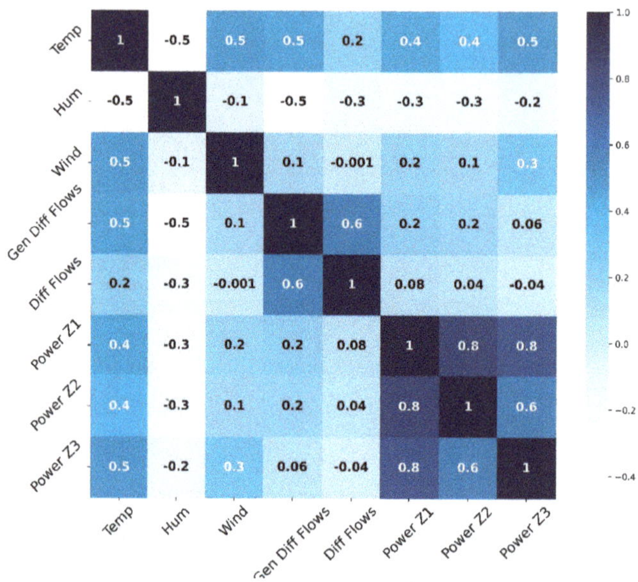

Figure 3. Pearson's correlation coefficient matrix comparing the dataset variables. Positive correlations are colored dark blue; negative correlations are light. The scale down the side of the graphic depicts the gradient of the correlation's strength and weakness from +1 to −1.

3.2. *Machine Learning Methods*

3.2.1. Linear Regression

Linear regression models the relationship between an output variable and one or more input variables. It is one of the most widely used techniques for data analysis and prediction. For the case of one input variable, we assume that the output variable is a linear function of that input variable. The equation of the simple linear regression model is

$$y = \beta_0 + \beta_1 x + \epsilon \tag{1}$$

where y is the dependent variable, x is the independent variable, β_0 is the intercept, β_1 is the slope, and ϵ is the error term.

The simple linear regression is scaled up to model the relationship between a set of multiple input variables to one output variable. In this case, we assume that the output variable is a linear combination of the input variables. The equation of the multiple linear regression model is

$$y = \beta_0 + \beta_1 x_1 + \beta_2 x_2 + \ldots + \beta_k x_k + \epsilon \tag{2}$$

The goal of linear regression is to estimate the values of the parameters $(\beta_0, \beta_1, \ldots, \beta_k)$ that best fit the data. There are different methods to perform this, such as ordinary least squares, maximum likelihood, or Bayesian inference.

3.2.2. Ridge Regression

Ridge regression enhances the linear regression by slightly changing its cost function, which results in less overfit models. It does so by adding a penalty term to the ordinary least squares (OLS) estimator, which shrinks the coefficients of the model to zero. This penalty term is proportional to the square of the L2-norm of the coefficients, also known as the ridge parameter. By choosing an appropriate value for the ridge parameter, we can trade off some bias for lower variance and improve the prediction accuracy of the model. The Ridge regression minimizes the following cost function:

$$\mathrm{J}(\phi) = \sum_{i=0}^{n} \left(\left(\sum_{k=0}^{p} \beta_k x_k \right) - y_i \right)^2 + \lambda \sum_{j}^{p} \beta_j^2 \quad (3)$$

where y is the actual output, λ is coefficient that controls the Ridge penalty applied to the regression model. Often Ridge regression is employed in scenarios where the input variables are highly correlated. Figure 3 shows Temp and Hum input variables with 0.5 or more correlation with other input variables.

3.2.3. Support Vector Regression

Support vector regression (SVR) is an ML technique that can be used to model the relationship between a dependent variable and one or more independent variables. SVR is based on the idea of finding a function that has at most epsilon deviation from the actual data points for all the data points and at the same time is as flat as possible 1. In other words, SVR tries to fit a smooth curve that minimizes the error between the predicted and observed values, while also avoiding overfitting the data.

SVR has some advantages over other regression methods, such as being able to handle nonlinear and high-dimensional data, being robust to outliers and noise, and having a unique solution that does not depend on the initial conditions. However, SVR also has some drawbacks, such as being computationally expensive, requiring careful tuning of the parameters, and being sensitive to the scale of the input features.

3.3. Deep Learning Methods

Deep Forwarded Neural Network (DFNN)

DFNN represents a classical model in DL research, revered for its ability to sift through extensive input variables and deliver highly accurate predictions in regression tasks [99]. Its architectural design is structured into three pivotal components: the input layer, the hidden layer, and the output layer. To ward off overfitting during training, a dropout layer is strategically inserted between the input and hidden layers, selectively pruning neurons at random intervals to enhance generalization performance [100]. DFNN's training process encompasses fine-tuning the hidden layers, neuron configurations, and the number of iterations. Rigorous cross-validation procedures are employed to scrutinize the model's performance, rigorously assessing its efficacy across test and training datasets.

4. Proposed Approach

Predicting electricity power consumption is crucial for enhancing the efficiency and productivity of utility systems. ML models are renowned for their accuracy in this context. The goal of our study is to predict the electricity power consumption every 10 min, and/or every hour with the determining objective of which approach is the most successful. The proposed methodology combines data preprocessing, DL model building, learning rate schedule, early stopping, and model evaluation techniques to train a DL model for regression tasks on the provided dataset, as shown in Figure 4.

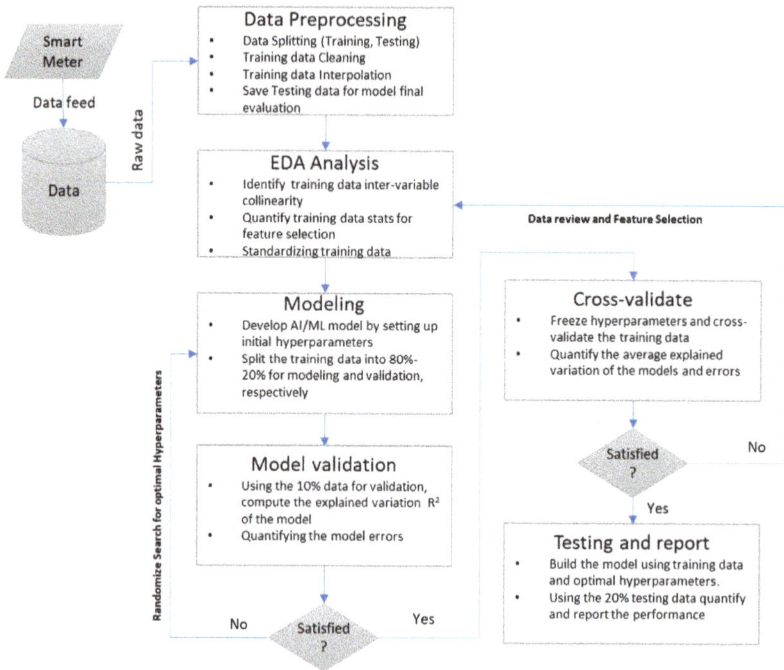

Figure 4. Methodology flowchart.

While our hybrid predictive model has been meticulously designed to enhance multivariate time series forecasting accuracy within the energy sector, its adaptability extends to other domains such as industry, residential, and commercial applications. The model's flexibility allows for customization to address the unique characteristics of each sector, leveraging techniques like forward DL, hyperparameter optimization, and feature significance analysis. Beyond the energy sector, the model's potential lies in optimizing operational efficiency, from production schedules in industries to demand-side management in residential areas and strategic energy planning for commercial establishments. Real-world applications and case studies in diverse settings can underscore the model's broader impact, showcasing its versatility in contributing to accurate forecasting across various sectors. While acknowledging the need to consider sector-specific factors in the adaptation process, our work suggests that the methodologies employed hold promise for advancing forecasting capabilities beyond the energy sector, offering a valuable tool for enhancing operational planning and resource allocation across different industries.

4.1. Data Preprocessing

In the data preprocessing stage, several techniques are employed to transform the input variable "DateTime" into more appropriate forms, including Year, Month, Day, Hour, and Minute. Moreover, the time scale is adjusted from 10 min intervals to 60 min intervals to enable short-term load forecasting for the subsequent hour. Additionally, standardization is applied to the input variables as part of the data preprocessing pipeline.

4.2. Model Development

Model development comprises different components, as summarized in the following subsections.

4.2.1. Deep Learning

In this study, a DL model was constructed using the Keras library [101,102], particularly the Sequential model, which facilitates the creation of a linear stack of layers. The model architecture comprises densely connected layers, known as Dense layers, which incorporate activation functions to introduce non-linearity and dropout regularization to prevent overfitting. The model was compiled using the mean squared error (MSE) loss function, which measures the discrepancy between predicted and actual values, and the RMSprop optimizer, which adjusts the model's parameters to minimize the loss function during training [103].

4.2.2. Learning Rate Scheduling

The ReduceLROnPlateau callback from the Keras library was employed in this study to implement the learning rate scheduling [104,105]. This technique dynamically adjusts the learning rate during the training process based on the validation loss. By monitoring the validation loss, the callback reduces the learning rate when the loss plateaus, aiming to enhance the model's convergence and overall performance. This adaptive adjustment of the learning rate facilitates efficient training by allowing the model to make smaller steps toward the optimal solution when progress becomes slower.

4.2.3. Early Stopping

The EarlyStopping callback from the Keras library was employed in this study to implement the early stopping technique [106]. During the training process, this callback continuously monitors the validation loss and halts the training if the loss does not improve for a predefined number of epochs. This technique helps prevent overfitting by stopping the model from further optimizing its performance on the training data at the expense of generalization. By selecting the model with the best performance on the validation set, early stopping allows for the retention of the model that exhibits optimal performance without compromising its ability to generalize to unseen data.

4.3. Model Training and Evaluation

To evaluate the efficacy of our proposed model, we partitioned the dataset into training and testing subsets, adhering to an 80–20 ratio. Subsequently, we conducted a comparative analysis by juxtaposing the predicted power consumption values against the corresponding ground truth data within identical time intervals. This rigorous assessment facilitated the evaluation of the model's accuracy and overall performance. The DL model is trained using the fit function, which iterates over the specified number of epochs. During training, mini-batches of size 64 are utilized, allowing for efficient processing of the training data [107]. The learning rate scheduling and early stopping callbacks are incorporated into the training process, ensuring dynamic adjustment of the learning rate, and stopping the training if the validation loss does not improve. This approach optimizes the model's convergence and prevents overfitting, leading to improved performance and generalization capabilities. Following the training phase, the trained model is employed to make predictions on the preprocessed testing set. The predictions obtained are then evaluated using commonly used regression evaluation metrics described in the next subsection. By examining these evaluation metrics, the performance and effectiveness of the trained model can be assessed.

4.4. Hyperparameter Optimization

To optimize the hyperparameters of the Keras model, we employed a combination of techniques. First, we utilized Randomized Search CV, which is a randomized search algorithm from scikit-learn, to perform a hyperparameter search. The search space included various hyperparameters such as the learning rate, dropout rate, number of epochs, batch size, and activation function. This allowed us to explore a range of hyperparameter combinations and identify the best configuration based on the specified evaluation metric, which was the negative mean squared error. To integrate the Keras model with the hyperparameter search, we used the Keras Regressor wrapper. This wrapper provided a scikit-learn compatible interface for the Keras model, enabling us to incorporate it into the Randomized Search CV process. The Keras Regressor wrapper allowed us to create and compile the Keras model within the create_model function, which defined the model architecture and optimization parameters based on the given hyperparameters. After performing the hyperparameter search and obtaining the best hyperparameters, we trained the Keras model with these optimal settings. The model was trained on preprocessed training data, using the best number of epochs and batch size determined by Randomized Search CV. The training process involved fitting the model to the training data and updating the model's weights and biases iteratively to minimize the mean squared error loss. Finally, we evaluated the performance of the trained model by making predictions on the preprocessed test set. The predicted values were compared with the actual target values using different evaluation metrics. These metrics provided insights into the accuracy and predictive capability of the best Keras model identified through the hyperparameter optimization process. By combining Randomized Search CV, the Keras Regressor wrapper, model training with the best hyperparameters, and model evaluation, we were able to efficiently search for and assess the performance of the optimal Keras model for the given dataset.

5. Results and Discussion

In this section, we present the comprehensive results of our study on household LF, showcasing the efficacy of our proposed hybrid DL model with hyperparameter optimization. We begin by examining the model's performance in predicting electricity consumption at both 10 min intervals and hourly intervals, shedding light on its capabilities in capturing intricate temporal patterns. Furthermore, we delve into a rigorous evaluation of the model's accuracy, utilizing a range of statistical metrics to quantify its forecasting precision. These results not only highlight the advancements achieved in household LF but also underline the potential for enhancing energy management systems with state-of-the-art predictive models. To assess the efficacy of our ML models, we employ five distinct statistical metrics that have been previously identified as valuable for power consumption forecasting. These metrics are defined as follows:

R^2 assesses the proportion of variance in the target variable that is explained by the model. It ranges from 0 to 1, with higher values indicating a better fit.

$$R^2 = 1 - \frac{SS_{res}}{SS_{tot}} \tag{4}$$

where SS_{res} is the sum of squared residuals (sum of squared differences between the actual and predicted values), and SS_{tot} is the total sum of squares (the sum of squared differences between the actual values and the mean of the actual values).

RMSE represents the standard deviation of the residuals and is expressed in the same units as the target variable.

$$RMSE = \sqrt{\frac{1}{n}\sum_{i=1}^{n}(y_i - \hat{y}_i)^2} \tag{5}$$

where n is the number of samples; y_i and $\hat{y}_i$ are the actual and predicted values of the target variable for the ith sample, respectively.

5.1. Machine Learning Methods

We assessed some baseline ML methods to analyze the input variables' relationship with the target variable and establish the baseline performance of traditional ML methods using the Tetouan City dataset. Table 3 presents the configuration of machine learning methods.

Table 3. Configuration of machine learning methods.

Machine Learning Method	Parameters
Linear Regression	Ordinary Least Square (OLS) method
Ridge Regression	Regularization alpha = 2
Support Vector Regression	Kernel = rbf, C = 2, degree = 3, gamma = scale

We built ML models and assessed them to establish a baseline performance using the Tetouan City dataset. Table 4 tabulates the performance of three known machine learning techniques. We noticed that coefficients of determination R^2 were low in all experiments. This affects the RMSE per model and indicates the need for better models.

Table 4. Performance baseline machine learning methods.

Method	Target	R^2-Score	RMSE
Linear Regression	PowerConsumption_Zone1	0.64	4236.84
	PowerConsumption_Zone2	0.58	3365.45
	PowerConsumption_Zone3	0.6	4150.29
Ridge Regression	PowerConsumption_Zone1	0.64	4236.83
	PowerConsumption_Zone2	0.58	3365.44
	PowerConsumption_Zone3	0.6	4150.28
Support Vector Regression	PowerConsumption_Zone1	0.44	5336.56
	PowerConsumption_Zone2	0.47	3799.05
	PowerConsumption_Zone3	0.29	5573.99

5.2. Deep Neural Network Design

In this experiment, we employ DL methods by constructing a neural network model, defining its architecture, training it with data, and evaluating its performance using appropriate metrics. The algorithm to build the DNN was stated by creating a sequential model using 'Sequential ()' from 'tensorflow.keras.models', which allows for building a neural network model by stacking multiple layers sequentially. The dense layers were added to the model to ensure full connection among the neurons in the consecutive layers. The model uses a rectified linear unit (relu) as an activation function. We applied regularization to the model's weights in the dense layers. In this experiment, L1 regularization with a regularization strength of 0.001 was used. Additionally, dropout regularization was utilized to avoid overfitting by randomly setting a fraction of input units to 0 during training to reduce the co-adaptation of neurons. The model was compiled with the loss function set to MSE metric to calculate the mean squared difference between the predicted and actual values. The RMSprop optimizer was incorporated as an adaptive learning rate optimization algorithm that helps in faster convergence. Lastly, Callbacks are used for dynamic adjustment of the learning rate and early stopping.

The main structure and number of parameters to learn per layer are summarized in Table 5. To avoid overfitting, the DNN was designed with dropout layers where the algorithm drops 20% of the computed information randomly to regularize the model. Moreover, the design uses the relu activation function due to it being able to be computed faster than other complex activation functions.

In this model, 'ReduceLROnPlateau' reduces the learning rate when a metric (in this case, validation loss) stops improving [31]. 'EarlyStopping' stops training when the metric (validation loss) does not improve for a certain number of epochs. Table 6 demonstrates the obtained performance measurements in the context of the three targets. In addition, it displays the RMSE associated with predicting the power load at its peak point.

Table 5. Deep neural network structure (learning rate = 0.1).

Layers	Layer Shape	Parameters per Layer	Activation Function
Dense	128 Neuron	1408	RELU
Dropout	NA	Drop rate: 0.2	NA
Dense	128 Neuron	16512	RELU
Dropout	NA	Drop rate: 0.2	NA
Dense	1 Neuron	129	Sigmoid

Table 6. Performance metrics using the DL model.

Target	R^2-Score	RMSE (Average)	RMSE (Peak Point)
PowerConsumption_Zone1	0.96	1466.49	1709.92
PowerConsumption_Zone2	0.96	1039.71	1362.11
PowerConsumption_Zone3	0.97	1215.52	1306.34

Figures 5–7 present distinct figures, each encapsulating the outcomes derived from our proposed DL model in the context of Power Consumption prediction for three distinct zones, as specified within our dataset. These figures collectively provide an intricate analysis of our DL model's predictive capabilities, offering valuable insights into its performance across different zones and sample sizes. Each figure consists of three subfigures: (top) comprehensively illustrates the results encompassing all testing samples, offering a holistic view of the model's performance over time, (middle) selectively focuses on a subset, specifically 10% of the testing samples, enabling a more detailed examination of predicted and actual data points, and (bottom) narrows the scope further, emphasizing only 1% of the testing samples. This deliberate reduction in sample size enhances the visual clarity of the plots, facilitating a meticulous assessment of the alignment between predicted and actual data points.

5.3. Prediction with Hyperparameters Optimization

In this experiment, we aim to perform hyperparameter optimization using Randomize Search CV to find the best configuration of hyperparameters for a DL model and to utilize a Keras Regressor wrapper for this purpose. The 'RandomizedSearchCV' randomly passes the set of hyperparameters calculates the score and gives the best set of hyperparameters which gives the best score as an output. Cross-validation is a resampling method used to test the model's generalization ability using out-of-the-sample data chunks. The hybrid framework trains the best model and evaluates its performance on the test data. The components of the optimization process are explained in the following:

(1) The Keras model architecture consists of two dense layers with specified activation functions, dropout regularization layers, and a final dense layer with one output unit. The model is compiled with the mean squared error loss function and an optimizer, as described above.
(2) Feature scaling on the input variables using a Standard Scaler which standardizes features by removing the mean and scaling to unit variance.
(3) Keras Regressor wrapper for compatibility with the hyperparameter tuning algorithm.
(4) A hyperparameter search space with different settings for the learning rate, dropout rate, number of epochs, batch size, and activation function.
(5) A Randomized Search CV object from sklearn.model_selection with the Keras Regressor wrapper, the hyperparameter search space, and other parameters like the number of cross-validation folds and scoring metric.

(6) Hyperparameter optimization using the scaled training data to search for the best combination of hyperparameters based on the specified scoring metric (negative mean squared error).
(7) Optimal hyperparameters and the corresponding best model from the Randomized Search CV object.
(8) Train the best model using the scaled training data and the best hyperparameters and lastly make predictions on the scaled test data using the trained best model.

The proposed hybrid model was applied to the power consumption dataset to predict the three targets independently. The hyperparameter search space given to the models includes the following settings: 'learning rate': [0.1, 0.01, 0.001], 'dropout rate': [0.2, 0.3, 0.4], 'epochs': [50, 100, 150], 'batch size': [32, 64, 128], and 'activation': ['relu', 'sigmoid']. The optimal parameters that were determined for each experiment are presented in Table 7.

Table 7. Optimal hyperparameters.

Target	Learning Rate	Epochs	Dropout Rate	Batch Size	Activation
Zone1-model	0.1	100	0.2	32	Sigmoid
Zone2-model	0.1	50	0.2	128	Sigmoid
Zone3-model	0.1	150	0.3	64	Sigmoid

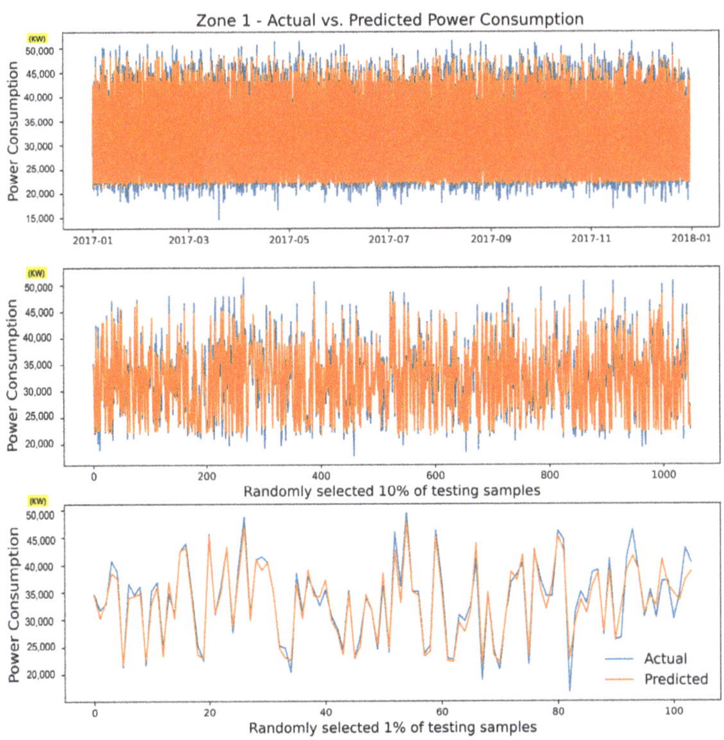

Figure 5. Zone-1 power consumption prediction over time using the Keres model. (**top**) All testing samples, (**middle**) with 10% of testing samples, and (**bottom**) 1% of testing samples.

The results obtained are presented in Table 8, demonstrating the advantage of optimizing the model. The table displays the RMSE associated with predicting the power load at its peak point. The prediction accuracy was improved significantly when comparing the results presented in Tables 7 and 8.

Table 8. Performance metrics using the optimized model.

Target	R^2-Score	RMSE (Average)	RMSE (Peak Point)
PowerConsumption_Zone1	0.97	1169.81	1255.72
PowerConsumption_Zone2	0.98	790.02	1014.36
PowerConsumption_Zone3	0.98	864.39	983.58

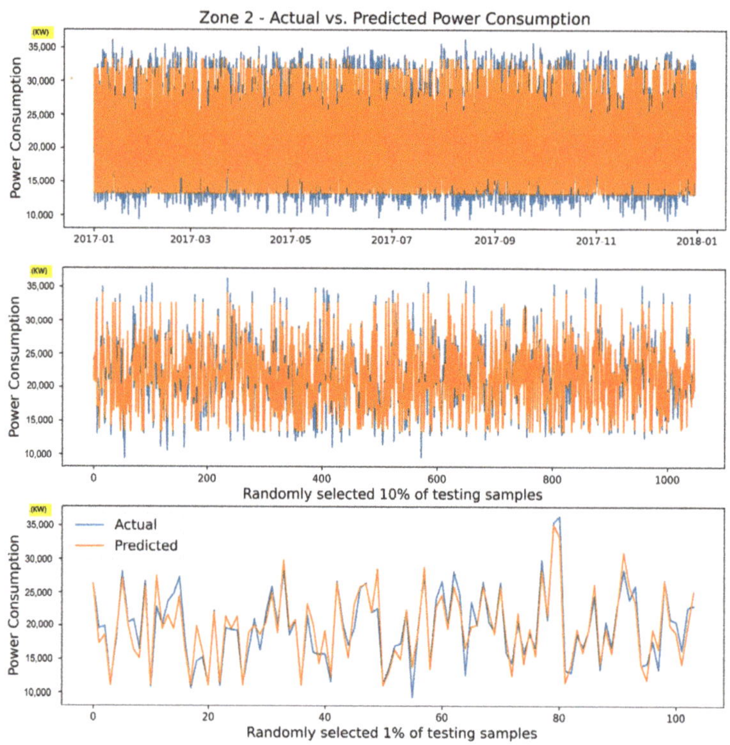

Figure 6. Zone-2 power consumption prediction over time using the Keres model: (**top**) all testing samples, (**middle**) with 10% of testing samples, and (**bottom**) 1% of testing samples.

Figures 8–10 individually depict the results obtained from the optimized Keres model for Power Consumption prediction across three distinct zones, as defined within our dataset. These figures collectively provide a comprehensive analysis of the model's predictive capabilities, delivering valuable insights into its performance variations across different zones and sample sizes. Each figure comprises three subfigures: (top) offers a comprehensive overview by displaying results for all testing samples, providing a holistic perspective of the model's performance over time; (middle) zooms in on a specific subset, precisely 10% of the testing samples, facilitating a more detailed examination of predicted and actual data points; and (bottom) further narrows the focus to a mere 1% of the testing samples, enhancing visual clarity within the plots and enabling meticulous evaluation of the alignment between predicted and actual data points.

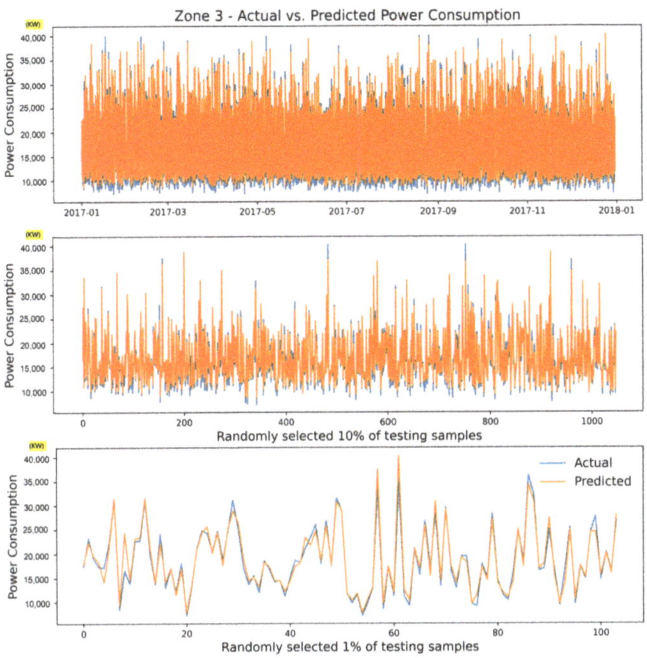

Figure 7. Zone-3 power consumption prediction over time using the Keres model. (**top**) All testing samples, (**middle**) with 10% of testing samples, and (**bottom**) 1% of testing samples.

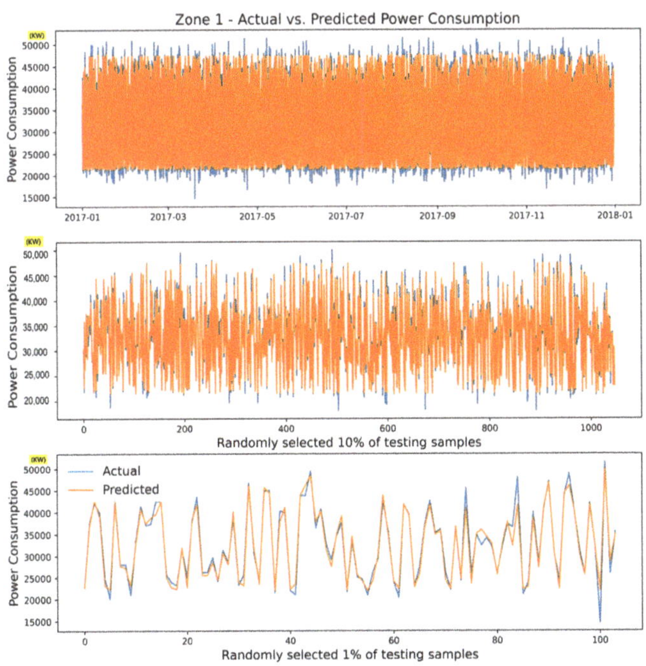

Figure 8. Zone-1 power consumption prediction over time using the optimized Keres model (**top**) all testing samples, (**middle**) with 10% of testing samples, (**bottom**) 1% of testing samples.

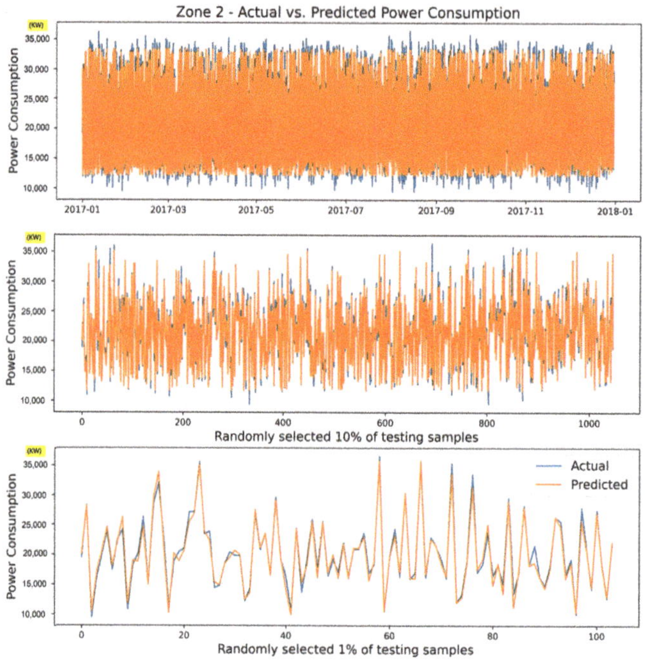

Figure 9. Zone-2 power consumption prediction over time using the optimized Keres model (**top**) all testing samples, (**middle**) with 10% of testing samples, (**bottom**) 1% of testing samples.

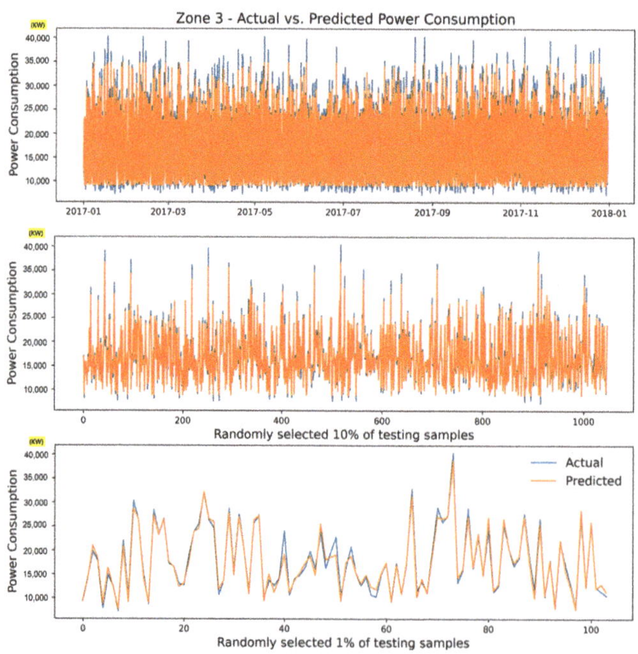

Figure 10. Zone-3 power consumption prediction over time using the optimized Keres model (**top**) all testing samples, (**middle**) with 10% of testing samples, (**bottom**) 1% of testing samples.

5.4. Comparison with Other Models

We performed a comparative analysis by comparing our findings against those of other models designed for the used dataset, as detailed in the scholarly work by Salam and Hibaoui [32]. To evaluate these models comprehensively, we employed the Root-Mean-Squared Error (RMSE) as the established performance criterion. It is worth noting that our model consistently demonstrates superior performance by consistently yielding the lowest RMSE in comparison to the models reported in the existing literature. This compelling evidence underscores the efficacy of our approach and its potential to set a new standard in the field. Table 9 presents the results of different methods applied on the dataset of Tetouan city.

Table 9. Experimental results using the dataset from the distribution network of Tetouan city [32].

Model	Median RMSE
DFFNN	7208
DFFNN-ResNet	7397
CNN	7191.9
CNN-ResNet	6874
CNN LSTM	6744.1
CNN-ResNet LSTM	6429.1
DFFNN LSTM	6547.5
DFFNN-ResNet LSTM	6941.4
DENSENET	10220
DENSENET LSTM	7443.9
EECP-CBL	8146.2
DFFNN LSTM	5876
Proposed Model-1	1215.5
Proposed Model-2	864.4

5.5. Potential Limitations

While our proposed hybrid predictive model demonstrated notable advancements in electric LF, it is essential to acknowledge its limitations. Understanding these shortcomings is crucial for refining the model and guiding future research endeavors in this domain.

One of the notable limitations of our model is its sensitivity to specific characteristics of the input data. The model's performance may vary when applied to datasets with different temporal patterns or levels of noise. Further research is needed to develop techniques that enhance the model's robustness across diverse datasets. The model's training and evaluation are based on a dataset obtained from the Distribution Network Station in Tetouan City, Morocco. While our results demonstrate superior performance within this context, generalizing the model to different geographic locations with distinct energy consumption patterns may pose challenges. Future work should explore methods for adapting the model to diverse regional characteristics. Furthermore, the proposed model heavily relies on DL techniques, which may present challenges in terms of interpretability. Interpretability is crucial, especially in applications where decisions impact critical infrastructure. Future research could explore hybrid models that incorporate both DL and interpretable ML techniques to strike a balance between accuracy and interpretability. Furthermore, additional metrics can be used to measuring the peak load prediction error.

6. Conclusions and Future Work

Efficient and accurate LF is crucial for modern power generation facilities to meet dynamic electricity demand. This work highlights the complexity of predicting electricity consumption due to the multifaceted factors influencing energy usage. Consequently, electricity utilities and governmental bodies are actively seeking advanced machine learning solutions to enhance LF.

A hybrid predictive model was designed to enhance the accuracy of multivariate time series forecasting for electricity consumption within the energy domain. The proposed model was compared with other state-of-the-art DL models using a dataset sourced from the Distribution Network Station of Tetouan City in Morocco. In the experiments, we found that a simple and shallow DNN achieved great prediction performance compared to other more complex models introduced in previous studies. In the future, we will focus on validating the accuracy of load-forecasting shallow models by incorporating additional data sources and refining existing algorithms. Exploring new ML techniques and considering factors such as economic indicators, and household lifestyle changes could lead to more precise predictions.

The implications of our research for policymakers are significant in the context of electric LF and the utilization of advanced DL techniques. Our study offers policymakers valuable insights into optimizing energy planning, resource allocation, and grid stability. The enhanced accuracy of our electric LF model can inform decisions related to infrastructure planning and resource optimization, allowing for more efficient deployment of both energy and computational resources. Policymakers can leverage this knowledge to implement measures that ensure a stable and reliable electricity grid, ultimately minimizing the risk of disruptions. Additionally, as the energy landscape evolves towards increased reliance on renewable sources, our findings provide policymakers with guidance on integrating renewable energy into the grid. The introduction of novel DL techniques prompts considerations for supportive policy frameworks that encourage the adoption of advanced technologies in the energy sector. Policymakers can also use the insights from our study to develop strategies that enhance resilience to demand variability, with proactive measures for predicted high-demand periods and the development of adaptive systems. Moreover, the environmental impact of energy generation can be addressed through more efficient energy use facilitated by accurate LF, aligning with sustainability and environmental goals. In summary, our research provides actionable insights for policymakers to shape policies that improve energy management, grid reliability, and environmental sustainability.

The limitations discussed in Section 4.4 open avenues for future research in the field of electric LF. Future investigations should focus on developing models that are more robust across diverse datasets, expanding the geographic applicability of the proposed model, and exploring hybrid approaches that prioritize interpretability without compromising predictive accuracy.

Author Contributions: Conceptualization, H.A.A.-J. and G.M.B.; Methodology, H.A.A.-J., G.M.B., M.Y.W. and M.A.H., Software, H.A.A.-J. and G.M.B., manuscript writing, and revising, H.A.A.-J., G.M.B., M.Y.W. and M.A.H. All authors have read and agreed to the published version of the manuscript.

Funding: This research was funded by Interdisciplinary Research Center for Renewable Energy and Power Systems (IRC-REPS) at KFUPM, grant number INRE2311.

Data Availability Statement: This study utilized a published energy consumption dataset. The dataset has been published and made available for the research community online via the link (https://www.kaggle.com/datasets/fedesoriano/electric-power-consumption/data), accessed date, 15 March 2023.

Acknowledgments: The authors would like to acknowledge the help and support provided by King Fahd University of Petroleum and Minerals (KFUPM). This research was supported by Interdisciplinary Research Center for Renewable Energy and Power Systems (IRC-REPS) at KFUPM in the terms of research.

Conflicts of Interest: The authors declare no conflict of interest.

References

1. Chen, J.; Liu, M.; Milano, F. Aggregated Model of Virtual Power Plants for Transient Frequency and Voltage Stability Analysis. *IEEE Trans. Power Syst.* **2021**, *36*, 4366–4375. [CrossRef]
2. Dewangan, F.; Abdelaziz, A.Y.; Biswal, M. Load Forecasting Models in Smart Grid Using Smart Meter Information: A Review. *Energies* **2023**, *16*, 1404. [CrossRef]
3. Muzaffar, S.; Afshari, A. Short-term load forecasts using LSTM networks. *Energy Procedia* **2019**, *158*, 2922–2927. [CrossRef]
4. Hammad, M.A.; Jereb, B.; Rosi, B.; Dragan, D. Methods, and Models for Electric Load Forecasting: A Comprehensive Review. *Logist. Sustain. Transp.* **2020**, *11*, 51–76. [CrossRef]
5. Zheng, J.; Xu, C.; Zhang, Z.; Li, X. Electric load forecasting in smart grids using long-short-term-memory based recurrent neural network. In Proceedings of the 2017 51st Annual Conference on Information Sciences and Systems (CISS), Baltimore, MD, USA, 22–24 March 2017; pp. 1–6.
6. Singla, M.K.; Nijhawan, P.; Oberoi, A.S.; Singh, P. Application of levenberg marquardt algorithm for short term load forecasting: A theoretical investigation. *Pertanika J. Sci. Technol.* **2019**, *27*, 1227–1245.
7. Mehta, S.; Basak, P. A comprehensive review on control techniques for stability improvement in microgrids. *Int. Trans. Electr. Energy Syst.* **2021**, *31*, 1–28. [CrossRef]
8. Hou, H.; Liu, C.; Wang, Q.; Wu, X.; Tang, J.; Shi, Y.; Xie, C. Review of load forecasting based on artificial intelligence methodologies, models, and challenges. *Electr. Power Syst. Res.* **2022**, *210*, 340–344. [CrossRef]
9. Kong, W.; Dong, Z.Y.; Jia, Y.; Hill, D.J.; Xu, Y.; Zhang, Y. Short-term residential load forecasting based on LSTM recurrent neural network. *IEEE Trans. Smart Grid* **2017**, *10*, 841–851. [CrossRef]
10. Li, Z.; Wu, L.; Xu, Y.; Moazeni, S.; Tang, Z. Multi-Stage Real-Time Operation of a Multi-Energy Microgrid with Electrical and Thermal Energy Storage Assets: A Data-Driven MPC-ADP Approach. *IEEE Trans. Smart Grid* **2022**, *13*, 213–226. [CrossRef]
11. Tan, M.; Hu, C.; Chen, J.; Wang, L.; Li, Z. Multi-node load forecasting based on multi-task learning with modal feature extraction. *Eng. Appl. Artif. Intell.* **2022**, *112*, 104856. [CrossRef]
12. Muhtadi, A.; Pandit, D.; Nguyen, N.; Mitra, J. Distributed Energy Resources Based Microgrid: Review of Architecture, Control, and Reliability. *IEEE Trans. Ind. Appl.* **2021**, *57*, 2223–2235. [CrossRef]
13. Conditions and Requirements for the Technical Feasibility of a Power System with a High Share of Renewables in France towards 2050. 2021. Available online: https://www.iea.org/reports/conditions-and-requirements-for-the-technical-feasibility-of-a-power-system-with-a-high-share-of-renewables-in-france-towards-2050 (accessed on 4 June 2023). [CrossRef]
14. Jacob, M.; Neves, C.; Vukadinović Greetham, D. *Forecasting and Assessing Risk of Individual Electricity Peaks*; Springer: Cham, Switzerland, 2020.
15. Liu, H.; Xiong, X.; Yang, B.; Cheng, Z.; Shao, K.; Tolba, A. A Power Load Forecasting Method Based on Intelligent Data Analysis. *Electronics* **2023**, *12*, 3441. [CrossRef]
16. Almalaq, A.; Edwards, G. A review of deep learning methods applied on load forecasting. In Proceedings of the 2017 16th IEEE International Conference on Machine Learning and Applications (ICMLA), Cancun, Mexico, 18–21 December 2017; pp. 511–516.
17. Proedrou, E. A comprehensive review of residential electricity load profile models. *IEEE Access* **2021**, *9*, 12114–12133. [CrossRef]
18. Burg, L.; Gürses-Tran, G.; Madlener, R.; Monti, A. Comparative analysis of load forecasting models for varying time horizons and load aggregation levels. *Energies* **2021**, *14*, 7128. [CrossRef]
19. Haben, S.; Arora, S.; Giasemidis, G.; Voss, M.; Greetham, D.V. Review of low voltage load forecasting: Methods, applications, and recommendations. *Appl. Energy* **2021**, *304*, 117798. [CrossRef]
20. Vanting, N.; Ma, Z.; Jørgensen, B. A scoping review of deep neural networks for electric load forecasting. *Energy Inform.* **2021**, *4*, 49. [CrossRef]
21. Azeem, A.; Ismail, I.; Jameel, S.M.; Harindran, V.R. Electrical load forecasting models for different generation modalities: A review. *IEEE Access* **2021**, *9*, 142239–142263. [CrossRef]
22. Mamun, A.A.; Sohel, M.; Mohammad, N.; Sunny, M.S.H.; Dipta, D.R.; Hossain, E. A comprehensive review of the load forecasting techniques using single and hybrid predictive models. *IEEE Access* **2020**, *8*, 134911–134939. [CrossRef]
23. Li, J.; Chen, W.; Chen, Y.; Sheng, K.; Du, S.; Zhang, Y.; Wu, Y. A survey on investment demand assessment models for power grid infrastructure. *IEEE Access* **2021**, *9*, 9048–9054. [CrossRef]
24. Kuster, C.; Rezgui, Y.; Mourshed, M. Electrical load forecasting models: A critical systematic review. *Sustain. Cities Soc.* **2017**, *35*, 257–270. [CrossRef]
25. Hong, T.; Pinson, P.; Wang, Y.; Weron, R.; Yang, D.; Zareipour, H. Energy forecasting: A review and outlook. *IEEE Open Access J. Power Energy* **2020**, *7*, 376–388. [CrossRef]
26. Acaroğlu, H.; Márquez, F. Comprehensive review on electricity market price and load forecasting based on wind energy. *Energies* **2021**, *14*, 7473. [CrossRef]
27. Ij, H. Statistics versus machine learning. *Nat. Methods* **2018**, *15*, 233.
28. Ongsulee, P. Artificial intelligence, machine learning and deep learning. In Proceedings of the 2017 15th International Conference on ICT and Knowledge Engineering (ICT&KE), Bangkok, Thailand, 22–24 November 2017; pp. 1–6.
29. Chahal, A.; Gulia, P. Machine learning and deep learning. *Int. J. Innov. Technol. Explor. Eng.* **2019**, *8*, 4910–4914.
30. Dab, K.; Agbossou, K.; Henao, N.; Dubé, Y.; Kelouwani, S.; Hosseini, S.S. A compositional kernel based gaussian process approach to day-ahead residential load forecasting. *Energy Build.* **2022**, *254*, 111459. [CrossRef]

31. Syah, R.; Davarpanah, A.; Elveny, M.; Karmaker, A.K.; Nasution, M.K.; Hossain, M.A. Forecasting daily electricity price by hybrid model of fractional wavelet transform, feature selection, support vector machine and optimization algorithm. *Electronics* **2021**, *10*, 2214. [CrossRef]
32. Fekri, M.N.; Patel, H.; Grolinger, K.; Sharma, V. Deep learning for load forecasting with smart meter data: Online Adaptive Recurrent Neural Network. *Appl. Energy* **2021**, *282*, 116177. [CrossRef]
33. Alrasheedi, A.; Almalaq, A. Hybrid Deep Learning Applied on Saudi Smart Grids for Short-Term Load Forecasting. *Mathematics* **2022**, *10*, 2666. [CrossRef]
34. Goodfellow, I.; Bengio, Y.; Courville, A. *Deep Learning*; MIT Press: Cambridge, MA, USA, 2016.
35. Langdon, W.B.; Gustafson, S.M. Genetic programming, and evolvable machines: Ten years of reviews. *Genet. Progr. Evol. Mach.* **2010**, *11*, 321–338. [CrossRef]
36. Akhtar, S.; Adeel, M.; Iqbal, M.; Namoun, A.; Tufail, A.; Kim, K.-H. Deep learning methods utilization in electric power systems. *Energy Rep.* **2023**, *10*, 2138–2151. [CrossRef]
37. Abdulrahman, M.L.; Ibrahim, K.M.; Gital, A.Y.; Zambuk, F.U.; Ja'afaru, B.; Yakubu, Z.I.; Ibrahim, A. A review on deep learning with focus on deep recurrent neural network for electricity forecasting in residential building. *Procedia Comput. Sci.* **2021**, *193*, 141–154. [CrossRef]
38. Dong, Y.; Ma, X.; Fu, T. Electrical load forecasting: A deep learning approach based on K-nearest neighbors. *Appl. Soft Comput.* **2021**, *99*, 106900. [CrossRef]
39. Farsi, B.; Amayri, M.; Bouguila, N.; Eicker, U. On short-term load forecasting using machine learning techniques and a novel parallel deep LSTM-CNN approach. *IEEE Access* **2021**, *9*, 31191–31212. [CrossRef]
40. Kouvelas, V.; Moschakis, M. Short-term Electric Load Forecasting using Engineering and Deep Learning techniques. In Proceedings of the 2022 2nd International Conference on Energy Transition in the Mediterranean Area (SyNERGY MED), Thessaloniki, Greece, 17–19 October 2022; pp. 1–5. [CrossRef]
41. Liu, F.; Dong, T.; Liu, Q.; Liu, Y.; Li, S. Combining fuzzy clustering and improved long short-term memory neural networks for short-term load forecasting. *Electr. Power Syst. Res.* **2024**, *226*, 109967. [CrossRef]
42. Zeyu, W.; Yueren, W.; Rouchen, Z.; Srinivasan, R.S.; Ahrentzen, S. Random Forest based hourly building energy prediction. *Energy Build.* **2018**, *171*, 11–25.
43. Touzani, S.; Granderson, J.; Fernandes, S. Gradient boosting machine for modelling the energy consumption of commercial buildings. *Energy Build.* **2018**, *158*, 1533–1543. [CrossRef]
44. Hadri, S.; Naitmalek, Y.; Najib, M.; Bakhouya, M.; Fakhiri, Y.; Elaroussi, M. A Comparative Study of Predictive Approaches for Load Forecasting in Smart Buildings. *Procedia Comput. Sci.* **2019**, *160*, 173–180. [CrossRef]
45. Vrablecová, P.; Bou Ezzeddine, A.; Rozinajová, V.; Šárik, S.; Sangaiah, A.K. Smart grid load forecasting using online support vector regression. *Comput. Electr. Eng.* **2018**, *65*, 102–117. [CrossRef]
46. Khan, S.; Javaid, N.; Chand, A.; Khan, A.B.M.; Rashid, F.; Afridi, I.U. Electricity Load Forecasting for Each Day of Week Using Deep CNN. *Adv. Intell. Syst. Comput.* **2019**, *927*, 1107–1119.
47. Chen, S.; Ren, Y.; Friedrich, D.; Yu, Z.; Yu, J. Prediction of office building electricity demand using artificial neural network by splitting the time horizon for different occupancy rates. *Energy AI* **2021**, *5*, 100093. [CrossRef]
48. Amber, K.P.; Ahmad, R.; Aslam, M.W.; Kousar, A.; Usman, M.; Khan, M.S. Intelligent techniques for forecasting electricity consumption of buildings. *Energy* **2018**, *157*, 886–893. [CrossRef]
49. Zhong, H.; Wang, J.; Jia, H.; Mu, Y.; Lv, S. Vector field-based support vector regression for building energy consumption prediction. *Appl. Energy* **2019**, *242*, 403–414. [CrossRef]
50. Martínez-Comesaña, M.; Febrero-Garrido, M.; Granada-Álvarez, E.; Martínez-Torres, J.; Martínez-Mariño, S. Heat Loss Coefficient Estimation Applied to Existing Buildings through Machine Learning Models. *Appl. Sci.* **2020**, *10*, 8968. [CrossRef]
51. Al-Gabalawy, M.; Hosny, N.S.; Adly, A.R. Probabilistic forecasting for energy time series considering uncertainties based on deep learning algorithms. *Electr. Power Syst. Res.* **2021**, *196*, 107216. [CrossRef]
52. Guo, J.; Lin, P.; Zhang, L.; Pan, Y.; Xiao, Z. Dynamic adaptive encoder-decoder deep learning networks for multivariate time series forecasting of building energy consumption. *Appl. Energy* **2023**, *350*, 121803. [CrossRef]
53. Chen, Q.; Zhang, W.; Zhu, K.; Zhou, D.; Dai, H.; Wu, Q. A novel trilinear deep residual network with self-adaptive dropout method for short-term load forecasting. *Expert Syst. Appl.* **2021**, *182*, 115272. [CrossRef]
54. Somu, N.; MR, G.R.; Ramamritham, K. A deep learning framework for building energy consumption forecast. *Renew. Sustain. Energy Rev.* **2021**, *137*, 110591. [CrossRef]
55. Mughees, N.; Mohsin, S.A.; Mughees, A.; Mughees, A. Deep sequence to sequence Bi-LSTM neural networks for day-ahead peak load forecasting. *Expert Syst. Appl.* **2021**, *175*, 114844. [CrossRef]
56. Wang, T.; Lai, C.S.; Ng, W.W.; Pan, K.; Zhang, M.; Vaccaro, A.; Lai, L.L. Deep autoencoder with localized stochastic sensitivity for short-term load forecasting. *Int. J. Electr. Power Energy Syst.* **2021**, *130*, 106954. [CrossRef]
57. Vaygan, E.K.; Rajabi, R.; Estebsari, A. Short-term load forecasting using time pooling deep recurrent neural network. In Proceedings of the 2021 IEEE International Conference on Environment and Electrical Engineering and 2021 IEEE Industrial and Commercial Power Systems Europe (EEEIC/I&CPS Europe), Bari, Italy, 7–10 September 2021; pp. 1–5.
58. Hu, Y.; Qu, B.; Wang, J.; Liang, J.; Wang, Y.; Yu, K.; Li, Y.; Qiao, K. Short-term load forecasting using multimodal evolutionary algorithm and random vector functional link network-based ensemble learning. *Appl. Energy* **2021**, *285*, 116415. [CrossRef]

59. Zhang, W.; Chen, Q.; Yan, J.; Zhang, S.; Xu, J. A novel asynchronous deep reinforcement learning model with adaptive early forecasting method and reward incentive mechanism for short-term load forecasting. *Energy* **2021**, *236*, 121492. [CrossRef]
60. Thejus, S.; Sivraj, P. Deep learning-based power consumption and generation forecasting for demand side management. In Proceedings of the 2021 Second International Conference on Electronics and Sustainable Communication Systems (ICESC), Coimbatore, India, 4–6 August 2021; pp. 1350–1357.
61. Wang, J.; Chen, X.; Zhang, F.; Chen, F.; Xin, Y. Building load forecasting using deep neural network with efficient feature fusion. *J. Mod. Power Syst. Clean. Energy* **2021**, *9*, 160–169. [CrossRef]
62. Irankhah, A.; Rezazadeh, S.; Moghaddam, M.H.Y.; Ershadi-Nasab, S. Hybrid deep learning method based on lstm-autoencoder network for household short-term load forecasting. In Proceedings of the 2021 7th International Conference on Signal Processing and Intelligent Systems (ICSPIS), Tehran, Iran, 29–30 December 2021; pp. 1–6.
63. Sinha, A.; Sawant, M.; Kochar, H.; Abhija, A.; Seth, R.; Sornagattu, P.R.; Vyas, O. Demand response optimization for microgrid clusters with deep reinforcement learning. In Proceedings of the 2021 12th International Conference on Computing Communication and Networking Technologies (ICCCNT), Kharagpur, India, 6–8 July 2021; pp. 1–7.
64. Mansoor, H.; Rauf, H.; Mubashar, M.; Khalid, M.; Arshad, N. Past vector similarity for short term electrical load forecasting at the individual household level. *IEEE Access* **2021**, *9*, 42771–42785. [CrossRef]
65. Shabbir, N.; Kütt, L.; Raja, H.A.; Ahmadiahangar, R.; Rosin, A.; Husev, O. Machine learning and deep learning techniques for residential load forecasting: A comparative analysis. In Proceedings of the 2021 IEEE 62nd International Scientific Conference on Power and Electrical Engineering of Riga Technical University (RTUCON), Riga, Latvia 15–17 November 2021; pp. 1–5.
66. Li, Y.; Wang, R.; Yang, Z. Optimal scheduling of isolated microgrids using automated reinforcement learning-based multi-period forecasting. *IEEE Trans. Sustain. Energy* **2021**, *13*, 159–169. [CrossRef]
67. Ibrahim, N.M.; Megahed, A.I.; Abbasy, N.H. Short-term individual household load forecasting framework using LSTM deep learning approach. In Proceedings of the 2021 5th International Symposium on Multidisciplinary Studies and Innovative Technologies (ISMSIT), Ankara, Turkey, 21–23 October 2021; pp. 257–262.
68. Cheng, L.; Zang, H.; Xu, Y.; Wei, Z.; Sun, G. Probabilistic residential load forecasting based on micrometeorological data and customer consumption pattern. *IEEE Trans. Power Syst.* **2021**, *36*, 3762–3775. [CrossRef]
69. He, Y.; Luo, F.; Ranzi, G.; Kong, W. Short-term residential load forecasting based on federated learning and load clustering. In Proceedings of the 2021 IEEE International Conference on Communications, Control, and Computing Technologies for Smart Grids (SmartGridComm), Aachen, Germany, 25–28 October 2021; pp. 77–82.
70. Bento, P.M.; Pombo, J.A.; Calado, M.R.; Mariano, S.J. Stacking ensemble methodology using deep learning and ARIMA models for short-term load forecasting. *Energies* **2021**, *14*, 7378. [CrossRef]
71. Salman, D.; Kusaf, M.; Elmi, Y.K. Using recurrent neural network to forecast day and year ahead performance of load demand: A case study of France. In Proceedings of the 2021 10th International Conference on Power Science and Engineering (ICPSE), Istanbul, Turkey, 21–23 October 2021; pp. 23–30.
72. Yaprakdal, F. An ensemble deep-learning-based model for hour-ahead load forecasting with a feature selection approach: A comparative study with state-of-the-art methods. *Energies* **2022**, *16*, 57. [CrossRef]
73. Zhang, G.; Bai, X.; Wang, Y. Short-time multi-energy load forecasting method based on CNN-Seq2Seq model with attention mechanism. *Mach. Learn. Appl.* **2021**, *5*, 100064. [CrossRef]
74. Fekri, M.N.; Grolinger, K.; Mir, S. Distributed load forecasting using smart meter data: Federated learning with Recurrent Neural Networks. *Int. J. Electr. Power Energy Syst.* **2022**, *137*, 107669. [CrossRef]
75. Lu, Y.; Wang, G.; Huang, S. A short-term load forecasting model based on mixup and transfer learning. *Electr. Power Syst. Res.* **2022**, *207*, 107837. [CrossRef]
76. Ahajjam, M.A.; Licea, D.B.; Ghogho, M.; Kobbane, A. Experimental investigation of variational mode decomposition and deep learning for short-term multi-horizon residential electric load forecasting. *Appl. Energy* **2022**, *326*, 119963. [CrossRef]
77. Hadjout, D.; Torres, J.; Troncoso, A.; Sebaa, A.; Martínez-Álvarez, F. Electricity consumption forecasting based on ensemble deep learning with application to the Algerian market. *Energy* **2022**, *243*, 123060. [CrossRef]
78. Abdel-Basset, M.; Hawash, H.; Sallam, K.; Askar, S.; Abouhawwash, M. STLFNet: Two-stream deep network for short-term load forecasting in residential buildings. *J. King Saud. Univ-Comput. Inf. Sci.* **2022**, *34*, 4296–4311.
79. Fernández, J.D.; Menci, S.P.; Lee, C.M.; Rieger, A.; Fridgen, G. Privacy-preserving federated learning for residential short-term load forecasting. *Appl. Energy* **2022**, *326*, 119915. [CrossRef]
80. Javed, U.; Ijaz, K.; Jawad, M.; Khosa, I.; Ansari, E.A.; Zaidi, K.S.; Rafiq, M.N.; Shabbir, N. A novel short receptive field based dilated causal convolutional network integrated with bidirectional LSTM for short-term load forecasting. *Expert Syst. Appl.* **2022**, *205*, 117689. [CrossRef]
81. Aouad, M.; Hajj, H.; Shaban, K.; Jabr, R.A.; El-Hajj, W. A CNN-sequence-to-sequence network with attention for residential short-term load forecasting. *Electr. Power Syst. Res.* **2022**, *211*, 108152. [CrossRef]
82. Sharma, A.; Jain, S.K. A novel seasonal segmentation approach for day-ahead load forecasting. *Energy* **2022**, *257*, 124752. [CrossRef]
83. Yang, W.; Shi, J.; Li, S.; Song, Z.; Zhang, Z.; Chen, Z. A combined deep learning load forecasting model of single household resident user considering multi-time scale electricity consumption behavior. *Appl. Energy* **2022**, *307*, 118197. [CrossRef]

84. Reddy, S.; Akashdeep, S.; Harshvardhan, R.; Kamath, S. Stacking deep learning and machine learning models for short-term energy consumption forecasting. *Adv. Eng. Inform.* **2022**, *52*, 101542.
85. Xiao, X.; Mo, H.; Zhang, Y.; Shan, G. Meta-ANN–A dynamic artificial neural network refined by meta-learning for Short-Term Load Forecasting. *Energy* **2022**, *246*, 123418. [CrossRef]
86. Yan, K.; Zhou, X.; Chen, J. Collaborative deep learning framework on IoT data with bidirectional NLSTM neural networks for energy consumption forecasting. *J. Parallel Distrib. Comput.* **2022**, *163*, 248–255. [CrossRef]
87. Abdallah, M.; Talib, M.A.; Hosny, M.; Waraga, O.A.; Nasir, Q.; Arshad, M.A. Forecasting highly fluctuating electricity load using machine learning models based on multimillion observations. *Adv. Eng. Inform.* **2022**, *53*, 101707. [CrossRef]
88. Tong, X.; Wang, J.; Zhang, C.; Wu, T.; Wang, H.; Wang, Y. LS-LSTM-AE: Power load forecasting via long-short series features and LSTM-autoencoder. *Energy Rep.* **2022**, *8*, 596–603. [CrossRef]
89. Deng, X.; Ye, A.; Zhong, J.; Xu, D.; Yang, W.; Song, Z.; Zhang, Z.; Guo, J.; Wang, T.; Tian, Y.; et al. Bagging–XGBoost algorithm based extreme weather identification and short-term load forecasting model. *Energy Rep.* **2022**, *8*, 8661–8674. [CrossRef]
90. Inteha, A.; Hussain, F.; Khan, I.A. A data driven approach for day ahead short-term load forecasting. *IEEE Access* **2022**, *10*, 84227–84243. [CrossRef]
91. Moradzadeh, A.; Moayyed, H.; Zare, K.; Mohammadi-Ivatloo, B. Short-term electricity demand forecasting via variational autoencoders and batch training based bidirectional long short-term memory. *Sustain. Energy Technol. Assess.* **2022**, *52*, 102209. [CrossRef]
92. Liu, M.; Sun, X.; Wang, Q.; Deng, S. Short-term load forecasting using EMD with feature selection and TCN-based deep learning model. *Energies* **2022**, *15*, 7170. [CrossRef]
93. Ibrahim, B.; Rabelo, L.; Gutierrez-Franco, E.; Clavijo-Buritica, N. Machine learning for short-term load forecasting in smart grids. *Energies* **2022**, *15*, 8079. [CrossRef]
94. Taleb, I.; Guerard, G.; Fauberteau, F.; Nguyen, N. A flexible deep learning method for energy forecasting. *Energies* **2022**, *15*, 3926. [CrossRef]
95. Alotaibi, M.A. Machine learning approach for short-term load forecasting using deep neural network. *Energies* **2022**, *15*, 6261. [CrossRef]
96. Luo, X.; Oyedele, L.O. A self-adaptive deep learning model for building electricity load prediction with moving horizon. *Mach. Learn. Appl.* **2022**, *7*, 100257. [CrossRef]
97. Zou, Y.; Feng, W.; Zhang, J.; Li, J. Forecasting of short-term load using the MFF-SAM-GCN model. *Energies* **2022**, *15*, 3140. [CrossRef]
98. Akhtar, S.; Shahzad, S.; Zaheer, A.; Ullah, H.S.; Kilic, H.; Gono, R.; Jasiński, M.; Leonowicz, Z. Short-term load forecasting models: A review of challenges, progress, and the road ahead. *Energies* **2023**, *16*, 4060. [CrossRef]
99. Arnold, T.B. kerasR: R Interface to the Keras Deep Learning Library. *J. Open Source Softw.* **2017**, *2*, 296. [CrossRef]
100. Ketkar, N.; Ketkar, N. Introduction to keras. In *Deep Learning with Python a Hands-on Introd*; Apress: Berkeley, CA, USA, 2017; pp. 97–111. [CrossRef]
101. Tarek, H.; Aly, H.; Eisa, S.; Abul-Soud, M. Optimized deep learning algorithms for tomato leaf disease detection with hardware deployment. *Electronics* **2022**, *11*, 140. [CrossRef]
102. Konar, J.; Khandelwal, P.; Tripathi, R. Comparison of various learning rate scheduling techniques on convolutional neural network. In Proceedings of the 2020 IEEE International Students' Conference on Electrical, Electronics and Computer Science (SCEECS), Bhopal, India, 22–23 February 2020; pp. 1–5.
103. Al-Kababji, A.; Bensaali, F.; Dakua, S.P. Scheduling techniques for liver segmentation: Reducelronplateau vs. onecyclelr. In *Proceedings of the International Conference on Intelligent Systems and Pattern Recognition*; Springer: Berlin/Heidelberg, Germany, 2022; pp. 204–212.
104. Bisong, E.; Bisong, E. Regularization for deep learning. In *Building Machine Learning and Deep Learning Models on Google Cloud Platform: A Comprehensive Guide for Beginners*; Apress: Berkeley, CA, USA, 2019; pp. 415–421. ISBN 9781484244708.
105. Dekel, O.; Gilad-Bachrach, R.; Shamir, O.; Xiao, L. Optimal Distributed Online Prediction Using Mini-Batches. *J. Mach. Learn. Res.* **2012**, *13*, 165–202.
106. Liu, Y.; Dou, S.; Du, Y.; Wang, Z. Gearbox Fault Diagnosis Based on Gramian Angular Field and CSKD-ResNeXt. *Electronics* **2023**, *12*, 2475. [CrossRef]
107. Salam, A.; El Hibaoui, A. Energy consumption prediction model with deep inception residual network inspiration and LSTM. *Math. Comput. Simul.* **2021**, *190*, 97–109. [CrossRef]

electronics

MDPI

Article

Predictive Maintenance for Distribution System Operators in Increasing Transformers' Reliability

Vasiliki Vita [1,*], Georgios Fotis [1], Veselin Chobanov [2], Christos Pavlatos [1] and Valeri Mladenov [2]

[1] Department of Electrical and Electronics Engineering Educators, ASPETE—School of Pedagogical and Technological Education, 14121 N. Heraklion, Greece

[2] Department Fundamentals of Electrical Engineering, Technical University of Sofia, 8 Kliment Ohridski Blvd., Block 12, 1000 Sofia, Bulgaria

* Correspondence: vasvita@aspete.gr

Abstract: Power transformers' reliability is of the highest importance for distribution networks. A possible failure of them can interrupt the supply to consumers, which will cause inconvenience to them and loss of revenue for electricity companies. Additionally, depending on the type of damage, the recovery time can vary and intensify the problems of consumers. This paper estimates the maintenance required for distribution transformers using Artificial Intelligence (AI). This way the condition of the equipment that is currently in use is evaluated and the time that maintenance should be performed is known. Because actions are only carried out when necessary, this strategy promises cost reductions over routine or time-based preventative maintenance. The suggested methodology uses a classification predictive model to identify with high accuracy the number of transformers that are vulnerable to failure. This was confirmed by training, testing, and validating it with actual data in Colombia's Cauca Department. It is clear from this experimental method that Machine Learning (ML) methods for early detection of technical issues can help distribution system operators increase the number of selected transformers for predictive maintenance. Additionally, these methods can also be beneficial for customers' satisfaction with the performance of distribution transformers, which would enhance the highly reliable performance of such transformers. According to the prediction for 2021, 852 transformers will malfunction, 820 of which will be in rural Cauca, which is consistent with previous failure statistics. The 10 kVA transformers will be the most vulnerable, followed by the 5 kVA and 15 kVA transformers.

Keywords: distribution system; distribution transformers; k-means clustering; machine learning; maintenance planning; predictive maintenance

1. Introduction

Power distribution transformers are crucial parts of power system equipment because they regulate the voltage to various levels on the system components from the generator to the final consumer [1]. Temporary or permanent failure of a transformer interrupts the power supply to end users, causing them problem in their work or everyday life activity. Additionally, the market value of the transformers is high enough, and any possible malfunction in them causes additional expenses to the Distribution System Operators (DSOs). It is essential to prevent potential failures and aid in the early detection of issues to prevent unplanned outages and maintain transformer operation reliability. These failures may cause extensive outages or even blackouts, affecting both the transmission [2] and distribution system [3]. Therefore, monitoring systems that consider the weather conditions with an energy management system must be integrated in the distribution system [4].

In recent research works, efficient allocation strategies have been proposed that can be also applied to power transformers. These strategies lead to the optimal target, according to the technical state of the art, allowing assignment of a failure rate target to different units and then to reach the desired reliability goals for the whole system. In [5], a guideline to determine the appropriate allocation method in relation to the chosen application, available resources, and needed accuracy is presented. In [6], a novel method is focused on the adequate distribution of maintenance budget to system units according to the primary variables impacting availability and maintenance of equipment. The manufacturing sector's decision-making procedures are being transformed by Industry 4.0 technology [7], where important maintenance policy trends include "remote maintenance" and the "autonomous maintenance".

Some reasons for insulation failure in transformers are overload conditions for long durations, overvoltages, overcurrents, and failure of cooling equipment [8]. Hence, power utilities consider the health assessment of transformers to be a crucial factor to have a dependable and effective operation [9]. Each unplanned power outage of a transformer results in financial losses for both the owner of the transformer and the energy consumers it supplies. Therefore, it is critical to identify any signals that could point to a potential transformer defect as soon as possible. No matter where the transformer installation is located, effective diagnostic procedure selection and accurate interpretation of the findings of various types of measurements are required.

In [10], a single-phase transformer's physical geometrical dimensions are modeled using 3D finite element analysis to mimic the operation of a real transformer. The paper in [11] describes the creation and use of a technology for the analysis of dissolved gases in oil for the identification of defects in power transformers. The work in [12] provides an expert system made to perform insulation diagnostics, and other researchers in [13] discuss the state and most recent developments in several power transformer diagnostic approaches. The purpose of [14] is to describe, analyze, and explain current physicochemical diagnostic procedures for evaluating the insulation state in old transformers. Under on-site operating settings, the proposed methodology in [15] enables quick, accurate, and secure partial discharge (PD) diagnostics in a power transformer. A Fourier transform infrared (FT-IR) spectrometer was used to construct an analytical instrument in [16], while [17] addresses the issue of on-line dissolved gas analysis (DGA) of a power transformer. Researchers in [18] investigate and contrast traditional and intelligent DGA interpretation techniques.

Data mining is one method used to develop fault prediction models. Data mining is a complex technique that includes both computer science and statistics to uncover hidden, undiscovered, and possibly important information from huge databases [19]. Data mining comprises several techniques that can be applied on varying datasets. Classification and regression are the two methods that are most frequently used in the development of predictive models, according to [20]. Classification classifies each item in a data set into one of the predefined classes or groups [21].

The major goal of maintenance is to minimize malfunctions and maintain the functionality of the system. Maintenance aims to cut down failures that may happen during regular equipment operation [22]. An unanticipated production delay, decreased efficiency, and occasionally other consequences might result from equipment failure. Reactive, preventive, predictive, and prescriptive maintenance procedures are all combined into effective maintenance [23]. Only when a functional failure is brought on by the function's deterioration are repairs or replacements considered reactive maintenance. The routine examination, alterations, cleaning, replacement of parts, and component repairs make up preventive maintenance. To evaluate the state of the equipment, predictive maintenance employs nonintrusive testing methods, visual inspection, performance data, and data analysis. Through better design, installation techniques, failure analysis, and scheduling, prescriptive maintenance improves equipment condition and rate of degradation [22]. All maintenance strategies are analytically presented in Figure 1.

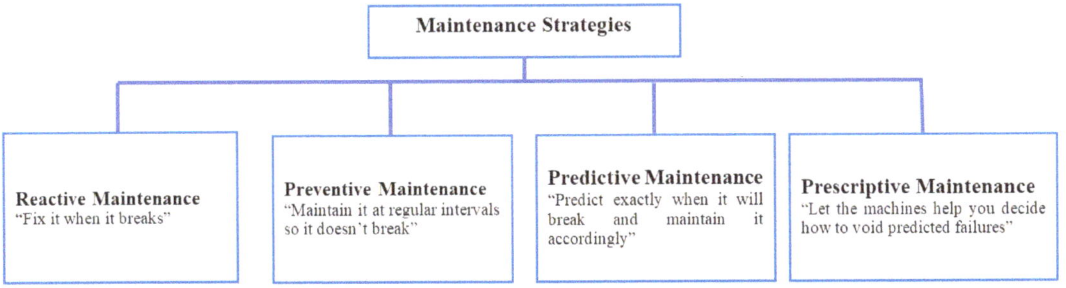

Figure 1. Maintenance strategies.

It is feasible to suggest cost reduction, machine failure and repair reduction, and inventory reduction methods through the treatment and analysis of these data [24]. Artificial Intelligence (AI)-based methods are some of the technologies used to examine the vast amount of data available [25]. In order to increase the power transformer's reliability, data communication, storage, and acquisition systems must be more reliable. Additionally, massive amounts of monitored data from intelligent devices must be analyzed. The ability of contemporary power systems to gather and retain enormous volumes of data from their constituent parts is advancing [26]. For the creation of scalable, adaptable, and pluggable data analysis and real-time self-monitoring systems for manufacturing environments, the suggested Intelligent Data Analysis and Real-Time Supervision (IDARTS) architecture is presented in [27].

Similar problems are tackled internationally using a variety of optimization strategies, including neural networks optimized by Genetic Algorithm (GA) and Fuzzy c-Means [28] or with self-adaptive strategies for diagnosing fault problems in transformers [29], with the drawback of requiring a heavier processing burden because of the deployed neural network. Fuzzy logic, developed by [30], is another tool for making decisions. According to [31], there are optimization techniques, such as linear programming, that use an objective function in order to maximize or reduce a result. Determining this objective function might be challenging in complicated systems, where it is unclear how the variables are related.

According to data from Compania Energetica de Occidente, 1297 transformers burned in 2016; replacement required substantial expenses and power supply disruptions [32,33]. There have been several recorded causes of burning, including atmospheric discharges, third-party manipulation, overload, and lack of secondary distribution line trimming. By eliminating superfluous repair tasks and fewer unexpected power outages, developing preventive maintenance plans can help cut costs. Due to the unpredictable nature of the dataset, this study suggests using ML methods as a classification strategy. Using these methods, it is possible to categorize and rank maintenance needs according to business requirements.

There have been plenty of research works on transformers predictive maintenance using various techniques. However, most of the research to date has been on the degradation of oil alone using dissolved gas analysis (DGA) for transformer health index assessment, whereas the integrated model for fault diagnosis using other diagnostic data has received little attention [9,10,12–14]. Major types of faults [18,20] include high- and low-energy arcing, partial discharge, and hot patches with a range of temperatures, but if negligent implementation is used, there is no region for a normal aging condition that might lead to a diagnostic of any of the faults. To avoid these issues, researchers collected different types of data than the insulating oil parameters for the power distribution transformers from the Compania Energetica de Occidente [32,33]. The variables were binary, continuous and categorical, such as the keraunic-level criticality or the earth discharge density. The authors proposed an AI technique for scheduling predictive maintenance of the power distribution transformers. The aim of this work is to propose a new methodology for the same prediction with higher prediction ability. With more accurate prediction of transformer failures, the reliability of the distribution system will be higher, providing more satisfied customers and fewer expenses for the DSO, both for maintenance or replacement of the power distribution transformers.

The motivation for this study comes from the need to improve the reliability of power transformers in distribution networks. Transformer failures can cause significant disruptions to the distribution network and result in costly outages and repairs. By enabling predictive maintenance through accurate failure prediction, distribution system operators can reduce the probability of transformer failures and minimize the impact of any failures that may occur. The research question of this paper was to investigate whether the proposed model can accurately predict transformer failures and thus enable distribution system operators to perform predictive maintenance increasing the reliability of their transformers.

The main contributions of this paper are as follows:

- Introducing a predictive maintenance approach for distribution system operators to increase the reliability of transformers;
- Proposing a novel model for predicting transformer failures that outperforms existing models;
- Demonstrating the effectiveness of the proposed approach through a case study on an existing distribution network.

The main advantages of using models to solve the problem of transformer failure prediction include:

- Increased accuracy: Models can often predict transformer failures with higher accuracy than traditional rule-based approaches.
- Early detection: Models can detect potential failures before they occur, enabling distribution system operators to perform preventive maintenance to avoid outages and costly repairs.
- Scalability: Models can be applied to large-scale distribution networks to identify potential failures across many transformers simultaneously.

The structure of this work is as follows. In Section 2, the most common transformer failures are discussed, while in Section 3 the model description is presented. The data collection and description of the data is reviewed in Section 4. Then, in Section 5, two different strategies for early MS detection are discussed: supervised learning using support vector machines (SVM) and non-supervised learning using k-means clustering. In Section 6, the proposed methodology estimates the predicted number of transformers that will present malfunction in the future. The concluding notes are provided in the two last sections.

2. Common Transformer Failures

The failure of a power distribution transformer may happen due to internal causes inside the transformer [34] or due to environmental conditions such as lightning. In [35], an effort was made to use an online overvoltage monitoring system to acquire the waveform characteristics of encroaching lightning impulses in power transformers. In another paper [36], a 35 kV distribution transformer that had been struck by lightning was used as the study object to determine the electromagnetic transient and the protective measures that should be taken for transformers when struck by lightning. In [37], the lightning protection of high-voltage transmission lines was approached as an optimization problem where optimal design parameters are calculated for the lines, relating their cost with the lightning failures' cost, aiming to reduce or even eliminate lightning failures. Another research team examines the developed overvoltages at the entrance of a distribution substation, due to lightning strike to the connected line, and computes them while considering various configurations [38]. Using the primary–secondary islanding technique for controlling the distributed generation units during grid-connected and islanding operation due to various causes, such as lightning, another work discusses the viability of planned islanding operation and looks into the impact of unplanned islanding [39].

Another factor that may affect a power transformer is extreme weather conditions. In [40], a risk assessment is performed, proving that incorporating load management in asset planning is a viable measure that would offset the probability of catastrophic failure of geomagnetic disturbances. Ref. [41] covers some of these impacts on the electric power system, specifically distribution transformers and underground cables, while [42] examines power quality issues in the distribution system. The primary components of the distribution transformer are the terminals of the magnetic and electrical circuits, the bushings, the tank, the oil, the radiator, the conservator, and the breather. Any of the components listed below that are failure-prone can cause the transformer to malfunction. Within the text each reference to the word "burned" is related to at least one of the malfunctions that are analytically described in 2.1 to 2.6. A typical power distribution transformer is depicted in Figure 2.

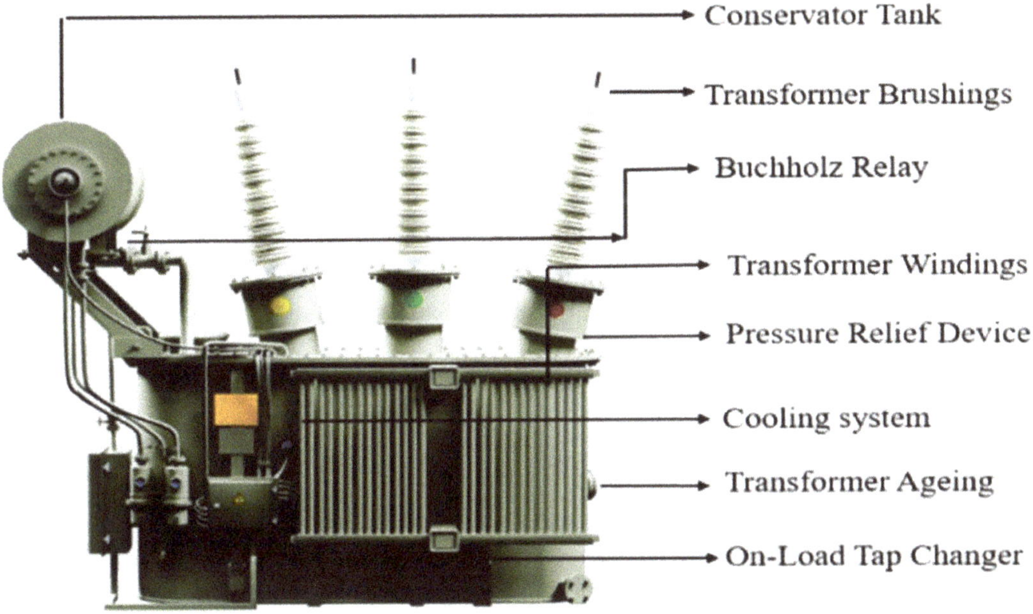

Figure 2. A typical power distribution transformer.

2.1. Core

The transformer's core both conducts magnetic flux and gives it mechanical strength. DC magnetization or displacement of the core steel during the transformer's construction are the two main causes of core failure.

2.2. Winding

The transformer's windings, which are positioned around the core limb as cylindrical shells, are responsible for carrying the current. Each strand of each winding is covered with paper insulation. The windings must be able to endure mechanical forces that can induce winding displacement in addition to dielectric stress and temperature requirements. These forces can manifest during lightning and short circuits. Most winding failures are caused by transient overvoltage or short circuit. The creation of hot spots, the production of copper sludge, low oil levels, or mechanical flaws in the windings during transformer construction are a few examples of the causes of winding short circuits. Transient overvoltage may be caused by lightning or improper transformer connection.

2.3. Tank

The tank physically protects the transformer core and windings and serves as a container for the cooling oil. It must be able to tolerate environmental pressures including solar rays, corrosive air, and high humidity. The tank is examined for leaks, corrosion, and other signs of abusive handling. A transformer's internal arcing can rapidly evaporate the surrounding oil, creating a high pressure inside the transformer that can cause the tank to break.

2.4. Solid Insulation

For electrical isolation, press board and paper formed of cellulose are employed as solid insulation between the windings. Long chains of glucose rings make up the structure of cellulose, which breaks down over time to form shorter chains. The average number of these rings in the chain, or degree of polymerization (DP), serves as a proxy for the condition of the paper [43].

The transformer insulation system's most vulnerable point is this sturdy insulation. Forces produced during short circuits or by the movement of the transformer can mechanically damage solid insulation. $CuSO_4$ production, hot spots produced by insufficient oil, or overloading of the transformer can all cause faults in insulating materials.

2.5. Insulation Oil

Insulation between the windings and the desired cooling of the transformer are both provided by the transformer oil [44]. There are two causes of cooling oil failure: either improper oil circulation or inadequate transfer of heat to the cooling circuit. As a result, the oil in the transformer becomes more viscous and the temperature in the cooling circuit becomes too high. The main factor for oil contamination and the production of conducting particles is moisture and oxygen combined with heat. As a result, the temperature inside the transformer will increase, and a short circuit will result from the oil insulation failing.

2.6. Bushings

To connect the transformer to the power system, bushings remove the winding terminals from the tank's outside and cover them with electrical insulation. Sliding bushings and capacitance graded bushings are the two main types of bushings employed. A center conductor and insulation made of porcelain or epoxy surround the solid bushing. Short circuit is the primary bushing failure mode. It can be a result of damage or insulation material flaws. Sabotage, shipment, or flying parts from other malfunctioning equipment can all cause damage. Damages, porcelain cracks, and faulty gaskets allow water to enter the bushing's insulation, which causes the bushing to fail.

3. Model Description

Computers are taught to learn from experience using ML, much as people do naturally. ML techniques do not rely on a mathematical model to describe the data; instead, they employ computational methods to learn information from the data. In general, AI has been applied in a great variety of technical problems. For example, the electromagnetic field prediction of electrostatic discharges can be conducted either by ML techniques [45] or by developing an ANN tool [46]. A heuristic technique for lowering the frequency of high-voltage substation outages caused by atmospheric overvoltages is presented in [47]. As the amount of data available for learning rises, they adaptively improve at performing their tasks. Optimized and predictive maintenance strategies are evolved to improve power availability for consumers [48]. Although SVM and k-means clustering are well-known techniques, their efficiency varies depending on the dataset and situation at hand. As a result, it is critical to assess their performance on an individual basis. We intended to compare the performance of these algorithms on a specific dataset and problem in this work, which we feel would be beneficial to people working in this area. Our findings show that our suggested model generation strategy based on k-means clustering outperformed the classic SVM method on our dataset in terms of classification accuracy [49]. Other researchers find that preventive maintenance has been proven effective in improving the continuity of service and reliability of customers [50]. The new method has higher accuracy and efficiency in predicting highlight dates' load rates and is used from [51].

To justify the use of numerical modeling in this study, several previous works have successfully employed this approach for analyzing transformer performance. For example, in one study [52], a numerical simulation was used to investigate the effects of different operating conditions on transformer oil temperature and winding hot spot temperature. Another study [53] utilized a finite element method to analyze the effect of thermal aging on the insulation properties of transformers. Additionally, a paper by [54] presented a numerical model for predicting the partial discharge inception voltage of power transformers. These previous works demonstrate the effectiveness and validity of using numerical modeling in transformer performance analysis, which justifies its use in this paper as well. Overall, the numerical modeling used in this study involves the development and training of an Artificial Neural Network (ANN) model using historical maintenance records and operational parameters, as well as the evaluation of the model's performance using various performance metrics.

There are several ML algorithms that can be used for predictive maintenance of transformers. Some examples include:

1. Regression algorithms: Linear and non-linear regression algorithms can be used to predict when a transformer component is likely to fail using multiclass classification [55] or ANN [56]. These algorithms can analyze historical data from sensors and other sources to identify patterns that indicate a component is nearing the end of its useful life.
2. Random Forest: Random Forest is an ensemble ML algorithm that can be used to predict the remaining useful life of transformer components [57]. It creates a set of decision trees and uses the majority vote of these decision trees to predict the outcome [58].
3. Gradient Boosting: The Gradient Boosting algorithm uses an ensemble of weak models, such as decision trees, to predict the remaining useful life of transformer components [59]. It works by iteratively adding new models to the ensemble and adjusting the weights of the previous models [60].
4. Deep Learning: Deep learning algorithms, such as convolutional neural networks and recurrent neural networks, can be used to analyze sensor data and predict when a transformer component is likely to fail [61]. These algorithms can learn to detect patterns in the data that are not visible to humans [62].
5. Anomaly Detection: Unsupervised ML algorithms such as One-Class SVM, Isolation Forest, and Autoencoder can be used to detect anomalies in the data, indicating a failure [63]. These algorithms can detect patterns in the data that are not visible to humans.
6. Predictive modeling: Predictive modeling algorithms such as the Markov Chain Monte Carlo (MCMC) [64] and Bayesian networks [65] can be used to predict the remaining useful life of transformer components. These algorithms use probabilistic models to estimate the likelihood of a failure occurring [66].

Overall, using ML algorithms for predictive maintenance of transformers can help to improve the efficiency, effectiveness, and reliability of the maintenance process. By analyzing data from sensors and other sources, ML algorithms can predict when maintenance is needed, optimize maintenance schedules, and identify the root cause of problems, thus improving the overall performance of the transformer model.

We have included these algorithms in the methodology section to provide a comprehensive overview of the different methods available for predictive maintenance of transformers. The inclusion of these methods may serve as a basis for future research and comparison with other approaches in the field.

In this paper, we used the k-means clustering algorithm to group transformers based on their behavior patterns and characteristics. We then used Support Vector Machine (SVM) as a machine learning algorithm to develop a predictive model to identify which transformers are at risk of failure. The SVM algorithm was trained on clustered data to predict the probability of failure for each transformer. We also evaluated the performance of the predictive model using metrics such as accuracy, precision, and recall. The results showed that the predictive model was able to identify the transformers at risk of failure with high accuracy and precision.

The use of machine learning algorithms such as k-means clustering and SVM can significantly improve the reliability and efficiency of transformer maintenance, reducing costs and minimizing outages.

k-means clustering is an unsupervised ML algorithm that can be used for the predictive maintenance of transformers. The general process for using k-means clustering for predictive transformer maintenance is as follows:

1. Data collection: Collect data from sensors and other sources that can be used to train the k-means clustering algorithm. This data could include information about the transformer's operating conditions, such as temperature, voltage, and current, as well as information about the transformer's components, such as the age and condition of the components. Additionally, these data could include the transformer's type, the location of its installation, the environmental conditions to which it is exposed, etc.
2. Data preprocessing: Prepare the data for use in the k-means clustering algorithm by cleaning and preprocessing them. This includes removing missing or duplicate data, normalizing the data, and transforming them into a format that can be used by the algorithm.
3. Feature selection: Select the features that will be used by the k-means clustering algorithm to group similar transformer components together. This includes selecting a subset of the available features or creating new features by combining or transforming existing features.
4. Clustering: Apply the k-means clustering algorithm to the preprocessed data to group similar transformer components together. The algorithm partitions the data into k clusters, where k is the number of clusters chosen.
5. Cluster evaluation: Evaluate the performance of the k-means clustering algorithm. This can be performed by measuring the quality of the clusters, such as by using the silhouette score, or by comparing the clusters to the labeled data if available.
6. Model deployment: Once the model has been trained and evaluated, it is deployed for use in the predictive maintenance process. This includes using the clusters to identify groups of similar transformer components that are likely to fail at the same time, and scheduling maintenance accordingly.
7. Model retraining: Retrain the model over time to account for new data and changes in the transformer's operating conditions. This helps to improve the accuracy of the predictions over time.

We used the k-means clustering algorithm in methodology for predictive transformer maintenance. The k-means clustering algorithm is used to group transformers based on their behavior patterns and characteristics. We used k-means clustering to identify groups of transformers that share similar characteristics, such as number of users, type of clients and electric power not supplied.

The k-means algorithm is an iterative process that involves the following steps:

- Initialization: Randomly select k data points as initial centroids.
- Assignment: Assign each data point to the nearest centroid.
- Recalculation: Recalculate the centroid of each cluster.
- Iteration: Repeat steps 2 and 3 until convergence.

In the case of our methodology, we initialized k (the number of clusters) based on the elbow method to find the optimal number of clusters. We then assigned each transformer to the nearest centroid and recalculated the centroid of each cluster. The process continued until the algorithm converged.

The k-means clustering algorithm helps us to identify which transformers are more likely to fail and which ones are performing well by grouping them based on their characteristics and behavior patterns. This information is then used to develop a predictive model that can identify which transformers are at risk of failure and require maintenance, allowing for proactive maintenance to prevent downtime and extend the life of the transformers.

Figure 3 displays the flowchart for the proposed model. For various values of K, Figure 3 depicts the average clustering accuracy of the suggested model creation technique utilizing k-means clustering (the number of clusters). The accuracy rose with rising K values, which is consistent with the iterative refining process of the k-means algorithm. Initial centroids are picked at random in stages 1–3 of the process, and data points are allocated to the nearest centroid. Steps 4–6 update the centroids to represent the mean of the data points allocated to each cluster. The method iterates through stages 4–6 until convergence is obtained in step 7. The findings in Figure 3 indicate that our suggested strategy of building models using k-means clustering can improve classification accuracy.

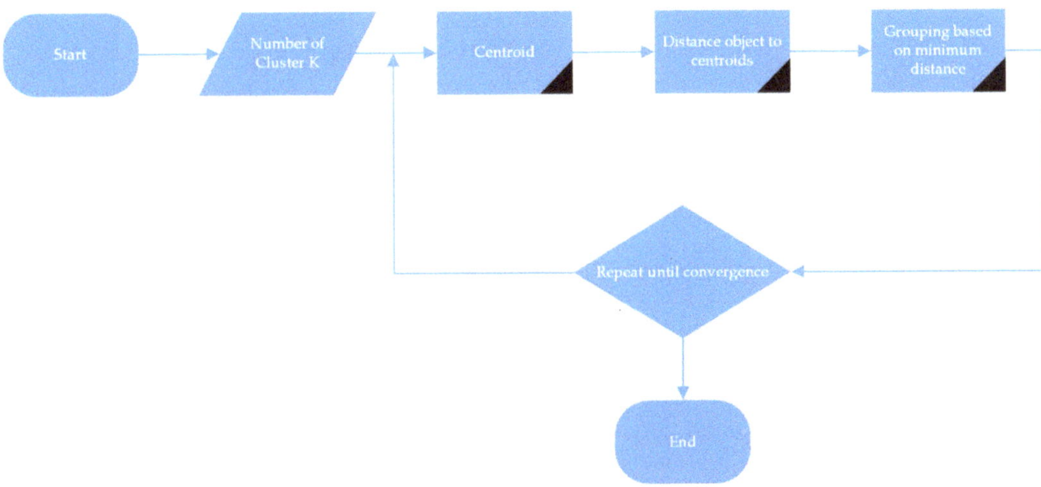

Figure 3. Flowchart of the proposed model.

Overall, using k-means clustering for predictive maintenance of transformers can help to improve the efficiency, effectiveness, and reliability of the maintenance process. By grouping similar transformer components together, the k-means clustering algorithm can help to identify groups of components that are likely to fail at the same time and schedule maintenance accordingly, thus improving the overall performance of the transformer model.

SVMs are a type of supervised ML algorithm used for classification and regression tasks. The goal of an SVM is to find a hyperplane that separates the data into different classes, or in the case of regression, to find the best hyperplane that fits the data.

The basic idea behind an SVM is to find a hyperplane that maximally separates the data into different classes. The equation of this hyperplane is represented as:

$$\mathrm{w} \cdot \mathrm{x} + \mathrm{b} = 0 \tag{1}$$

where w represents the weights of the features, x represents the input features, and b represents the bias term. The weights and bias are learned during the training process.

SVMs also have a concept of margin, which is the distance between the hyperplane and the closest data points from each class, called support vectors. The objective of an SVM is to find the hyperplane with the largest margin.

The optimization problem for an SVM can be represented as:

$$minimize\left(\frac{1}{2}\right)\cdot\|w\|^2 \tag{2}$$

Subject to:

$$\mathrm{y}\cdot(\mathrm{w}\cdot\mathrm{x}+\mathrm{b}) \geq 1 \text{ for } \mathrm{i} = 1, 2, \ldots, \mathrm{n} \tag{3}$$

where n is the number of data points, y is the class label (-1 or 1), and $\|w\|$ is the norm of the weights.

The above optimization problem is a quadratic programming problem and can be solved using optimization techniques such as Sequential Minimal Optimization (SMO).

In the case of non-linearly separable data, SVMs use the kernel trick to map the data into a higher dimensional space where the data become linearly separable. The kernel function is represented as:

$$\mathrm{K}(\mathrm{x}, \mathrm{y}) = \varphi(\mathrm{x})\cdot\varphi(\mathrm{y}) \tag{4}$$

where φ is a mapping function that maps the input data into a higher dimensional space, and K(x, y) is the dot product of the mapped data. Some commonly used kernel functions are the linear, polynomial, and radial basis function (RBF) kernels.

k-means clustering is an unsupervised ML algorithm that is used to group similar data points together into clusters. The goal is to partition the data into k clusters, where k is the number of clusters chosen.

The basic idea behind k-means clustering is to find k cluster centroids, which are the mean value of the data points in each cluster. These centroids are used to define the boundaries of each cluster. The algorithm iteratively assigns each data point to the cluster whose centroid is closest to it, and then updates the centroids based on the new assignment of points.

The process of k-means can be formalized in the following steps:

1. Initialize k centroids randomly: The k centroids are initialized randomly from the data points.
2. Assign each data point to the nearest centroid: Each data point is assigned to the cluster whose centroid is closest to it. This can be completed by calculating the Euclidean distance between the data point and each centroid.
3. Update the centroids: The centroid of each cluster is updated by taking the mean of all the data points assigned to that cluster.
4. Repeat steps 2 and 3 until the centroids do not change anymore or a stopping criterion is reached.

The algorithm can be mathematically represented by the following:

1. Initially, k centroids are chosen randomly from the data points. Let the k centroids be represented by $c_1, c_2, \ldots, c_k$
2. Assign each data point x to the closest centroid, which can be represented by:

$$\mathrm{argmin}(1 \leq \mathrm{j} \leq \mathrm{k})\|\mathrm{x} - \mathrm{c_i}\|^2 \tag{5}$$

3. Update the centroids by taking the mean of all the data points assigned to that cluster.

$$\mathrm{c_j} = \left(\frac{1}{\mathrm{n_i}}\right)\cdot\sum_{\mathrm{j}}^{1}\mathrm{x}(\mathrm{j}) \tag{6}$$

4. Repeat steps 2 and 3 until the centroids do not change anymore or a stopping criterion is reached.

Figure 4 depicts a thorough block diagram presenting the suggested methodology's flow and the interconnections between its many components.

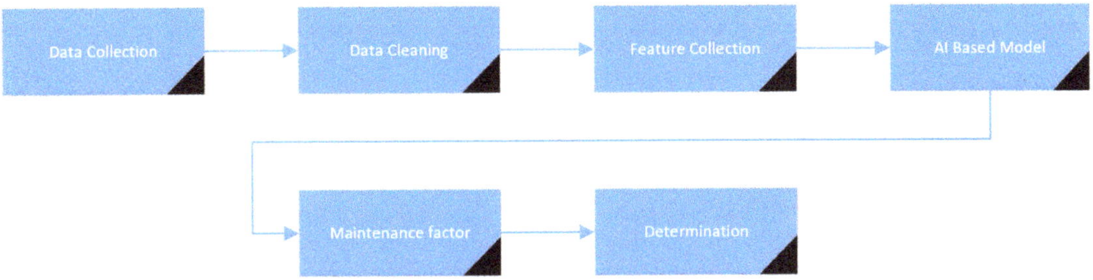

Figure 4. Block diagram of the proposed methodology.

As machine learning techniques become more prevalent in various fields, the evaluation and validation of these techniques have become increasingly important. Performance metrics such as root-mean-square error (RMSE), mean absolute error (MAE), and root-mean-square deviation (RMSD) are commonly used to evaluate the accuracy of machine learning models [67].

Furthermore, the use of machine learning techniques, such as ANNs, has been found to be effective in predicting the remaining useful life (RUL) of various engineering systems, including transformers [68]. In addition, previous studies have demonstrated the effectiveness of ANNs [69] in predicting transformer faults and estimating the remaining life of transformers [70]. Our proposed AI-based model is based on an ANN approach and is tailored to the specific problem of determining the maintenance factor for distribution transformers. The presented approach in this work is well-justified and will provide a significant improvement over existing methods.

This paper proposes a methodology that uses k-means clustering and Support Vector Machine (SVM) algorithms for predictive maintenance of transformers. Its main advantages are:

- Non-linear relationships: The SVM algorithm can capture non-linear relationships between the input features and the output labels, which is useful when dealing with complex systems like transformers.
- Scalability: k-means clustering is computationally efficient and can handle large datasets, making it suitable for industrial applications with large amounts of data.
- Interpretable results: k-means clustering provides interpretable results that can be visualized in the form of clusters, which can help engineers understand the underlying patterns in the data.

Despite the above-mentioned advantages, the proposed methodology also has some limitations compared to other methods. These main disadvantages are as follows:

- Feature engineering: The performance of the SVM algorithm is highly dependent on the quality and relevance of the input features. This requires significant effort and expertise in feature engineering, which may not be available in all applications.
- Sensitivity to hyperparameters: Both k-means clustering and SVM require tuning of hyperparameters, such as the number of clusters and regularization parameter, respectively. The performance of the model can be sensitive to these hyperparameters, and selecting optimal values requires careful experimentation.
- Limited to labeled data: The SVM algorithm is a supervised learning method and requires labeled data for training. This can be a limitation in applications where labeled data are scarce or expensive to obtain.

The specific needs for a custom initialization method depend on the specific characteristics of the proposed model, such as the number and type of layers, the activation functions used, and the size of the input and output layers. In addition, the specific data used to train the model also influence the choice of initialization method. For example, if a section of the data is highly unbalanced or noisy, a custom initialization method is designed to help address these issues. Ultimately, the specific needs for a custom initialization method depend on the details of the model and data used in the study.

Some potential disadvantages of using a customized initialization method include the increased complexity and time required to develop and implement the method, as well as the possibility that the customized method may not generalize well to other datasets or models. Additionally, if the customized method is not carefully designed or implemented, it may lead to over fitting or under fitting of the model, which can negatively impact its performance. It is also possible that the customized method may not result in significant improvements over standard initialization methods, in which case the additional effort and complexity may not be justified.

4. Distribution Transformers Data at Cauca Department of Colombia

In the current work, AI techniques have been applied on open access data [15] that other researchers have similarly used to predict future malfunctions of the distribution transformers, helping them to create their maintenance schedule. A total of 15,873 distribution transformers of the Cauca Departments of Colombia are included in the data chosen for the analysis presented in this work [71].

These distribution transformers located in the rural and urban areas of the 42 municipalities are connected to the operator's network at voltage levels of 13.2 kV and 34.5 kV. There are 13,112 transformers in the urban areas and 2761 in the rural areas. In Table 1, the names and classification of variables for the dataset of distribution transformers of the Cauca Departments of Colombia are presented. There are 16 variables (binary, continuous, and categorical), which pertain to the years 2019 and 2020. Next to each variable, a short description follows. Many variables, such as temperature during the transformer's operation, the level of oil, and overloads, could not be measured, but are nonetheless crucial for classification. Additionally, several transformers could malfunction for unknown reasons, such as electrical discharges or wrong connections.

The technical records of 15,873 transformers were used, out of which 2761 belong to urban areas, and 13,112 to residential customers. The raw data include history, containing the reported terms for the transformers and transformers' technical data: rated power, number of customers connecting, type of installation, etc. The analysis data used in this paper's ML classifiers (SVM and k-means clustering) include the following: the top 16 reported technical concerns for the problematic transformers population from the raw data, which are location, rated power, self-protection, average and maximum earth discharge density, burning rate, keraunic level criticality, detachable connectors, type of clients, number of users, electric power not supplied, type of installation, air network, circuit queue, length of network, and burned transformers.

The rated power of the transformers range is between 5 to 2000 kVA, as shown in Table 2. Also, in Figure 5, both the number of transformers for each rated power and the number of the burned transformers for the years 2019 and 202 are presented.

Table 1. Names and classification of variables for the dataset of distribution transformers of the Cauca Departments of Colombia.

Name of Variable	Type of Variable				Short Description
	Binary		Continuous	Cate-gorical	
	1	0			
Location	Urban area	Rural area	-	-	Location of the transformer
Power [kVA]	-	-	X	-	Transformer capacity
Self-protection	Self-protected	Not self-protected	-	-	Inbuilt switch for low voltage (LV) protection in the transformer or not
Average earth discharge density [Rays/km^2 year]	-	-	X	-	Typical annual rate of lightning strikes per km^2
Maximum earth discharge density [Rays/km^2 year]	-	-	X	-	The annual average for lightning strikes per km^2
Burning rate	-	-	X	-	The quantity of component failures per unit of recording time.
Keraunic level criticality	High risk	Low risk	-	-	Variable product of a prior study conducted by other parties on behalf of the distribution company
Detachable connectors	There are detachable connectors	No detachable connectors	-	-	Removable medium voltage connectors for easy repair of the transformer
Type of clients	-	-		X	Residential, commercial, or industrial consumers
Number of users	-	-	X	-	Number of clients the particular transformer is supplying
Electric power not supplied [kWh]	-	-	X	-	The energy that the DSO ceases to sell when the transformer is out of service.
Installation type	-	-		X	Indicates whether the installed transformer is in a cabin, in a H-type structure, if it has a macro with an anti-fraud net, if it is a pad mounted type, if it is in a simple pole-type structure, an anti-fraud net pole, a metal tower or others
Air network	Aerial type	Non aerial type	-	-	Identifies if the LV network of the transformers is of the aerial type or not
Circuit queue	Position in the terminal	Position in a passing point	-	-	Shows whether the transformer is situated at a circuit's terminal point within the medium voltage network
Length of network [km]	-	-	X	-	Length of the distribution lines that the transformer feeds
Burned transformers	Burned	Not burned	-	-	Shows whether the transformer has burned this year

Table 2. Transformer data and number of burned transformers for 2019 and 2020.

Rated Power [kVA]	Number of Transformers	Damaged Transformers in 2019	Damaged Transformers in 2020
5	1571	23	52
10	3511	423	296
15	3981	252	118
20	13	0	10
25	2651	58	87
30	322	4	6
37.5	1057	17	29
45	686	8	14
50	305	2	2
75	1134	1	11
100	4	0	0
112.5	576	1	4
125	4	3	0
150	27	0	0
200	2	0	0
225	14	0	0
250	1	0	0
300	5	0	0
400	1	0	0
500	1	0	0
630	3	0	0
1000	1	0	0
1125	1	0	0
1250	1	0	0
2000	1	0	0
Total	**15,873**	**792**	**629**

ML algorithms are divided into two categories: controlled training and uncontrolled training. A collection of training data is utilized to train the algorithm for controlled training, which enables it to identify the earliest indications of technical problems, follow their progression, and create a predictive model that can help identify whether the transformer is at risk of malfunction. An effort was made to cluster the data for unsupervised learning so that transformers at danger and transformers that are not at risk belong to different clusters.

The extracted data frequently contain gaps, omissions, confusing information, noise interruptions, and other issues that have an impact on how well the prediction models function. Therefore, to prevent complications in the future, they must be pre-processed and validated. It could take a while and be tedious to extract variables from the data of the transformers. However, the necessary variables from the raw data using statistical analysis software have been extracted, and then the data that will be the most useful for our needs have been formatted. Transformer values that were missing were handled by deleting the associated technical record. Each reported issue for the technical history has been made to constitute a separate column after the data have been transformed to one record per transformer. A value of "1" is used to indicate the presence of a documented technical issue for the technical history and "−1" to indicate its absence.

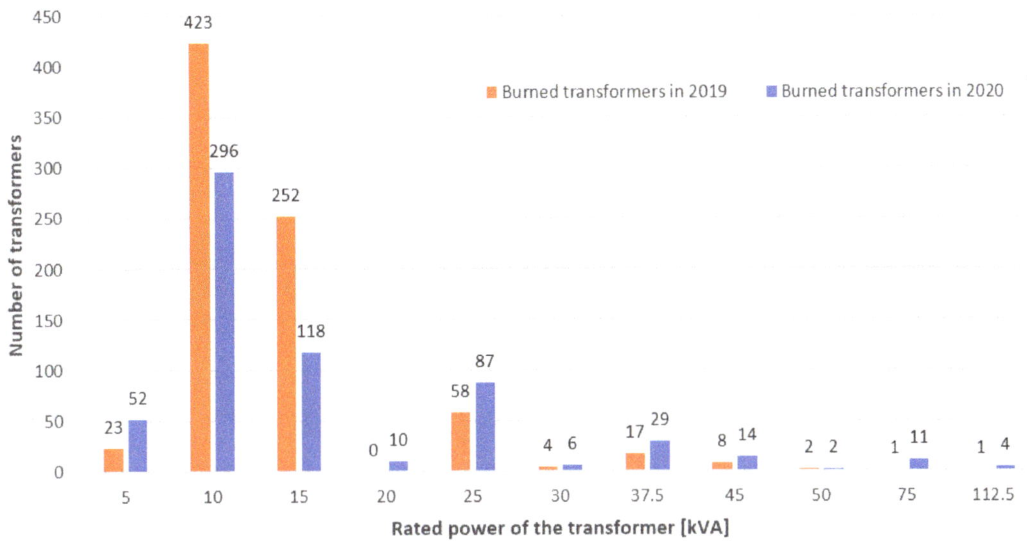

Figure 5. Transformer data and number of burned transformers for 2019 and 2020.

5. AI Methods for Early Transformer Issue Detection

In this study, we aim to investigate the use of AI methods, such as natural language processing (NLP) and ML, to automatically analyze technical trial eligibility databases and electronic technical data bases of DSOs, find matches between active technical trials and suitable transformers, and recommend these matches to DSOs and investigators for a particular prediction of transformer failure. We use the gathered dataset to apply two well-known techniques—SVM and k-means clustering—to analyze the data to enhance the maintenance process for transformers and ensure that customers have a reliable supply of energy.

The paper proposes a methodology for predictive maintenance of transformers using Support Vector Machine (SVM) algorithms and k-means clustering. The methodology consists of several steps. Firstly, we preprocess the data by selecting relevant features and normalizing the data. The relevant features include operational and environmental variables such as nominal power of the transformer, earth discharge density and type of network (aerial or non-aerial type), which have been found to affect the health of transformers. Normalization is performed to ensure that all variables have the same scale and range.

Then, k-means clustering is applied to group the data into clusters based on similarity in the feature space. The number of clusters is determined using the elbow method, which selects the number of clusters that minimizes the within-cluster sum of squares. The resulting clusters are labeled and used as input for the SVM algorithm. In the SVM step, a binary classification model is trained to predict the health state of each transformer based on the labeled clusters. The model is trained using a labeled dataset, which consists of historical data on transformer health and corresponding cluster labels. The SVM algorithm uses a non-linear kernel function to capture non-linear relationships between the input features and the output labels.

Finally, the performance of the proposed methodology is evaluated using various metrics such as accuracy, precision, recall. The evaluation is carried out on a test dataset that was not used during the training phase to ensure the generalizability of the model.

5.1. Support Vector Machines (SVMs)

SVM is a supervised learning method that analyzes the data used in regression and classification studies. A label, with numbers +1 belonging to the appropriate class and −1 not, is used when there are two classes being classified. In our study, we used two different methods to select the features for the SVM and k-means models. For the SVM model, we used a method called sequential forward feature selection, which selects the most informative features by iteratively adding one feature at a time based on their performance on a cross-validation set. This process continues until the desired number of features is reached. For the k-means model, we used a method called mutual information-based feature selection, which selects the features that have the highest mutual information with the target variable (in our case, the class label) while minimizing the redundancy among the selected features. So, even though the same dataset was used to train both models, the features used for each model were selected using different methods. Transformers in our situation are classified as either +1, meaning with technical issues, or −1, meaning without technical concerns.

The dataset is split into two subsets: 14,873 transformers for training and 1000 transformers for testing. The Matlab ML toolbox is used to produce the results. Figure 6 displays the training's outcomes for years 2019 and 2020, respectively. Although different supervised learning models are employed, the SVM provides the best accuracy of 95.60% and 96.93% for the years 2019 and 2020, respectively, as they are depicted in Figure 6. Successfully and unsuccessfully learned points are shown in Figure 6 as well. It is obvious that 104 (year 2019) and 102 (year 2020) transformers (points) are unsuccessfully taught for class −1, whereas 551 (year 2019) and 355 (year 2020) transformers (points) are poorly learned for class +1.

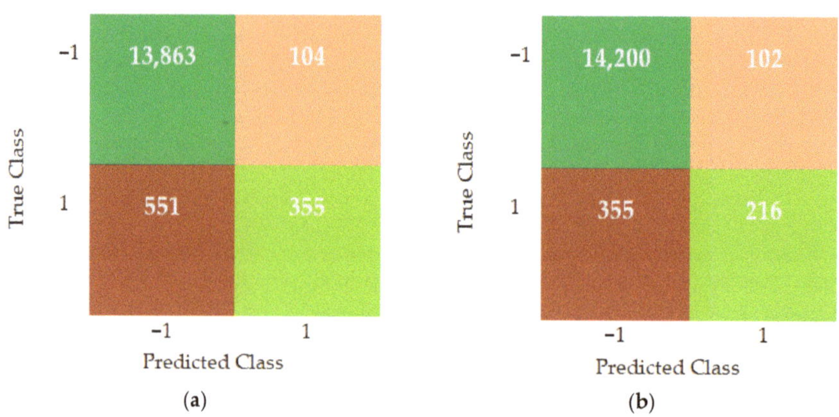

Figure 6. (**a**) The percentages of successfully and unsuccessfully learned points for both classes (Year 2019). (**b**) The percentages of successfully and unsuccessfully learned points for both classes (Year 2020).

All 1000 transformers utilized for testing are appropriately categorized according to the obtained classifier. In addition, we tested the SVM learning while eliminating some features. The accuracy of learning increased to 96.74% and 97.25% for the years 2019 and 2020, respectively, when the following features were removed: location, power, removable connectors, electric power not supplied, air network, and circuit queue. We can infer from the foregoing that the reported terms under consideration should not have a significant impact on the transformers' technical problems. Additionally, the learning accuracy is higher than this presented in [33], in which it was 95.43% for 2019 and 90.62% for 2020.

5.2. k-Means Clustering

In unsupervised learning, a hidden structure in the data is found when the correct response is not known up front. A natural grouping of the data is produced by the clustering technique, and items from the same cluster have a higher degree of similarity than those from other clusters. In k-means clustering, a "prototype" data point serves as a representation for each cluster. Figure 7 depicts the clustering in clusters 2, 3, and 4. The clusters' average value indicates that two clusters are the ideal quantity. It is appropriate given that there are just two classes to which the transformers belong. The first one is for transformers that have technical problems, and the second one is for transformers that do not. The intention of this work is to explain that the performance of the proposed model construction method using k-means clustering was evaluated using the leave-one-out cross-validation method. In this method, each data point is left out in turn, and the model is trained using the remaining data points. The left-out data point is then classified using the trained model, and the process is repeated for each data point. The overall accuracy of the model is calculated as the proportion of correctly classified data points. This evaluation method allows us to assess the robustness and generalizability of the proposed model construction method.

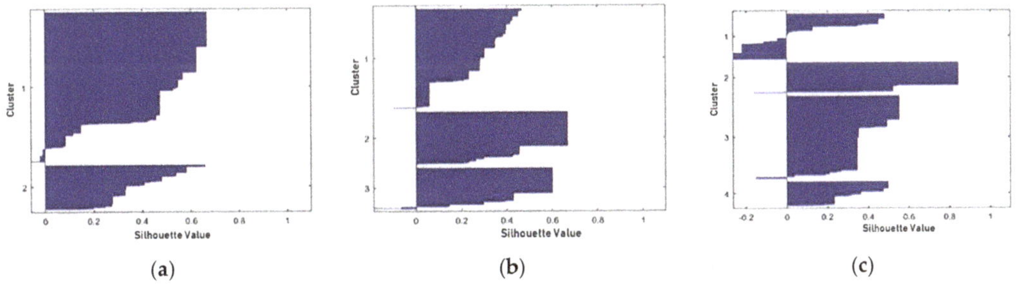

Figure 7. Clustering in: (**a**) 2 clusters, (**b**) 3 clusters and (**c**) 4 clusters.

Our proposed approach is based on a customized initialization method for the parameters of the model. The main advantage of this method is that it takes into account the specific needs of our problem and optimizes the initial values of the parameters accordingly. To implement this method, we first analyze the characteristics of the data and the architecture of the model. We then design a customized initialization strategy that takes into account the specific needs of our problem. More specifically, we start by defining the activation functions and the number of hidden layers for the neural network. Next, we initialize the weight and bias parameters of each layer based on a customized initialization method. We then train the model using back propagation with a suitable loss function. Our customized initialization method is based on a combination of heuristics and domain knowledge.

The paper also discusses the practical implications of the proposed methodology for distribution system operators. By using predictive maintenance, operators can detect potential failures in transformers before they occur, allowing for timely maintenance and repair. This can lead to cost savings by reducing unplanned downtime and extending the lifespan of transformers.

In summary, our proposed approach is based on a customized initialization method that takes into account the specific needs of our problem. By analyzing the characteristics of the data and the architecture of the model, we design a customized initialization strategy that optimizes the initial values of the parameters. While our method requires significant domain expertise and experimentation, we believe that it offers several advantages over standard initialization methods for deep learning models. The proposed methodology offers a promising approach to predictive maintenance of transformers in the electrical power industry and has the potential to improve the reliability and efficiency of distribution systems.

6. Maintenance Scheduling for 2021

According to the prediction for 2021, using the previously presented methodology, there will be 852 transformers that will present malfunction, 820 of which will be in Cauca's rural areas, which is consistent with past failure statistics. From Figure 8 and the relevant Table 3, it is obvious that the 10 kVA transformers remain a priority at risk, with 5 kVA and 15 kVA following. Additionally, in Table 3, the percentage results of the failures in transformers, related to the total transformer number (on each rated power), are presented as well. It is obvious that the higher the absolute number of the installed transformers (per rated power) the higher the percentage failure for the specific rated power. The residential sector receives the majority of the transformers' (96.2%) energy, making its consumers the most exposed to and impacted by the frequency of unexpected power outages. For transformers with a rated power of 100 kVA and between 125 kVA and 2000 kVA, there is no predicted transformer that will present malfunction. The impact of failure in a high-rated power transformer in comparison to a low one has some significant differences. First of all, in a high-rated power transformer, the number of non-power-supplied customers is greater, and consequently, the profit losses of the power companies are also higher. Additionally, the maintenance cost and replacement cost of a high-rated power transformer are also higher than a low-rated one.

As can be seen in Figure 8 and Table 3, the proposed methodology is compared to the methodology proposed in [33]. The methodology proposed in the current work predicts in general in every transformer's power, rating a smaller number of transformers that may present problems in comparison to [33]. The total predicted burned transformers for the methodology presented in [33] is 910, while for the AI methodology presented in this work, the number is 852. This difference of 58 transformers is not negligible. Taking into consideration that the proposed methodology presents a higher accuracy rate than that in [33], it has a positive impact on the maintenance of these transformers. The maintenance of the transformers that may be burned is more expensive than periodic maintenance with fewer spare parts that must be replaced and with fewer working hours. Consequently, the proposed methodology saves a considerable amount of money to the DSO that may be used in investments.

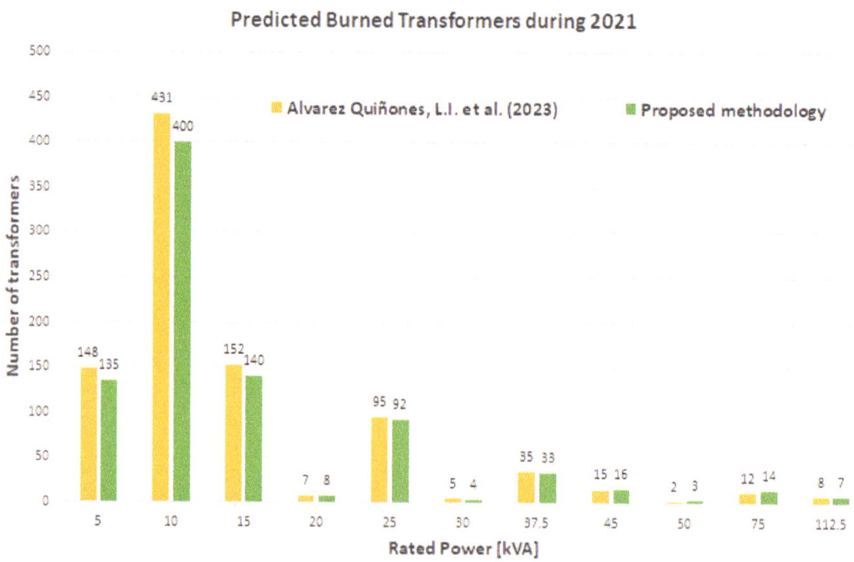

Figure 8. Predicted burned transformers during 2021 for both the methodology in [33] and the proposed methodology.

Table 3. Transformer data and predicted burned transformers during 2021 for both the methodology in [33] and the proposed methodology.

Rated Power [kVA]	Number of Transformers	Number of Predicted Burned Transformers			
		Methodology in [33]		Proposed Methodology	
			[%] *		[%] *
5	1571	148	0.93	135	0.85
10	3511	431	2.72	400	2.52
15	3981	152	0.96	140	0.88
20	13	7	0.04	8	0.05
25	2651	95	0.60	92	0.58
30	322	5	0.03	4	0.03
37.5	1057	35	0.22	33	0.21
45	686	15	0.09	16	0.10
50	305	2	0.01	3	0.02
75	1134	12	0.08	14	0.09
100	4	0	0.00	0	0.00
112.5	576	8	0.05	7	0.04
125	4	0	0.00	0	0.00
150	27	0	0.00	0	0.00
200	2	0	0.00	0	0.00
225	14	0	0.00	0	0.00
250	1	0	0.00	0	0.00
300	5	0	0.00	0	0.00
400	1	0	0.00	0	0.00
500	1	0	0.00	0	0.00
630	3	0	0.00	0	0.00
1000	1	0	0.00	0	0.00
1125	1	0	0.00	0	0.00
1250	1	0	0.00	0	0.00
2000	1	0	0.00	0	0.00
Total	**15,873**	**910**	5.73	**852**	5.37

*: Expresses the percentage of the transformer of the specific rated power to the total number of the installed transformers, which is 15,873.

7. Discussion and Limitations

Since power transformers are the foundation of the power system, which is a complex network, their efficient performance is essential to the system's dependable and secure operation. They are highly expensive and take a lot of time to maintain and replace if they are damaged because they are critical components. The biggest issues with power transformers are the various flaws that develop in them. These devices are subject to mechanical, thermal, and electrical stresses because of fluctuating loading and weather conditions. In the worst-case scenario, these shifting variables could cause several defects that would create abnormal circumstances and cascade failure. Transformers can be maintained in a variety of methods, including predictive, corrective, and preventative maintenance.

There are certain limitations in the proposed methodology. First of all, for the power transformers that break down, their related data are sparse, and traditional trained models perform poorly since there are not enough characteristics that can be learned. Additionally, the available data were for just two years (2019 and 2020). Although important for classification, several factors, such as the temperature during transformer operation, the oil level, and overloads, could not be measured and many transformers may also fail for unexplained reasons with no correlation with those mentioned in this work. Modern predictive maintenance tools should use a real-time monitoring system that analyzes gases using a variety of DGA techniques, collecting temperature from the transformer's winding and the environment, collecting data from the relays that protect the transformer for various threats (such as overvoltage, over frequency, overcurrent, etc.), and performing risk analysis by comparing measured data to historical databases. In the future, the use of such a system will help to improve prediction in transformer failure, saving costs for the DSOs.

From the current work, the following conclusions can be obtained:

(a) The majority of fault detection techniques focus on evaluating a single failure; however, many failures may occur simultaneously and are advised to be further studied.

(b) Other key and essential techniques for diagnosing transformer faults include acoustic signal processing and image identification, which have garnered considerable interest from power companies, academic institutions, and equipment operating units.

(c) The accuracy of prediction may be greatly increased by using the mined association rules between dissolved gas content and additional data (such as oil temperature, load, and winding temperature).

(d) As previously described, the suggested methodology uses a classification predictive model to identify the minimum distribution transformers that are vulnerable to failure. This methodology provides better accuracy than in [33] for the years 2019 and 2020 as they are depicted in Figure 6. Consequently, it will also present better prediction results for 2021 than the other researchers described in [33].

Consequently, (a), (b), and (c) need further study. Future work should collate these additional data, which must be gathered by a DSO on which the proposed methodology will be applied.

8. Conclusions

The recommended methodology employs a classification predictive model to identify with minimal error the number of transformers in the Cauca Department of Colombia that are very susceptible to failure. This was verified by training, testing, and validation using real data in Cauca. In accordance with prior failure statistics, the prognosis for 2021 states that 852 transformers would malfunction, 820 of which will be in rural Cauca. The 10 kVA transformers, and then the 5 kVA and 15 kVA transformers, will be the most at risk.

The reported results for application of ML methods to early detection of technical issues not only can help distribution system operator to increase the number of selected transformers for predictive maintenance but also can be beneficial for customer satisfaction to improve the amount of delivered energy. Early recognition and accurate diagnosis of technical issues are crucial to delay expensive problems as much as possible and improve the reliability of the network. Due to predictive maintenance, the mean time between failures improves the performance of distribution power transformers and it increases the expected lifetime of the transformers, a fact that both delays the transformer's replacement for some more years and saves funds for the distribution system operators.

The results illustrate that the use of ML on transformers' technical history data could speed up the process of technical maintenance of transformers and help find transformers for which major technical issues can occur. As future research, the proposed methodology could be applied to the Greek Distribution Network or/and the Greek Transmission System, taking into consideration the same parameters and some more (e.g., the dielectric strength of the transformer's insulation oil). A more cost-effective maintenance schedule for electric power distribution companies might be created with the help of a precise estimation of the usable life left in transformers.

Author Contributions: Conceptualization, V.V., G.F., C.P., V.C. and V.M.; methodology, V.V., G.F., V.C. and V.M.; software, V.V., C.P. and V.C.; validation, V.V., G.F., C.P., V.C. and V.M.; formal analysis, V.V. and V.M.; investigation V.V., G.F. and V.M.; resources, V.V., G.F., C.P., V.C. and V.M.; data curation, V.V., V.C. and V.M.; writing—original draft preparation, G.F. and V.C.; writing—review and editing, V.V., C.P. and V.M.; visualization, V.V., G.F., C.P., V.C. and V.M.; supervision, V.V. and V.M.; All authors have read and agreed to the published version of the manuscript.

Funding: This research received no external funding.

Conflicts of Interest: The authors declare no conflict of interest.

References

1. Kulkarni, S.V.; Khaparde, S.A. *Transformer Engineering Design, Technology, and Diagnostics*, 2nd ed.; CRC Press: Boca Raton, FL, USA, 2013.
2. Fotis, G.; Vita, V.; Maris, T.I. Risks in the European Transmission System and a Novel Restoration Strategy for a Power System after a Major Blackout. *Appl. Sci.* **2023**, *13*, 83. [CrossRef]
3. Vita, V.; Fotis, G.; Pavlatos, C.; Mladenov, V. A New Restoration Strategy in Microgrids after a Blackout with Priority in Critical Loads. *Sustainability* **2023**, *15*, 1974. [CrossRef]
4. Zafeiropoulou, M.; Mentis, I.; Sijakovic, N.; Terzic, A.; Fotis, G.; Maris, T.I.; Vita, V.; Zoulias, E.; Ristic, V.; Ekonomou, L. Forecasting Transmission and Distribution System Flexibility Needs for Severe Weather Condition Resilience and Outage Management. *Appl. Sci.* **2022**, *12*, 7334. [CrossRef]
5. Forcina, A.; Silvestr, I.L.; Di Bona, G.; Silvestri, A. Reliability allocation methods: A systematic literature review. *Qual. Reliab. Eng. Int.* **2020**, *36*, 2085–2107. [CrossRef]
6. Di Bona, G.; Forcina, A.; Falcone, D. Maintenance strategy design in a sintering plant based on a multicriteria approach. *Int. J. Manag. Decis. Mak.* **2018**, *17*, 29–49. [CrossRef]
7. Di Bona, G.; Cesarotti, V.; Arcese, G.; Gallo, T. Implementation of Industry 4.0 technology: New opportunities and challenges for maintenance strategy. *Procedia Comput. Sci.* **2021**, *180*, 424–429. [CrossRef]
8. Rajendra Prasad, U.; Vyjayanthi, C.; Jaison, K. Modeling and Detection of Inter-turn Faults in Distribution Transformer. In Proceedings of the 2019 8th International Conference on Power Systems (ICPS), Jaipur, India, 20–22 December 2019.
9. Hashemnia, N.; Abu-Siada, A.; Islam, S. Improved power transformer winding fault detection using FRA diagnostics—Part 1: Axial displacement simulation. *IEEE Trans. Dielectr. Electr. Insul.* **2015**, *22*, 556–563. [CrossRef]
10. Hashemnia, N.; Abu-Siada, A.; Islam, S. Improved power transformer winding fault detection using FRA diagnostics—Part 2: Radial deformation simulation. *IEEE Trans. Dielectr. Electr. Insul.* **2015**, *22*, 564–570. [CrossRef]
11. Rolim, J.R.; Morais, D.R. A hybrid tool for detection of incipient faults in transformers based on the dissolved gas analysis of insulating oil. *IEEE Trans. Power Deliv.* **2006**, *21*, 673–680.
12. Sarkar, S.; Sharma, T.; Baral, A.; Chatterjee, B.; Dey, D.; Chakravorti, S. An expert system approach for transformer insulation diagnosis combining conventional diagnostic tests and PDC, RVM data. *IEEE Trans. Dielectr. Electr. Insul.* **2014**, *21*, 882–891. [CrossRef]
13. Tenbohlen, S.; Coenen, S.; Djamali, M.; Müller, A.; Samimi, M.; Siegel, M. Diagnostic Measurements for Power Transformers. *Energies* **2016**, *9*, 347. [CrossRef]
14. N'cho, J.; Fofana, I.; Hadjadj, Y.; Beroual, A. Review of physicochemical-based diagnostic techniques for assessing insulation condition in aged transformers. *Energies* **2016**, *9*, 367. [CrossRef]
15. Kunicki, M.; Cichon, A.; Borucki, S. Measurements on partial discharge in on-site operating power transformer: A case study. *IET Gener. Transm. Distrib.* **2018**, *12*, 2487–2495. [CrossRef]
16. Christina, A.J.; Salam, M.A.; Rahman, Q.M.; Wen, F.; Ang, S.P.; Voon, W. Causes of transformer failures and diagnostic methods—A review. *Renew. Sustain. Energy Rev.* **2018**, *82*, 1442–1456.
17. Tang, X.; Wang, W.; Zhang, X.; Wang, E.; Li, X. On-Line Analysis of Oil-Dissolved Gas in Power Transformers Using Fourier Transform Infrared Spectrometry. *Energies* **2018**, *11*, 3192. [CrossRef]
18. Faiz, J.; Soleimani, M. Assessment of Computational Intelligence and Conventional Dissolved Gas Analysis Methods for Transformer Fault Diagnosis. *IEEE Trans. Dielectr. Electr. Insul.* **2018**, *25*, 1798–1806. [CrossRef]
19. Agarwal, S. Data Mining: Data Mining Concepts and Techniques. In Proceedings of the 2013 International Conference on Machine Intelligence and Research Advancement, Katra, India, 21–23 December 2013. [CrossRef]
20. Jiang, Y.; Cukic, B.; Ma, Y. Techniques for evaluating fault prediction models. *Empir. Softw. Eng.* **2008**, *13*, 561–595. [CrossRef]
21. Kesavaraj, G.; Sukumaran, S. A study on classification techniques in data mining. In Proceedings of the 4th International Conference on Computing, Communications and Networking Technologies (ICCCNT), Tiruchengode, India, 4–6 July 2013. [CrossRef]
22. Gill, P. *Electrical Power Equipment Maintenance and Testing*, 2nd ed.; CRC Press: Boca Raton, FL, USA, 2009.
23. Shayesteh, E.; Hilber, P. Reliability-centered asset management using component reliability importance. In Proceedings of the International Conference on Probabilistic Methods Applied to Power Systems (PMAPS), Beijing, China, 16–20 October 2016. [CrossRef]

24. Biswal, S.; Sabareesh, G.R. Design and development of a wind turbine test rig for condition monitoring studies. In Proceedings of the International Conference on Industrial Instrumentation and Control (ICIC), Pune, India, 28–30 May 2015; pp. 891–896.
25. Çınar, Z.M.; Abdussalam Nuhu, A.; Zeeshan, Q.; Korhan, O.; Asmael, M.; Safaei, B. Machine Learning in Predictive Maintenance towards Sustainable Smart Manufacturing in Industry 4.0. *Sustainability* **2020**, *12*, 8211. [CrossRef]
26. Erl, T.; Khattak, W.; Buhler, P. *Big Data Fundamentals Concepts, Drivers & Techniques*; Pearson Education Limited: New York, NY, USA, 2016.
27. Peres, R.S.; Dionisio Rocha, A.; Leitao, P.; Barata, J. Idarts towards intelligent data analysis and real-time supervision for industry 4.0. *Comput. Ind.* **2018**, *101*, 138–146. [CrossRef]
28. Zhang, K.; Yuan, F.; Guo, J.; Wang, G. A Novel Neural Network Approach to Transformer Fault Diagnosis Based on Momentum-Embedded BP Neural Network Optimized by Genetic Algorithm and Fuzzy c-Means. *Arab. J. Sci. Eng.* **2016**, *41*, 3451–3461. [CrossRef]
29. Yi, J.-H.; Wang, J.; Wang, G.-G. Improved probabilistic neural networks with self-adaptive strategies for transformer fault diagnosis problem. *Adv. Mech. Eng.* **2016**, *8*, 1687814015624832. [CrossRef]
30. Naresh, R.; Sharma, V.; Vashisth, M. An integrated neural fuzzy approach for fault diagnosis of transformers. *IEEE Trans. Power Deliv.* **2008**, *23*, 2017–2024. [CrossRef]
31. Freund, Y.; Schapire, R.E. Experiments with a new boosting algorithm. In Proceedings of the 13th International Conference on International Conference on Machine Learning, ICML, Bari, Italy, 3–6 July 1996; Morgan Kaufmann Publishers: San Francisco, CA, USA; pp. 148–156.
32. Diego-A Bravo, M.; Laura-I Alvarez, Q.; Carlos-A Lozano, M. Dataset of distribution transformers for predictive maintenance. *Data Brief* **2021**, *38*, 107454. [CrossRef]
33. Alvarez Quiñones, L.I.; Lozano-Moncada, C.A.; Bravo Montenegro, D.A. Machine learning for predictive maintenance scheduling of distribution transformers. *J. Qual. Maint. Eng.* **2022**, *29*, 188–202. [CrossRef]
34. Sambhi, S.; Sharma, H.; Bhadoria, V.; Kumar, P.; Chaurasia, R.; Chaurasia, G.S.; Fotis, G.; Vita, V.; Ekonomou, L.; Pavlatos, C. Economic Feasibility of a Renewable Integrated Hybrid Power Generation System for a Rural Village of Ladakh. *Energies* **2022**, *15*, 9126. [CrossRef]
35. Sun, P.; Sima, W.; Yang, M.; Lan, X.; Wu, J. Study on voltage-number characteristics of transformer insulation under transformer invading non-standard lightning impulses. *IEEE Trans. Dielectr. Electr. Insul.* **2015**, *22*, 3582–3591. [CrossRef]
36. Chen, Z.; Zhou, Q.; Du, B.; Zhang, Y.; Ding, L. Electromagnetic Transient Calculation and Protective Measures of Transformers Under Lightning Overvoltage. *IEEE Trans. Dielectr. Electr. Insul.* **2022**, *29*, 718–726. [CrossRef]
37. Christodoulou, C.A.; Ekonomou, L.; Fotis, G.; Harkiolakis, N.; Stathopulos, I.A. Optimization of Hellenic overhead high voltage transmission lines lightning protection. *Energy J.* **2009**, *34*, 502–509. [CrossRef]
38. Christodoulou, C.A.; Vita, V.; Ekonomou, L. Studies for the more effective protection of MV/LV substations against lightning overvoltages. *Int. J. Circuits Electron.* **2017**, *2*, 11–15.
39. Ekonomou, L.; Fotis, G.; Vita, V.; Mladenov, V. Distributed Generation Islanding Effect on Distribution Networks and End User Loads Using the Master-Slave Islanding Method. *J. Power Energy Eng.* **2016**, *4*, 1–24. [CrossRef]
40. Naim, W.; Hilber, P.; Shayesteh, E. Impact of geomagnetic disturbances on power transformers: Risk assessment of extreme events and data availability. *Life Cycle Reliab. Saf. Eng.* **2022**, *11*, 11–18. [CrossRef]
41. Abi-Samra, N.C.; Forsten, K.R.; Entriken, R. Sample Effects of extreme weather on power systems and components part I: Sample effects on distribution systems. In Proceedings of the IEEE PES General Meeting, Minneapolis, MN, USA, 25–29 July 2010; pp. 1–3. [CrossRef]
42. Adewumi, O.B.; Fotis, G.; Vita, V.; Nankoo, D.; Ekonomou, L. The Impact of Distributed Energy Storage on Distribution and Transmission Networks' Power Quality. *Appl. Sci.* **2022**, *12*, 6466. [CrossRef]
43. Linhjell, D.T.; Painter, J.; Lundgaard, L.E.; Hansen, W. Aging of oil impregnated paper in power transformers. *IEEE Trans. Power Deliv.* **2004**, *19*, 230–239. [CrossRef]
44. Muhamad, N.A.; Phung, B.T.; Blackburn, T.R.; Lai, K.X. Comparative Study and Analysis of DGA Methods for Transformer Mineral Oil. In Proceedings of the IEEE Lausanne Power Tech, Lausanne, Switzerland, 1–5 July 2007; pp. 45–50. [CrossRef]
45. Fotis, G.; Vita, V.; Ekonomou, L. Machine Learning Techniques for the Prediction of the Magnetic and Electric Field of Electrostatic Discharges. *Electronics* **2022**, *11*, 1858. [CrossRef]
46. Fotis, G.; Ekonomou, L.; Maris, T.I.; Liatsis, P. Development of an artificial neural network software tool for the assessment of the electromagnetic field radiating by electrostatic discharges. *IEE Proc. Sci. Meas. Technol.* **2007**, *1*, 261–269. [CrossRef]
47. Christodoulou, C.A.; Vita, V.; Voglitsis, D.; Milushev, G.; Ekonomou, L. A heuristic method for the reduction of the outage rate of high-voltage substations due to atmospheric overvoltages. *Appl. Sci.* **2018**, *8*, 273. [CrossRef]
48. Venkataswamy, R.; Rao, K.U.; Meena, P. Internet of things-based metaheuristic reliability centered maintenance of distribution transformers. In *IOP Conference Series: Earth and Environmental Science*; IOP Publishing Ltd.: Bristol, UK, 2020; Volume 463.
49. Sarajcev, P.; Jakus, D.; Vasilj, J. Optimal scheduling of power transformers preventive maintenance with Bayesian statistical learning and influence diagrams. *J. Clean. Prod.* **2020**, *258*, 120850. [CrossRef]
50. Abbasi, M.K.; Dezfuli, H. Smart Maintenance Planning for Distribution Transformers Using Discrete-time Markov Chain. In Proceedings of the 26th International Electrical Power Distribution Conference (EPDC), Tehran, Iran, 11–12 May 2022; pp. 8–17.

51. Xie, H.; Yingjie, T.; Zhu, W.; Zhongyu, H. Heavy overload forecasting of distribution transformers based on neural network. In Proceedings of the 2019 International Conference on Computer Science Communication and Network Security (CSCNS2019), Sanya, China, 22–23 December 2019; Volume 309.
52. Yang, Z.; Liu, J.; Chen, Z. Numerical analysis of transformer temperature based on computational fluid dynamics. *J. Eng. Thermophys.* **2018**, *39*, 2187–2191.
53. Ameli, A.; Agheb, M.; Jafari, M. Assessment of transformer insulation life using finite element method. *IEEE Trans. Dielectr. Electr. Insul.* **2019**, *26*, 1234–1244.
54. Babaei, E.; Rashidi, R. A numerical model for predicting partial discharge inception voltage in power transformers. *High Volt.* **2019**, *4*, 154–159.
55. Huang, G.; Zhou, H.; Ding, X.; Zhang, R. Extreme Learning Machine for Regression and Multiclass Classification. *IEEE Trans. Syst. Man Cybern. Part B Cybern.* **2012**, *42*, 513–529. [CrossRef] [PubMed]
56. Xiao, Z.; Liang, S.; Wang, J.; Chen, P.; Yin, X.; Zhang, L.; Song, J. Use of General Regression Neural Networks for Generating the GLASS Leaf Area Index Product from Time-Series MODIS Surface Reflectance. *IEEE Trans. Geosci. Remote Sens.* **2014**, *52*, 209–223. [CrossRef]
57. Scornet, E. Random forests and Kernel methods. *IEEE Trans. Inf. Theory* **2016**, *62*, 1485–1500. [CrossRef]
58. Breiman, L. Random forests. *Mach. Learn.* **2001**, *45*, 5–32. [CrossRef]
59. Natekin, A.; Knoll, A. Gradient boosting machines, a tutorial. *Front. Neurorobotics* **2013**, *7*, 21. [CrossRef]
60. Li, X.; Bai, R.B. Freight Vehicle travel time prediction using gradient boosting regression tree. In Proceedings of the 2016 15th IEEE International Conference on Machine Learning and Applications, Anaheim, CA, USA, 18–20 December 2016; IEEE: Piscataway, NJ, USA, 2016; pp. 1010–1015.
61. LeCun, Y.; Bengio, Y.; Hinton, G. Deep learning. *Nature* **2015**, *521*, 436–444. [CrossRef]
62. Espadoto, M.; Hirata, N.S.T.; Telea, A.C. Deep learning multidimensional projections. *Inf. Vis.* **2020**, *19*, 247–269. [CrossRef]
63. Mokhtari, S.; Abbaspour, A.; Yen, K.K.; Sargolzaei, A. A Machine Learning Approach for Anomaly Detection in Industrial Control Systems Based on Measurement Data. *Electronics* **2021**, *10*, 407. [CrossRef]
64. López-Gonzales, J.L.; Castro Souza, R.; Leite Coelho da Silva, F.; Carbo-Bustinza, N.; Ibacache-Pulgar, G.; Calili, R.F. Simulation of the Energy Efficiency Auction Prices via the Markov Chain Monte Carlo Method. *Energies* **2020**, *13*, 4544. [CrossRef]
65. Nam, S.; Hur, J. Probabilistic Forecasting Model of Solar Power Outputs Based on the Naïve Bayes Classifier and Kriging Models. *Energies* **2018**, *11*, 2982. [CrossRef]
66. Mosavi, A.; Salimi, M.; Faizollahzadeh Ardabili, S.; Rabczuk, T.; Shamshirband, S.; Varkonyi-Koczy, A.R. State of the Art of Machine Learning Models in Energy Systems, a Systematic Review. *Energies* **2019**, *12*, 1301. [CrossRef]
67. Mohanty, S.; Subudhi, B. A critical appraisal of performance metrics for machine learning based predictive models: A survey. *Artif. Intell. Rev.* **2019**, *51*, 93–129.
68. Saxena, A.; Celaya, J.R.; Saha, B. Machine learning-based remaining useful life prediction techniques for equipment maintenance: A review. *Mech. Syst. Signal Process.* **2018**, *104*, 799–834.
69. Kovalenko, I.; Bozhko, S. Fault diagnosis of power transformers based on artificial neural networks. *Electr. Eng.* **2019**, *101*, 943–952.
70. Tsai, M.F.; Lin, C.Y.; Chen, Y.C. Estimation of the remaining life of transformers using an adaptive neuro-fuzzy inference system. *Energies* **2014**, *7*, 2925–2937.
71. Bravo, M.; Diego, A.; Lozano, C.; Alvarez, L. Dataset of Distribution Transformers at Cauca Department (Colombia). *Mendeley Data* **2021**, *4*. [CrossRef]

electronics

MDPI

Article

Long Short-Term Memory Network-Based HVDC Systems Fault Diagnosis under Knowledge Graph

Qian Chen [1], Jiyang Wu [1], Qiang Li [1], Ximing Gao [2], Rongxing Yu [3], Jianbao Guo [4], Guangqiang Peng [4] and Bo Yang [3,*]

[1] EHV Power Transmission Company of China Southern Power Grid Co., Ltd., Guangzhou 510530, China
[2] China Southern Power Grid Co., Ltd., Guangzhou 510530, China
[3] EHV Power Transmission Company of China Southern Power Grid Co., Ltd., Dali Bureau, Dali 671000, China
[4] Maintenance and Test Center of CSG EHV Power Transmission Company of China Southern Power Grid Co., Ltd., Guangzhou 510530, China
* Correspondence: yangbo_ac@outlook.com

Abstract: To enhance the precision of fault diagnosis for high-voltage direct-current (HVDC) systems by effectively extracting various types of fault characteristics, a fault diagnosis method based on the long short-term memory network (LSTM) is proposed in this paper. The method relies on a knowledge graph platform and is developed using measured data from four fault types in an HVDC substation located in southwest China. Firstly, a knowledge graph for the HVDC systems is constructed, then the fault waveform data is preprocessed and divided into a training set and a test set. Various optimizers are employed to train and test the LSTM. The proposed strategy's accuracy is calculated and compared with recurrent neural network (RNN), eXtreme Gradient Boosting (XGBoost), support vector machine (SVM), Naive Bayes classifier, probabilistic neural networks (PNN), and classification learner (CL), which are commonly used in fault diagnosis. Results indicate that the proposed method achieves an accuracy of over 95%, which is 30% higher than RNN, 8% higher than XGBoost, 4% higher than SVM, 7% higher than Naive Bayes, 40% higher than PNN, and 42% higher than classification learner (CL), respectively; the method also has the minimum time cost, fully demonstrating its superiority and effectiveness compared to other methods.

Keywords: knowledge graph; HVDC systems; fault diagnosis; LSTM; RNN; XGBoost; SVM; Naive Bayes; classifier; PNN; CL

1. Introduction

With the accentuation of the world's energy problems and the development of new energy generation, energy transmission methods are being transformed [1,2]. High-voltage direct-current (HVDC) transmission systems in long-distance transmission have numerous advantages; e.g., no inductive resistance, no synchronization, etc., compared to the traditional high-voltage AC transmission method, which is an important guarantee for the construction of long-distance, large-scale, large-capacity grid interconnection and power exchange. The fault diagnosis of HVDC systems is different from the traditional transmission method, so it is momentous to quickly and safely diagnose the fault of HVDC systems. In recent years, many fault diagnosis methods have been developed and applied to HVDC systems. For example, Reference [3] studied the impact of the lightning current peak and grounding resistance on shielding fault flashover in Yunnan to Guizhou 500 kV high-voltage direct current transmission systems. Reference [4] analyzed the mechanism of high short circuit current in the DC near areas caused by converter transformer during single-phase grounding faults. Work [5] focused on studying lightning overvoltage at the neutral point of the HVDC converter transformer to ensure the safe and stable operation of the HVDC system. Additionally, work [6] analyzed the grounding mode of the neutral point of the converter transformer to improve the stability of the 800 kV HVDC system.

With the change of power grid structure, higher requirements are increasingly put on the table for the performance of power grid operation. Along with the popularization of information technology, fault prediction and diagnosis methods based on the Internet of things and artificial intelligence have begun to be applied. Artificial intelligence can learn and adapt to people's processing experience and realize human-machine collaborative operation, so it can also be solved well in the face of complex and diverse problems. Artificial neural networks have started to be used well in power systems fault diagnosis in recent years due to their efficient processing of noisy data. The literature [7] uses a support vector machine (SVM) that can implement nonlinear classification and regression, which have been applied in some data modeling fields. Currently, the problems in the development of SVM are low accuracy and poor utilization of hidden information of data. Moreover, a convolutional neural network (CNN)-based fault diagnosis method for power grids is presented in the literature [8]. The network is gradually tested by filtering and layer-by-layer incremental stacking construction, and then the network parameters are adjusted using a network layer optimization strategy, and the deep fault features are mined to minimize cross-entropy. In the literature [9], considering the effect of random noise on the measurement results, a collaborative filter is used to filter the output of the HVDC systems, and then virtual faults are introduced according to the state equation of the HVDC to construct a fault tracking estimator. Work [10] applies eXtreme Gradient Boosting (XGBoost) to fault diagnosis in actual HVDC systems, providing a reliable tool for classifying fault data sets in power grids. Study [11] applies classification learner (CL) to the operation and maintenance of intelligent distribution system equipment to improve the intelligence level of detection, significantly improving detection efficiency and the distribution network equipment management level. The effective use of the above-mentioned artificial intelligence methods has ensured the safe operation of the power systems to a certain extent and has been superior to the earlier diagnostic methods [12,13].

In recent years, knowledge graph-based fault diagnosis methods for power systems have been continuously proposed and have had an active effect on the fault diagnosis of power systems [14,15]. With four characteristics of dynamism, spatiality, correlation, and knowledge dependency, the knowledge graph can not only visualize knowledge in the form of directed graphs and obtain the relationships among them through visualization models, but can also complete the accurate search of massive knowledge information in a very short time through the search function of computers and perform statistical analysis on them [16,17]. By combining database technology and data mining methods, the connections and rules between data can be discovered, thus improving the various performances of fault diagnosis. When a large amount of data is accumulated to a certain extent, after analyzing and processing these data people can find effective information of interest from these data [18,19].

The fault knowledge graph of HVDC systems is a normal domain knowledge graph with vivid concepts and relationship models, which can realize the continuous accumulation of power systems knowledge. The key knowledge elements extracted from the fault data collected by various means can be effectively integrated through standardized representation and various relationships, thus continuously expanding the scope of domain knowledge, and also providing basic elements for intelligent application and the visual display of knowledge [20,21]. The literature [22] proposed a knowledge graph-based intelligent fault diagnosis method for substation equipment, which established a fault diagnosis framework consisting of five stages, i.e., fault data governance, domain dictionary construction, knowledge graph construction, distributed vector representation, and fault relationship inference. In the literature [22], a knowledge graph-based knowledge base construction method for power equipment faults is proposed for complex power equipment and its operation and maintenance involving a large amount of data such as equipment information, fault information, real-time monitoring information, and maintenance information.

The distributed word vector representation of natural language words provides a new basis for the application of different artificial intelligence methods in natural language processing. Knowledge graph relational reasoning is effective for knowledge validation, prediction, and inference. This research aims to develop a fault diagnosis technology framework based on small sample machine learning and multi-parameter fusion to address the lack of collection carriers and intelligent means for fault anomaly analysis in HVDC systems.

This paper raises a fault diagnosis strategy for HVDC systems based on the LSTM under the knowledge graph and classifies faults into four categories, i.e., single-phase faults of DC-side transmission lines, phase-to-phase faults of DC-side transmission lines, faults of converter valve arms, and faults of converter valve groups [20]. The advantages of neural networks in data classification applications include high classification accuracy and fast running speed [18,19]. By extracting the fault characteristics of fault waveforms, the LSTM network can be applied to quickly and accurately classify various types of faults and compare them with recurrent neural network (RNN) [20], XGBoost, SVM [23], Naive Bayes [24], probabilistic neural networks (PNN) [25], and classification learner (CL) [26]; this solves the shortcomings of RNN that tend to forget earlier fault information when the fault sequence is too long, and solves the poor performance of SVM in multi-classification situations. Consequently, the test results show that the raised strategy has excellent behavior and high accuracy in the fault diagnosis of HVDC systems.

2. Knowledge Graph of HVDC Systems

The knowledge graph is a kind of abandonment of traditional text-based matching search, which displays structured entity information corresponding to the retrieved content after understanding the user's search intent. The knowledge graph is a knowledge base with a directed graph structure that allows the representation of natural language in a structured graph for the storage, management, and representation of the knowledge base [27,28].

Knowledge graphs form graph-structured fact databases with nodes and edges between nodes. The nodes refer to entities or concepts in the data source, and the edges represent the relationships between entities or concepts. They work by extracting the semantic and structured data from textual information and expressing the information in the data in the form of an "entity-relationship-entity" knowledge triad. Finally, a web-like knowledge structure is built, which can store knowledge and express semantics more accurately at the same time [29]. This structure has the advantages of easy understanding and presentation.

As shown in Figure 1, the construction of HVDC systems knowledge graphs includes four steps: knowledge extraction, knowledge fusion, knowledge computing, and knowledge application.

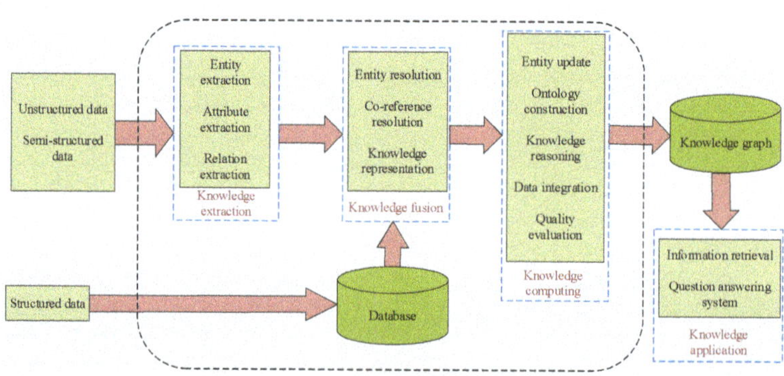

Figure 1. Steps of knowledge graph construction.

Knowledge data mainly includes some power industry standards and specifications, as well as some fault data [30,31]. Knowledge extraction is a process of searching and extracting needed data from massive, disorganized data with different sources in an automated way. Knowledge fusion is to integrate the description information of the same entity or concept from multiple data sources and eliminate the connotation conflict. Knowledge computing is a dynamic process which requires the quality assessment of the integrated new knowledge to add the part that meets the requirements into the knowledge base, conduct knowledge reasoning, expand the existing knowledge, and obtain new knowledge. The knowledge graph focuses on the realization of knowledge visualization based on data visualization, so that the knowledge in complex data relations can be intuitively represented. In practical application, the concrete form of visualization is often combined with the characteristics of the problem to be solved to carry out the diversified design.

Knowledge application is the main goal of knowledge graph construction. Through knowledge application, fault characteristics can be analyzed quickly and accidents can be located accurately. By combining fault data with the knowledge graph, fault causes can be rapidly discovered and solved, which greatly improves the management, operation, and maintenance level and efficiency.

Combining artificial intelligence techniques with traditional databases can constitute a knowledge graph. It is an intelligent database that allows knowledge to be managed according to a certain structure [32]. By introducing a knowledge graph in HVDC systems, relevant data from fault data information can be mined and useful information can be extracted. It is also possible to aggregate the scattered knowledge, thus improving the ability to analyze data. By developing and constructing industry-leading bottom-up human-machine collaborative DC knowledge systems based on large models and driven by big data, the scale, quality, and construction efficiency of the knowledge graph can be significantly improved compared with the traditional top-down graph construction technology [33,34], as shown in Figure 2.

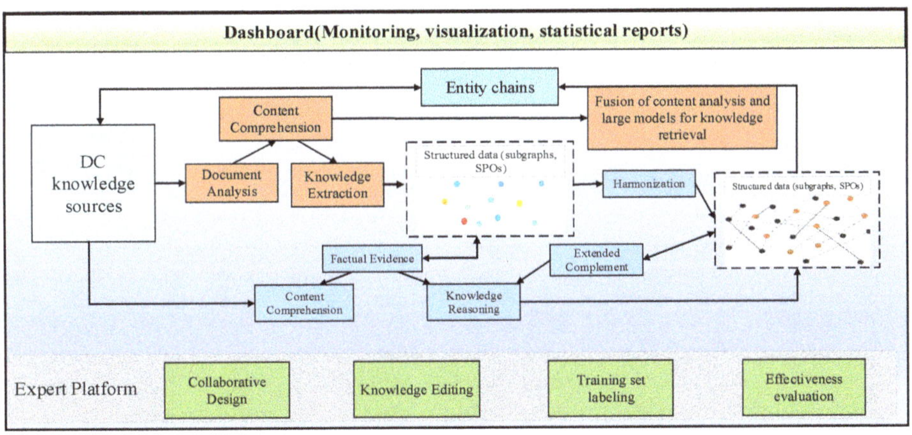

Figure 2. Diagram of construction of DC knowledge systems.

Here, the DC knowledge source is to accumulate massive DC source data, including systems and standards, operation and maintenance information, engineering information, major technical research information, etc. The DC knowledge base is DC knowledge for business personnel to query, browse and learn, which is produced by fragmented reorganization based on DC knowledge sources and expert experience precipitation. The DC knowledge graph is the DC knowledge for machine understanding and reasoning application, which is produced by the latest bottom-up human-machine collaborative graph construction technology [35].

In HVDC systems, knowledge comes from a wide range of sources. One part is the production data in the operation and maintenance process, and the other part is the technical update to continuously enrich the HVDC knowledge systems. As the knowledge comes from a wide range of sources and in various formats, it is necessary to sort out the knowledge to better explore the application value of knowledge. The construction is to create a graph by collecting and processing relevant knowledge and exploring the relationship between knowledge, which can quickly retrieve relevant information according to keywords and enhance the efficiency of fault diagnosis.

To address the lack of data collection carriers and intelligent means for fault and abnormality analysis in DC transmission systems, and to develop a fault diagnosis method, risk analysis, and decision-making technology for systems, the article uses small sample machine learning and multi-parameter fusion to build a fault diagnosis technology architecture. Figure 3 illustrates the knowledge graph-based framework for fault handling and risk analysis in the Tianshengqiao-Guangzhou system. The high accuracy and security requirements for fault diagnosis in this system are efficiently met with the help of the knowledge graph. The knowledge graph also allows for rapid fault treatment.

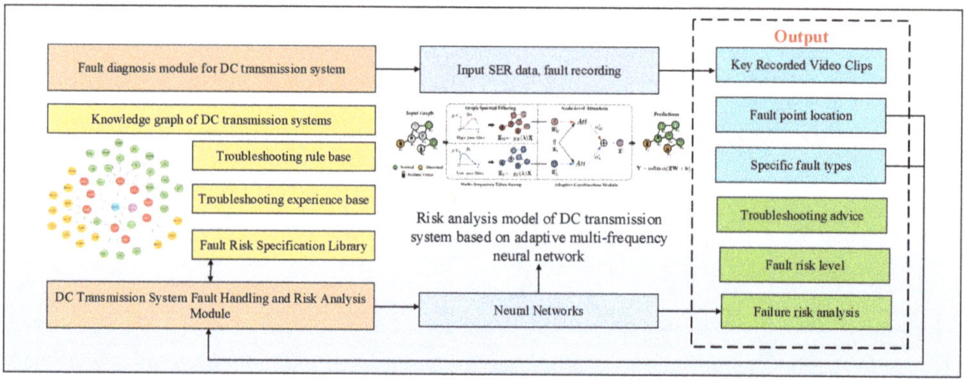

Figure 3. Fault handling and risk analysis framework based on knowledge graph of DC transmission systems.

The abnormalities are recorded in the Sequence of Events Record (SER) data, which is unstructured document data. The relevant information on the equipment is stored in the resource management library, which is structured data. Meanwhile, each manufacturer has product documentation and alarm descriptions, which are semi-structured data [36,37]. Based on these data, we extract and fuse them to build the knowledge graph and extract the knowledge elements from the data and store them in the pattern layer and data layer of the knowledge base [38]. The knowledge graph model of HVDC systems fault diagnosis is constructed for fault discrimination and analysis. By establishing the knowledge graph, one can directly access the graph information, which can significantly enhance the capability and efficiency of the system in troubleshooting, and improve the stable operation of the system.

The article raises a fault diagnosis strategy based on LSTM under the knowledge graph of DC transmission systems and realizes intelligent fault diagnosis through artificial intelligence technology [39], which provides an important guarantee for stable operation and efficient management of HVDC systems.

The construction of the knowledge graph has greatly promoted the development of the power system [40]. Fault diagnosis is a core purpose of the knowledge graph [41], as shown in Figure 4. By diagnosing various faults and integrating them into the system, future similar faults can be quickly and accurately analyzed, greatly improving the intelligence of power system operation management.

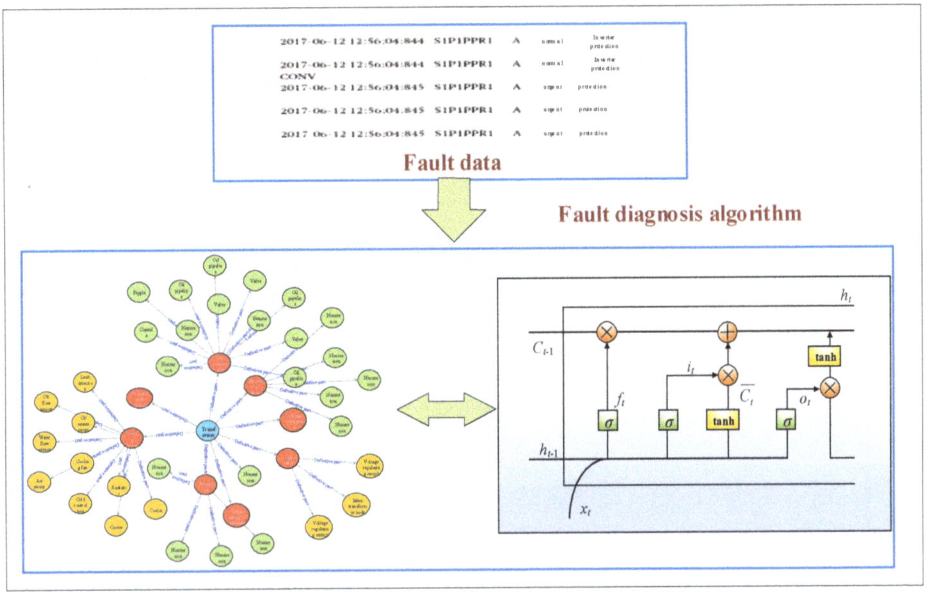

Figure 4. Application of knowledge graph in fault diagnosis.

3. Long Short-Term Memory Network

LSTM is a special recurrent neural network structure [42]. LSTM has a memory function and is suitable for modeling sequential data. When the individual sequence used for training is too long, the traditional RNN will easily forget the information from the previous more distant period, which largely limits the application of RNN. Therefore, LSTM corrects the traditional RNN by designing gating units. The structure of LSTM cyclic units is shown in Figure 5.

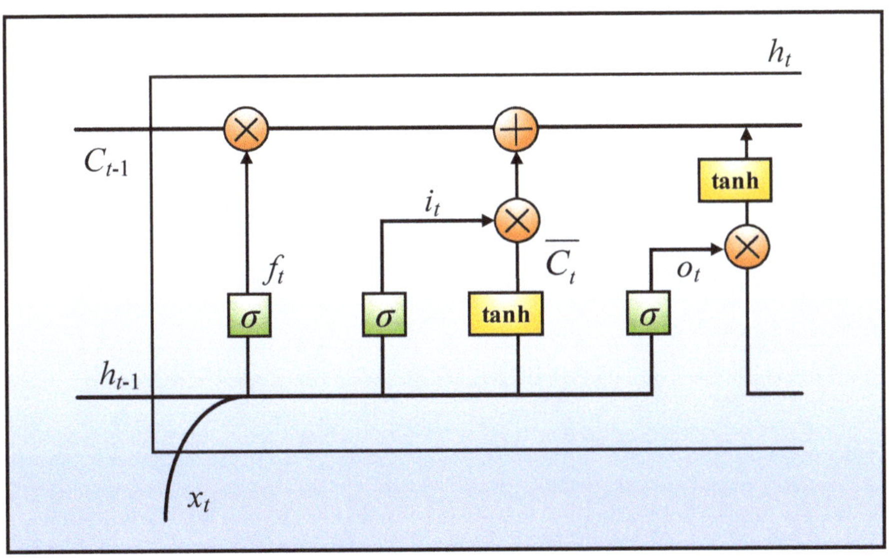

Figure 5. Structure of LSTM network unit.

LSTM solves the problem of long-term dependence, which is common in general recurrent neural networks, by setting forgetting gates, input gates, and output gates to flexibly transfer and express information in a long-term sequence without causing useful information from long ago to be forgotten. The LSTM long-term control structure [42] is shown in Figure 6.

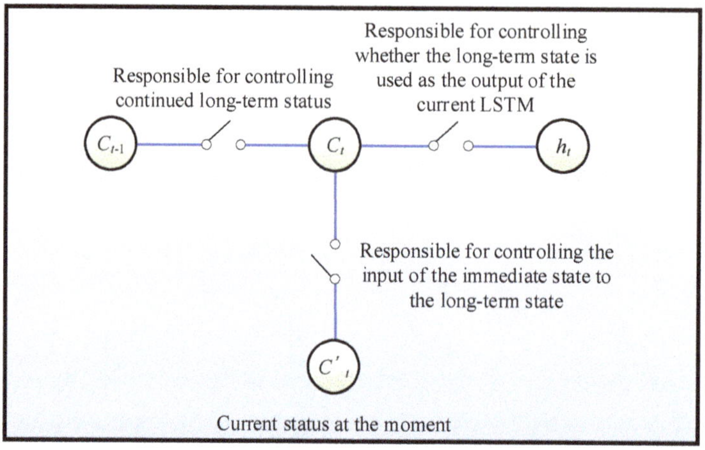

Figure 6. LSTM long-term state control structure diagram.

Longer time series of model inputs need to be considered when using the training model for the following reasons:

(1) Due to the high reliability of HVDC systems and few fault samples, previous data should be considered in model training, which is conducive to improving the accuracy of model training;

(2) The HVDC systems record the voltage U and the current I. Failures at different locations of the HVDC systems will affect the voltage U and the current I at subsequent recording locations. To ensure the accuracy of network training, it is necessary to consider the input of a longer time series.

The LSTM proposed in this paper solves the problem of long-term dependence, which is common in general recurrent neural networks, by setting forgetting gates, input gates, and output gates to flexibly transfer and express information in long-time sequences and to not cause useful information from long ago to be forgotten [43]. At the same time, the proposed fault diagnosis method based on the LSTM model does not require feature extraction and screening, which not only reduces the difficulty of using machine learning for fault diagnosis training, but also avoids fault prediction caused by improper feature selection. Therefore, it is very suitable for HVDC systems fault diagnosis.

In this paper, the sigmoid function is used as the activation function of the gating unit, and the inverse hyperbolic tangent function is designed as the activation function of the unit state and output [44].

4. Fault Diagnosis Method of HVDC Systems Based on Long Short-Term Memory Network under Knowledge Graph

LSTM is used to diagnose faults in HVDC systems based on all stored fault data by the China Southern Power Grid. The project in question is the Tianshengqiao (Guangxi Province, China)-Guangzhou (Guangdong Province, China) power transmission project, with a voltage level of ±500 kV, a length of 960 km, and a rated power of 1800 MW. Figure 7 shows the circuit diagram of the HVDC project, while Figure 8 shows the specific electrical diagram of fault points and types in the HVDC system.

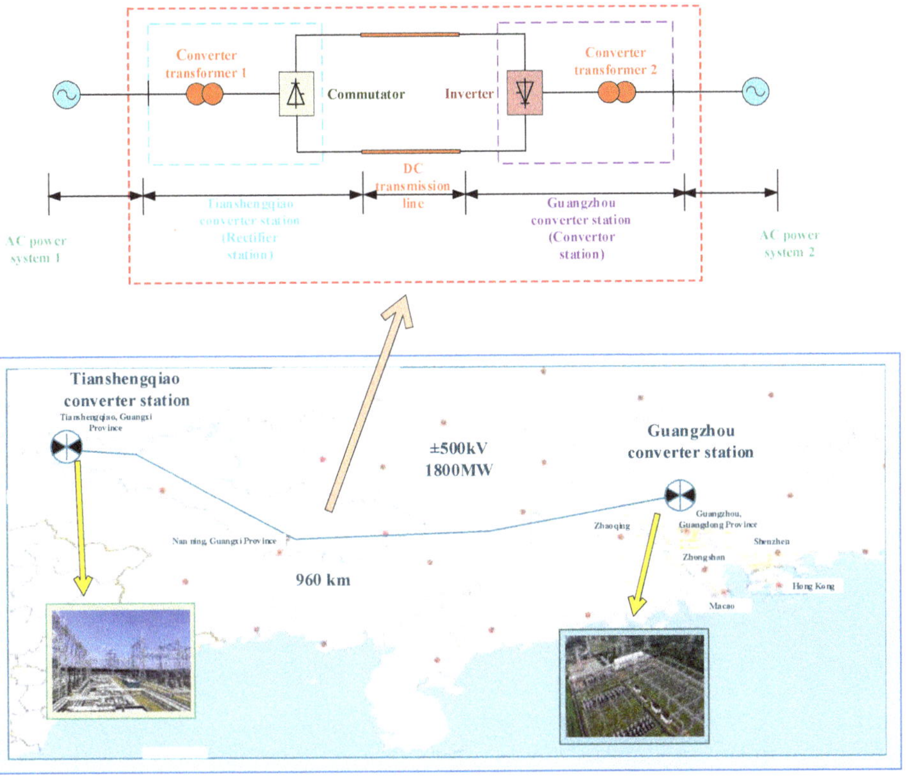

Figure 7. Schematic diagram of Tianshengqiao-Guangzhou HVDC project.

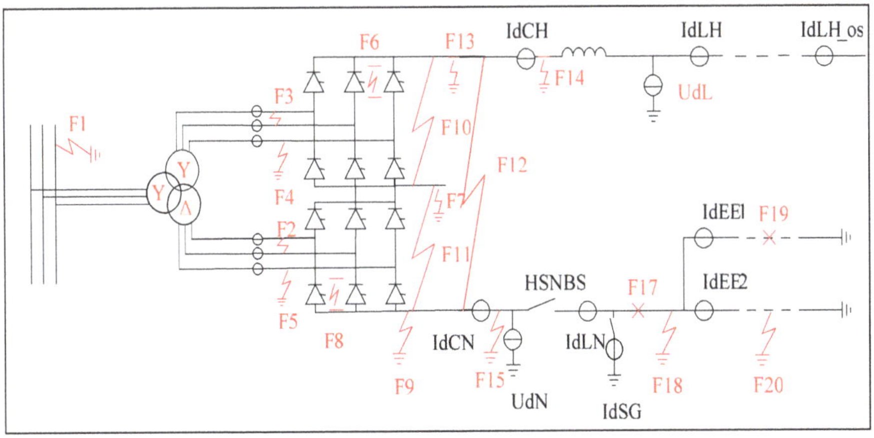

Figure 8. Main fault points of a substation in the southwest power grid of China.

Table 1 summarizes fault types corresponding to each point number. The original data set includes waveform data for 15 cycles before and after each fault, totaling 0.5 s. The data preprocessing involves concatenating 11 channel data of each sample for each fault type and stacking them to create a full fault data set. Next, 80% of the data is randomly selected for training and 20% for testing.

Table 1. Fault type of a substation fault point in Southwest Power Grid.

Fault Point	Fault Type	Fault Point	Fault Type
F1	single-phase ground short circuit	F1	Three-phase grounding short circuit
F1	Interphase short circuit	F3	Interphase short circuit
F2	Interphase short circuit	F4	single-phase short circuit to ground
F5	single-phase short circuit to ground	F6	Y1 bridge short circuit
F6	Y2 bridge short circuit	F6	Y3 bridge short circuit
F6	Y4 bridge short circuit	F6	Y5 bridge short circuit
F6	Y6 bridge short circuit	F8	D1 bridge short circuit
F8	D2 bridge short circuit	F8	D3 bridge short circuit
F8	D4 bridge short circuit	F8	D5 bridge short circuit
F8	D6 bridge short circuit	F9	outlet fault at high-pressure side of Y valve
F10	Y valve short circuit	F11	D valve short circuit
F12	valve short circuit	F13	outlet fault at high-pressure side of Y valve
F14	high voltage bus fault	F14	high voltage bus fault
F15	neutral bus fault	F16	line ground fault
F17	neutral busbar disconnection	F18	neutral bus grounding
F19	ground electrode line disconnection	F20	grounding electrode line grounding

In the extraction of the recorded data, 11 representative signal channels are collected, and the specific signal meaning descriptions are shown in Table 2. Note that the sign "n.s." in Table 2 indicates not specified.

Table 2. Signal name and meaning description.

Signal Name	Signal Meaning Description	Signal Name	Signal Meaning Description
UAC_IN_L1	A-phase AC voltage, V	IVD_L1	AC at valve side A of bridge D, A
UAC_IN_L2	B-phase AC voltage, V	IVD_L2	AC at valve side B of bridge D, A
UAC_IN_L3	C-phase AC voltage, V	IVD_L3	AC at valve side B of bridge D, A
IVY_L1	A-phase AC at Y-bridge valve side, A	UDL	DC line voltage, V
IVY_L2	B-phase AC at Y-bridge valve side, A	UDN	Neutral bus voltage, V
IVY_L3	C-phase AC at Y-bridge valve side, A	n.s.	n.s.

The fault diagnosis strategy of HVDC systems based on LSTM under the knowledge graph is used for fault diagnosis [45,46], and the validation of the presented method is confirmed; the LSTM flow is shown in Figure 9.

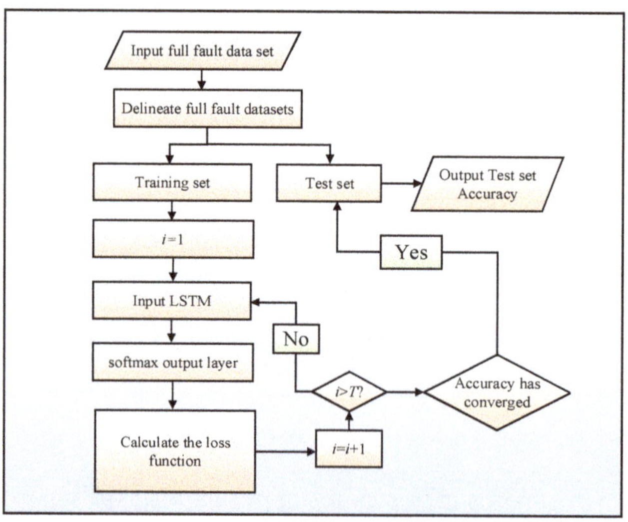

Figure 9. Flow chart of LSTM-based fault diagnosis algorithm.

The specific implementation process: first, the full failure data set is extracted according to the fault waveform, and then the 11 channels of each fault data sample are concatenated in turn, and stacked according to the number of samples to form a full fault data set. The collected fault data are processed in the format of [*datatem*, *target*], where *datatem* is the collected fault data and *target* is the various fault type labels corresponding to the fault category to which the fault data in *datatem* belongs [47].

After preprocessing the data, the sample data are randomly divided into 20% and 80% of the test and training sets. By continuously learning the training set, the model can mine the intrinsic relationship between the systems fault data and the fault categories and thus can predict the type of faults on the test set. For instance, 11 channel data waveforms corresponding to the four types of faults about HVDC systems are shown in Figure 10.

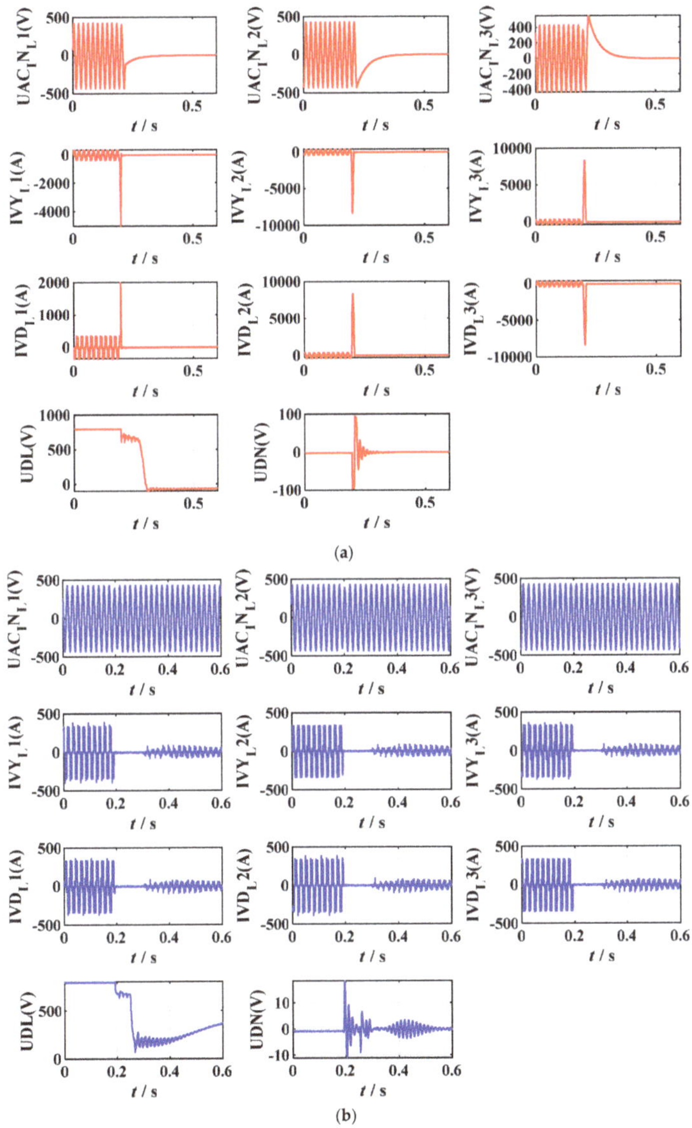

Figure 10. *Cont.*

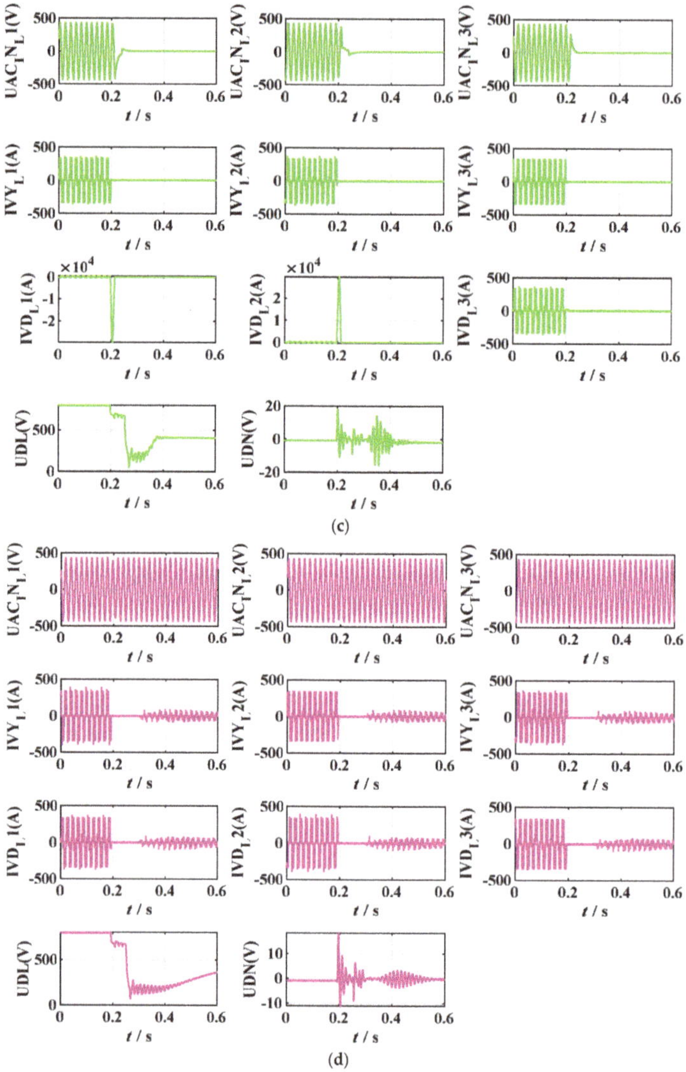

Figure 10. Diagnosis waveform of HVDC four fault types. (**a**) DC-side transmission line single-phase fault; (**b**) fault of converter valve arm; (**c**) fault of converter valve group; and (**d**) DC-side transmission line interphase fault.

5. Case Studies

All simulation experiments in this paper are run under the Python Constant Source Cloud_GPUSHARE environment on a personal computer configured with a 2.90 GHz Intel (R) Core (TM) i5-9400 CPU, 32.0 GB RAM, and 64-bit Windows 10.

5.1. LSTM Network Parameter Settings

The fault data is substituted into the knowledge graph to analyze and process the fault data. The fault data is then divided into 409 samples with 33,000 dimensions and combined with the probability of previous failures in the knowledge graph database; the data is divided into training data sets and test data sets with the optimal solution; four fault types are extracted according to the knowledge graph; and the output target dimension is set as [1–4], where 1, 2, 3, 4 represent single-phase faults of DC-side transmission lines, faults of converter valve arms, faults of converter valve groups, and phase-to-phase faults of DC-side transmission lines, respectively. Among these, the test data set will be used to verify its performance. In addition, 11 channel data waveforms measured from the fault recording device installed along the transmission line of Tianshengqiao-Guangzhou and the converter station (Niucong and Xindong) fault data from 2018–2022, which correspond to four types of faults in HVDC systems, are shown in Figure 11. It can be seen from the graph that the waveform diagrams of the four types of faults are very inconsistent and all have their unique characteristics. The setting of the hidden layer parameters is crucial to the training of the network and will directly determine the final fault classification performance, and overfitting and underfitting may also occur if improperly chosen.

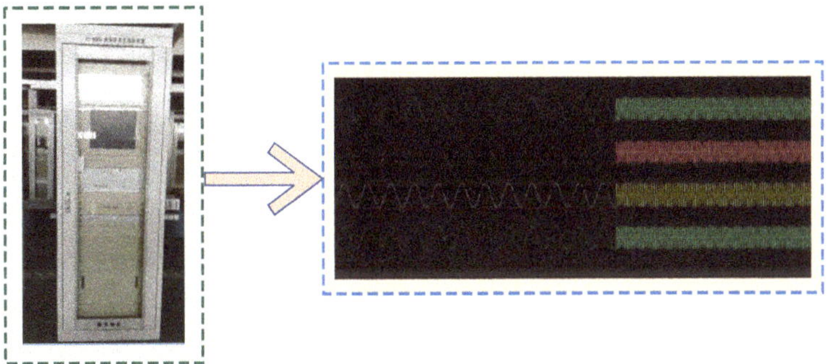

Figure 11. Fault recording device diagram.

In the training process of the LSTM network, the hyper-parameters that have a significant impact on the fault classification accuracy are learning rate, training times, and optimizer. By adjusting these parameters, the fault prediction accuracy is finally obtained after continuous iterations.

The batch size affects the training speed and model optimization. The variance of the gradient is expressed as:

$$Var(g) = Var(\frac{1}{m}\sum_{i=1}^{m} g(x_i, y_i)) = \frac{1}{m^2}Var(g(x_2, y_2) + g(x_2, y_2) + \ldots + g(x_m, y_m)) \quad (1)$$

where m is the value set by the batch size.

The increasing batch size can reduce the gradient variance. If the batch size is set as the total number of fault samples, it is equivalent to directly training the entire sample data set. This will lead to a long training time, but the gradient is more accurate, so it is only suitable for small sample training. If the batch size is set too small, the gradient change fluctuates greatly, and the network is not easy to converge.

Since the input LSTM fault data set is relatively large, this paper set batch size = 64 through the trial-and-error method. At the same time, to achieve higher training network accuracy, the epoch is increased appropriately, thus increasing the training time.

There is usually no definite selection method for the setting of LSTM parameters, which can be set by empirical formulas and continuous experiments; the specific parameter settings in this paper are shown in Table 3.

Table 3. LSTM parameter settings.

Parameters	Values
Matrix size of input fault data	409 by 33,000
The number of hidden layers	2
Output labels	[1–4]
Optimizer	Adaptive moment estimation (Adam)
Epoch	200
Number of neurons	128
Activation function	Sigmoid and inverse hyperbolic tangent
Batch size	64

5.2. Performance Comparison of Optimizers on Diagnostic Results

There are many kinds of optimization algorithms for neural networks, mainly based on gradient descent type, such as root mean square prop (RMSprop), adaptive moment estimation (Adam), stochastic gradient descent (SGD), etc.

To improve the accuracy and convergence of the model, various gradient optimization algorithms are employed to optimize the neural network. Specifically, we selected three optimizers, namely RMSprop, Adam, and SGD to optimize the weight coefficients and bias coefficients of the LSTM. Through experimentation, we evaluated the effectiveness of each optimizer in terms of fault diagnosis accuracy, as presented in Table 4.

Table 4. The final classification accuracy of the three optimizers.

Optimizers	Prediction Accuracy
Adam	95.06%
RMSprop	90.43%
SGD	87.37%

The best optimizer sought should make the loss function of the LSTM model converge fast and have high classification accuracy. As shown in Table 4, it can be seen that for various optimizers, Adam has a better optimization effect, faster convergence speed, and higher fault diagnosis accuracy, so it is chosen as the optimizer of the LSTM model proposed in this paper.

5.3. Analysis of Diagnostic Results and Comparison of Programs

In this section, all stored fault data of the Tianshengqiao-Guangzhou HVDC transmission project is used as the input of LSTM, which contains 409 fault samples. The input fault samples are the voltage and current waveform after the failure, and the length of each fault sample sequence is 33,000.

To prove the efficiency of the fault diagnosis, RNN, XGBoost, SVM, Naive Bayes classifier, PNN, and CL are taken to compare the effect of fault diagnosis, and the parameter settings of RNN, XGBoost [10], SVM, Naive Bayes classifier, PNN, and CL are shown in Tables 5–9.

Table 5. RNN parameter settings.

Parameters	Values
The number of hidden layers	2
Output labels	[1–4]
Optimizer	Adam
Epoch	200
Hidden layer	100
Dropout probability	0.1
Activation function	Sigmoid and inverse hyperbolic tangent
Batch size	64

Table 6. Parameter settings for XGBoost.

Parameters	Values
gamma	0.4
max_depth	8
reg_lambda	2
subsample	0.7
colsample_bytree	0.7
min_child_weight	3
eta	0.1
seed	1000
N-thread	4

Table 7. Parameter settings for SVM.

Parameters	Values
Multi-Classification Support Vector Machine Model	One-versus-One
Kernel function	quadratic
Nuclear scales	Automatic
Box Constraint Level	1

Table 8. Parameter settings for Naive Bayes.

Parameter Name	Parameter Values
Kernel function	Gaussian kernel
Support	No Borders

Table 9. Parameter settings for PNN and CL.

Method	Parameter Name	Parameter Setting
PNN	spread	1.5
CL	Max_split tree	100

It is worth noting that the total measured fault data, e.g., from 2018–2022, are all used to better train LSTM and other alternatives (these data are all the stored fault data collected from the Tianshengqiao transmission project of the China Southern Power Grid).

For fault 1, 84 samples were trained and 20 samples were tested. Additionally, the overall training set and test set are summarized in Table 10.

Table 10. Split of the fault data set.

Fault Type	Fault Labels	Training Set	Test Set
DC-side transmission line single-phase faults	1	84	20
faults in the converter valve arm	2	64	17
faults in the converter valve bank	3	118	29
DC-side transmission line phase-to-phase faults	4	62	15

Note that because the fault data set is relatively small, the selection of hyper-parameters in the seven methods used in this study is the optimal result after adjustment using the uniform design method [48].

The RNN, XGBoost, SVM, Naive Bayes, PNN, and CL are trained using the same training data set, and the same test data set is used for accuracy testing after training. The diagnostic accuracies of the seven methods are shown in Table 11. The five evaluating indicators of F1-score, precision score, recall score, AUC score, and test time are shown in Table 12.

Table 11. Comparison of diagnostic accuracy among LSTM, RNN, XGBoost, SVM, Naive Bayes, PNN and CL.

Fault Type	LSTM	RNN	XGBoost	SVM	Naive Bayes	PNN	CL
single-phase faults of DC-side transmission lines	100%	70.00%	100%	100%	100%	75.00%	70.00%
faults of converter valve arms	94.10%	52.90%	70.60%	82.40%	70.60%	47.05%	41.18%
faults of converter valve groups	93.10%	89.70%	93.10%	93.10%	100%	62.07%	55.17%
phase-to-phase faults of DC-side transmission lines	93.30%	33.30%	80.00%	86.70%	73.30%	46.67%	40.00%
total	95.06%	66.67%	87.65%	91.36%	88.89%	46.91%	53.07%

Table 12. Performance comparison of 7 methods.

Evaluating Indicator \ Method	LSTM	RNN	XGBoost	SVM	Naive Bayes	PNN	CL
F1-score	0.86	0.52	0.84	0.45	0.61	0.53	0.55
AUC score	0.88	0.53	0.83	0.48	0.64	0.59	0.61
Precision score	0.90	0.59	0.89	0.49	0.62	0.47	0.51
Recall score	0.82	0.56	0.81	0.46	0.65	0.61	0.63
Test time	73.04 s	78.04 s	75.03 s	97.64 s	85.77 s	122.33 s	270.69 s

To visualize the fault diagnosis accuracy of the test, the confusion matrix is used for analysis. The fault diagnosis results of the seven methods are shown in Figure 12. Although the seven methods are subject to misdiagnosis, the misdiagnosis rate of the LSTM method is significantly lower than that of the other methods.

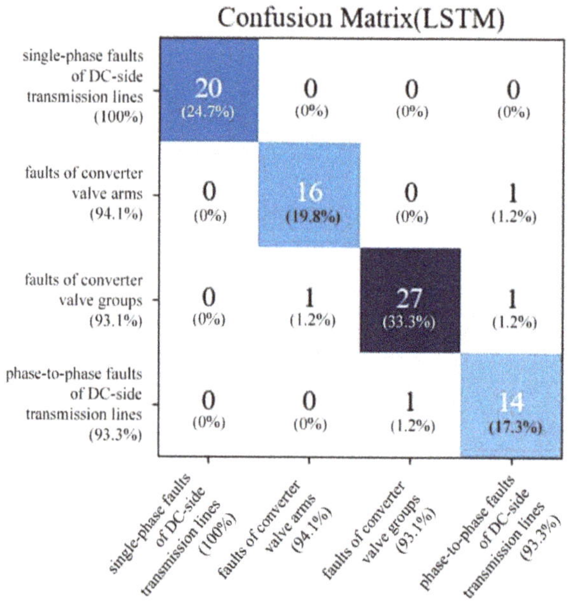

(a)

Figure 12. *Cont.*

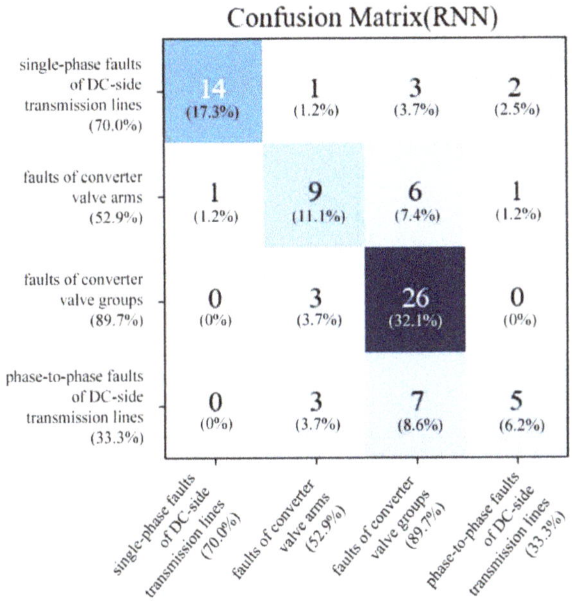

(**b**)

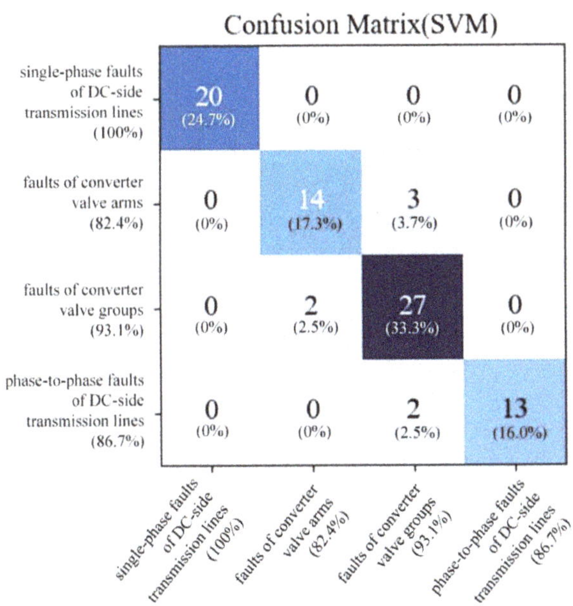

(**c**)

Figure 12. *Cont.*

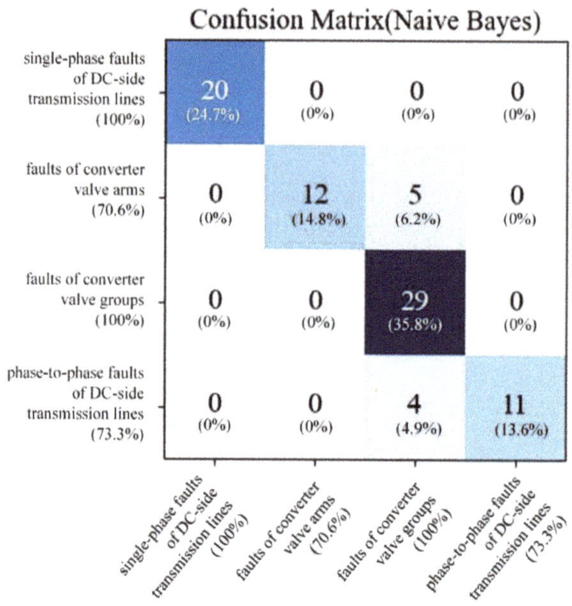

(d)

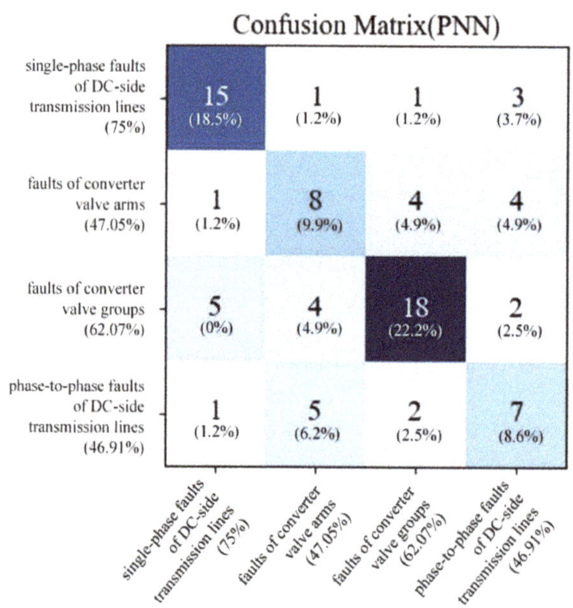

(e)

Figure 12. *Cont.*

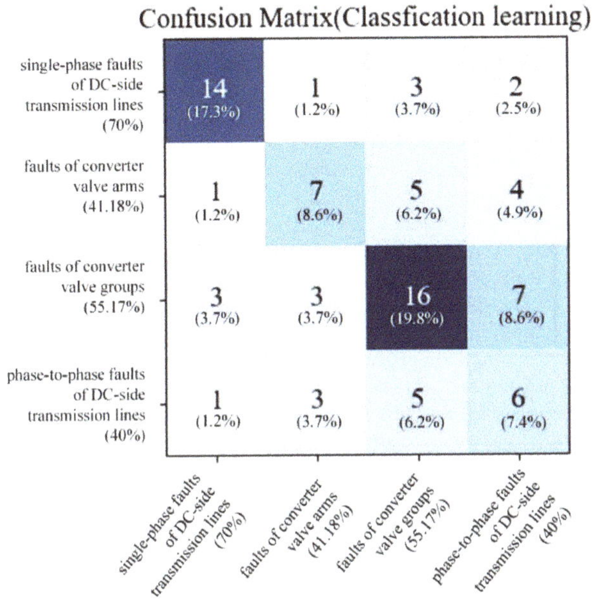

(f)

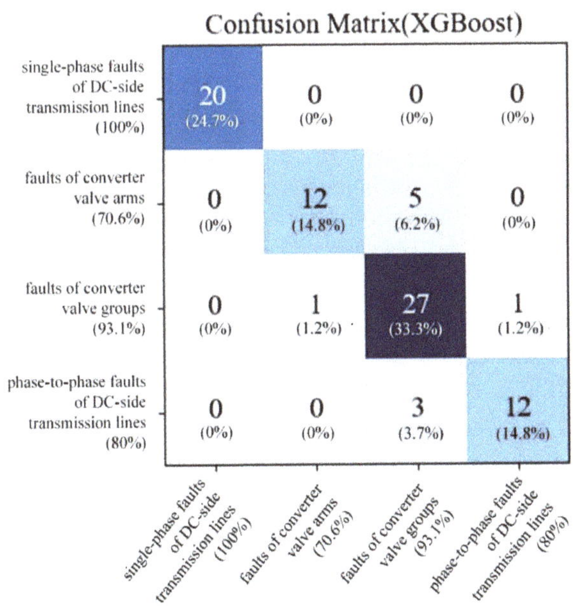

(g)

Figure 12. Confusion matrix of the diagnosis results of the seven methods. Results of: (**a**) LSTM method; (**b**) RNN method; (**c**) SVM method; (**d**) Naive Bayes method; (**e**) PNN method; (**f**) CL method; and (**g**) XGBoost method.

It can be observed from Figure 12a that 1 misdiagnosis data appears in faults of converter valve arms, 2 misdiagnosis data appear in faults of converter valve groups, and 1 misdiagnosis data appears in phase-to-phase faults of DC-side transmission lines in the results of the LSTM method. Furthermore, for the results of the RNN method in Figure 12b, 6 misdiagnosis data appear in single-phase faults of DC-side transmission lines, 8 misdiagnosis data appear in faults of converter valve arms, 3 misdiagnosis data appear in faults of converter valve groups, and 10 misdiagnosis data appear in phase-to-phase faults of DC-side transmission lines. In addition, from the result of the SVM method in Figure 12c, 3 misdiagnosis data appear in faults of converter valve arms, 2 misdiagnosis data appear in faults of converter valve groups, and 2 misdiagnosis data appear in phase-to-phase faults of DC-side transmission lines. Then it can be observed from Figure 12d that 0 misdiagnosis data appear in single-phase faults of DC-side transmission lines, 5 misdiagnosis data appear in faults of converter valve arms, 0 misdiagnosis data appear in faults of converter valve groups, and 4 misdiagnosis data appear in phase-to-phase faults of DC-side transmission lines in the Naive Bayes method. After that, from the result of the PNN method in Figure 12e, 5 misdiagnosis data appear in single-phase faults of DC-side transmission lines, 9 misdiagnosis data appear in faults of converter valve arms, 11 misdiagnosis data appear in faults of converter valve groups, and 8 misdiagnosis data appear in phase-to-phase faults of DC-side transmission lines. From the results of the SVM method in Figure 12f, 6 misdiagnosis data appear in single-phase faults of DC-side transmission lines, 10 misdiagnosis data appear in faults of converter valve arms, 13 misdiagnosis data appear in faults of converter valve groups, and 9 misdiagnosis data appear in phase-to-phase faults of DC-side transmission lines. Lastly, for the results of the XGBoost method in Figure 12g, 0 misdiagnosis data appear in single-phase faults of DC-side transmission lines, 5 misdiagnosis data appear in faults of converter valve arms, 2 misdiagnosis data appear in faults of converter valve groups, and 3 misdiagnosis data appear in phase-to-phase faults of DC-side transmission lines.

The parameters of the seven methods were optimized, and the results showed that the diagnostic accuracy of the LSTM method is 95.06%.

Because RNN is prone to gradient disappearance, it cannot process a long input sequence, so traditional RNN easily forgets the information of the previous relatively distant period, resulting in the failure of training accuracy convergence. This limits the use of RNN to a large extent. Therefore, the diagnostic accuracy of the RNN method is limited to 66.67%, and it is difficult to improve the diagnostic accuracy.

LSTM corrects the traditional RNN by designing a gated unit, solves the problem of long-term dependence common in general cyclic neural networks, and enables information to be transmitted and expressed flexibly in a long time series, without causing useful information from long ago to be forgotten, which is suitable for modeling sequential data. At the same time, the proposed fault diagnosis method based on the LSTM model does not require feature extraction and screening, which not only reduces the difficulty of using machine learning for fault diagnosis training, but also avoids fault prediction caused by improper feature selection.

The accuracy of XGBoost, SVM, Naive Bayes, PNN, and CL is 87.65%, 91.36%, 88.89%, 46.91%, and 53.07%, respectively, but it is still lower than that of the LSTM method. Therefore, this paper puts forward the advanced fault diagnosis method of HVDC systems.

6. Discussion and Limitation

6.1. Discussion

The research data is based on the fault monitoring data of the Tianshengqiao-Guangzhou transmission project of the China Southern Power Grid; the fault data is all the stored fault data collected from the HVDC system (from 2018–2022). During fault diagnosis, it is very obvious that when the data set used for training is larger, the final diagnostic results will be more accurate. Therefore, the number of fault samples is very important for fault diagnosis. In future research on fault diagnosis, it is essential to collect data and use reasonable methods for data preprocessing, which is also a new direction for future research in this field. Because of the large number of data samples needed to train the LSTM network to ensure high accuracy of fault diagnosis, the accuracy of the raised LSTM-based fault diagnosis strategy is limited to 95.06%. However, the actual system power supply reliability of the HVDC systems is very high—about 99.7116% [49]. The fault probability of HVDC systems is very low, so few HVDC systems fault data samples can be used to train LSTM, which will affect the accuracy of the fault diagnosis method proposed, to some extent. However, compared with six comparison methods, LSTM-based fault diagnosis accuracy is still very high. At the same time, with the increase of using time, more and more fault data samples of trained LSTM can further enhance the accuracy of fault diagnosis of HVDC systems based on LSTM. In addition, the study is aimed at the fault diagnosis of an actual HVDC system project. This research has high accuracy and is very suitable for fault diagnosis in actual power systems. It can replace some traditional fault diagnosis methods in power systems, such as traditional neural networks RNN, Naive Bayes, etc.

By combining the fault diagnosis with the knowledge graph technology, the detected fault data can be directly transmitted to the knowledge graph, which is analyzed and processed, and the fault solution can be obtained, thus realizing the visualization of the fault diagnosis technology in the HVDC systems. At the same time, fault diagnosis technology is one of the core technologies of the knowledge graph, so its combination with the knowledge graph leads to the continuous improvement and development of the knowledge graph.

6.2. Limitations

HVDC systems fault diagnosis is a problem of small sample data. The fault data samples were divided into 80% training set and 20% test set with the optimal solution. LSTM requires a large amount of data for training, so if the training samples are too small, the training results will be unsatisfactory and the final fault diagnosis accuracy will be affected. If the proportion of training set is too large and the proportion of test set is too small, the reliability of the final fault diagnosis accuracy will decrease. When the ratio of the training set and test set is 8:2, the training accuracy can converge to a higher level in the training process; thus, the ratio of the training set and test set is 8:2, which is very appropriate.

At the same time, the fault data set only includes four types of faults, but does not cover all types of faults, such as transformer faults and generator faults in HVDC systems, which affects the accuracy of fault diagnosis to a certain extent, meaning the proposed method has certain limitations for some special fault prediction.

7. Conclusions and Perspectives

Relying on the knowledge graph platform, the article raises a fault diagnosis method based on the LSTM network under the knowledge graph, using the fault data of four kinds of faults in a southwest HVDC substation as the data set. The method can accurately classify each type of fault in tests, showing better fault diagnosis performance, and the specific contributions are summarized as follows:

(1) The knowledge graph of HVDC systems is established. By diagnosing various types of faults and blending them in the system, the fault analysis can be carried out quickly when faults appear in the future, which improves the efficiency of power system operation management;

(2) A fault diagnosis strategy of HVDC systems based on LSTM networks is proposed, which overcomes the shortcomings of traditional RNN that tend to forget earlier fault information when the fault sequence is too long; and the method can achieve accurate classification of all kinds of faults;

(3) Using the RNN, XGBoost, SVM, Naive Bayes, PNN, and CL for comparison, the results show that the accuracy of the LSTM method is as high as 95.06%, and the accuracy of the RNN, XGBoost, SVM, and Naive Bayes, PNN, and CL is 66.67%, 87.65%, 91.36%, 88.89%, 46.91%, and 53.07%, respectively. The test results show that the LSTM-based fault diagnosis is more accurate and can effectively improve the reliability of HVDC operation.

On the basis of the LSTM-based fault diagnosis model for HVDC systems, future research will be conducted as follows:

(1) The function of the fault diagnosis model for fault location will be developed, and will strive to locate the fault point more quickly;

(2) In practice, to further improve the accuracy of LSTM, more fault data sets need to be used for training. At the same time, there are many fault types in the HVDC systems. To improve the feasibility, the amount of data and fault types will be further increased;

(3) The fault diagnosis research in this article can be directly applied to other HVDC systems, such as VSC-HVDC systems;

(4) The development of smart grids, the knowledge graph and the fault diagnosis research in this article can not only be applied to HVDC systems in the future, but also provide a reference for fault research for the entire power system.

Author Contributions: Q.C.: writing the original draft and editing. J.W., Q.L., X.G. and B.Y.: conceptualization. R.Y., J.G. and G.P.: visualization and contributed to the discussion of the topic. All authors have read and agreed to the published version of the manuscript.

Funding: This research was funded by key science and technology projects of the China Southern Power Grid grant number (CGYKJXM20210309, CGYKJXM20220343).

Acknowledgments: The authors gratefully acknowledge the support of key science and technology projects of the China Southern Power Grid (CGYKJXM20210309, CGYKJXM20220343).

Conflicts of Interest: Authors Qiang Li, Qian Chen, and Jiyang Wu are employed by EHV Power Transmission Company of China Southern Power Grid Co., Ltd.; the remaining authors declare that the research was conducted in the absence of any commercial or financial relationships that could be construed as a potential conflict of interest.

References

1. Yang, B.; Liu, B.; Zhou, H.; Wang, J.; Yao, W.; Wu, S.; Shu, H.; Ren, Y. A critical survey of technologies of large offshore wind farm integration: Summarization, advances, and perspectives. *Prot. Control Mod. Power Syst.* **2022**, *7*, 17. [CrossRef]
2. Yang, B.; Li, Y.; Li, J.; Shu, H.; Zhao, X.; Ren, Y.; Li, Q. Comprehensive summarization of solid oxide fuel cell: Control: A state-of-the-art review. *Prot. Control Mod. Power Syst.* **2022**, *7*, 36. [CrossRef]
3. Zalhaf, A.; Zhao, E.; Han, Y.; Yang, P.; Almaliki, A.; Aly, R. Evaluation of the transient overvoltages of HVDC transmission lines caused by lightning strikes. *Energies* **2022**, *15*, 1452. [CrossRef]
4. Zhao, E.; Han, Y.; Liu, Y.; Zalhaf, A.; Wang, C.; Yang, P. Feasibility analysis of neutral grounding by small reactor of HVDC converter transformer. *Energy Rep.* **2022**, *8*, 392–399. [CrossRef]
5. Hu, Z.; Han, Y.; Yang, P.; Wang, C.; Zalhaf, A. Evaluation of lightning overvoltage at neutral point of HVDC converter transformer based on EMTP. *Energy Rep.* **2022**, *8*, 274–283. [CrossRef]
6. Fu, J.; Han, Y.; Yang, P.; Wang, C.; Zalhaf, A. Analysis of fault current and overvoltage at the neutral point of ±800 kV high-voltage DC converter transformer. *Energy Rep.* **2022**, *8*, 292–300. [CrossRef]
7. Ma, L. Support vector machine algorithms in nonlinear classification and regression based problems. *J. Tianshui Norm. Coll.* **2009**, *29*, 44–47.
8. Ding, J.; Shao, Q.; Qi, Z.; Xie, M.; Gao, B.; Yu, Y. Migration learning based convolutional neural network for grid fault diagnosis. *Sci. Technol. Eng.* **2022**, *22*, 5653–5658.
9. Yan, B.; Liu, X.; Tian, Z.; Shi, S.; Yu, F. Application of co-filter and support vector machine in HVDC system fault diagnosis. *Chin. J. Electr. Eng.* **2008**, *28*, 23–29.
10. Li, Q.; Chen, Q.; Wu, J.; Qiu, Y.; Zhang, C.; Huang, Y.; Jian, B.; Yang, B. XGBoost-based intelligent decision making of HVDC system with knowledge graph. *Energies* **2023**, *16*, 2405. [CrossRef]
11. Chen, J.; Li, Y.; Chen, J.; Liu, D.; Yang, Y. Identification of typical partial discharge defects of distribution system equipment based on classification learner. In Proceedings of the 2022 7th Asia Conference on Power and Electrical Engineering (ACPEE), Hangzhou, China, 15–17 April 2022; pp. 2025–2029.
12. Fan, Q.; Zhang, J.; Wang, G.; Ren, W. Research on intelligent fault diagnosis of substation based on knowledge graph. *Electron. Technol. Softw. Eng.* **2022**, *20*, 109–112.
13. Chen, Y.; Yang, B.; Guo, Z.; Wang, J.; Zhu, M.; Li, Z.; Yu, T. Dynamic reconfiguration for TEG systems under heterogeneous temperature distribution via adaptive coordinated seeker. *Prot. Control Mod. Power Syst.* **2022**, *7*, 38. [CrossRef]
14. Liu, J.; Du, N.; Xu, J.; Liu, X.; Song, Y.; Qiu, L.; Zhao, Y.; Sun, M. Application and research of knowledge graph in electric power field. *Power Inf. Commun. Technol.* **2020**, *18*, 60–66. [CrossRef]
15. Mohan, M. A comprehensive review of DC fault protection methods in HVDC transmission systems. *Prot. Control Mod. Power Syst.* **2021**, *6*, 1.

16. Sebastian, P.; Benjamin, S.; Dirk, W.; Johannes, K. Revealing interactions between HVDC cross-area flows and frequency stability with explainable AI. *Prot. Control Mod. Power Syst.* **2022**, *5*, 46.
17. Xing, J.; Bian, J.; Kang, J.; Qi, K.; Feng, P. Hot spots and trends of domestic and international network security assessment research–a visual analysis of knowledge graph based on citespace. *Comput. Knowl. Technol.* **2022**, *18*, 37–40.
18. Niri, M.F.; Bui, T.M.; Dinh, T.Q.; Hosseinzadeh, E.; Yu, T.F.; Marco, J. Remaining energy estimation for lithium-ion batteries via gaussian mixture and markov models for future load prediction. *J. Energy Storage* **2020**, *28*, 101271. [CrossRef]
19. Niri, M.F.; Dinh, T.Q.; Yu, T.F.; Marco, J.; Bui TM, N. State of power prediction for lithium-ion batteries in electric vehicles via Wavelet-Markov load analysis. *IEEE Trans. Intell. Transp. Syst.* **2021**, *22*, 5833–5848. [CrossRef]
20. Zhang, D.; Zhang, X.; Sun, H.; He, J. Fault diagnosis of AC/DC transmission system based on convolutional neural network. *Autom. Electr. Power Syst.* **2022**, *46*, 132–145.
21. Gong, Y.; Li, B.; Li, D.; Yang, X.; Chen, Q. A knowledge base construction method for fault knowledge base of power equipment based on knowledge graph. *Electron. Prod. Reliab. Environ. Test.* **2021**, *39*, 72–77.
22. Guo, Z.; Yang, M. Application of RNN diagnosis method to motor bearing and misalignment compound fault. *J. Nanjing Univ. Aeronaut. Astronaut.* **2022**, *54*, 87–93.
23. Truong, M.; Nicolas, H.; Truong, Q. Baseline strategy for remaining range estimation of electric motorcycle applications. In Proceedings of the 2022 25th International Conference on Mechatronics Technology, Kaohsiung, Taiwan, 18–21 November 2022; pp. 1–4.
24. Shu, Y.; Guo, W.; Fan, B.; Kang, J.; Xu, S. Based on the instance and electrical fault attribute weighted Naive Bayes classification study. *Comput. Meas. Control* **2022**, *30*, 169–180.
25. Yang, X. Review of performance metrics of classification learning algorithms. *Comput. Sci.* **2021**, *48*, 209–219.
26. Cheng, Y.; Zuo, G. Research on fault diagnosis system of CVT hydraulic system based on PNN. *Small Intern. Combust. Engine Veh. Technol.* **2018**, *47*, 18–21.
27. Wang, C.; Li, Y.; Fei, C.; Huang, X. A review of knowledge graph platforms. *Comput. Appl. Res.* **2022**, *39*, 3201–3210.
28. Pu, T.; Tan, Y.; Peng, G.; Xu, H.; Zhang, Z. Construction and application of knowledge graph in electric power domain. *Power Grid Technol.* **2021**, *45*, 2080–2091.
29. Wang, Q.; Zhang, Z. Knowledge graph-based fault diagnosis method for signal equipment. *Railw. Stand. Des.* **2022**, *66*, 149–156.
30. Gao, H.; Miao, L.; Liu, J.; Liu, J.; Lin, X.; Dong, K.; He, X. A review of research on knowledge graph and its application in power system. *Guangdong Electr. Power* **2020**, *33*, 66–76.
31. Lu, F.; Leng, Y. Knowledge graph data indexing and compressed storage algorithm supported by RDF graph model. *J. Bohai Univ. (Nat. Sci. Ed.)* **2021**, *42*, 277–282.
32. Deng, Z. Artificial intelligence-based knowledge graph construction techniques and applications. *Radio Eng.* **2022**, *52*, 766–774.
33. Li, Z.; Dong, X.; Zhou, D.; Tong, T. Research on human-machine collaborative construction method and application of knowledge graph in adaptive learning system. *Mod. Educ. Technol.* **2019**, *29*, 80–86.
34. Guo, R.; Yang, Q.; Liu, S.; Li, W.; Yuan, X.; Huang, X. Research and application of knowledge graph construction for power grid fault disposal. *Power Grid Technol.* **2021**, *45*, 2092–2100.
35. Liu, Q.; Li, Y.; Duan, H.; Liu, Y.; Qin, Z. A review of knowledge graph construction techniques. *Comput. Res. Dev.* **2016**, *53*, 582–600.
36. Jiang, T.; Xie, J.; Hu, J.; Ding, S.; Liu, G.; Xie, Q. Analysis and processing of chaotic timing of event sequence records in intelligent substations. *Yunnan Electr. Power Technol.* **2021**, *49*, 9–12.
37. Zhang, C. Resolution of power system event sequence records and detection of real-time signals of component actions. *Power Grid Technol.* **1991**, *4*, 38–43.
38. Li, J.; Zhang, C.; Zhao, H.; Huang, T.; Wan, Y.; Wang, X. Knowledge graph construction for technical supervision of power grid equipment based on multi-source data fusion. *Electr. Eng. Electr.* **2021**, *9*, 60–63.
39. Yang, B.; Sang, Y.; Shi, K.; Yao, W.; Jiang, L.; Yu, T. Design and real-time implementation of perturbation observer based sliding-mode control for VSC-HVDC systems. *Control Eng. Pract.* **2016**, *56*, 13–26. [CrossRef]
40. Yang, B.; Jiang, L.; Yao, W.; Wu, Q. Perturbation observer based adaptive passive control for damping improvement of multi-terminal voltage source converter-based high voltage direct current systems. *Trans. Inst. Meas. Control* **2017**, *39*, 1409–1420. [CrossRef]
41. Yang, B.; Yu, T.; Zhang, X.; Huang, L.; Shu, H.; Jiang, L. Interactive teaching-learning optimizer for parameter tuning of VSC-HVDC systems with offshore wind farm integration. *IET Gener. Transm. Distrib.* **2018**, *12*, 678–687. [CrossRef]
42. Zhao, Y.; Sun, S.; Liu, X.; Nie, Y. Improved CNN-LSTM-based wide-band oscillation identification for power systems. *Intell. Power* **2022**, *50*, 96.
43. Pang, C.; Zhang, B.; Yu, J. Short-term electric load forecasting based on LSTM recurrent neural network. *Power Eng. Technol.* **2021**, *40*, 175–180, 194.
44. Yang, J.; Xiao, D.; Li, H.; Yu, M.; Yi, B. 1000 kV extra high voltage line loss prediction based on improved gray correlation analysis and LSTM. *Electr. Technol.* **2020**, *19*, 131–136.
45. Wang, Y.; Liu, B.; Li, Y. An LSTM neural network-based method for electric load forecasting. *Lab. Res. Explor.* **2020**, *39*, 41–45.
46. Shao, Q.; Guo, L.; Liu, Y.; Xie, M.; Dai, C.; Wang, T.; Zhang, J.; Cong, Z. Single-phase ground fault identification method for distribution network based on LSTM model. *Guangdong Electr. Power* **2019**, *32*, 100–106.

47. Yang, B.; Jiang, L.; Yu, T.; Shu, H.; Zhang, C.; Yao, W.; Wu, Q. Passive control design for multi-terminal VSC-HVDC systems via energy shaping. *Int. J. Electr. Power Energy Syst.* **2018**, *98*, 496–508. [CrossRef]
48. Pang, Y.; Zhou, X.; He, W.; Zhong, J.; Hui, O. Uniform design-based gaussian process regression for data-driven rapid fragility assessment of bridges. *J. Struct. Eng.* **2021**, *147*, 04021008. [CrossRef]
49. National Power Reliability Report in the First Half of 2020. Available online: http://prpq.nea.gov.cn/gzdt/4638.html (accessed on 18 September 2020).

electronics

MDPI

Article

Detection and Classification of Rolling Bearing Defects Using Direct Signal Processing with Deep Convolutional Neural Network

Maciej Skowron [1], Oliwia Frankiewicz [1], Jeremi Jan Jarosz [1], Marcin Wolkiewicz [1], Mateusz Dybkowski [1,*], Sebastien Weisse [2], Jerome Valire [2], Agnieszka Wyłomańska [3], Radosław Zimroz [4] and Krzysztof Szabat [1]

1 Department of Electrical Machines, Drives and Measurements, Wroclaw University of Science and Technology, Wyb. Wyspianskiego 27, 50-370 Wroclaw, Poland; maciej.skowron@pwr.edu.pl (M.S.); oliwia.frankiewicz@pwr.edu.pl (O.F.); jeremi.jarosz@pwr.edu.pl (J.J.J.); marcin.wolkiewicz@pwr.edu.pl (M.W.); krzysztof.szabat@pwr.edu.pl (K.S.)

2 SAFRAN Electrical & Power, Parc d'activité d'Andromède, 1, rue Louis Blériot, 31702 Blagnac Cedex, France; sebastien.weisse@safrangroup.com (S.W.); jerome.valire@safrangroup.com (J.V.)

3 Department of Pure Mathematics, Wroclaw University of Science and Technology, Wyb. Wyspianskiego 27, 50-370 Wroclaw, Poland; agnieszka.wylomanska@pwr.edu.pl

4 Department of Mining, Wroclaw University of Science and Technology, Wyb. Wyspianskiego 27, 50-370 Wroclaw, Poland; radoslaw.zimroz@pwr.edu.pl

* Correspondence: mateusz.dybkowski@pwr.edu.pl

Abstract: Currently, great emphasis is being placed on the electrification of means of transportation, including aviation. The use of electric motors reduces operating and maintenance costs. Electric motors are subjected to various types of damage during operation, of which rolling bearing defects are statistically the most common. This article focuses on presenting a diagnostic tool for bearing conditions based on mechanic vibration signals using convolutional neural networks (CNN). This article presents an alternative to the well-known classical diagnostic tools based on advanced signal processing methods such as the short-time Fourier transform, the Hilbert–Huang transform, etc. The approach described in the article provides fault detection and classification in less than 0.03 s. The proposed structures achieved a classification accuracy of 99.8% on the test set. Special attention was paid to the process of optimizing the CNN structure to achieve the highest possible accuracy with the fewest number of network parameters.

Keywords: induction motor drive; fault diagnosis; rolling bearing faults; artificial intelligence; convolutional neural networks

1. Introduction

In response to the energy crisis and the need to reduce the negative impact of public transport on the environment, there is now a strong emphasis on the electrification of various modes of transportation, including aircrafts [1]. By replacing conventional internal combustion engines with electric motors, operating costs can be reduced by replacing jet fuel with electricity and reducing maintenance costs for these machines [2]. Despite the high quality of the materials and design methods of electric machines, they are subject to emerging defects. The effect of machine defects can range from reduced functionality to complete failure. Due to the need to ensure the safety of electric vehicles, the diagnosis and prediction of defects in electric machines is an important issue [3]. The correct diagnosis and detection of damage at its initial stage significantly reduce the time of possible machine downtime, avoid harmful, sometimes catastrophic, consequences, and reduce financial losses [4]. The induction motors most commonly used in industrial drive systems consist of many components. Each of these components can fail due to overload, abrasion, electrical, mechanical, and thermal stresses, or as a result of an unbalanced load. According to the results of statistical studies shown in [5,6], rolling bearing damage is the most common recurring failure of electric machines. Bearing fault diagnosis is therefore crucial to ensure the proper maintenance and trouble-free operation of electric motors. This issue is particularly important for aviation safety, as well as for forecasting and planning maintenance operations [7].

Superior control systems impose several restrictions on the signals used that carry information about the machine's condition. In the case of bearing damage diagnostics, the most commonly used diagnostic signals are vibration [8–10], current [11,12], or acoustic emission [13–15]. A vibration signal is a very good carrier of information and enables the early detection of mechanical damage [16]. Vibration analysis techniques used to detect bearing failures in electric drives are most often divided into four categories: time domain, frequency domain, time–frequency domain, and other methods [17]. Time domain signal analysis includes the analysis of statistical parameters such as RMS, Crest factor, and kurtosis [18]. However, a significant drawback of these methods is their sensitivity to noise and their inability to determine the location of the fault. Frequency domain analysis techniques mainly include fast Fourier transform analysis and envelope analysis [19,20]. However, there are some limitations to these techniques that make them unsuitable for analyzing non-stationary signals. Time–frequency analysis combines the advantages of both methods and includes wavelet transforms, short-time Fourier transform (STFT), and Hilbert–Huang transform, among others [21,22]. However, it should be noted that these methods are more computationally complex, which can lengthen the fault detection process.

The shortest possible time between the occurrence of a defect and its detection is crucial to ensure safety, especially in critical drives. In addition, modern control systems enforce the need for the full automation of the fault detection process, at the same time ensuring a short response time to the appearance of a defect while maintaining high precision in its assessment. Therefore, to meet these requirements, but also to increase the reliability of diagnostic systems, artificial intelligence techniques are increasingly used [23]. Artificial neural networks are now a very good tool to partially replace humans in the decision-making process, based on signal analysis [10,24], allowing them to automate and maintain the diagnostic process [25,26].

The most widely used neural structure in diagnostic applications is the multilayer perceptron (MLP), whose use and good precision performance have been described in [27–29], among others. These networks perform the primary function of learning data approximation and perform well in simple diagnostic tasks based on signal preprocessing. Other widely used types of shallow neural networks are self-organizing Kohonen maps (SOM) [30,31], networks with radial activation functions (RBF) [32], or recurrent structures [33]. However, these solutions base their operation on the extraction of classical symptoms, which implies the use of analysis methods whose limitations have been mentioned above.

A natural development step in automating the decision-making process of diagnostic systems was to use methods that would allow the direct use of the diagnostic signal. One solution with good results was the use of deep neural networks [10,34–37]. The structure of deep neural networks is based on the use of many different neural layers [15], each of which introduces a certain level of abstraction by extracting successive features from the data coming from the previous layer, starting from the input layer [38,39]. This also makes use of features extracted from processed diagnostic signals as an input for deep network work [10,40]; however, an important advantage of deep networks is their ability to extract features directly from the diagnostic signal and their ability to process them for appropriate classification [38,39,41,42].

The most widely used deep learning network structures are autoencoders [43], long short-term memory (LSTM) [7], and convolutional neural networks (CNNs) [36,44–46]. Compared to the shallow structures mentioned above, CNNs show higher accuracy when operating directly on the diagnostic signal presented in the form of multidimensional arrays or vectors [38,45], further reducing the time of the diagnostic process [36,37]. CNNs also provide automatic symptom extraction, reducing the role of an expert in the diagnostic process. Due to the direct processing of diagnostic signals, fault response times are many times faster than known classical detection methods. Furthermore, the technique performs well in detection during steady-state and transient conditions, which is extremely important for modern drive systems. The topic of bearing damage detection using CNNs with a direct diagnostic signal, such as vibrations, has been addressed in publications [10,15,46,47], among others. However, in this paper, the authors used signals for a larger number of degrees of different damage, which allows an increase in the sensitivity of the neural structure for the initial stage of damage [15].

In addition, in the article [46], time–frequency analysis was used to develop the input matrix of the network. This fact adversely affects the diagnostic process due to the significant computational load of the applied combination of continuous wavelet analysis (CWT) and a deep convolutional network. Furthermore, the signal acquisition time declared in [46] is 0.5 s, which is 25 times longer than the time presented in this article. Also noteworthy is the very elaborate structure of the fully connected layer presented in [46], which is not justified, especially in the context of the initial symptom extraction applied using CWT. The article [47] proposed an approach based on the analysis of the vibration signal in the time domain. Feature extraction was enhanced by the statistical analysis of vibration samples contained in the measurement vector. However, the disadvantage of the described approach is the use of a ready-made AlexNet structure without taking into account the possibility of optimization. The CNN structure presented in [47] contained more than 2.5 billion parameters adapted to the training process. In addition, the transition between convolutional layers containing more than 3.3 million parameters and a classifier containing more than 2.6 billion parameters was not protected against a loss of generalization. It should be noted that the lack of an optimization algorithm between the layers of the feature detector (convolutional layers) and the layers of the classifier (fully connected layers) results in an excessive dependence of the state of one neuron on the others. In the approach proposed in this article, a structure with 64 thousand parameters is used. In addition, a dropout layer [10,38] and stochastic network training methods were used to avoid a loss of generalization ability.

Recognizing damage at a possible early stage is extremely crucial for critical propulsion systems (aviation) given the early prediction of required maintenance work to ensure system reliability [10]. Due to the application of ready-made neural structures with an excessive number of neural connections presented in the literature, this article presents the optimization of the CNN structure to maximize the accuracy of performance and minimize the required time and computational resources. Due to the crucial role played in modern diagnostic systems by the immunity of the solution to external disturbances [45] and the stability of the system's operation, it is important to optimize the neural structure that is a key element of the diagnostic application [41]. A reduced number of network parameters translates directly into the ability to implement the solution and response time to an emerging defect. So far, this issue has not been discussed in the literature concerning rolling element-bearing diagnostics, so this article describes a study showing the possibility of deep network optimization for diagnostic tasks.

2. Rolling Bearing Damage—Analysis of the Fault Detection Problem

2.1. Extraction of Damage Symptoms Using Spectral Analysis

When damage occurs on the surface of any of the bearing elements, each time one of the rolling elements rolls through the damaged area, a brief impulsive force is generated that causes the bearing to vibrate. If the speed is constant, these pulses occur periodically. Periodic changes in the vibration signal resulting from rolling bearing defects provide excellent information to determine the nature of the damage. The analysis of the impact of periodically occurring changes in signals, which can be understood as the evaluation of the contribution of damage-related features to the measured signal, is now mainly implemented using the fast Fourier transform. With the FFT, it is possible to assess the trend of amplitude changes associated with rolling bearing defects that occur at specific frequencies of the spectrum. For a ball bearing in which the inner race rotates and the outer race is stationary, the characteristic frequencies for each type of defect are as follows [16,48]:

$$f_C = 0.5 \cdot f_r \cdot \left(1 - \frac{d \cdot cos\vartheta}{D}\right), \tag{1}$$

$$f_B = \frac{D}{2d} \cdot f_r \cdot \left(1 - \left(\frac{d \cdot cos\vartheta}{D}\right)^2\right), \tag{2}$$

$$f_O = \frac{N_B}{2} \cdot f_r \cdot \left(1 - \frac{d \cdot cos\vartheta}{D}\right), \tag{3}$$

$$f_I = \frac{N_B}{2} \cdot f_r \cdot \left(1 + \frac{d \cdot cos\vartheta}{D}\right), \tag{4}$$

where f_r is the rotational frequency, f_C is the frequency associated with cage failure, f_B is the frequency associated with rolling element failure, f_O is the frequency associated with outer race failure, f_I is the frequency associated with inner race failure, N_B is the number of rolling elements, D is the pitch diameter of the bearing, d is the diameter of the rolling element, and ϑ is the operating angle of the bearing.

2.2. Methodology of the Conducted Experimental Research

The test bench (Figure 1) used for the experimental tests consisted of an *INDUKTA Sh90L-4* induction motor (Celma Indukta S.A., Cantoni Group, Cieszyn, Poland), which was mechanically coupled to a *PZB b44b DC* external motor. Load control is achieved by varying the motor arm current at a constant excitation current. A triaxial accelerometer type *4506-B-003* placed on the counter-drive side and a uniaxial sensor type *4514-001* placed on the drive side were used to measure mechanical vibrations. The measured diagnostic signal in the form of a voltage signal was fed directly to a National Instruments measurement card. A single measurement was performed in 10 s with a sampling rate of 50 kHz, which ensured a high resolution of the spectrum. Based on the measurements performed on the object, the measured signal was measured and processed. For this purpose, a measurement and diagnostic application was developed in the *LabVIEW 2019* and *MATLAB 2022a* environments.

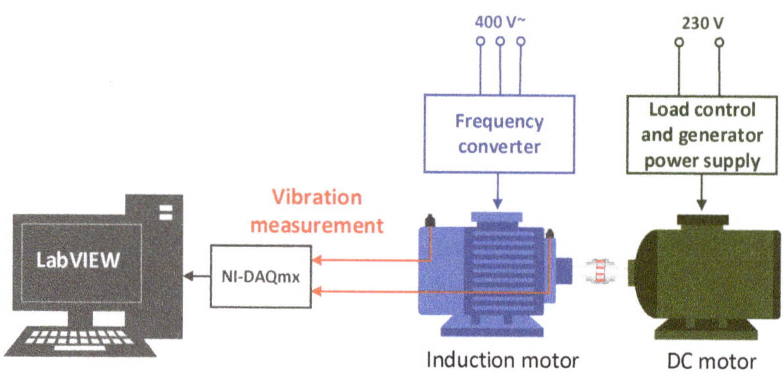

Figure 1. Diagram of the test bench.

Two bearings from *SKF 6205-Z* are mounted in the engine under study, the design dimensions of which are shown in Table 1. During the tests, the damaged bearings were mounted on the counter-drive side. The classification and photos of all the damages tested are shown in Figure 2. The following types of damage were investigated for the outer and inner races:

- Longitudinal scratch at a length of 3 mm;
- A spot indentation 1 mm deep;

- Two spot indentations 1 mm deep;
- Transverse scratch.

Table 1. Dimensions of construction of the *SKF 6205-Z* bearing.

Bearing Element	Description	Value	Unit
Diameter of the rolling element	d	8	mm
Bearing pitch diameter	D	39	mm
Number of rolling elements	N_B	9	-
Bearing operating angle	ϑ	0	°

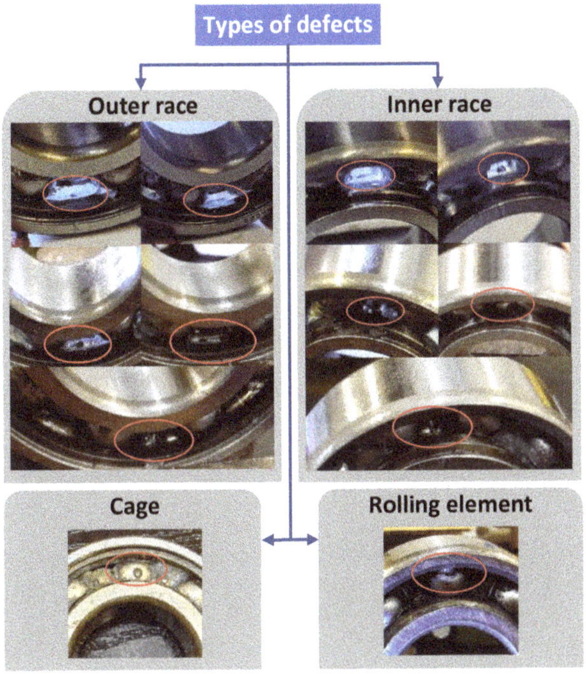

Figure 2. Classification of damage to the bearing analyzed.

The conduct of tests for different stages of damage made it possible to assess the effectiveness and precision of the proposed solution for the initial and advanced stages of the mechanical degradation of the bearing. For each of the types of damage analyzed, measurements were carried out for the operation of the induction motor under different load conditions (in the range of 0–T_{LN}). Additionally, to compare the effect of an external machine mechanically coupled to the motor under study, measurements were made in the absence of this coupling. This eliminated the situation in which the auxiliary machine asymmetry was transferred to the test machine. To analyze the impact of individual rolling bearing failures, a spectral analysis of mechanical vibrations was carried out. The results of the analysis are presented in the next section.

2.3. Spectral Analysis of Mechanical Vibration Signal

The algorithm to calculate the envelope of a signal involves averaging it with a bandpass filter with an appropriately selected bandwidth, then using the Hilbert function, an analytical signal is calculated, the absolute value of which is the envelope signal [49].

The band selection was determined by the technique provided by the bearing manufacturer (Bruel&Kjaer, Nærum, Denmark). For the induction motor used in the research work, used to install the bearing node described in the manufacturer's documentation, the frequency was determined experimentally as 1600 Hz. It should be emphasized that the bandwidth was individually determined for each machine based on experimental measurements of the natural frequency of the bearing node. By filtering the signal and averaging it, it is possible to remove interference that can interfere with the extraction of the symptoms of the damage under study.

A comparison of the frequency spectrum of the envelope for an undamaged bearing and four different types of damage at a load equal to half the rated load and a rotational speed of 1450 rpm is shown in Figures 3–6. For each of the cases studied, it is possible to extract the characteristic frequencies of the damage. However, during the frequency analysis of the signal, the accuracy of the analysis is affected by the resolution of the spectrum under study. This parameter depends on the number of samples of the measured signal, that is, the sampling frequency and the measurement time. To increase the resolution of the spectrum at a constant sampling frequency, it is necessary to increase the measurement time. However, an important limitation is that the measurement must take place under constant load conditions and supply voltage frequency (steady state). This makes signal analysis methods based on the fast Fourier transform unsuitable for applications in which the operating conditions of the drives under testing change dynamically [50].

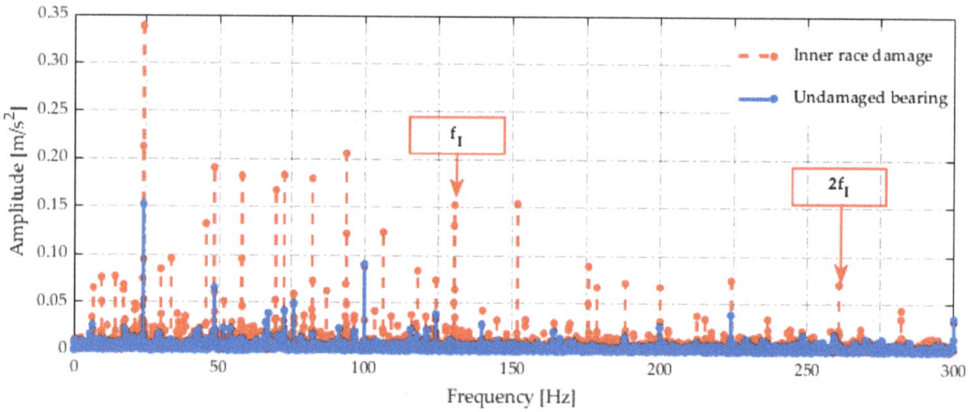

Figure 3. Envelope spectrum—undamaged bearing and inner race damage, $T_L = 0.5T_{LN}, f_s = 50$ Hz.

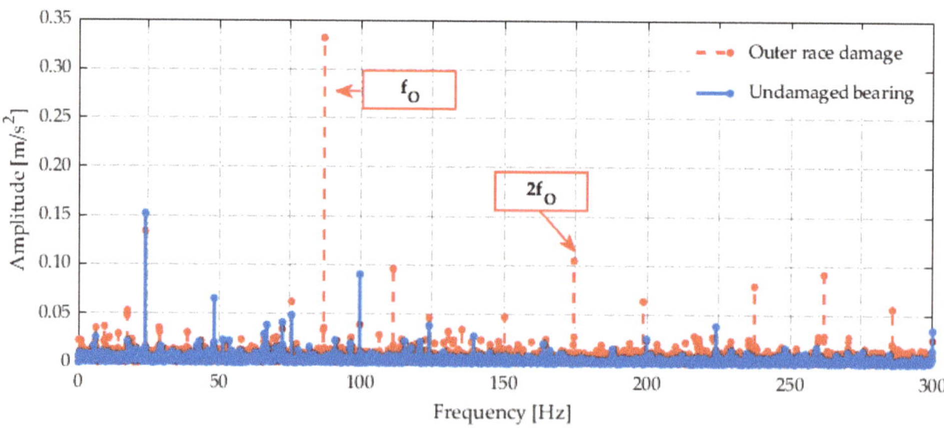

Figure 4. Envelope spectrum—undamaged bearing and outer race damage, $T_L = 0.5T_{LN}, f_s = 50$ Hz.

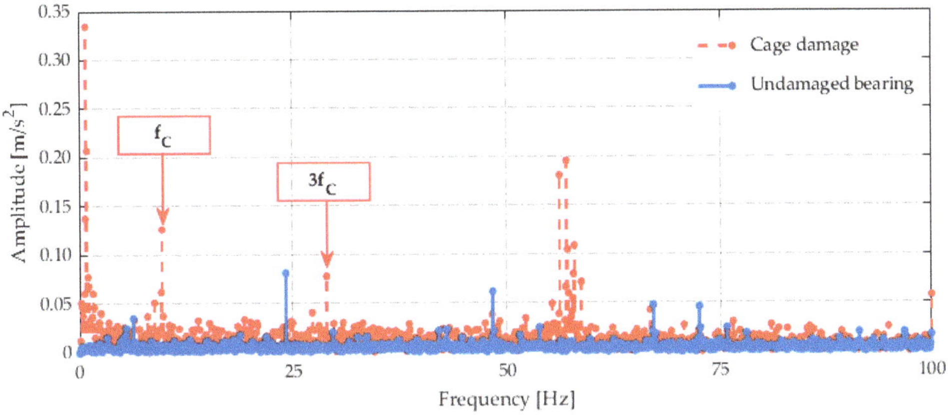

Figure 5. Envelope spectrum—undamaged bearing and cage damage, $T_L = 0.5T_{LN}, f_s = 50$ Hz.

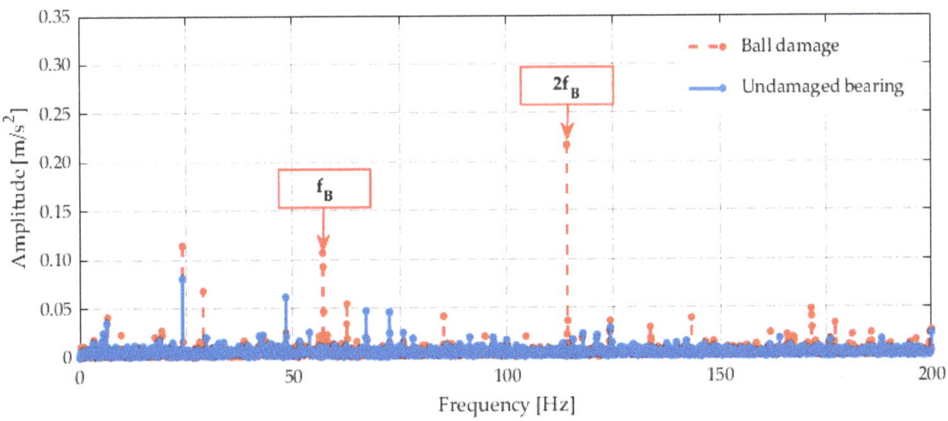

Figure 6. Envelope spectrum—undamaged bearing and rolling element damage, $T_L = 0.5T_{LN}, f_s = 50$ Hz.

3. Bearing Fault Detection and Classification System Based on a Convolutional Neural Network

Convolutional neural networks (CNNs) are currently being used in an increasing number of applications due to their high precision in automatic data analysis. Initially, they were used mainly in image processing, but with the appropriate signal transformations, they are increasingly finding widespread use in electrical machine diagnostics, among other applications. With the ability to directly analyze diagnostic signals, CNNs are defining increasingly abstract sets of features, enabling the generation of high-level patterns and, ultimately, allowing appropriate signal classification. The performance of the structure is strongly dependent on many factors, including the input signal, the selected number of layers, and appropriately selected hyperparameters, which affect not only the accuracy of the structure's performance, but also the processing time of the input information, so optimizing the structure and the parameters of the training process is an important step in the development of a diagnostic application.

3.1. Development of Deep Network Input Information

The operation of the convolutional structure forces the processing of input information in the form of a two- or three-dimensional matrix (Figure 7). Therefore, the appropriate processing of diagnostic signals is aimed at making optimal use of the properties of CNN.

The diagnostic approach proposed in the article used signals recorded from a triaxial sensor. Given this, the collected data included three time series for the X, Y, and Z axes, respectively. In each measurement series, 1000 samples were recorded, which corresponded to a signal acquisition time of 0.02 s. The vectors were then transformed into a 25 × 40 matrix. The use of such a matrix shape allows the use of filters in convolution layers with small dimensions. In addition, the developed structure does not require the use of the zero-padding technique. Thus, the entirety of the detected simple and higher-order features is taken into account in the final classification.

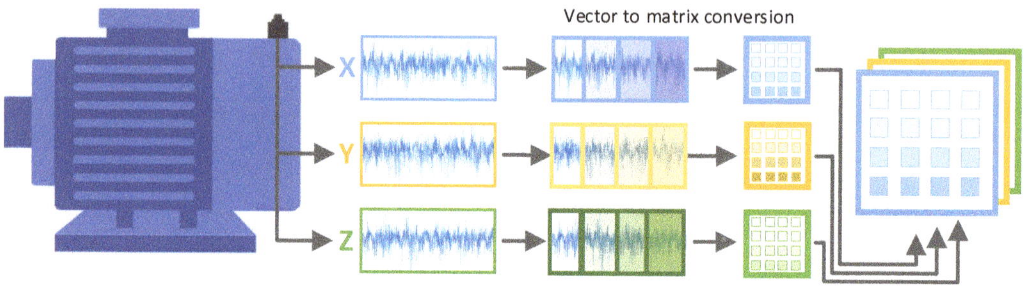

Figure 7. Preparation of the CNN input matrix: idea diagram.

An equally important aspect of preparing the signals for input to the CNN was the normalization of vectors containing samples of the measured mechanical vibrations. Overestimated values affect the updates of the network weights and significantly increase computation time, and thus training time. This fact is due to very large gradient jumps known in the literature as an "exploding gradient." In the final stage of processing, the data were combined into a 3D matrix, and in this form, they were fed to the input of the structure. In total, 19,500 samples were collected (1500 cases for each of the 13 damage categories). The developed data set was randomly divided into three packages (keeping the same number of samples in the considered class):

- Training package used in the training process,
- Validation package used to analyze the stability of the learning process and avoid loss of generalization (analysis of learning curves),
- Testing package used to determine the additional precision coefficient of the network (after the training process).

Table 2 shows the exact distribution of data allocated to the training, validation, and testing processes for each piece of damage under investigation, where the sets were chosen to contain different loads, from 0 to nominal in 20% increments. This was done to ensure the good generalization of the network being trained.

Table 2. Summary of the number of samples for each type of damage and process.

Type of Fault	Number of Samples (Cases)		
	Training	**Validation**	**Test**
No fault	500	500	500
Inner race	2500	2500	2500
Outer race	2500	2500	2500
Rolling element	500	500	500
Cage	500	500	500
Summary	6500	6500	6500

3.2. Development of Deep Network Structure

CNNs are steadily gaining popularity due to their ability to use raw data in the classification process. Their architecture in general usually includes layers such as a convolution layer, which is responsible for converting the provided data into new information with a higher degree of abstraction, a pooling layer, which is responsible for selecting the information created in the convolution layer, thus leading to a reduction in the dimension of the data, and a fully connected layer, which is ultimately responsible for classifying the input data based on the features detected by the convolution layers. However, the proposed CNN structure also includes additional layers to ensure the restoration of non-linear dependencies and the stabilization of the training process (Table 3).

Table 3. Parameters of the convolutional neural network structure used.

Parameter Name	Parameter Value	Structure Scheme
Number of convolution layers	3	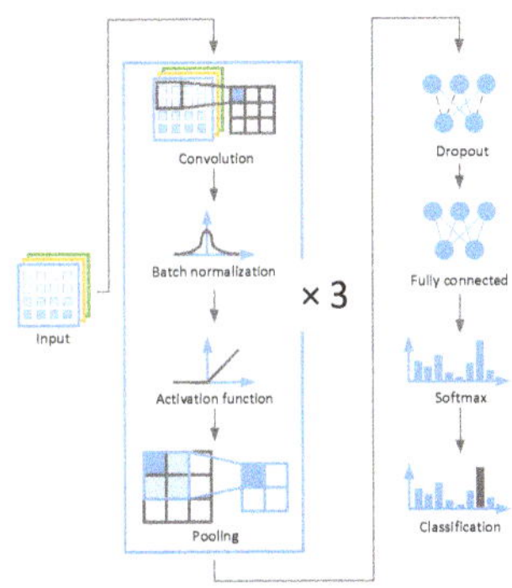
Number of filters	20-40-60	
Dimension of filters	5 × 5	
Stride	(1 × 1), (2 × 2), (2 × 2)	
Number of normalization layers	3	
Value of the coefficient ε	0.001	
Number of activation layers	3	
Activation function	ReLU	
Number of pooling layers	3	
Pooling method	maximum	
Window size	3 × 3	
Stride	(1 × 1), (2 × 2), (2 × 2)	
Dropout probability	0.5	
Number of fully connected layers	2	
Number of fully connected neurons	(60), (13)	

- Convolution layer: Consisting of a set of different filters, each of which is responsible for extracting a different selected feature (by tuning the window parameters). The filter window determines the output features using a convolution operation of the filter g and the set h to which the filter is applied:

$$C = g[x,y] * h[x,y] = \sum_i \left(\sum_j (g[i,j] \cdot h[x-i, y-j]) \right) \tag{5}$$

  where C is the resulting matrix of higher-order features found with the selected filter.
- Batch normalization layer: Used to speed up the network training process and increase accuracy by reducing the internal variation of the data range. During the training process, the mean and standard deviation are calculated for each mini-packet and provide the normalization of the convolution layers' weighting factors to the 0–1 range.
- Activation function: Ensures that the network correctly reproduces non-linear relationships. For CNNs, the most commonly used activation function is the Rectified Linear Unit (ReLU). ReLU is most commonly used because of the simplicity of calculating both the result and the derivative, which accelerates the training process.
- The pooling layer: Determines which information is useful in context to evaluate the class of the input matrix. In addition, it allows the dimensionality of the data to be reduced, leading to lower computing power requirements and improved generalization capabilities.
- Dropout layer: involves removing selected neural connections at the input of the first fully connected layer, which allows one to speed up the training process and, above

all, to make the state of individual neurons independent of each other (improving generalization ability).

- Fully connected layer: Is responsible for determining the contribution of matrix features to the final evaluation of category membership. The most common way to use the final classification is to use the softmax function, which determines the probabilities of a given input belonging to each of the analyzed classes.

3.3. *Convolutional Neural Networks—Training Process Hyperparameters*

One of the most commonly used algorithms in the training process is stochastic gradient descent (SGD), which is characterized by calculating an averaged gradient for individual mini-batches of learning data. However, a limitation of the SGD algorithm is the high variance of the gradient update, which can lead to slow convergence (getting stuck at the local minimum or the so-called saddle). A popular enhancement to this algorithm is the addition of a "momentum" factor, which introduces gradient-matching adaptation by referring to the history of gradient changes in earlier learning iterations (Table 4). This extension is referred to as stochastic gradient descent with momentum (SGDM), which allows not only for the better convergence of the network learning process, but also for bypassing local minima of the objective function. According to the SGDM algorithm, in each iteration, the average gradient was determined for 90 randomly selected samples (mini-batch) from the entire training data set. The number of iterations was selected so that all training data samples were presented at each epoch. Moreover, after the end of each epoch, the mini-batch was shuffled, thanks to which the gradient was averaged based on different samples. Updates to network parameters are based on the following formula.

$$\boldsymbol{\theta}_{t+1} = \boldsymbol{\theta}_t - \boldsymbol{v}_{t+1} \tag{6}$$

where

$$\boldsymbol{v}_{t+1} = \mu \cdot \boldsymbol{v}_t + \eta \cdot \boldsymbol{\nabla} \boldsymbol{J}(\boldsymbol{\theta}_t) \tag{7}$$

and where $\boldsymbol{\theta t}$ is the network parameters in step t, $\boldsymbol{\nabla J}$ is the gradient of the objective function, η is the learning rate, $\boldsymbol{vt}$ is the velocity vector in step t, and μ is the momentum factor.

Table 4. Parameters of the CNN training process.

Parameter Name	Parameter Value
Learning method	SGDM
Momentum value	0.95
Initial value of learning rate	0.002
Number of learning epochs	500
Decreasing period	10
Input matrix size	25 × 40
Execution environment	GPU
Mini-batch size	90
Size of training data set	6500
Number of considered classes	13

4. CNN-Based Diagnostic System for Bearing Faults

Fault diagnostic systems that use direct signal processing are characterized by an extended structure compared to classical solutions. The extensive network architecture enables the extraction of the characteristics of the input matrices for assignment to one of the damage categories considered. Deep neural networks are distinguished by their lack of formal rules for the selection of network hyperparameters, so these structures in diagnostic applications are often too extensive. Therefore, it is important to optimize the number of neuronal connections. Of key importance for a CNN is the selection of the number of filters that perform the function of extracting the features of the input matrix. The applications of deep neural networks in electrical motor diagnostics encountered in the literature are characterized by the large number of filters that significantly increase the number of parameters required for adaptation during the training process. Another approach described in the literature is the use of pre-trained structures developed for image recognition tasks such as AlexNet, RespNet, and GoogLeNet. The result of the elaborate structure is a significant lengthening of the process of the adaptation of weighting factors of convolutional layers. To eliminate this phenomenon, the research assumed a minimum precision threshold of the network with the selection of parameters dedicated to the development of the smallest possible structure that achieves the assumed efficiency threshold. Moreover, it is important to adapt the structure of the deep network to the changing conditions of the training process such as available data packets. Only in the absence of a strict dependence on the precision of the diagnostic system on the size and quality of the available information is it possible to ensure correct fault detection [51]. During the experimental study, structures with three convolutional layers and one classifier layer were analyzed. The process was limited to changing the number of filters of three convolutional layers. Optimization included the amount of information that went to the classifier, which allowed the input matrix to be properly assigned to a class. A total of 125 deep convolutional network structures were analyzed (changing the number of filters in each layer from 20 to 100 with a step of 20). For each of the analyzed structures, the number of neural connections, the number of parameters required for tuning, as well as the training time, and the final precision achieved for the test data were determined. To analyze the accuracy of the training process, the impact of available training data on the precision of the bearing damage detection system was determined. Research included the use of variable sizes of training samples from the available data package in the process of adapting the weight coefficients of the network. To show the influence of the amount of information (λ coefficient: training data size/training packet in percent) on the effectiveness of fault classification, the same CNN structure was used in each case. The research used a range of coefficient changes from 5% to 49% with a 2% step of change. The results of the conducted analyses are presented in Figure 8b. The test results are shown in the dependence of the network's accuracy on the number of its parameters in the figure below. As can be seen in Figure 8a, increasing the number of parameters does not necessarily translate into an increased accuracy of network performance. In addition, outlier samples are observed which, despite an increase in the number of neural connections, did not result in correct adaptation. Nevertheless, the trend of changes allows a limited increase in the precision of the damage class assessment. This means that the choice of network parameters should be a compromise between the number of parameters and the assumed minimum precision of the detection system. Therefore, in further studies, out of the 125 structures analyzed, those selected were the ones that met the assumed quality criterion with the lowest possible number of neural connections. Moreover, the research has shown that the use of a training data package containing over 25% of available samples provides less than a 99% level of damage classification precision (Figure 8b). This means that despite the available information obtained as a result of a short acquisition time, it is possible to develop sufficient sets of training data. Moreover, the high efficiency for the variable conditions of the training process (available data) confirms the high quality of the automatic extraction of damaged features directly visible in mechanical vibration signals.

The classification performance was determined based on a data set that contained samples for 13 categories (Appendix A) with a total dimension of 6500 cases. Based on the results of neural computations for 125 CNN structures, those that met certain assumptions regarding the precision of damage classification were selected (Table 5).

The juxtaposition of the obtained results presented in Table 5 allows us to observe that as the number of neuronal connections increases, the ability of the structure to recognize individual classes of damage increases. However, achieving a precision of more than 99.8% requires the use of a much more extensive structure with a large number of convolution filters. However, it should be emphasized that the training time did not increase with increasing network parameters. This fact is related to the much simpler extraction of features from the input matrix with an increased number of filters. The elaboration of universal features contained in the input information by a CNN structure with a small number of neural connections requires greater precision in the selection of the network's weighting coefficients. Given this, the process is limited by the need to adjust the learning rate to values that allow for small changes in the weights of the network connections. This problem does not occur in structures with a much larger number of filters that enable the memorization of many features of the input matrix. Taking into account the implementation of CNN in programmable systems, it is crucial to provide as small several parameters as possible to ensure a high level of efficiency. Therefore, the adjustment of the precision threshold should be closely related to the task implemented by the neural structure.

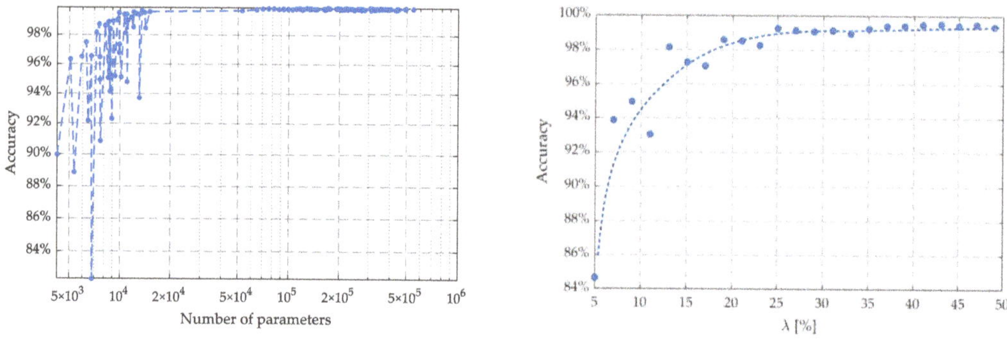

Figure 8. Dependency of network accuracy on (**a**) the number of its parameters and (**b**) the training set size: λ = training data size/training packet.

Table 5. Summary of selected CNN structures.

Assumed Accuracy	Achieved Accuracy	Convolutional Layers			CNN Learnable Parameters	Training Time [s]
		1 Layer	2 Layers	3 Layers		
90.0%	96.323%	20	20	40	5071	1281
92.0%	96.323%	20	20	40	5071	1281
94.0%	96.323%	20	20	40	5071	1281
96.0%	96.323%	20	20	40	5071	1281
98.0%	98.185%	20	40	60	7203	1246
99.0%	99.062%	20	60	80	9535	1212
99.5%	99.569%	20	80	60	9815	1279
99.8%	99.815%	80	20	20	64,413	1263
99.9%	99.908%	100	20	80	127,753	1256

In the neural calculations implemented, the network structures with a variable number of parameters in the range were analyzed: 4245–545,253. Of particular note, the highest precision of the neural structure (99.923%) was obtained for a network with 207,493 parameters, which is less than half of the analyzed range. Expanding the number of neural connections twice (545,253 parameters) did not result in such high precision (99.877%). Furthermore, increasing the number of parameters beyond 12,000 in the described diagnostic application resulted in a maximum increase in the classification precision of 0.25%. Therefore, increasing the network architecture should only be done up to a certain range, where a clear increase in efficiency due to an increase in the number of tuneable parameters is observable. In practical applications, the process of parameter selection is carried out while observing learning curves for the test data. Example waveforms of the curves for the structures described in Table 5 are shown in Figure 9.

The analysis of the learning curves shown in Figure 9 clearly shows a much higher level of precision of the diagnostic system based on extended structures. However, the analysis makes it possible to observe that regardless of the structure used, the training process converges. As the number of neuronal connections increases, a reduced level of oscillation of the learning curves for testing data is noticeable. In addition, in the case of a reduced structure (red color), much lower dynamics of the learning process were observed. This means that the structure requires a larger number of epochs to tune the classifier parameters for the reduced number of diagnostic symptoms extracted from the convolution layers. The approximation shown in Figure 9 allows us to see that increasing the structures has an effect only up to a certain range, which confirms the results shown in Table 5.

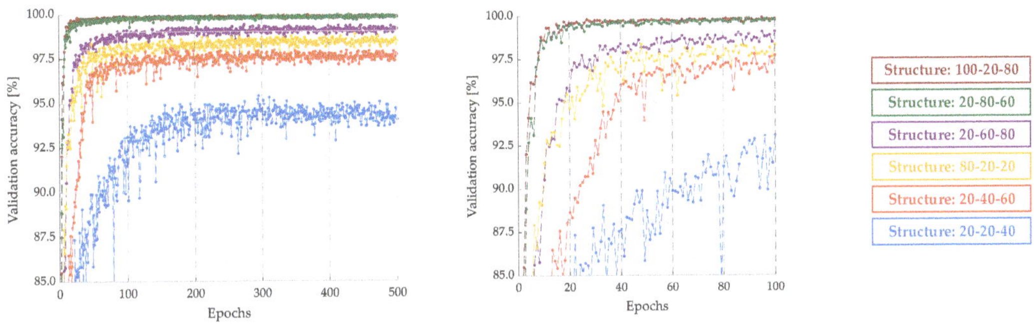

Figure 9. CNN training process—learning curves.

Concerning the importance of fault detection systems, the limitations associated with the use of CNNs should be noted. The implementation of CNNs in the diagnostic system results in difficulties in the form of a lack of formal rules for selecting hyperparameters for the structure and training process, the need for large learning datasets capable of providing automatic symptom extraction, the long process of training the network, the risk of losing its generalization capability, and the time to compute the response depending on the input information and network structure. However, these limitations were addressed in the study by optimizing the network structure and using the hyperparameter selection technique presented in [52]. Next, running the study on 1000 samples over a period, with a measurement lasting 10 s and a sampling rate of 50 kHz, yielded 500 cases from a single measurement, whereas using classical methods such as FFT would yield only one case; so, despite the need for a large training data set, it was simple and quick to develop. Further, the training process was optimized by using the SGDM algorithm based on mini-batches of data to average the gradient (speeding up the learning process, compared to classical approaches where usually the gradient is calculated for each sample separately), and the network training itself was performed using a GPU, giving a training time of slightly more than 20 min. Subsequently, the risk of losing the generalization of the network was eliminated through several approaches: the use of a stochastic learning technique (giving efficient exploration of the solution space and avoiding local minima), the analysis of learning curves for training and validation data (which helps verify that the model does not begin to over-fit the training data), and the use of a dropout layer (involving random resetting of the neuron weights, which forces the network to learn more elaborate and robust representations of the data). Finally, the study showed an average response time for the optimized network of 0.03 s. This time can be considered constant due to the constant size of the input matrix and the invariant number of operations performed on the network. Additionally, the network response was further accelerated by optimizing the structure, which in its smallest version has only 5071 parameters (with an accuracy of more than 96%, Table 5).

To verify the performance of CNN in fault diagnostic application, the next stage of the research concerns the analysis of the network's response to test packets containing samples obtained for the 13 classes. The responses of the developed neural structures were summarized in the form of confusion matrices shown in Figure 10.

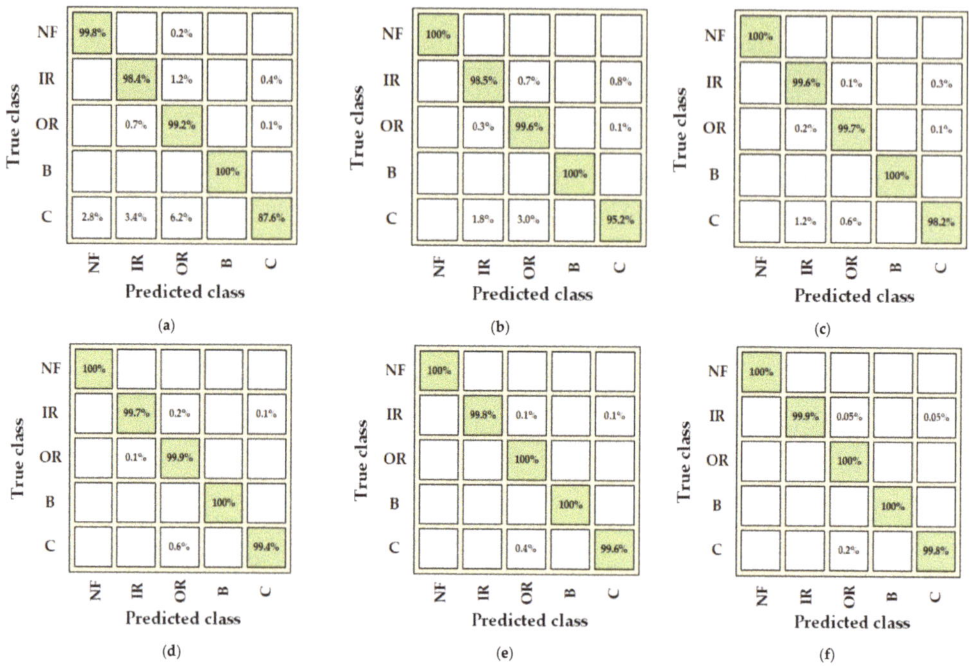

Figure 10. Verification of the proposed CNN structures—confusion matrix for different numbers of convolutional filter: (**a**) 20-20-40; (**b**) 20-40-60; (**c**) 20-60-80; (**d**) 20-80-60; (**e**) 80-20-20; (**f**) 100-20-80; NF—no fault, IR—inner race fault, OR—outer race fault, B—ball defect, C—cage defect.

The key task of diagnostic systems is to detect and evaluate the type of damage, while the precise determination of the degree of the defect is a secondary function. Therefore, in the first step, the responses of the network were analyzed in the form of division into each category of damage: inner race (IR), outer race (OR), ball (B), and cage (C). In the confusion matrices shown in Figure 10, the percentage effectiveness of the systems for each of the categories considered was represented. On this basis, the initial verification of the proposed structures was determined.

As can be observed in Figure 10, as the number of filters in each convolution layer increases, the proportion of false information obtained in the CNN output decreases. However, it should be emphasized that each of the structures presented, except for 20-20-40 (Figure 10a), was characterized by almost 100% defect detection precision, understood as the recognition between defect and no-defect states. Furthermore, an increase in the number of filters increased the effectiveness of the classification of the type of fault. Based on the analysis of the results shown in Figure 10, as well as the number of parameters of the structure (Table 5) and the analysis of the training process (Figure 9), it was decided that the 80-20-20 structure should be used in further studies. This network was characterized by a small number of parameters, a short weight adaptation time, and high detection and classification precision. To verify the selected structure, tests were carried out, including the classification of the type of defect and evaluation of the degree of rolling bearing degradation. The results obtained for different loads are shown in Figure 11.

The experimental verification of the developed detection system based on a deep neural network was carried out for defects of different kinds as well as degrees. As bearing damage cannot be modeled during drive operation, the course of mechanical vibration signals on the axis was artificially modeled by combining fragments of signals measured on the real object. As a result, it was possible to determine the response time of the neural structure to the occurrence of bearing damage.

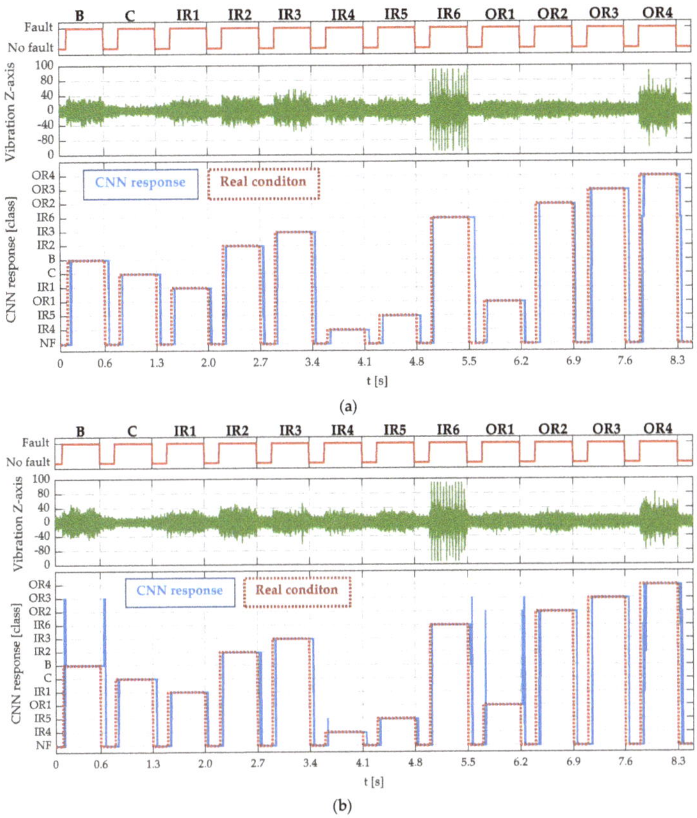

Figure 11. Verification of the proposed CNN structures (80-20-20): (**a**) $T_L = 0.5T_{LN}, f_s = 50$ Hz; (**b**) $T_L = T_{LN}$, $f_s = 50$ Hz.

The analysis of the results of the experimental verification shown in Figure 11 unambiguously confirms the high level of precision of the developed diagnostic method. The selected structure of the convolutional neural network is characterized by the high detection of damage and the assessment of the degree of fault. In addition, the short response time to an emerging defect is particularly notable, even in the case of damage at an early stage. Based on the analysis of CNN's response to the given input matrix, an average detection time of about 0.03 s was determined. As can be observed in Figure 11a, the response of the system is delayed concerning the moment the defect disappears. The fact is related to the presence in the input data buffer (data frame) of the samples characteristic of the damage state. Due to this, the neural structure still has information on part of the features attributable to the damage state. However, it should be noted that, from a practical point of view, damage decay does not occur and this study aimed to assess the response of CNN to dynamically changing input information. Only then is it possible to determine the response time, as well as the resistance to changes in the technical state of the bearing, and the operating conditions of the motor (load moment). The course of the network response, shown in Figure 11b, makes it possible to notice the false information about the technical condition of the bearings. An in-depth analysis of the CNN confirmed that the cause of the anomalies that appear is the previously described method of modeling mechanical vibrations. The use of a combination of diagnostic signal vectors results in the lack of an unambiguous response of the network when the input data buffer is half full of samples characteristic of the fault condition and its absence. The response of the network determined by the probability of belonging to one of the categories is then ambiguous. However, in the practical implementation of the diagnostic system, such a situation will not occur.

5. Conclusions

The proposed diagnostic approach based on CNN's direct processing of mechanical vibration signals in rolling bearing diagnostics is an alternative to current methods that use advanced signal processing methods. Furthermore, the optimization of the neural structure allowed the reduction of the number of parameters to the necessary minimum, while ensuring a very high level of precision in the short time of damage detection and classification. In addition, the developed diagnostic system was characterized by a high sensitivity to a change in the degree of damage, so the application can be used in safety-critical systems. Future research will include an investigation into the applicability of current signals in rolling bearing damage diagnostics, which is not currently achievable using classical diagnostic methods such as the short-time Fourier transform, the Hilbert–Huang transform, etc. In addition, work on the application of a convolutional neural network in the diagnosis of bearing damage during transients (start-up, braking, and dynamic load changes) is planned to be carried out.

Author Contributions: Conceptualization, M.S. and M.D.; methodology, M.W. and O.F.; software, M.S. and J.J.J.; validation, M.S., J.J.J. and O.F.; formal analysis, M.D., K.S., S.W. and J.V.; data curation, M.W.; writing—original draft preparation, M.S., O.F. and J.J.J.; writing—review and editing, M.D., M.W., K.S., O.F., M.S. and A.W.; project administration, K.S., R.Z., M.D. and S.W. All authors have read and agreed to the published version of the manuscript.

Funding: Funded by the European Union under GA no 101101961—HECATE. The views and opinions expressed are, however, those of the author(s) only and do not necessarily reflect those of the European Union or Clean Aviation Joint Undertaking. Neither the European Union nor the granting authority can be held responsible for them. This project is supported by the Clean Aviation Joint Undertaking and its Members.

Data Availability Statement: Data are contained within the article.

Conflicts of Interest: Authors Sebastien Weisse and Jerome Valire was employed by the company SAFRAN Electrical & Power. The remaining authors declare that the research was conducted in the absence of any commercial or financial relationships that could be construed as a potential conflict of interest.

Appendix A

Table A1. Description and designations of the investigated damages.

Type of Damage	Label	Parameters
Rolling element	B	Spot indentation 0.5–1 mm deep
Cage	C	Spot indentation 2 mm deep
Inner race	IR1	Spot indentation 1 mm deep
	IR2	Spot indentation 1 mm deep
	IR3	Two spot indentations 1 mm deep
	IR4	Longitudinal scratch at a length of 3 mm
	IR5	Transverse scratch
Outer race	OR1	Spot indentation 1 mm deep
	OR2	Spot indentation 1 mm deep
	OR3	Two spot indentations 1 mm deep
	OR4	Longitudinal scratch at a length of 3 mm
	OR5	Transverse scratch
	NF	No fault

References

1. Xiong, R.; Sun, W.; Yu, Q.; Sun, F. Research progress, challenges and prospects of fault diagnosis on battery system of electric vehicles. *Appl. Energy* **2020**, *279*, 115855. [CrossRef]

2. Brelje, B.J.; Martins, J.R.R.A. Electric, hybrid, and turboelectric fixed-wing aircraft: A review of concepts, models, and design approaches. *Prog. Aerosp. Sci.* **2019**, *104*, 1–19. [CrossRef]
3. Nandi, S.; Toliyat, H.A.; Li, X. Condition Monitoring and Fault Diagnosis of Electrical Motors—A Review. *IEEE Trans. Energy Convers.* **2005**, *20*, 719–729. [CrossRef]
4. Bellini, A.; Filippetti, F.; Tassoni, C.; Capolino, G.-A. Advances in Diagnostic Techniques for Induction Machines. *IEEE Trans. Ind. Electron.* **2008**, *55*, 4109–4126. [CrossRef]
5. Gangsar, P.; Tiwari, R. Signal based condition monitoring techniques for fault detection and diagnosis of induction motors: A state-of-the-art review. *Mech. Syst. Signal Process.* **2020**, *144*, 106908. [CrossRef]
6. Singh, G.K.; Kazzaz, S.A.S.A. Induction machine drive condition monitoring and diagnostic research—A survey. *Electr. Power Syst. Res.* **2003**, *64*, 145–158. [CrossRef]
7. Li, Y.; Wang, H.; Li, J.; Tan, J. A 2-D Long Short-Term Memory Fusion Networks for Bearing Remaining Useful Life Prediction. *IEEE Sens. J.* **2022**, *22*, 21806–21815. [CrossRef]
8. Rubini, R.; Meneghetti, U. Application Of The Envelope And Wavelet Transform Analyses For The Diagnosis Of Incipient Faults In Ball Bearings. *Mech. Syst. Signal Process.* **2001**, *15*, 287–302. [CrossRef]
9. Stack, J.R.; Habetler, T.G.; Harley, R.G. Fault-signature modeling and detection of inner-race bearing faults. *IEEE Trans. Ind. Appl.* **2006**, *42*, 61–68. [CrossRef]
10. Luo, X.; Wang, H.; Han, T.; Zhang, Y. FFT-Trans: Enhancing Robustness in Mechanical Fault Diagnosis With Fourier Transform-Based Transformer Under Noisy Conditions. *IEEE Trans. Instrum. Meas.* **2024**, *73*, 2515112. [CrossRef]
11. Hoang, D.T.; Kang, H.J. A Motor Current Signal-Based Bearing Fault Diagnosis Using Deep Learning and Information Fusion. *IEEE Trans. Instrum. Meas.* **2020**, *69*, 3325–3333. [CrossRef]
12. Schoen, R.R.; Habetler, T.G.; Kamran, F.; Bartfield, R.G. Motor bearing damage detection using stator current monitoring. *IEEE Trans. Ind. Appl.* **1995**, *31*, 1274–1279. [CrossRef]
13. Caesarendra, W.; Kosasih, B.; Tieu, A.K.; Zhu, H.; Moodie, C.A.S.; Zhu, Q. Acoustic emission-based condition monitoring methods: Review and application for low speed slew bearing. *Mech. Syst. Signal Process.* **2016**, *72–73*, 134–159. [CrossRef]
14. Pandya, D.H.; Upadhyay, S.H.; Harsha, S.P. Fault diagnosis of rolling element bearing with intrinsic mode function of acoustic emission data using APF-KNN. *Expert Syst. Appl.* **2013**, *40*, 4137–4145. [CrossRef]
15. Yakkati, R.R.; Yeduri, S.R.; Tripathy, R.K.; Cenkeramaddi, L.R. Multi-Channel Time-Frequency Domain Deep CNN Approach for Machinery Fault Recognition Using Multi-Sensor Time-Series. *IEEE Access* **2023**, *11*, 116570–116580. [CrossRef]
16. Immovilli, F.; Bellini, A.; Rubini, R.; Tassoni, C. Diagnosis of Bearing Faults in Induction Machines by Vibration or Current Signals: A Critical Comparison. *IEEE Trans. Ind. Appl.* **2010**, *46*, 1350–1359. [CrossRef]
17. Patidar, S.; Soni, P.K. An Overview on Vibration Analysis Techniques for the Diagnosis of Rolling Element Bearing Faults. *Int. J. Eng. Trends Technol.* **2013**, *4*, 1804–1809.
18. Tandon, N. A comparison of some vibration parameters for the condition monitoring of rolling element bearings. *Measurement* **1994**, *12*, 285–289. [CrossRef]
19. Ewert, P.; Kowalski, C.T.; Orlowska-Kowalska, T. Low-Cost Monitoring and Diagnosis System for Rolling Bearing Faults of the Induction Motor Based on Neural Network Approach. *Electronics* **2020**, *9*, 1334. [CrossRef]
20. Liang, B.; Iwnicki, S.D.; Zhao, Y. Application of power spectrum, cepstrum, higher order spectrum and neural network analyses for induction motor fault diagnosis. *Mech. Syst. Signal Process.* **2013**, *39*, 342–360. [CrossRef]
21. Verstraete, D.; Ferrada, A.; Droguett, E.L.; Meruane, V.; Modarres, M. Deep Learning Enabled Fault Diagnosis Using Time-Frequency Image Analysis of Rolling Element Bearings. *Shock Vib.* **2017**, *2017*, 5067651. [CrossRef]
22. Ewert, P.; Kowalski, C.T.; Wolkiewicz, M. The application of wavelet analysis and neural networks in the diagnosis of rolling bearing faults in induction motors. *Przegląd Elektrotechniczny* **2013**, *89*, 124–127.
23. Filippetti, F.; Franceschini, G.; Tassoni, C. Vas, Recent developments of induction motor drives fault diagnosis using AI techniques. *IEEE Trans. Ind. Electron.* **2000**, *47*, 994–1004. [CrossRef]
24. Kowalski, C.T. *Diagnostyka Układów Napędowych z Silnikiem Indukcyjnym z Zastosowaniem Metod Sztucznej Inteligencji*; Oficyna Wydawnicza Politechniki Wrocławskiej: Wrocław, Poland, 2013.
25. Kowalski, C.T.; Orlowska-Kowalska, T. Neural networks application for induction motor faults diagnosis. *Math. Comput. Simul.* **2003**, *63*, 435–448. [CrossRef]
26. Ghate, V.N.; Dudul, S.V. Optimal MLP neural network classifier for fault detection of three phase induction motor. *Expert Syst. Appl.* **2010**, *37*, 3468–3481. [CrossRef]
27. Asfani, D.A.; Muhammad, A.K.; Syafaruddin; Purnomo, M.H.; Hiyama, T. Temporary short circuit detection in induction motor winding using combination of wavelet transform and neural network. *Expert Syst. Appl.* **2012**, *39*, 5367–5375. [CrossRef]
28. Hamdani, S.; Touhami, O.; Ibtiouen, R.; Fadel, M. Neural network technique for induction motor rotor faults classification-dynamic eccentricity and broken bar faults. In Proceedings of the 8th IEEE Symposium on Diagnostics for Electrical Machines, Power Electronics Drives, Bologna, Italy, 5–8 September 2011.
29. Taibi, Z.M.; Hasni, M.; Hamdani, S. Optimization of the feedforward neural network for rotor cage fault diagnosis in three-phase induction motors. In Proceedings of the IEEE International Electric Machines & Drives Conference (IEMDC), Niagara Falls, ON, Canada, 15–18 May 2011.

30. Coelho, D.N.; Barreto, G.A.; Medeiros, C.M.S. Detection of Short Circuit Faults in 3-Phase Converter-Fed Induction Motors Using Kernel SOMs. In Proceedings of the 12th International Workshop on Self-Organizing Maps and Learning Vector Quantization, Clustering and Data Visualization (WSOM), Nancy, France, 28–30 June 2017.
31. Khalfaoui, N.; Salah, M.; Hamid Amiri, S. The SOM tool in mechanical fault detection over an electric asynchronous drive. In Proceedings of the 4th International Conference on Control Engineering & Infonnation Technology, Hammamet, Tunisia, 16–18 December 2016.
32. Ghate, V.N.; Dudul, S.V. Cascade Neural-Network-Based Fault Classifier for Three-Phase Induction Motor. *IEEE Trans. Ind. Electron.* **2011**, *58*, 1555–1563. [CrossRef]
33. Gao, X.Z.; Ovaska, S.J.; Dote, Y. Motor fault detection using Elman neural network with genetic algorithm-aided training. In Proceedings of the IEEE International Conference on Systems, Man and Cybernetics 'Cybernetics Evolving to Systems, Humans, Organizations, and Their Complex Interactions', Nashville, TN, USA, 8–11 October 2000.
34. Goodfellow, I.; Bengio, Y.; Courville, A. *Deep Learning*; MIT Press: Cambridge, MA, USA, 2016.
35. Kao, I.-H.; Wang, W.-J.; Lai, Y.-H.; Perng, J.-W. Analysis of Permanent Magnet Synchronous Motor Fault Diagnosis Based on Learning. *IEEE Trans. Instrum. Meas.* **2019**, *68*, 310–324. [CrossRef]
36. Chattopadhyay, P.; Saha, N.; Delpha, C.; Sil, J. Deep Learning in Fault Diagnosis of Induction Motor Drives. In Proceedings of the Prognostics and System Health Management Conference (PHM-Chongqing), Chongqing, China, 26–28 October 2018.
37. Afrasiabi, S.; Afrasiabi, M. Real-Time Bearing Fault Diagnosis of Induction Motors with Accelerated Deep Learning Approach. In Proceedings of the 10th International Power Electronics, Drive Systems and Technologies Conference (PEDSTC), Shiraz University, Iran, 12–14 February 2019.
38. Mahesh, T.R.; Chandrasekaran, S.; Ram, V.A.; Kumar, V.V.; Vivek, V.; Guluwadi, S. Data-Driven Intelligent Condition Adaptation of Feature Extraction for Bearing Fault Detection Using Deep Responsible Active Learning. *IEEE Access* **2024**, *12*, 45381–45397. [CrossRef]
39. Kozma, R.; Ilin, R.; Siegelmann, H.T. Evolution of Abstraction Across Layers in Deep Learning Neural Networks. *Procedia Comput. Sci.* **2018**, *144*, 203–213. [CrossRef]
40. Ince, T.; Kiranyaz, S.; Eren, L.; Askar, M.; Gabbouj, M. Real-Time Motor Fault Detection by 1-D Convolutional Neural Networks. *IEEE Trans. Ind. Electron.* **2016**, *63*, 7067–7075. [CrossRef]
41. Li, C.; Xu, J.; Xing, J. A Frequency Feature Extraction Method Based on Convolutional Neural Network for Recognition of Incipient Fault. *IEEE Sens. J.* **2024**, *24*, 564–572. [CrossRef]
42. Shao, S.; Sun, W.; Wang, P.; Gao, R.X.; Yan, R. Learning features from vibration signals for induction motor fault diagnosis. In Proceedings of the International Symposium on Flexible Automation, Cleveland, OH, USA, 1–3 August 2016.
43. Principi, E.; Rossetti, D.; Squartini, S.; Piazza, F. Unsupervised Electric Motor Fault Detection by Using Deep Autoencoders. *IEEE/CAA J. Autom. Sin.* **2019**, *6*, 441–451. [CrossRef]
44. Han, S.; Sun, S.; Zhao, Z.; Luan, Z.; Niu, P. Deep Residual Multiscale Convolutional Neural Network With Attention Mechanism for Bearing Fault Diagnosis Under Strong Noise Environment. *IEEE Sens. J.* **2024**, *24*, 9073–9081. [CrossRef]
45. Wang, H.; Zhang, X. Fault Diagnosis Using Imbalanced Data of Rolling Bearings Based on a Deep Migration Model. *IEEE Access* **2024**, *12*, 5517–5533. [CrossRef]
46. Chen, Z.; Gryllias, K.; Li, W. Mechanical fault diagnosis using Convolutional Neural Networks and Extreme Learning Machine. *Mech. Syst. Signal Process.* **2019**, *133*, 106272. [CrossRef]
47. Pinedo-Sánchez, L.A. Vibration analysis in bearings for failure prevention using CNN. *J. Braz. Soc. Mech. Sci. Eng.* **2020**, *42*, 628. [CrossRef]
48. Eren, L.; Ince, T.; Kiranyaz, S. A Generic Intelligent Bearing Fault Diagnosis System Using Compact Adaptive 1D CNN Classifier. *J. Signal Process. Syst.* **2018**, *91*, 179–189. [CrossRef]
49. McInerny, S.A.; Dai, Y. Basic vibration signal processing for bearing fault detection. *IEEE Trans. Educ.* **2003**, *46*, 149–156. [CrossRef]
50. Randall, R.B. *Vibration-Based Condition Monitoring*; John Wiley & Sons: Hoboken, NJ, USA, 2011.
51. Magadán, L.; Roldán-Gómez, J.; Granda, J.C.; Suárez, F.J. Early Fault Classification in Rotating Machinery With Limited Data Using TabPFN. *IEEE Sens. J.* **2023**, *23*, 30960–30970. [CrossRef]
52. Skowron, M.; Kowalski, C.T.; Orlowska-Kowalska, T. Impact of the Convolutional Neural Network Structure and Training Parameters on the Effectiveness of the Diagnostic Systems of Modern AC Motor Drives. *Energies* **2022**, *15*, 7008. [CrossRef]

electronics

MDPI

Article

Novel Neural-Network-Based Fuel Consumption Prediction Models Considering Vehicular Jerk

Licheng Zhang [1,*], Jingtian Ya [1], Zhigang Xu [1], Said Easa [2], Kun Peng [1], Yuchen Xing [3] and Ran Yang [1]

1 School of Information Engineering, Chang'an University, Xi'an 710018, China; 2022224006@chd.edu.cn (J.Y.); xuzhigang@chd.edu.cn (Z.X.)
2 Department of Civil Engineering, Toronto Metropolitan University, Toronto, ON M5B 2K3, Canada
3 School of Computing, Australian National University, Australian Capital Territory, Canberra, ACT 2601, Australia
* Correspondence: lichengzhang@chd.edu.cn

Abstract: Conventional fuel consumption prediction (FCP) models using neural networks usually adopt driving parameters, such as speed and acceleration, as the training input, leading to a low prediction accuracy and a poor correlation between fuel consumption and driving behavior. To address this issue, the present study introduced jerk (an acceleration derivative) as an important variable in the training input of four selected neural networks: long short-term memory (LSTM), recurrent neural network (RNN), nonlinear auto-regressive model with exogenous inputs (NARX), and generalized regression neural network (GRNN). Furthermore, the root-mean-square error (RMSE), relative error (RE), and coefficient of determination (R^2) were used to evaluate the prediction performance of each model. The results from the comparison experiment show that the LSTM model outperforms the other three models. Specifically, the four selected neural network models exhibited an improved accuracy in fuel consumption prediction after the jerk was added as a new variable to the training input. LSTM exhibited the greatest improvement under the high-speed expressway scenario, in which the RMSE decreased by 14.3%, the RE decreased by 28.3%, and the R^2 increased by 9.7%.

Keywords: eco-driving; fuel consumption forecast; neural networks; driving behavior; jerk

1. Introduction

The World Meteorological Organization (WMO) [1] reported that the concentrations of primary greenhouse gases have continued to rise over the past two years, with the global carbon dioxide concentration exceeding 410 ppm. Furthermore, with the rapid development of the transportation industry, the greenhouse gas emissions from vehicles are an essential factor causing air pollution. The resulting energy shortages and environmental pollution problems are becoming increasingly severe. As a result, the eco-driving research has focused on controlling vehicle speed and acceleration, to promote sustainable and low-emission transportation, and reduce the impacts of energy consumption and exhaust emissions on air pollution and climate change. Therefore, predicting fuel consumption, considering vehicle driving parameters, holds significant importance.

Currently, several classic models are used to solve the problem of fuel consumption predictions. Typical traditional models include the mobile source model [2], the computer program to calculate emissions from road transport (COPERT) model [3], the emission factor (EMFAC) model [4], the international vehicle emissions (IVE) model [5], the comprehensive modal emissions model (CMEM) [6–8], the vehicle-specific power (VSP) model [9], and the microscopic energy and emission model developed by Virginia Tech (VT-Micro) [10]. The first three models mentioned above obtain emission factors via engine dynamometer testing. However, as this emission factor is not relevant to the actual roads, it cannot accurately represent real road emissions, resulting in considerable differences between the predicted results and actual values. The IVE fuel consumption and emission model considers two real-time vehicle operating parameters: the vehicle power ratio VSP, and the engine load. This model calculates fuel emissions based on the average driving speed and the time proportions of the driving state in different modules, but engine load data are challenging to collect. The CMEM fuel consumption emission model calculates exhaust emissions and fuel consumption in real time, through the second-by-second driving mode, and real-time engine operating condition data. However, obtaining actual data is difficult, due to the model's excessively detailed vehicle classification. Moreover, the model's excessive input parameters can lead to a low operational efficiency in practical applications. The VSP-based and VT-Micro fuel consumption emission models require numerous coefficients that need to be calibrated, with the VT-Micro model containing 32 calibration parameters. Consequently, while researchers have conducted several studies on the fuel consumption emission model, and achieved satisfactory results, the calibration of coefficients remains cumbersome.

With the rapid growth in artificial intelligence technology, many researchers are committed to using traditional artificial neural networks to predict fuel consumption. Rahimi-Ajdadi et al. [11] used a large number of experimental data from tractor laboratories to train a neural network repeatedly, established a tractor fuel consumption model, and highlighted the limitations of multiple regressions. Zhao et al. [12] extracted the microscopic driving behavior data of taxi drivers, using a vehicle-mounted terminal acquisition system, and established a taxi fuel consumption model, using the principal component analysis (PCA) algorithm and back-propagation (BP) neural network, accurately predicting the fuel consumption of taxis on expressways. Wu et al. [13] proposed a fuel consumption prediction system using a BP neural network. The prediction results showed that the system was effective. Jakov Topi'c et al. [14] proposed a neural network model based on vehicle velocity, acceleration, and road slope time series inputs, and the test results proved that the method is suitable for various applications, such as vehicle routing optimization, etc.

Although these studies have achieved good results, this neural network has higher input feature requirements, requires a longer training time, and suffers from a lower accuracy in its predictions, and an inferior generalization performance. To solve the defects of FCP models based on traditional neural networks, four neural networks, LSTM, RNN, NARX, and GRNN, were selected for this study. Among them, LSTM can capture time series characteristics over a longer period, and overcome the problem of gradient disappearance. Hence, this model is considered effective for long-term time series predictions [15–19], such as pedestrian trajectory predictions [20], and traffic flow predictions [21]. The RNN circulating neural network has a memory function, i.e., calculating the state at the current time point depends on the calculation results at the previous time point. NARX with external input is considered a suitable algorithm for modelling discrete nonlinear dynamic systems. NARX and LSTM belong to the category of RNNs, and their prediction effects depend on the actual scene. GRNN is an improved radial basis function network, established based on mathematical statistics. The network model offers robust nonlinear mapping capabilities, and a fast learning speed, and can be used to process unstable data. Zhang et al. [22] proposed a new data-driven fuel consumption model that considers vehicular speed, acceleration, and jerk. The authors reported a significant correlation between the jerk and fuel consumption. Xu et al. [23] developed a generalized regression neural network that implicitly established the relationship between the truck fuel consumption obtained from the internet of vehicles, and the driving behaviors of the truck drivers. However, jerk was not considered as the training input. The present study introduced jerk as an essential training input for the experiments, and used the above-mentioned neural networks to evaluate the impact of jerk on the fuel consumption prediction results.

This study's main contributions are threefold. Firstly, four combinations, i.e., speed, speed–acceleration, speed–acceleration–jerk, and rotating speed, are taken as the neural network's input variables for the fuel consumption prediction models, and the effects of introducing jerk as an input variable on the model performance are evaluated. The experiments demonstrate that the model obtained through adding the jerk variable offers a higher accuracy in its predictions. Secondly, three different experimental scenarios, i.e., a low-speed campus; a low- and medium-speed city; and an all-speed expressway with low, medium, and high speeds, are selected, to compare and analyze the performance of the various fuel consumption prediction models using a neural network, and to explore a model with a higher prediction accuracy and robustness. The results show that the LSTM model is suitable for different road conditions, with a greater robustness, and superior accuracy. Lastly, the jerk can be used to classify driving behaviors in more detail, thereby providing more instructive information for eco-driving and speed controller design in smart cars.

2. Research Framework

The overall framework of this study is shown in Figure 1a, and involves the following tasks:

Task 1: Establish a data acquisition system, and obtain the raw data (e.g., speed, rotating speed, and fuel consumption) for three road scenarios.

Task 2: Establish normalized datasets (speed, acceleration, jerk, rotating speed, and fuel consumption) using preprocessing data tools, such as derivation and normalization.

Task 3: Classify driving behaviors based on the jerk, and analyze the effects of various driving behaviors on the fuel consumption.

Task 4: Select four typical neural network models (LSTM, RNN, NARX, and GRNN), and four parameter combinations (speed, speed–acceleration, speed–acceleration–jerk, and rotating speed), which are shown in Figure 1b.

Task 5: Train and verify the fuel consumption prediction models in turn. Each neural network model input contains test training sets under three driving scenarios: the low-speed campus scenario; low– and medium–speed city scenario; and expressway driving scenario with low, medium, and high speeds.

Task 6: Evaluate the jerk's effect on the accuracy of the fuel consumption prediction models, using RMSE, RE, and R^2.

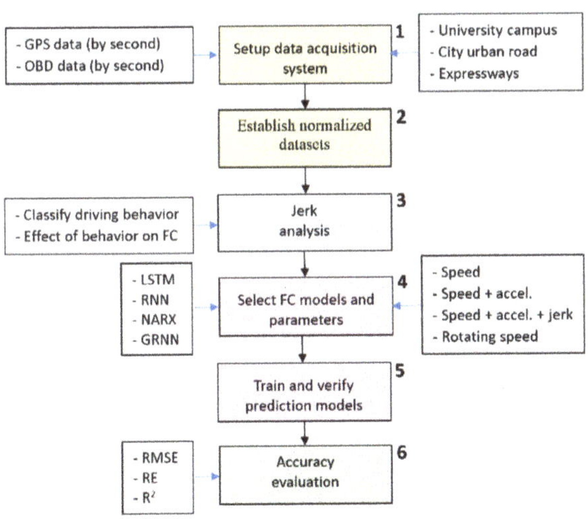

(a)

Figure 1. *Cont.*

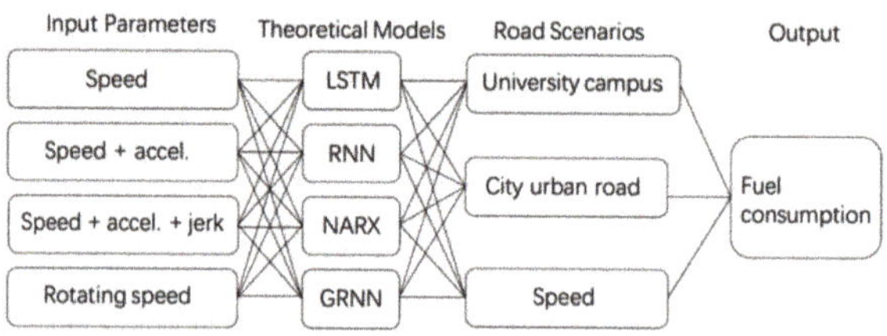

(b)

Figure 1. Research framework: (**a**) the task flow; (**b**) the evaluated combinations of input parameters, theoretical models, and road scenarios.

3. Data Description and Preprocessing

3.1. Data Description

The experimental road conditions used in this study included low speeds on university campuses (0–40 km/h); low and medium speeds on urban roads (0–70 km/h); and all speeds on expressways with low, medium, and high speeds (0–120 km/h). On-board diagnostics (OBDs) and a global positioning system (GPS) were used to collect data under every working condition, and the data were accurate to two decimal places. The dataset included 13 vehicle driving parameters: latitude and longitude, speed, acceleration, jerk, and instantaneous fuel consumption. The dataset samples are shown in Table 1. The data in the third and sixth columns were obtained via GPS, and the data in the seventh and tenth columns were obtained via OBDs. The data acquisition platform and GPS tracks are shown in Figures 2a and 2b, respectively.

Table 1. Sample datasets.

Date	Time	Lon [1] (°N)	Lat [2] (°E)	Alt [3] (km)	Speed (km/h)	RS [4] (r/min)	Ins Fuel [5] (L/h)	Cum Fuel [6] (L)	Mileage (km)
16 January 2021	18:52:02	3413.911	10,856.648	377.8952	16.76367	1119	0.92	224.90558	1,677,555
16 January 2021	18:52:03	3413.912	10,856.644	379.1028	15.85518	902	0.88	224.90590	1,677,561
16 January 2021	18:52:04	3413.912	10,856.641	379.4774	14.73993	859	0.94	224.90612	1,677,565
16 January 2021	18:52:05	3413.912	10,856.639	379.5281	12.65565	864	0.96	224.90636	1,677,568
16 January 2021	18:52:06	3413.912	10,856.637	379.4510	10.48305	875	0.93	224.90668	1,677,572
16 January 2021	18:52:07	3413.912	10,856.635	379.2913	7.57523	840	0.94	224.90692	1,677,574
16 January 2021	18:52:08	3413.912	10,856.633	379.1885	6.20904	749	0.93	224.90724	1,677,577

[1] Lon = longitude (°N), [2] Lat = latitude (°E), [3] Alt = altitude (km), [4] RS = rotating speed (r/min), [5] Ins Fuel = instantaneous fuel consumption (L/h), [6] Cum fuel = cumulative fuel consumption (L).

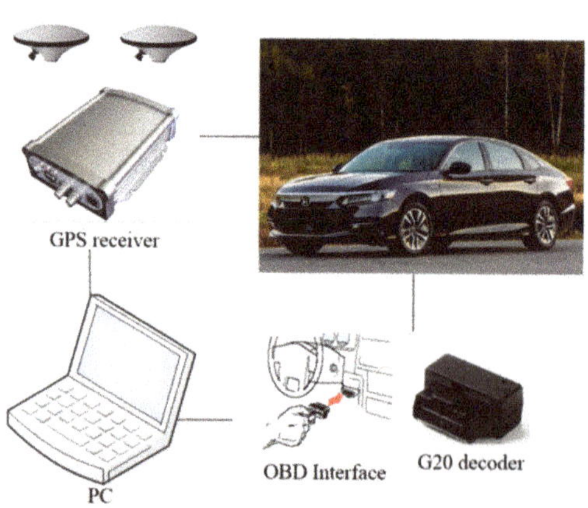

(a)

Figure 2. *Cont.*

(b)

Figure 2. The data acquisition platform and global positioning system(GPS) tracks: (**a**) the data acquisition platform: a Honda car and equipment (global positioning system(GPS) and On-board diagnostics(OBDs)); (**b**) the campus, city, and expressway GPS tracks.

3.2. Data Analysis

The dynamic changes in driving parameters under the low, medium, and high road scenarios are shown in Figure 3a–c, and an analysis of the statistical characteristics of the driving parameters is shown in Table 2. The characterization values of acceleration and jerk are derived through subtracting the speed and acceleration values before and after a one-second interval.

Ahn et al. [24] fitted a linear regression curve, and concluded that the higher the speed, the smaller the acceleration. This is because a vehicle engine must do more work to maintain the same acceleration at higher speeds, to overcome the increased air resistance. Therefore, the vehicle's ability to accelerate or decelerate naturally decreases at higher speeds. The distribution maps of acceleration and jerk with speed are provided, to verify the rationality of the dataset in this study, as shown in Figure 4. As noted, both the acceleration and jerk decreased gradually with an increase in speed, so the dataset is reasonable, at least to some extent.

3.3. Data Preprocessing

Due to the different dimensionalities and dimensionality units of the parameters investigated, as well as the relatively larger variance in the speed, compared to those of other features in several orders of magnitude, speed occupies a dominant position in the learning algorithm, leading to an excessive speed weight in algorithm learning, and affecting the data analysis results. To address this issue, data standardization was used in this study for preprocessing, to eliminate the dimensionality impact between the data indicators, and ensure their comparability.

Table 2. Statistical characteristics of the main driving parameters under the different road scenarios.

Input	Campus			City			Expressway		
	V [1]	A [2]	J [3]	V [1]	A [2]	J [3]	V [1]	A [2]	J [3]
Average	15.48	0.04	0.67	30.76	1.52×10^{-4}	−0.01	53.26	0.01	0.01
Max	33.28	3.41	4.49	82.72	2.83	6.44	119.49	4.94	8.14
Min	0.01	−2.22	−4.29	0	−3.10	−5.31	0	−1.82	−2.99
Variance	49.97	0.34	0.59	311.60	0.20	0.24	1.80×10^3	0.12	0.17

[1] V = speed (km/h), [2] A = acceleration (km/h^2), [3] J = jerk (km/h^3).

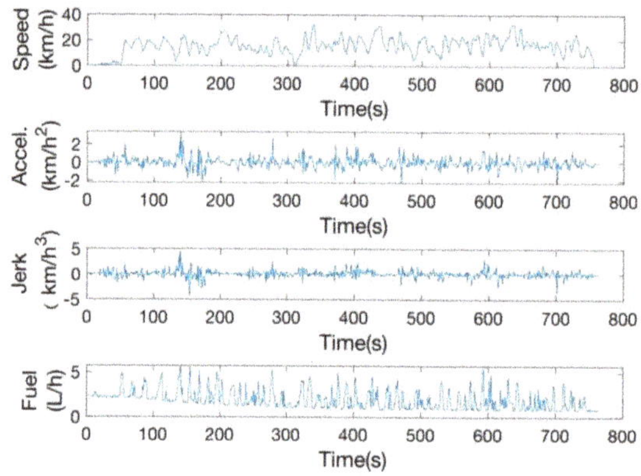

(**a**)

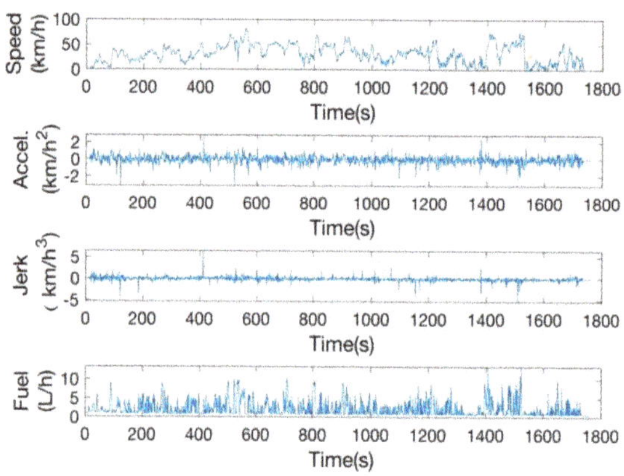

(**b**)

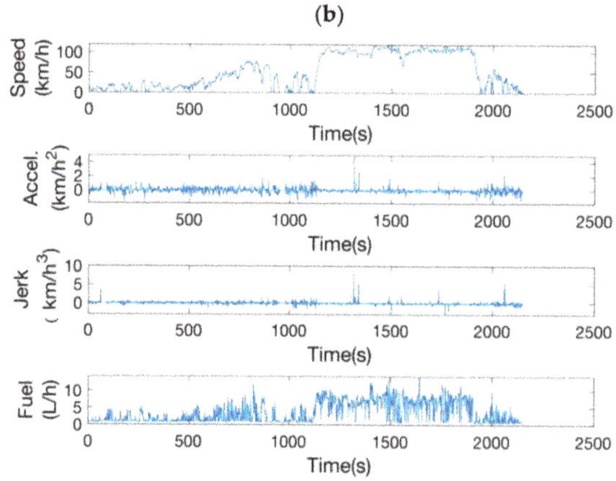

(**c**)

Figure 3. Dynamic changes in the main parameters under the various road scenarios: (**a**) the main data for the low-speed campus scenario, (**b**) the main data for the low- and medium-speed urban scenario, (**c**) the all-speed data for the low-, medium-, and high-speed expressway scenario.

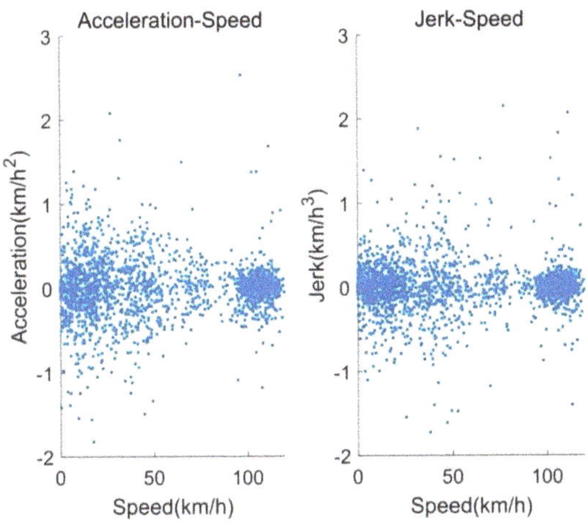

Figure 4. Relationship of the acceleration and jerk with speed.

Min–max normalization, also known as deviation standardization, was used to linearly transform the raw data, achieving values within $[-1, 1]$. The conversion function is shown in Equation (1).

$$f(x) = 2(x - Min)/(Max - Min) - 1 \quad (1)$$

where Min and Max are the minimum and maximum values of the sample data, respectively.

Some data samples, before and after normalization, are shown in Table 3. As noted, after the raw data were subjected to data standardization, all parameters remained within $[-1, 1]$. Here, all indicators have the same order of magnitude, and are suitable for a comprehensive comparative evaluation. As the variances in the new data are normalized, the dimensionalities of each dimension are equivalent. Each dimension conforms to a normal distribution, with a mean of 0 and a variance of 1. This distribution helps prevent the speed range from being too large, and the training time from being too long, due to the initialization falling in a specific direction, and thereby avoiding an enormous impact on the fuel consumption prediction caused by the selection of different dimensionalities. After normalization, the identification of the optimal solution was expedited, and the accuracy of the models was improved.

Table 3. Data before and after normalization.

Raw Data				Normalized Data			
Speed (km/h)	**Acceleration (km/h^2)**	**Jerk (km/h^3)**	**Fuel (L)**	**Speed**	**Acceleration**	**Jerk**	**Fuel**
15.9000	−0.1000	0.5000	0.8800	0.1338	0.2537	0.2963	0.0148
14.7000	−0.2000	−0.3000	0.9400	0.1237	0.2388	0.2222	0.0192
12.7000	−0.6000	−0.2000	0.9600	0.1069	0.1791	0.2315	0.0207
10.5000	−0.2000	0.2000	0.9300	0.0884	0.2388	0.2685	0.0185
7.6000	−0.7000	−0.1000	0.9400	0.0640	0.1642	0.2407	0.0192

4. Classification of Driving Behaviors Based on Jerk and Its Effects on Fuel Consumption

4.1. Introduction of Jerk

According to Newton's second law and conservation of energy, the vehicle jerk is the rate of change of the resultant force exerted on the vehicle, and the vehicle's power ultimately comes from fuel combustion work, so jerk is related to energy consumption.

In physics, jerk refers to the speed at which the acceleration of an object changes with time, and is usually represented by the symbol j, with units in m/s^3. As a vector, the jerk can be expressed as the first derivative of acceleration, the second derivative of speed, or the third derivative of displacement, as Equation (2).

$$j(t) = \frac{da(t)}{dt} = \frac{d^2v(t)}{dt^2} = \frac{d^3r(t)}{dt^3} \quad (2)$$

where a is acceleration, v is speed, r is displacement, and t is time. As noted, jerk represents the abrupt movement of vehicles. The jerk profile shows changes in the acceleration and deceleration rates, unlike the acceleration profile, which shows an increase or decrease in speed. The jerk profile indicates the driver's abrupt changes during the driving operation.

4.2. Driving Behavior Classification Based on Jerk

Equation (2) shows that the jerk, as the second derivative of speed, has a strong characterization effect on the fluctuation degree of the speed–time curve. In addition, the fluctuation degree of the speed–time curve significantly affects fuel consumption. Figure 5a classifies the jerk into nine types (a to i). Considering the speed–time curve of an expressway as an example, Figure 5b presents various jerk types in the speed–time curve, with different line types, according to the classifications outlined in Figure 5a.

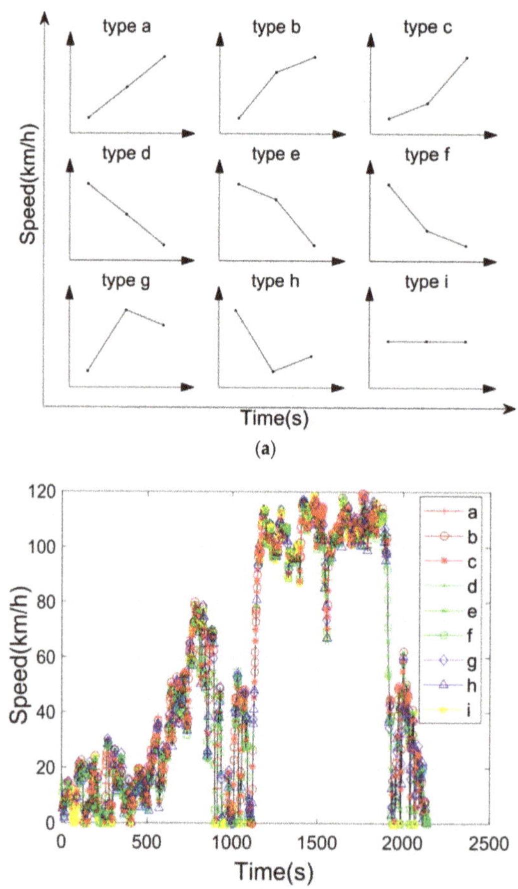

Figure 5. Relationship of acceleration and jerk with speed. Classification of jerk: (**a**) schematic diagram of nine jerk types, and (**b**) expressway speed curves marked with different types of jerk.

4.3. Effect of Jerk on Fuel Consumption

The occurrence frequency of various types of jerk, and the corresponding fuel consumption in the expressway scenario, were counted, and a histogram was plotted. Figure 6a–c show the effect of the jerk on the fuel consumption. As noted, the occurrence frequencies of different jerk types were different, and the corresponding fuel consumption of each type was also different. Thus, the jerk not only reflects driving behavior, but is also an essential factor affecting fuel consumption. Hence, it is of great significance to introduce jerk into neural networks as one of the inputs.

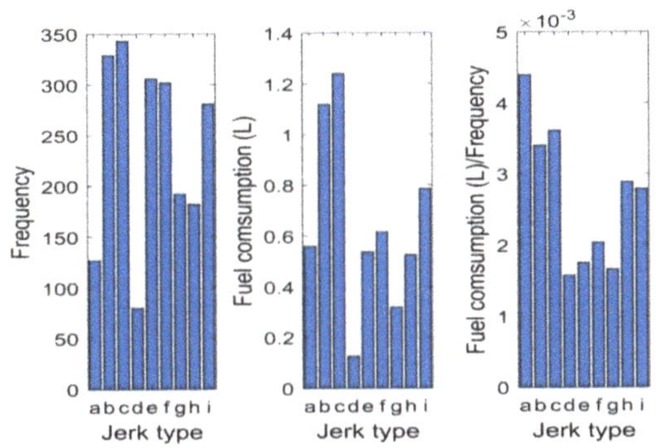

Figure 6. Relationship of acceleration and jerk with speed. Effect of the jerk type on fuel consumption: (**a**) frequency, (**b**) fuel consumption, and (**c**) fuel consumption per frequency.

The speed, acceleration, and jerk are the main manifestations of driving behavior closely associated with fuel consumption, and the acceleration is the speed's first derivative, and the jerk is the acceleration's derivative. Therefore, these three variables depend on each other, and using any one of them will impact the prediction results. The following sections describe, in detail, the effects of different combinations on the prediction results.

5. Experimental Modelling

5.1. Modelling

The input and output variables of the neural network models are described in Table 4. This study selected four neural network models: LSTM, RNN, NARX, and GRNN. This experiment sought to study the effects on fuel consumption prediction under different neural network models, after introducing the jerk. Therefore, parameters such as the speed, acceleration, jerk, and rotating speed were selected for the experiment, and combined as the model inputs, and the fuel consumption was set as the output parameter. The parameter setting of each neural network model is provided in Table 5.

Table 4. Description of input and output variables.

	Variable	Variable Description
Input	$v(t)$	Vehicle speed
	$a(t)$	Vehicle acceleration speed
	$j(t)$	Vehicle jerk speed
	$y(t)$	Fuel consumption at time t
	$r(t)$	Rotating speed
Output	$\hat{y}(t+1)$	Fuel consumption at the next time step

Table 5. Parameter setting of each neural network model.

Neural Network	Input	Network Layer	Parameter Setting	Output
LSTM	Speed, acceleration, jerk, rotating speed	Hidden neurons	60 × 180 × 60	Fuel consumption
		Dropout layers	0.2 × 0.3 × 0.2	
RNN		Hidden neurons	10	
NARX		Hidden neurons	10	
		Delays d	2	
GRNN		Hidden neurons	Number of samples	

5.2. Model Calibration and Verification

Four input combinations were selected (speed, speed–acceleration, speed–acceleration–jerk, and rotating speed) to determine the parameters of the best input combination. Under the three road scenarios, the fuel consumption prediction performance of each group of the four neural network models, LSTM, RNN, NARX, and GRNN, was quantitatively analyzed. Therefore, it was necessary to carry out 4 × 4 × 3 = 48 groups of experiments. In each experimental group, 70% of the datasets were used for training, 15% for verifying the accuracy of the models, and 15% for testing. The calibration and verification of each model under the input condition combination of speed–acceleration–jerk are shown in Figure 7a–d.

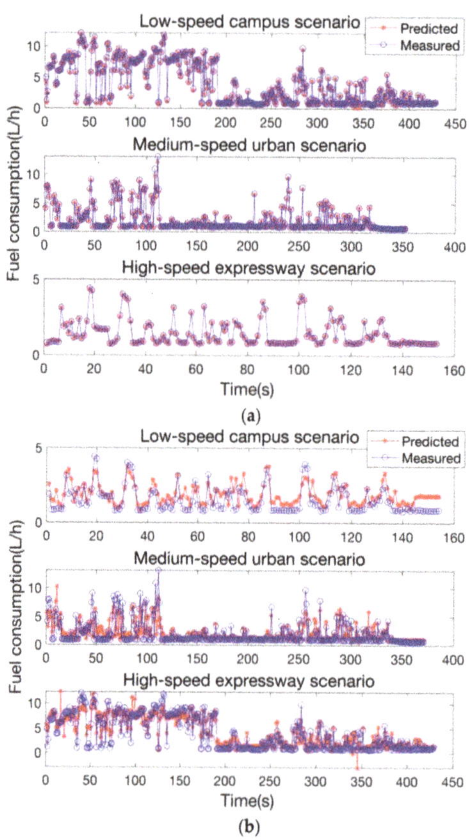

Figure 7. *Cont.*

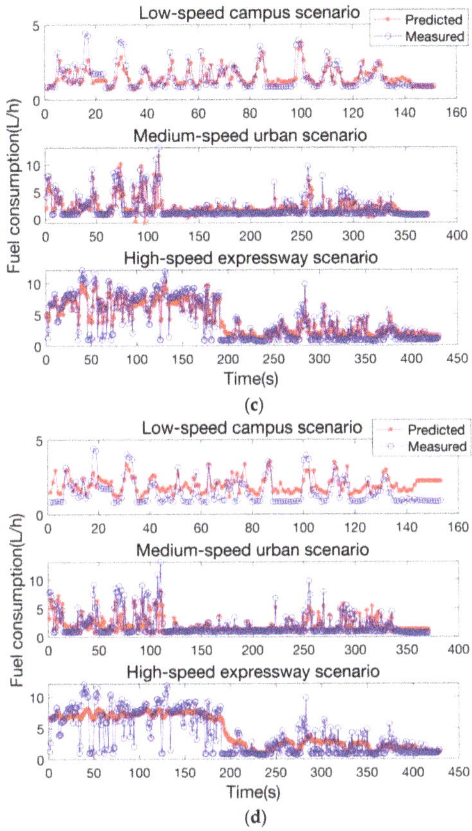

Figure 7. The model calibration and verification of each neural network model: (**a**) LSTM, (**b**) RNN, (**c**) NARX, (**d**) GRNN.

6. Analysis of Experimental Results

6.1. Evaluation Indices

Three indices were selected to evaluate the fuel consumption prediction results, as Equations (3)–(5).

$$RMSE = \sqrt{\frac{1}{N}\sum_{t=1}^{N}\left(y_{real_t} - y_{pre_t}\right)^2} \tag{3}$$

$$RE = \frac{1}{N}\sum_{t=1}^{N}\frac{\left|y_{real_t} - y_{pre_t}\right|}{y_{real_t}} \tag{4}$$

$$R^2 = 1 - \frac{\sum_{t=1}^{N}\left(y_{real_t} - y_{pre_t}\right)^2}{\sum_{t=1}^{N}\left(y_{real_t} - \overline{y}\right)^2} \tag{5}$$

where N is the sample size, y_{pre_t} is the predicted value, y_{real_t} is the actual value, and $\overline{y}$ is the average value. When the $RMSE$ and RE are small, and the R^2 is closer to 1, the data fitting is better, which indicates that the independent variables offer a higher degree of explanation for the dependent variables.

6.2. Experimental Analysis of Each Neural Network Model under Different Input Conditions

According to the analysis in Section 4.2, the jerk should be introduced into the input sequence of the neural network models as a factor. Figure 8a–d graphically show the absolute error diagrams of different input combinations (speed, speed–acceleration, speed–

acceleration–jerk) for each neural network under three working conditions (campus, urban road, and expressway). As noted, when the speed, acceleration, and jerk are simultaneously used as the input characteristic variables, the prediction errors of each neural network are the smallest.

To further analyze the performance of different input variables for the four fuel consumption prediction models using a neural network under different road scenarios, the evaluation indices in Section 6.1 were calculated, as shown in Table 6. As noted, the prediction performance of each fuel consumption prediction model under different road scenarios gradually improved when speed, speed–acceleration, and speed–acceleration–jerk were selected as the training input combinations. The bold data in the Table 6 show the data results of the best performing model.

Table 6. The prediction performance of different models under three road scenarios.

Parameter Combination	Model	Driving Scenario								
		Campus			City			Expressway		
		RMSE	RE	R^2	RMSE	RE	R^2	RMSE	RE	R^2
Rotating speed	LSTM	0.030	0.033	0.998	0.029	0.018	0.998	0.090	0.067	0.994
	RNN	0.485	0.219	0.796	0.748	0.299	0.822	1.359	0.548	0.779
	NARX	0.485	0.229	0.795	1.704	0.535	0.773	1.670	0.624	0.665
	GRNN	0.521	0.247	0.765	0.884	0.425	0.820	1.679	0.613	0.740
Speed–acceleration–jerk	LSTM	**0.033**	**0.017**	**0.998**	**0.026**	**0.014**	**0.998**	**0.048**	**0.033**	**0.996**
	RNN	0.466	0.200	0.811	1.271	0.374	0.610	1.242	0.385	0.842
	NARX	0.377	0.153	0.875	1.510	0.647	0.451	1.607	0.489	0.736
	GRNN	0.545	0.234	0.743	1.528	0.506	0.463	1.543	0.483	0.781
Speed–acceleration	LSTM	0.040	0.024	0.997	0.044	0.044	0.991	0.056	0.046	0.991
	RNN	0.512	0.225	0.771	1.448	0.457	0.517	1.450	0.450	0.806
	NARX	0.574	0.267	0.712	1.688	0.686	0.318	1.840	0.640	0.688
	GRNN	0.624	0.330	0.663	1.581	0.528	0.424	1.709	0.520	0.731
Speed	LSTM	0.054	0.047	0.995	0.055	0.065	0.988	0.065	0.051	0.988
	RNN	0.732	0.345	0.674	1.915	0.494	0.479	2.070	0.764	0.664
	NARX	0.753	0.301	0.576	1.827	0.746	0.307	1.906	0.713	0.609
	GRNN	0.698	0.423	0.574	1.724	0.689	0.405	1.928	0.638	0.694

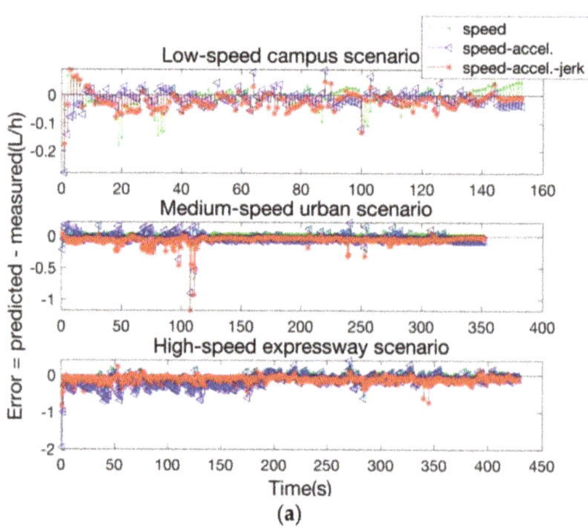

(a)

Figure 8. *Cont.*

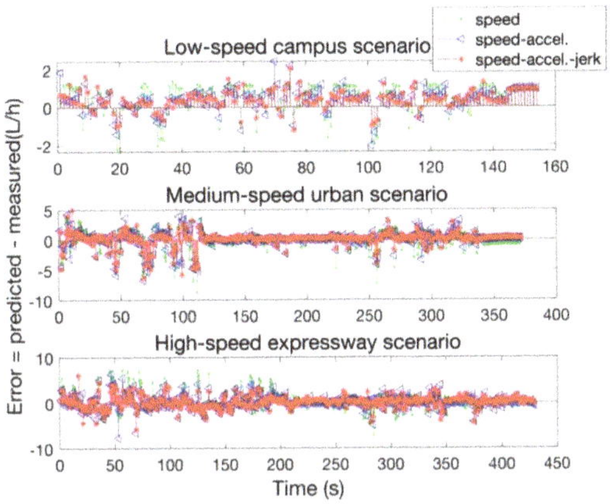

(**b**)

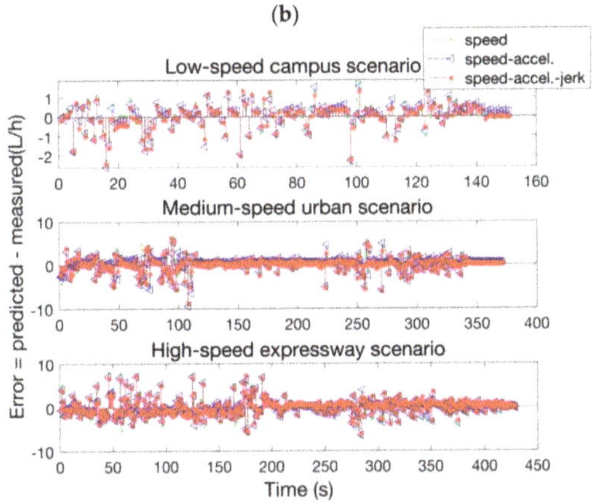

(**c**)

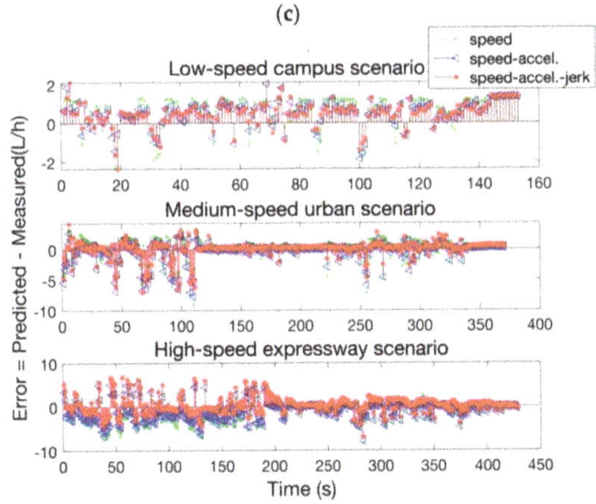

(**d**)

Figure 8. Absolute prediction error diagrams of each neural network model: (**a**) LSTM, (**b**) RNN, (**c**) NARX, (**d**) GRNN.

The prediction performance improvements in the four neural network models after considering the jerk are shown in Table 7 as percentages. As noted, for a low speed, medium speed, and high speed, each neural network offered the best fuel consumption prediction effects with the speed–acceleration–jerk as the combination input. The bold data in the Table 7 indicate the maximum and minimum values of the corresponding indicators. Here, the prediction results of each model improved after introducing jerk as an input, with the RMSE decreasing by up to 40.9% (LSTM, urban scenario), the RE decreasing by up to 68.2% (LSTM, urban scenario), and the R^2 increasing by up to 41.8% (NARX, urban scenario).

Table 7. Analysis of the model prediction performance improvements after considering jerk.

	Driving Scenario								
	Campus			City			Expressway		
	RMSE	RE	R^2	RMSE	RE	R^2	RMSE	RE	R^2
LSTM	−17.5%	−29.2%	+0.1%	**−40.9%**	**−68.2%**	+0.7%	**−14.3%**	**−28.3%**	**+9.7%**
RNN	−8.9%	−11.0%	+5.2%	−12.2%	−18.0%	+18.0%	−14.3%	−14.4%	+4.5%
NARX	**−34.3%**	**−43.0%**	**+22.9%**	−10.5%	−5.7%	**+41.8%**	−12.7%	−23.6%	+7.0%
GRNN	−12.7%	−29.0%	+13.3%	−3.4%	−4.2%	+9.2%	−9.7%	−7.1%	+6.8%

Specifically, under the high-speed expressway scenario, LSTM achieved the most remarkable improvement, with the RMSE decreasing by 14.3%, the RE decreasing by 28.3%, and the R^2 increasing by 9.7%. Under the low-speed campus scenario, NARX achieved the most remarkable improvement, with the RMSE decreasing by 34.3%, the RE decreasing by 43.0%, and the R^2 increasing by 22.9%. Under the medium-speed urban scenario, LSTM achieved the greatest improvement in the RMSE and RE, with the RMSE decreasing by 40.9%, and the RE decreasing by 68.2%. NARX achieved the greatest improvement in the R^2, with an increase of 41.8%.

Most of the large relative errors in prediction occurred in the following two cases: (1) when the vehicle came to a stop, the acceleration and the fuel consumption were not 0, and (2) a sudden acceleration or deceleration led to overly large relative prediction errors. The fuel consumption predictions of various neural networks could be properly trained, and the relative errors in fuel consumption prediction were also reduced when the jerk was introduced.

6.3. Comparison of FCP Models Using Neural Network

According to the above analysis, the prediction performance of each fuel consumption prediction model under different road scenarios gradually improved when the speed, speed–acceleration, and speed–acceleration–jerk were selected as input combinations. The effect of the jerk on the improvement of the fuel consumption prediction performance was deeply analyzed. This section reports a further quantitative analysis of the prediction results among the four neural network models. Among the LSTM, RNN, NARX, and GRNN neural network models, the prediction performance of the LSTM model outperformed the other three models under different input combinations (rotating speed, speed, speed–acceleration, speed–acceleration–jerk) and driving scenarios (low-speed campus scenario, medium-speed urban scenario, and high-speed expressway scenario). The RMSE and RE values of the LSTM model were the smallest (less than 0.1).

The RMSE values of the other three models were 11 to 17 times the value of LSTM in the low-speed campus scenario, 26 to 59 times the value of LSTM in the medium-speed urban scenario, and 15 to 33 times the value of LSTM in the high-speed expressway scenario. The RE of the other three models was 6 to 14 times the LSTM value in the low-speed campus scenario, 8 to 46 times the LSTM value in the medium-speed urban scenario, and 9 to 15 times the LSTM value in the high-speed expressway scenario. The R^2 of LSTM was the largest, reaching about 0.99, while the values of the other three models were between 0.3 and 0.8. Notably, the rotating speed and fuel consumption were highly correlated, but the rotating speed was not always observable. Thus, the rotating speed was only used for performance comparisons in this study. Each performance index of the LSTM-based FCP model with the combination of speed–acceleration–jerk as the training input was equivalent to, or better than, the results when the rotating speed was the training input (Table 6).

Figure 9 graphically shows a comparison of the absolute prediction errors among the different models, considering jerk, for the expressway condition. As noted, all four models offered an excellent performance in predicting fuel consumption, but the LSTM neural network showed the best performance in all three evaluation indices.

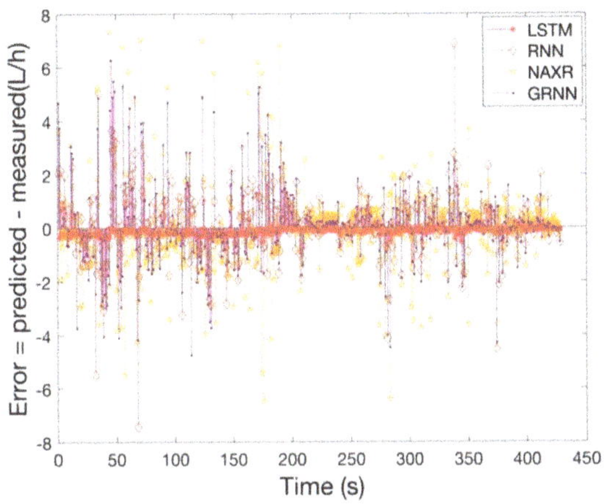

Figure 9. Comparison of the prediction results among the different models, considering jerk, under the expressway condition.

7. Conclusions

This study involved the collection of datasets under three road scenarios to facilitate experimental analysis, with modelling of the long-term dependence characteristics of time series data via the selection of suitable neural network parameters. Furthermore, the effects of four combinations of input variables, under three road scenarios and four FCP models, were compared, to determine the accuracy of their fuel consumption prediction. Based on this study, the following conclusions can be drawn.

1. Among the LSTM, RNN, NARX, and GRNN neural network models, the prediction performance of the LSTM model was best under the different input combinations (rotating speed, speed, speed–acceleration, speed–acceleration–jerk) and different driving scenarios (low-speed campus scenario, medium-speed urban scenario, and high-speed expressway scenario). The RMSE value and RE value of the LSTM model were the smallest (less than 0.1). The RMSE values of the other three models were 11 to 17 times the RMSE of LSTM in the low-speed campus scenario, 26 to 59 times that of LSTM in the medium-speed urban scenario, and 15 to 33 times that of LSTM in the high-speed expressway scenario. The RE values of the other three models were 6 to 14 times the LSTM value in the low-speed scenario, 8 to 46 times the LSTM in the medium-speed urban scenario, and 9 to 15 times the LSTM in the high-speed expressway scenario. The R^2 of LSTM was the largest, reaching about 0.99, while the values of the other three models were between 0.3 and 0.8.

2. After including the jerk as a new variable in the training input, all the neural network models improved in their fuel consumption accuracy. Notably, under the high-speed expressway scenario, LSTM achieved the most remarkable improvements, in which the RMSE decreased by 14.3%, the RE decreased by 28.3%, and the R^2 increased by 9.7%. Under the low-speed campus scenario, NARX achieved the most remarkable improvement, in which the RMSE decreased by 34.3%, the RE decreased by 43.0%, and the R^2 increased by 22.9%. Under the medium-speed urban scenario, LSTM achieved the greatest improvement in the RMSE and RE, with the RMSE decreasing by 40.9%, and the RE decreasing by

68.2%. Additionally, NARX achieved the greatest improvement in the R^2, with an increase of 41.8%.

Author Contributions: Conceptualization, L.Z.; methodology, J.Y. and Z.X.; formal analysis, S.E.; validation, K.P.; writing—review and editing, Y.X.; writing—original draft, R.Y. All authors have read and agreed to the published version of the manuscript.

Funding: Financial support for this research was provided by the National Key Research and Development Program of China (Nos. 2021YFB2501200 and 2018YFB0105104); the 111 project (No. B14043), the Joint Laboratory of Internet of Vehicles of the Ministry of Education and China Mobile (No. 2012-364-812-105); the National Natural Science Foundation of China (No. 51278058); and the Fundamental Research Funds for the Central Universities, CHD (Nos. 300102240503 and 300102242502).

Data Availability Statement: The data used to support the findings of this study have not been made available because these data still need to be used in other unfinished studies.

Conflicts of Interest: The authors declare no conflict of interest.

References

1. *The State of the Global Climate*; World Meteorological Organization: Washington, DC, USA, 2020.
2. Fu, L.; He, K.; He, D.; Tang, Z.; Hao, J. A study on models of mobile source emission factors. *Acta Sci. Circumstantiae* **1997**, *17*, 474–479. (In Chinese)
3. Ma, Y.; Lau, A.K.H.; Louie, P.K.K.; Li, T.; Luan, S. Application of vehicular emission models and comparison of their adaptability. *Acta Sci. Nat. Univ. Pekin.* **2008**, *44*, 308–316.
4. California Air Resource Board. *EMFAC User's Guide*; California Air Resource Board: Sacramento, CA, USA, 2020.
5. Guo, H.; Zhang, Q.; Shi, Y.; Wang, D. Evaluation of the International Vehicle Emission (IVE) model with on-road remote sensing measurements. *J. Environ. Sci.* **2007**, *19*, 818–826. [CrossRef] [PubMed]
6. Barth, M.; An, F.; Norbeck, J.; Ross, M. Modal emissions modelling: A physical approach. *J. Transp. Res. Board* **1996**, *1520*, 81–88. [CrossRef]
7. An, F.; Barth, M.; Norbeck, J.; Ross, M. Development of comprehensive modal emissions model: Operating under hot-stabilized conditions. *J. Transp. Res. Board* **1997**, *1587*, 52–62. [CrossRef]
8. Barth, M.; Younglove, T.; Wenzel, T.; Score, G.; An, F.; Ross, M.; Norbeck, J. Analysis of modal emissions from diverse in-use vehicle fleet. *Transp. Res. Rec. J. Transp. Res. Board* **1997**, *1587*, 73–84. [CrossRef]
9. Jiménez-Palacios, L.J. *Understanding and Quantifying Motor Vehicle Emissions with Vehicle Specific Power and TILDAS Remote Sensing*; Massachusetts Institute of Technology: Cambridge, MA, USA, 1999.
10. Rakha, H.; Ahn, K.; Trani, A. Development of VT-Micro model for estimating hot stabilized light duty vehicle and truck emissions. *Transp. Res. Part D Transp. Environ.* **2004**, *9*, 49–74. [CrossRef]
11. Rahimi-Ajdadi, F.; Abbaspour-Gilandeh, Y. Artificial neural network and stepwise multiple range regression method for predicting fuel consumption of tractors. *Measurement* **2011**, *44*, 2104–2111. [CrossRef]
12. Zhao, X.; Yao, Y.; Wu, Y.; Chen, C.; Rong, J. Research on combined prediction model of driving energy consumption based on principal component analysis and BP neural network. *J. Transp. Syst. Eng. Inf. Technol.* **2016**, *16*, 185–204.
13. Wu, J.; Liu, J. Development of a predictive system for car fuel consumption using an artificial neural network. *Expert Syst. Appl.* **2011**, *38*, 4967–4971. [CrossRef]
14. Topić, J.; Škugor, B.; Deur, J. Neural Network-Based Prediction of Vehicle Fuel Consumption Based on Driving Cycle Data. *Sustainability* **2022**, *14*, 744. [CrossRef]
15. Li, Y.; Chen, M.; Zhao, W. Investigating long-term vehicle speed prediction based on BP-LSTM algorithms. *IET Intell. Transp. Syst.* **2019**, *13*, 1281–1290.
16. Fitters, W.; Cuzzocrea, A.; Hassani, M. Enhancing LSTM prediction of vehicle traffic flow data via outlier correlations. In Proceedings of the 2021 IEEE 45th Annual Computers, Software, and Applications Conference (COMPSAC), Madrid, Spain, 12–16 July 2021; pp. 210–217.
17. Zhu, W.; Wu, J.; Fu, T.; Wang, J.; Shangguan, Q. Dynamic prediction of traffic incident duration on urban expressways: A deep learning approach based on LSTM and MLP. *J. Intell. Connect. Veh.* **2021**, *4*, 80–91. [CrossRef]
18. Hochreiter, S.; Schmidhuber, J. Long Short-Term Memory. *Neural Comput.* **1997**, *9*, 1735–1780. [CrossRef] [PubMed]
19. Phan, H.; Andreotti, F.; Cooray, N.; Chén, O.Y.; De Vos, M. SeqSleepNet: End-to-end hierarchical recurrent neural network for sequence-to-sequence automatic sleep staging. *IEEE Trans. Neural Syst. Rehabil. Eng.* **2019**, *27*, 400–410. [CrossRef] [PubMed]
20. Quan, R.; Zhu, L.; Wu, Y.; Yang, Y. Holistic LSTM for pedestrian trajectory prediction. *I-EEE Trans. Image Process.* **2021**, *30*, 3229–3239. [CrossRef] [PubMed]
21. Doğan, E. Analysis of the relationship between LSTM network traffic flow prediction performance and statistical characteristics of standard and nonstandard data. *J. Forecast.* **2020**, *39*, 1213–1228. [CrossRef]

22. Zhang, L.; Peng, K.; Zhao, X.; Asad, J. New fuel consumption model considering vehicular speed, acceleration, and jerk. *J. Intell. Transp. Syst.* **2023**, *27*, 174–186. [CrossRef]
23. Xu, Z.; Wei, T.; Easa, S.; Zhao, X.; Qu, X. Modelling relationship between truck fuel consumption and driving behavior using data from internet of vehicles. *Comput-Aided Civ. Infrastruct. Eng.* **2018**, *33*, 209–219. [CrossRef]
24. Ahn, K.; Rakha, H.; Trani, A.; Van Aerde, M. Estimating vehicle fuel consumption and emissions based on instantaneous speed and acceleration levels. *J. Transp. Eng.* **2002**, *128*, 182–190. [CrossRef]

electronics

MDPI

Article

Optimizing Parameter Extraction in Grid Information Models Based on Improved Convolutional Neural Networks

Xintong Li [1,*] and Xiangjun Liu [2]

1 International Education Institute, North China Electric Power University, Beijing 102226, China
2 School of Electrical and Electronic Engineering, North China Electric Power University, Beijing 102226, China; lxjun@ncepu.edu.cn
* Correspondence: xintong_li2024@163.com

Abstract: With the rapid advancement of digital technology, three-dimensional designs of Grid Information Models (GIMs) are increasingly applied in the power industry. Addressing the challenges of extracting key parameters during the GIM's process for power grid equipment, this paper explores an innovative approach that integrates artificial intelligence with image recognition technologies into power design engineering. The traditional methods of "template matching, feature extraction and classification, and symbol recognition" have enabled the automated processing of electrical grid equipment engineering drawings, allowing for the extraction of key information related to grid equipment. However, these methods still rely on manually designed and selected feature regions, which limits their potential for achieving full automation. This study introduces an optimized algorithm that combines enhanced Convolutional Neural Networks (CNNs) with Depth-First Search (DFS) strategies, and is specifically designed for the automated extraction of crucial GIM parameters from power grid equipment. Implemented on the design schematics of power engineering projects, this algorithm utilizes an improved CNN to precisely identify component symbols on schematics, and continues to extract text data associated with these symbols. Utilizing a scene text detector, the text data are matched with corresponding component symbols. Finally, the DFS strategy is applied to identify connections between these component symbols in the diagram, thus facilitating the automatic extraction of key GIM parameters. Experimental results demonstrate that this optimized algorithm can accurately identify basic GIM parameters, providing technical support for the automated extraction of parameters using the GIM. This study's recognition accuracy is 91.31%, while a traditional CNN achieves 71.23% and a Faster R-CNN achieves 89.59%. Compared to existing research, the main innovation of this paper lies in the application of the combined enhanced CNN and DFS strategies for the extraction of GIM parameters in the power industry. This method not only improves the accuracy of parameter extraction but also significantly enhances processing speed, enabling the rapid and effective identification and extraction of critical information in complex power design environments. Moreover, the automated process reduces manual intervention, offering a novel solution in the field of power design. These features make this research broadly applicable and of significant practical value in the construction and maintenance of smart grids.

Keywords: GIM; 3D design; drawing identification; image recognition technology; convolutional neural network

1. Introduction

Advancements in neural networks and other cutting-edge technologies have enabled the widespread application of image recognition in various real-world scenarios [1]. Text recognition, facial recognition, smart healthcare, non-destructive testing, and agricultural product classification are just a few examples [2,3]. In this context, the power industry has also emerged as a crucial domain for the application of image recognition technology, offering innovative solutions in various aspects. By leveraging image recognition techniques, we can monitor the real-time status of power equipment and swiftly identify any faults [4]. Additionally, image recognition technology exhibits tremendous potential in the recognition and extraction of design drawings and information within electric power systems.

Information technology's rapid development has greatly propelled the level of intelligence in the power grid while also fueling the growing demand for digitization in grid engineering. Harnessing advanced digital technologies such as computers and communications is crucial for making traditional power systems smarter and more efficient [5]. The integration of new technologies can also enhance the competitiveness of industry products [6]. In terms of operations and maintenance, countries like the United States and Canada have already embraced smart meter systems to analyze users' power consumption patterns and detect energy theft incidents [7]. Some substations in China have started to combine GIS and digital twin technology to simulate and model equipment in order to monitor the operational status of equipment in real time [8]. Additionally, the application of 3D modeling technology in power systems, as opposed to traditional 2D drawings, has effectively eliminated inefficiencies and the high occurrence of human errors [9]. Since the release of the Digitalized Design Application Guidelines for Substations and Power Transformation Projects by the State Grid Corporation of China in 2018, the Grid Information Model (GIM) has gained widespread attention as a digital model that integrates all aspects of power grid engineering, including grid elements and geographic information. The GIM, with its visual, standardized, and information-based characteristics, not only facilitates effective information sharing in grid projects but also enhances the synergy of information throughout the entire project lifecycle, thus improving engineering management capabilities. The GIM can describe the three-dimensional information and engineering attributes of substations, converter stations, transmission lines, and cable projects through one or more files. Moreover, it plays a crucial role in deepening the integration of "information flow and business flow" within grid projects [10–12].

The GIM relies primarily on key technologies such as 3D modeling, model coding, and databases, with 3D modeling being a crucial step in mapping grid information to the digital model. Currently, the 3D modeling of grid engineering projects is mainly based on 2D drawings. Designers use software like Computer-Aided Design (CAD) to create 2D design drawings, which are then manually inputted into 3D modeling software during the digital delivery phase, including parameters such as equipment information and topological structure. This process is time-consuming and inefficient, requiring significant manpower. While there are some plugins available on the market that automate the conversion from 2D to 3D, they have certain limitations, often require substantial investment, and are often unable to accurately identify components in non-standard drawings [13].

Traditional image-based recognition techniques for power grid equipment design drawings primarily employ methods such as template matching, feature extraction, and classification. These techniques aim to extract device parameters and identify interconnection relationships among devices [14–17].

Template matching is a fundamental technique in the field of image recognition, which involves comparing patterns in engineering design drawings with pre-defined pattern templates [14,15]. By identifying the maximum similarity between the two, this method enables the recognition of power grid equipment in engineering drawings. This approach is favored for its intuitiveness and simplicity. However, it relies heavily on the image quality of the drawings and the accuracy of the pre-defined template library.

Feature extraction and classification techniques are considered to be more complex pathways in the recognition of drawings. The process begins by utilizing image processing techniques to preprocess engineering drawings, accurately extracting key features of power grid equipment. Subsequently, machine learning algorithms such as clustering and decision trees are employed for classification to recognize different categories of power grid devices. Despite its remarkable accuracy and ability to handle complex scenarios, this technique relies on a large amount of training data and computational resources. These requirements may pose limitations in practical applications [16,17].

Symbol recognition involves using detection algorithms to identify symbols such as transformers, casings, and lightning arresters. Additionally, by combining Optical Character Recognition (OCR) technology, text information can be extracted. This process converts symbols and textual content in drawings into structured information for further processing and analysis [17]. Overall, although traditional image-based methods in power grid equipment engineering design drawings enable automated processing and extraction of key information, they still rely on manual design and the manual selection of feature areas, which limits the possibility of achieving complete automation. Furthermore, these traditional methods for recognizing power grid engineering design drawings also need improvements in accuracy and computational efficiency.

Therefore, the accurate and efficient identification and extraction of various types of electrical equipment, along with their corresponding parameter information and interconnection relationships from electrical grid engineering drawings, holds significant importance in the GIM 3D modeling process.

With the widespread application of computer technology and artificial intelligence, advanced image recognition techniques have become an important means for identifying and processing power grid engineering design drawings. This technology allows for the extraction of key parameters, such as equipment information, connection relationships, and operational parameters of the power GIM with higher accuracy and efficiency. This significantly improves the design efficiency and operational performance of power systems [18–20]. Currently, commonly used solutions for image recognition include Convolutional Neural Networks (CNNs), Support Vector Machines (SVMs), K-Nearest Neighbor (KNN) classifiers, and Artificial Neural Networks (ANNs) [21]. Among them, CNNs are the most widely used solution in the field of image processing [22]. The Depth-First Search (DFS) algorithm can effectively identify the connection methods of components in engineering drawings. This paper proposes an optimized algorithm for the automatic extraction of key parameters in the power GIM based on an improved Convolutional Neural Network + Depth-First Search (CNN + DFS) approach. The algorithm employs a symbol detection algorithm based on CNN models to recognize electrical component symbols, followed by the identification of textual information within the design diagram and its association with respective component symbols. Finally, it utilizes DFS to identify the connection relationships among component symbols. This algorithm effectively enhances the efficiency and accuracy of grid modeling and is particularly suitable for application in wiring diagrams found in electrical schematics.

This paper analyzes the parameters of drawings in Section 2 and explains the importance of parameter extraction in GIM use. In Section 3, an optimization algorithm for the automatic extraction of key parameters in GIM, based on an improved CNN + DFS method, is introduced. The components of the algorithm are also detailed. Section 4 presents a comparative analysis using an example to demonstrate the performance of the improved algorithm against traditional algorithms. Finally, Section 5 summarizes the research findings and discusses the limitations of the study.

2. Analysis of Key Parameters of GIM

2.1. Key Parameters of GIM

The GIM is an information model for power systems and their equipment, aiming to comprehensively describe the information content and relationships of the grid, equipment, and operations. This model is primarily applied in the field of power transmission and transformation projects, encompassing a wide range of digital design elements, including equipment, structures, and facilities within the substations, as well as towers, conductors, and infrastructure along the transmission lines.

Therefore, crucial parameters in building the GIM for the grid include engineering information of substations, parameter information of equipment, the parameters of substation structures and facilities, and relevant parameters of towers, conductors, and foundations along the transmission lines. Taking substations as an example, their three-dimensional modeling involves not only geometric models but also physical models. Thus, the parameter encompasses not only the geometric information describing the shape, structure, and dimensions of physical objects but also the parameters of engineering equipment, materials, structures, and other facilities.

2.2. Representation of Key Parameters in GIM in Engineering Design Drawings

The acquisition of key parameters is crucial in the construction of the GIM for the power grid, and these parameters are primarily obtained from engineering design drawings. Typically, engineering design drawings provide detailed information about the electrical characteristics, connection methods, and installation positions of grid equipment. These pieces of information have a close correspondence with the parameters in the GIM. For example, information such as equipment models and rated voltages from the design drawings can directly correspond to the equipment types and voltage parameters in the GIM. Additionally, parameters regarding equipment installation positions from the design drawings can be directly applied to the equipment location parameters in the GIM, enabling an accurate representation of the layout of the grid equipment.

Therefore, the crucial parameters of the GIM can be found in the engineering design drawings. Applying artificial intelligence technology to automatically identify and extract the key parameters for GIM use from the design drawings, instead of relying on tedious manual data entry, is beneficial in reducing labor and time costs, improving the accuracy and consistency of parameter input, and subsequently enhancing the speed and quality of GIM establishment.

2.3. Characteristics of Representation in Power Grid Equipment Engineering Design Drawings

Taking the electrical main single-line diagram of a substation as an example, as shown in Figure 1, this diagram primarily includes equipment layout, electrical connections, equipment parameter tables, and other additional notes. Among them, the equipment layout is the main part of the drawing, describing the overall structural layout of the substation. This includes not only the power supply locations of electrical equipment, such as transformers and reactive power compensation devices, but also the routing of power transmission lines and the distribution and usage of customer equipment. The electrical connections between equipment characterize the interconnection relationships, providing detailed information on the starting and ending points of various power transmission lines, as well as the specifications and ratings of the lines. The equipment parameter table records the electrical parameters of each device, including rated voltage, rated power, protection level, insulation level, and other relevant information. Meanwhile, other additional notes are usually found in blank areas of the drawing and are provided in the form of annotations using text or symbols, offering supplementary explanations for special design requirements or equipment specifications. Figure 1 shows the electrical circuit of a converter station in a certain ultra-high-voltage direct current (UHVDC) transmission project. This circuit, starting from the 66 kV busbar, sequentially passes through a single grounding disconnector, a current transformer, a station service transformer, and a zinc oxide arrester, before being routed via a 10 kV cable to the 10 kV distribution room of the converter station.

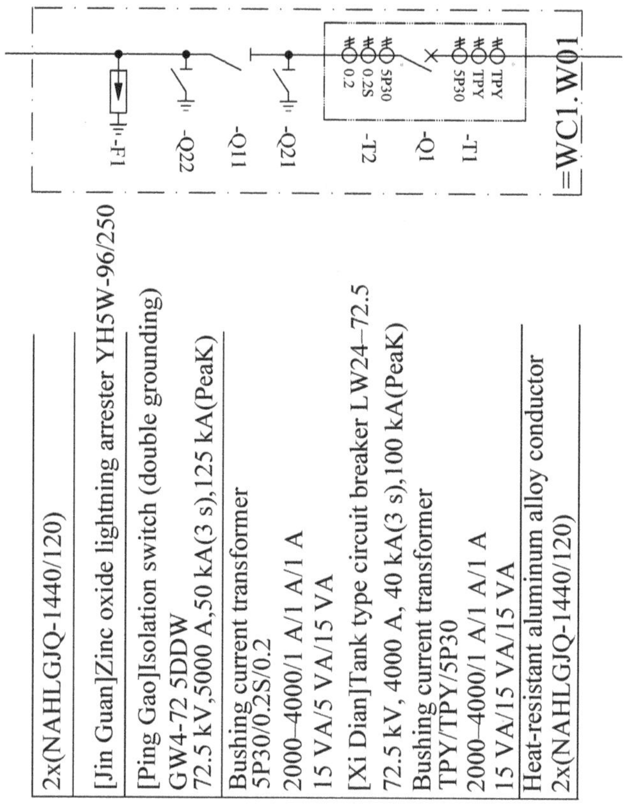

Figure 1. Partial electrical main wiring diagram of a certain substation.

3. Optimization Algorithm for Automatic Extraction of Key Parameters in GIM Based on Improved CNN + DFS

Given the limitations of traditional methods for extracting information from drawings, this paper aims to develop a new method that can accurately and efficiently extract key parameter information for the GIM in a fully automated manner. Taking into consideration the unique characteristics of design drawings, this paper combines a CNN with a Depth-First Search algorithm to propose an optimized algorithm for automatically extracting key parameters for the GIM. This method aims to improve the accuracy and efficiency of information extraction and overcome the shortcomings of traditional methods.

In this paper, we optimize an algorithm for automatically extracting key parameters for the GIM, based on a CNN, which consists of three main modules: component symbol detection, text recognition and association, and connection detection. Focusing on the processing of the electrical main single-line diagram of a substation in the grid engineering drawings, this technique first crops the substation's electrical main single-line diagram to generate images with consistent dimensions. Next, an improved CNN model is used to recognize and extract information from the component symbols. Subsequently, the text in the drawing is detected using a neural network algorithm, allowing for the establishment of a scene text detector to ensure the correct association between the text and the corresponding component symbols. Finally, a Depth-First Search method is employed to identify the connections between the various component symbols in the engineering drawings.

3.1. Component Symbol Detection

The component symbol detection module employs a CNN model to automatically identify the component symbols in electrical elementary drawings of substation main wiring diagrams. These drawings consist of the symbol elements of various electrical equipment, such as transformers, reactors, capacitors, and distribution devices, along with their corresponding device name labels, which are combined with electrical wiring to create the substation's main wiring diagram. Therefore, this paper focuses on achieving precise detection of these component symbols.

Firstly, the dataset undergoes symbol cropping. This dataset comprises two parts: the component symbol dataset and the composite symbol label dataset. We extract these from the collection of electrical main wiring drawings at the substation, marking all component symbols and their composite symbols in each electrical main wiring diagram. Given the significant differences between component symbols and composite symbols in the drawings, we choose an appropriate pixel window for individual marking and cropping of all electrical main wiring diagrams. Additionally, addressing situations where some drawings lack corresponding equipment text labels for component symbols or where their semantics cannot be clearly identified, we establish an "unsigned" cropping dataset to store cropped images in such special cases, as shown in Figure 2.

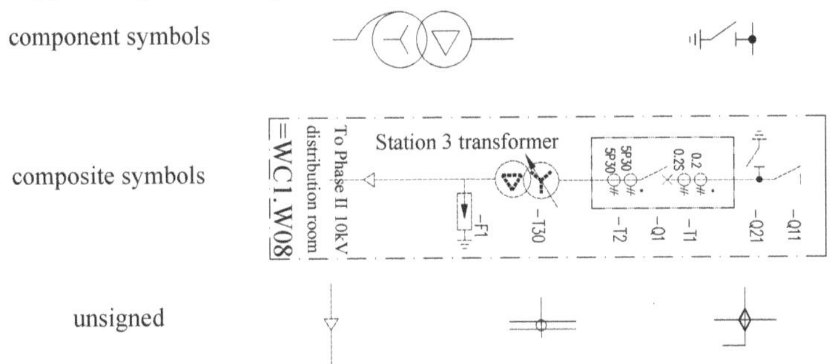

Figure 2. Symbol cropping dataset illustration.

Building upon the compiled symbol-cropped dataset, this paper employs a CNN model for image classification to determine whether input images contain component symbols, composite symbols, or neither. Recognizing the complexity and diversity of graphical symbols, we propose an enhanced CNN architecture for symbol detection, as illustrated in Figure 3. In the figure, dashed boxes represent a part as a whole module, arrows represent the direction of tensor transmission, and asterisk represents the number of executions.

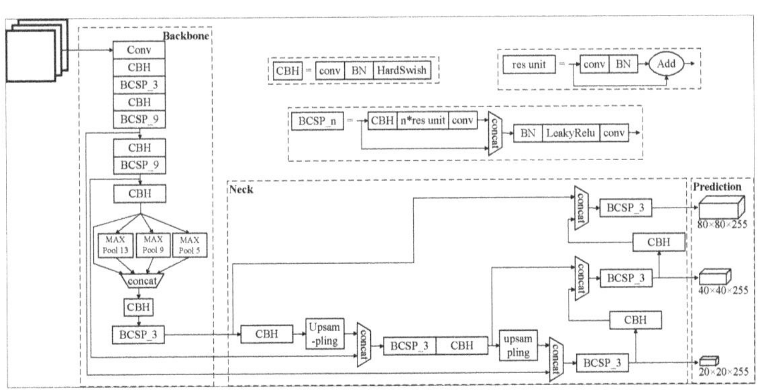

Figure 3. Improved CNN architecture for symbol detection.

The equivalent calculation formula for the convolution operation is shown in Equation (1) [19]:

$$C^{(k)} = B^{(k)} * A^{(k-1)} + H^{(k)} \quad (1)$$

In the equation, $A^{(k-1)}$ represents the input image of the k-th layer, $B^{(k)}$ is the weight matrix of the convolutional kernel, $H^{(k)}$ is the bias vector of the k-th layer, and $C^{(k)}$ is the output image after the convolution operation of the k-th layer [19].

In the enhanced CNN architecture proposed in this paper for symbol detection, the overall framework consists of four parts: the input end, Backbone network, Neck, and prediction sections. The input terminal receives images as input for the algorithm. The Backbone is typically a pre-trained Convolutional Neural Network with strong capabilities in extracting image features. The Neck further processes or merges the features extracted by the Backbone, with common structures such as FPN, PAN, ASPP, etc. The prediction module is used for object detection, usually comprising classification and regression branches to predict the class and position of the target, and box objects. These four components work together to form the basic architecture of image object detection algorithms, enabling the algorithm to automatically extract target location and class information from images. Specifically, in the input end of the network, considering the limited number of training samples, the Mosaic data augmentation method is employed. This technique randomly selects several images from the training set and recombines them using methods such as scaling, cropping, and rearrangement, effectively enhancing the network's robustness. Additionally, during the network training process, the auto-anchor mechanism is utilized to automatically determine the optimal anchor boxes for the current training set, accelerating the convergence speed of the network.

In the Backbone section, the architecture is constructed using slice convolution and Cross Stage Partial (CSP) modules. Slice convolution processes images through channel shuffling operations, integrating odd rows/odd columns, odd rows/even columns, even rows/even columns, and even rows/odd columns before conducting convolution operations, aiming to preserve the original data characteristics of graphical symbols to the maximum extent. The CSP module first divides the underlying feature maps into two parts and then effectively merges them using skip connections, thereby significantly reducing the computational complexity of the network while maintaining the accuracy of symbol detection.

In the Neck section, the network structure integrates the advantages of Feature Pyramid Networks (FPNs) and Path Aggregation Network (PANs). The FPN structure propagates high-level feature information in a top-down manner, transmitting strong semantic features through upsampling, and then integrates with the PAN structure, which can transmit strong localization features in a bottom-up manner. Through the combination of these two structures, feature fusion is performed on different feature layers of the Backbone and different detection layers, enhancing the network's ability to extract features related to graphical symbols.

In the prediction section, the bounding box loss function adopts the Generalized Intersection over Union Loss (GIoU_Loss) function, which effectively enhances the model's performance without increasing costs, as shown in Equation (2) [23]:

$$L_{GIoU} = 1 - IoU + \frac{|\, C \backslash (A \cup B) \,|}{|\, C \,|} \quad (2)$$

In this equation, A represents the area of the ground truth box; B represents the area of the predicted box; C represents the area of the minimum rectangle containing both A and B; and IoU is the Intersection over U nion of A and B [23].

The improved model structure and its parameter settings are shown in the Table 1.

Table 1. Network structure and parameter setting of model.

Index	Input Layer	Number of Modules	Number of Parameters	Module Name	Parameter Settings
0	−1	1	3520	Conv	[3, 32, 6, 2, 2]
1	−1	1	20,736	Rep_Block	[32, 64, 3, 2]
2	−1	1	18,816	C3	[64, 64, 1]
3	−1	1	82,432	Rep_Block	[64, 128, 3, 2]
4	−1	1	74,560	MT_Block	[128, 128, 1]
5	−1	1	328,704	Rep_Block	[128, 256, 3, 2]
6	−1	1	296,704	MT_Block	[256, 256, 1]
7	−1	1	1,312,768	Rep_Block	[256, 512, 3, 2]
8	−1	1	1,182,976	MT_Block	[512, 512, 1]
9	−1	1	656,896	SPPF	[512, 512, 5]
10	−1	1	131,584	Conv	[512, 256, 1, 1]
11	−1	1	0	Upsampling	[None, 2, 'nearest']
12	[1, 6]	1	0	Concat	[1]
13	−1	1	391,984	C3	[512, 256, 1, False]
14	−1	1	33,024	Conv	[256, 128, 1, 1]
15	−1	1	0	Upsampling	[None, 2, 'nearest']
16	[1, 4]	1	0	Concat	[1]
17	−1	1	90,880	C3	[256, 128, 1, False]
18	−1	1	6448	CA_Block	[128, 128, 8]
19	−1	1	147,712	Conv	[128, 128, 3, 2]
20	[1, 14]	1	0	Concat	[1]
21	−1	1	296,448	C3	[256, 256, 1, False]
22	−1	1	12,848	CA_Block	[256, 256, 16]
23	−1	1	590,336	Conv	[256, 256, 3, 2]
24	[1, 10]	1	0	Concat	[1]
25	−1	1	1,182,720	C3	[512, 512, 1, False]
26	−1	1	25,648	CA_Block	[512, 512, 32]
27	[18, 22, 26]	1	24,273	Detect	[4,[[...], [...], [...]], [...]]

The symbol cropping dataset was randomly divided into a training set (60%), a validation set (20%), and a test set (20%) for training the network model. The training results are shown in Figure 4. It can be observed that, in the initial stages of training, the model loss exhibits significant variation, indicating that the model is unable to effectively recognize unseen new data. This is because the model is just starting to learn and does not yet have a thorough understanding of the data. This phenomenon is common in most machine learning models, especially when the training dataset is complex or has many features. However, as the number of training epochs increases, the loss variation decreases significantly, and the tendency of the model to overfit is reduced. This indicates that the model continuously learns and adapts to the training data, gradually reducing the prediction error. The continuous decline in training loss is expected, as the model's performance on the training set is continuously optimized. Therefore, by comparing the loss changes between the training set and the validation set, it can be observed that using the enhanced CNN model proposed in this paper for symbol detection makes it easier for the model to learn effective features, thereby improving the model's performance. The decline in training loss indicates that the model is better at fitting the training data, while the decline in validation loss shows that the model possesses good generalization ability. The combination of both indicates that the improved Convolutional Neural Network model can more effectively extract features for symbol detection, enhancing the overall performance of the model.

It is worth noting that, to effectively use the trained CNN model for component symbol detection in new drawings, three prediction feature layers of different scales are designed in this study to adapt to various sizes of electrical components. Considering the high sparsity of most drawings, the module automatically filters out over 90% of empty windows and symbols lacking clear semantic representation, classifying them into the "unsigned" category. Finally, a non-maximum suppression algorithm is employed to merge the detection results from multiple prediction feature layers, ensuring that the output layer presents only unique and accurate detected symbols. This effectively avoids the issue of repetitive recognition of the same symbol in different feature layers.

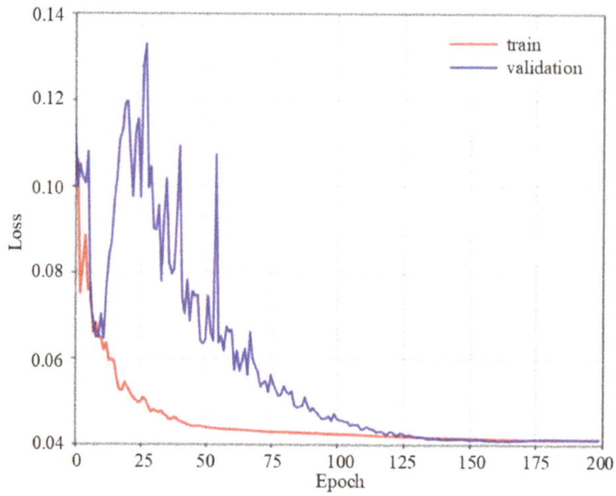

Figure 4. Training and validation losses converge after 200 rounds of training.

In the end, the component symbol detection module creates thresholds for the predicted probabilities based on preset thresholds and categorizes them into discrete symbols. Image windows with prediction probabilities below all thresholds are defined as non-symbols. Figure 5 and Table 2 shows the symbol detection results after inputting a specific drawing segment. It can be observed that all preset symbols are accurately classified, and composite symbols are also accurately recognized.

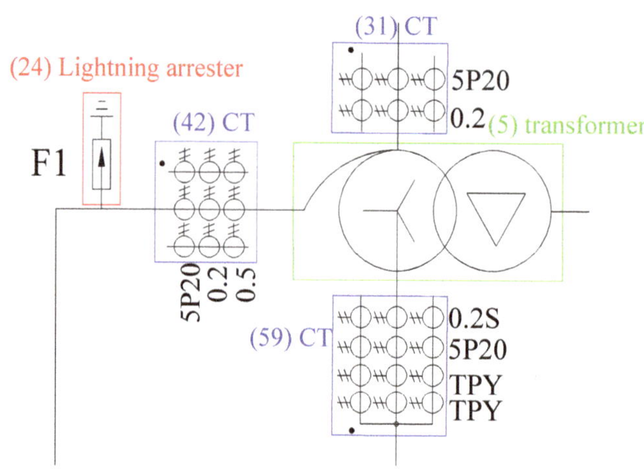

Figure 5. Symbol detection results after inputting the drawing.

Table 2. Symbol detection results after inputting the drawing.

Symbol Number	Symbol Name
(1)	Wind farm output circuit
(34)	Reactor circuit
(5)	transformer
(24)	Lightning arrester
(31)	CT
(42)	CT
(59)	CT

3.2. Text Recognition and Association

In the electrical primary wiring diagrams of substations, textual elements play a crucial role. They identify and describe various electrical equipment types, voltage levels, and design annotations within the drawings. These texts typically include the names of devices and the parameters of the devices in parameter tables placed next to the electrical equipment. Together, this information clearly defines the engineering and parameter details of the electrical equipment. Therefore, the accurate identification and parsing of these texts, along with the correct association with recognized component symbols on the drawings, are essential for the automatic extraction of key parameters in the GIM. The lack of this step would significantly reduce the extraction effectiveness.

Therefore, to ensure the effective identification of text in power grid engineering drawings and its accurate association with corresponding component symbols, this paper introduces a specially designed scene text detector based on a neural network algorithm in the optimization of key parameter automatic extraction for the GIM. The detector utilizes a CNN to generate bounding boxes indicating the positions of text in the image. It then identifies relevant text based on the proximity threshold between component symbols and text bounding boxes. Finally, Tesseract OCR is employed for text recognition. For text boxes in different orientations, a detection enhancement method is applied to extract text from various directions. The accuracy of the text content is ensured by comparing multiple extraction results of the same text box. Subsequently, these texts are associated with the corresponding symbols, achieving a structured representation of symbols and text information, as illustrated in Figure 6 and Tables 3 and 4.

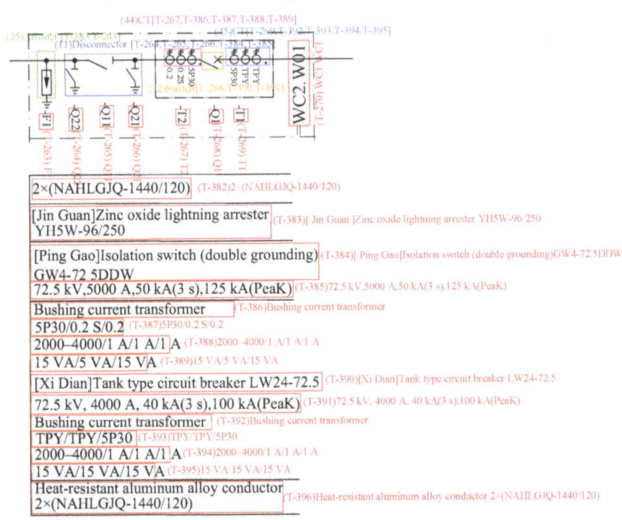

Figure 6. Symbol and text recognition results after inputting the drawing.

Table 3. Symbol recognition results after inputting the drawing.

Text Number	Recognized Text Content	Text Number	Recognized Text Content	Text Number	Recognized Text Content
(T-169)	[Jin Guan] Metal oxide arrester	(T-170)	WA.ST1	(T-171)	YH10W-204/532
(T-172)	F2	(T-173)	2× (NAHLGJQ-1440/120)	(T-174)	[Heng Bian] Three-phase integrated on-site assembly transformer
(T-239)	1000/1000/334 MVA	(T-240)	525/230 ± 2 × 2.5%/66 kV	(T-241)	YN, a0, d11, ODAF
(T-242)	U1-3 = 67%, U1-2 = 20%	(T-243)	F1	(T-244)	U2-3 = 40%
(T-245)	High voltage bushing CT:5P20/0.2/0.5	(T-246)	5P20	(T-247)	0.2
(T-248)	0.5	(T-249)	2000/1 A 15 VA	(T-250)	Medium voltage bushing CT: 5P20/0.2
(T-251)	4000/1 A 15 VA	(T-252)	Low voltage bushing CT: TPY/TPY/5P20/0.2	(T-253)	5P20
(T-254)	0.2	(T-255)	0.2	(T-256)	5P20
(T-257)	TPY	(T-258)	TPY	(T-259)	0.2S
(T-260)	5P20	(T-261)	TPY	(T-262)	TPY
(T-263)	F1	(T-264)	Q22	(T-265)	Q11
(T-266)	Q21	(T-267)	T2	(T-268)	Q1
(T-269)	T1	(T-270)	WC1.W01	(T-375)	4000/1A 15VA
(T-376)	72.5 kV, 5000 A	(T-377)	2000/4000/1 A 15 VA	(T-378)	No.1 main transformer
(T-379)	[Jin Guan] Metal oxide arrester	(T-380)	YH20W-420/1046 kV	(T-381)	2× (NAHLGJQ-1440/120)
(T-382)	2× (NAHLGJQ-1440/120)	(T-383)	[Jin Guan] Zinc oxide lightning arrester YH5W-96/250	(T-384)	[Ping Gao] Isolation switch (double grounding) GW4-72.5DDW
(T-385)	72.5 kV, 5000 A, 50 kA (3 s), 125 kA (Peak)	(T-386)	Bushing current transformer	(T-387)	5P30/0.2S/0.2
(T-388)	2000-4000/1A/1A/1A	(T-389)	15VA/5VA/15VA	(T-390)	Tank-type circuit breaker LW24-72.5
(T-391)	72.5 kV, 4000 A,40 kA (3 s), 100 kA (Peak)	(T-392)	Bushing current transformer	(T-393)	TPY/TPY/5P30
(T-394)	2000-4000/1 A/1 A/1 A	(T-395)	15 VA/15 VA/15 VA	(T-396)	Heat-resistant aluminum alloy conductor 2× (NAHLGJQ-1440/120)

Table 4. Symbol recognition and text association results after inputting drawings.

Symbol Number	Symbol Name	Associated Text	Symbol Number	Symbol Name	Associated Text
(23)	NoSymbol	None	(5)	Transformer	[T-174]
(16)	GRD	None	(31)	Switch	[T-268, T-390, T-391]
(11)	Disconnector	[T-264, T-265, T-266, T-384, T-385]	(31)	CT	[T-250, T-251, T-253, T-254]
(14)	Disconnector	None	(42)	CT	[T-245, T-246,T-247, T-248, T-249]
(17)	Arrester	[T-169, T-172]	(43)	CT	[T-252,T-255, T-256, T-257, T-258, T-375]
(24)	Arrester	[T-243, T-397]	(44)	CT	[T-267, T-386, T-387, T-388, T-389]
(25)	Arrester	[T-383, T-263]	(45)	CT	[T-269, T-392, T-393, T-394, T-395]
(39)	Arrester	[T-379]	(59)	CT	[T-259, T-260, T-261, T-262, T-376, T-377]

3.3. Connection Detection

In the field of power grid engineering, the interconnection of various grid devices is primarily achieved through transmission lines such as cables and conductors. In engineering drawings, the physical connections between devices are represented by solid line segments. The connection detection module, building upon the symbol detection step, further identifies which symbols are interconnected by these lines. This allows for the determination of the spatial and connection relationships between power grid devices. This process is crucial for reconstructing the mutual relationships between devices and establishing the hierarchical structure of power grid assets.

The optimization extraction method proposed in this paper achieves symbol connection detection through a graph search algorithm. The thresholded images of device component symbols are treated as graphical representations, with each pixel in the image corresponding to a node in the graph. Each node contains information about its color and whether it belongs to a device component symbol based on its thresholded pixel intensity. The connections between adjacent pixels form the edges of the graph, with each node having at most eight edges. Within this framework, device component symbols are represented in the graph by a group of nodes corresponding to the pixels forming the symbol.

Utilizing the graphical representation described above, the connection detection module employs a DFS strategy to identify connections between device component symbols. For each detected symbol, a DFS process is initialized from a node within the symbol. This process traverses along the black nodes in the graph while simultaneously recording and tracking encountered connections between symbols along its path. The search automatically terminates once all valid paths have been explored.

Figure 7 illustrates the results of connection detection on image segments, where the source symbols are highlighted in red, and the connected symbols are highlighted in green. From the figure, it can be observed that, apart from the labeled "unsigned" clipped set, all detected symbols are determined to be connected to the source symbol.

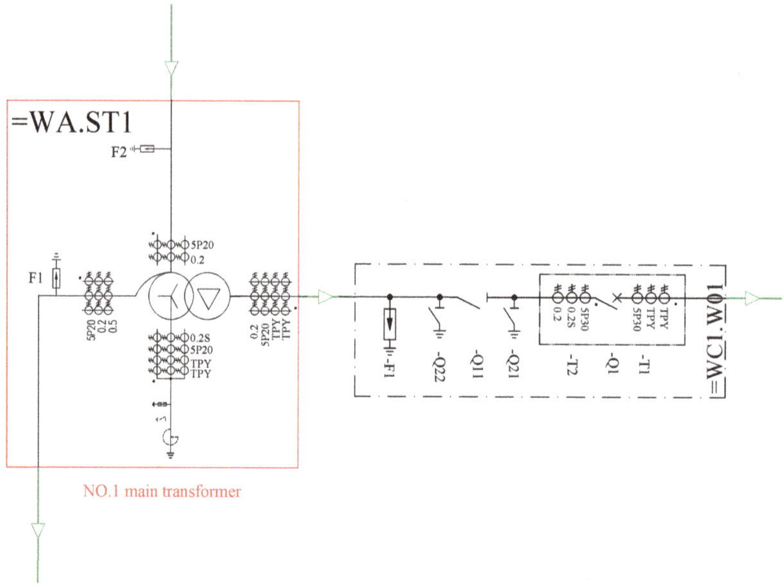

Figure 7. Results of connection detection on image segments.

4. Example Analysis

In order to verify the effectiveness of the proposed method, this study used 100 electrical main wiring diagrams of a substation with voltage levels of 220 kV and above. The proposed optimized algorithm based on the improved CNN + DFS method for key parameter automatic extraction of a power grid GIM was used for recognition and key element extraction of the diagrams, and the effectiveness of the method was evaluated. The diagrams were divided into training and test sets in a ratio of 4:1. After the experiment, the confusion matrix, F1-score curve, and Mean Average Precision (mAP) curve were drawn to analyze the prediction ability and results of the model from multiple aspects.

The confusion matrix in Figure 8 presents the confusion matrix of the recognition system, reflecting the recognition performance and confusion degree of different symbol categories. The recognition of unsigned and component symbols is less affected by interference and is not easily confused with the background or other categories. This indicates that the features of these two types of symbols are more distinct and less affected by background interference. Therefore, we can conclude that the feature extraction and classification algorithms for unsigned and component symbols are highly reliable in practical applications. On the other hand, composite symbols easily interfere with the background, with a probability of 22% of being misclassified as background. This higher misclassification rate suggests that the features of composite symbols are more easily confused with background features, leading to lower recognition accuracy. This may be due to the complex structure of composite symbols and the diverse background environments.

To effectively quantify the validity of the recognition results, this paper establishes the following evaluation criteria: a detected symbol is considered correctly identified if its category matches the ground truth label and if the bounding box of the detected symbol has at least a 0.5 Intersection over Union (IOU) with the bounding box of the ground truth symbol. The mAP@0.5 metric measures the average precision of the model at an Intersection over Union (IoU) threshold of 0.5, that is, the accuracy when the bounding boxes detected by the model overlap by 50% with the true bounding boxes. Generally, mAP@0.5 is one of the commonly used evaluation metrics in object detection tasks, utilized to gauge the precision and accuracy of the model. The results indicate that the validation set, comprising 20 sets of diagrams with 400 different categories of symbols, achieves an mAP@0.5 of 0.832 when using a classification probability threshold of 0.5 for symbol recognition, as illustrated in Figure 9. Although the improved CNN performs well on the test set, the performance of the modified model on other types of drawings has not yet been tested, and further experiments are needed to determine this.

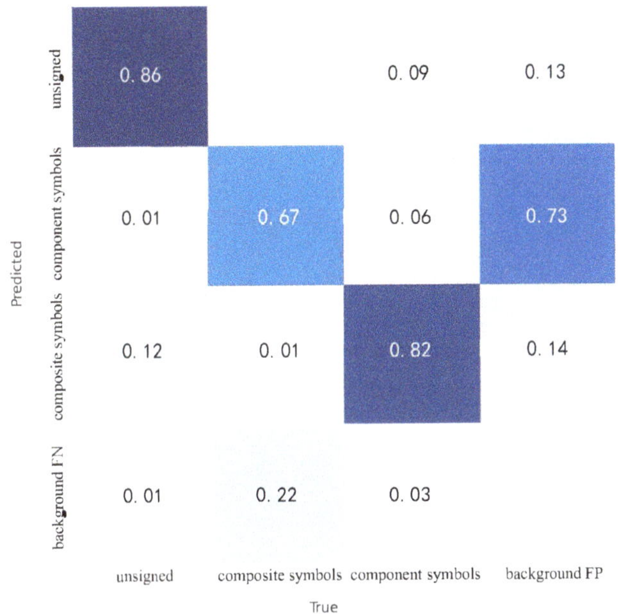

Figure 8. Validation set of confusion matrix.

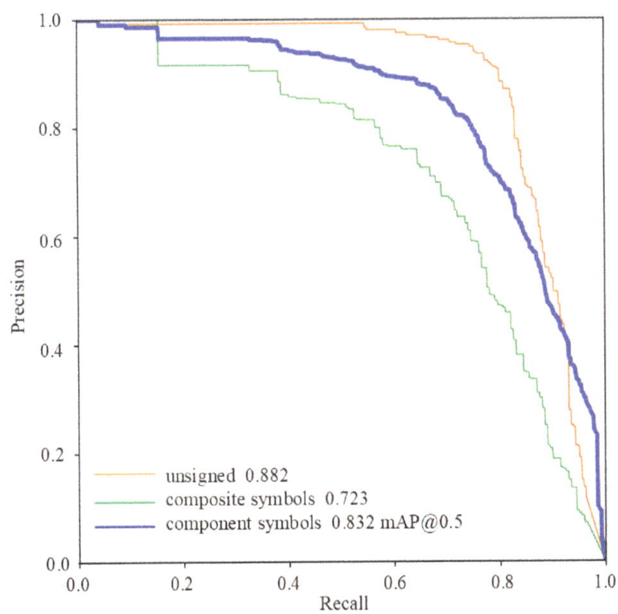

Figure 9. mAP test results of validation image set.

To measure the robustness of the model, we drew the F1-score curve based on the harmonic mean of precision and recall. As shown in Figure 10, the F1 curves for unsigned, combination symbols, and element symbols all performed well and were not significantly affected by the imbalance of the circuit diagram dataset. This indicates that the model has good robustness and overall performance.

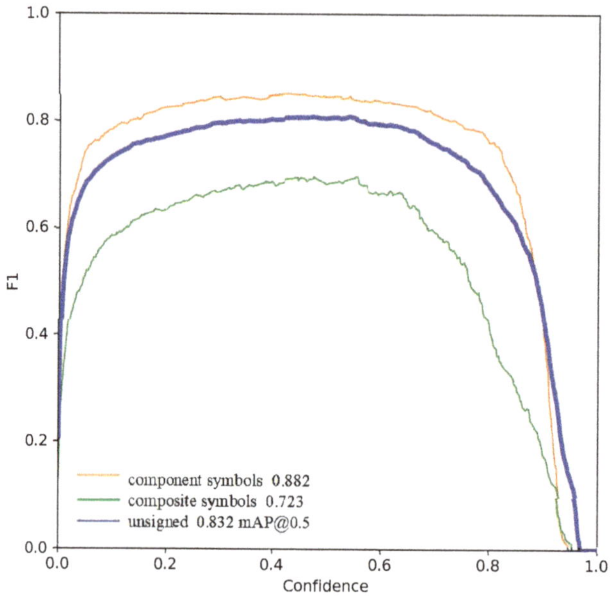

Figure 10. F1-score curve.

Additionally, from the above figure, it is evident that the performance of unsigned symbol recognition is significantly better than that of component symbol recognition. This discrepancy arises due to the fewer categories and samples for unsigned symbols, as well as the relatively complex composition and representation of component symbols, making them prone to confusion with other symbols. Comparisons between the proposed algorithm and traditional CNN models, as well as the Faster Regions with CNN features (R-CNN) model, are presented in Table 5. In this study, the traditional Convolutional Neural Network (CNN) model has a parameter count of 229.00 M and a computational cost of 220.0 G. The Faster R-CNN model has a parameter count of 315.00 M and a computational cost of 267.0 G. In contrast, our proposed CNN + DFS model significantly reduces both parameters and computational requirements, with a parameter count of 138.1 M and a computational cost of 89.3 G. The results indicate that, out of a total of 1623 component symbol samples tested, the drawing symbol recognition accuracy using the proposed improved CNN is the highest, achieving an overall accuracy of 91.31%. This surpasses the accuracy of traditional CNN models (71.23%) and the Faster R-CNN model (89.59%), demonstrating the effectiveness of the proposed improved CNN architecture for symbol detection.

In this study, a comparison was conducted among three algorithms. The results indicate that the traditional CNN algorithm yielded lower accuracy in the recognition of all types of component symbols when compared to the other two algorithms, demonstrating inferior performance. In contrast, the proposed optimization algorithm exhibited better performance in the recognition of the majority of component symbols when compared to the Faster R-CNN algorithm. Analysis of the F1-score curve leads to the conclusion that the improved algorithm demonstrates good robustness and overall performance.

Table 5. Accuracy of symbol recognition in power grid engineering drawings under different algorithms.

Drawing Component Symbols	Number of Samples	Accuracy of Drawing Symbol Recognition under Different Algorithms		
		Traditional CNN	Faster R-CNN	Optimized Algorithm
1	107	66.36	85.98	90.65
2	136	72.06	88.24	91.18
2	143	73.43	90.91	91.61
2	263	69.20	88.97	90.87
2	274	70.80	91.61	91.56
4	304	68.75	86.84	90.79
5	102	74.51	91.18	92.16
3	294	75.17	91.84	91.80
all	1623	71.23	89.59	91.31

5. Conclusions

To address the challenge of automatically extracting key parameters in the GIM, this paper proposes an optimization algorithm based on artificial intelligence image recognition technology, utilizing a CNN model. The proposed approach, which is based on an improved CNN + DFS framework, innovatively enhances traditional CNN methods by incorporating the Mosaic data augmentation technique and the GIoU_Loss loss function. These enhancements aim to improve the effectiveness, robustness, and computational speed of the neural network model. Simulation results demonstrate that compared to traditional CNN and Faster R-CNN algorithms, the proposed optimization algorithm achieves higher accuracy in character recognition and detection.

Compared to traditional manual input and simple image recognition techniques, this algorithm can automatically process design drawings, reducing labor costs and time, while reducing error rates. Moreover, the optimization algorithm introduced in this paper, based on the DFS strategy, enables the detection of connections between device symbols in power grid engineering drawings. This capability facilitates the intelligent recognition of power grid topological architecture in engineering drawings. In summary, the proposed optimization algorithm accurately identifies device information and topological structure information, among other key parameters, from engineering design drawings of power grid devices, thereby providing a reference for the automatic extraction of parameters in GIM modeling.

In addition to its application in GIM use, this key parameter extraction method has various other wide-ranging applications. In scenarios involving blueprint recognition and parameter extraction, as long as the blueprint category is ensured to be wiring diagrams and the extracted parameters are formatted to meet the actual requirements, it can be extended to other scenarios. However, it is important to note that the current algorithm focuses on the automatic extraction of key parameters in the GIM from power grid engineering design drawings and has not yet achieved automatic entry of detected and recognized data into the GIM's process. This limitation arises because some specialized software does not provide data interfaces to facilitate automated workflows, which introduces significant difficulties. This aspect will be explored in future research endeavors.

Author Contributions: Conceptualization, X.L. (Xintong Li) and X.L. (Xiangjun Liu); methodology, X.L. (Xintong Li); software, X.L. (Xintong Li); validation, X.L. (Xiangjun Liu) and X.L. (Xintong Li); formal analysis, X.L. (Xintong Li); investigation, X.L. (Xintong Li); resources, X.L. (Xiangjun Liu); data curation, X.L. (Xintong Li); writing—original draft preparation, X.L. (Xintong Li); writing—review and editing, X.L. (Xintong Li); visualization, X.L. (Xintong Li) and X.L. (Xiangjun Liu); supervision, X.L. (Xiangjun Liu); project administration, X.L. (Xiangjun Liu); funding acquisition, X.L. (Xiangjun Liu) All authors have read and agreed to the published version of the manuscript.

Funding: This research received no external funding.

Data Availability Statement: The data presented in this study are available on request from the corresponding author due to privacy.

Conflicts of Interest: The authors declare no conflicts of interest.

References

1. Vinnikov, V.; Pshehotskaya, E. Deficiencies of Computational Image Recognition in Comparison to Human Counterpart. In Proceedings of the Seventh International Congress on Information and Communication Technology, London, UK, 21–24 February 2022 ; Springer: Singapore, 2023; Volume 447, pp. 483–491.
2. Yang, M.; Kumar, P.; Bhola, J.; Shabaz, M. Development of image recognition software based on artificial intelligence algorithm for the efficient sorting of apple fruit. *Int. J. Syst. Assur. Eng. Manag.* **2022**, *13*, 322–330. [CrossRef]
3. Kwak, D.; Choi, J.; Lee, S. Rethinking Breast Cancer Diagnosis through Deep Learning Based Image Recognition. *Sensors* **2023**, *23*, 2307. [CrossRef] [PubMed]
4. Sinha, P.; Maharana, M.K.; Jena, C.; Kumar, A.P.; Akkenaguntla, K. Power System Fault Detection Using Image Processing And Pattern Recognition. In Proceedings of the 2021 IEEE 2nd International Conference on Applied Electromagnetics, Signal Processing, & Communication (AESPC), Bhubaneswar, India, 26–28 November 2021; Volume 5.
5. Mishra, M.; Biswal, M.; Bansal, R.C.; Nayak, J.; Abraham, A.; Malik, O.P. Intelligent Computing in Electrical Utility Industry 4.0: Concept, Key Technologies, Applications and Future Directions. *IEEE Access* **2022**, *10*, 100312–100336. [CrossRef]
6. Krasnyansky; Matveykin, M.; Dmitrievsky, V.; Kobelev, B.; Terekhova, A.; Kobeleva; V. Digitalization of Energy Management in an Industrial Enterprise. In Proceedings of the 2021 3rd International Conference on Control Systems, Mathematical Modeling, Automation and Energy Efficiency (SUMMA), Lipetsk, Russia, 10–12 November 2021; pp. 633–635.
7. Praanesh, K.S.; Vardhan, V.V.; Varun, C.M.; Naik, B.B.; Kulkarni, B.; Sailaja, V. Tariff Digitalization for Power Theft Detection in Transmission Lines. In Proceedings of the 2022 6th International Conference on Electronics, Communication and Aerospace Technology, Coimbatore, India, 1–3 December 2022; pp. 400–405.
8. Wang, R.; Wu, X.; Leng, Y.;Hou, H.; Wu, S.; Qiu, J. A review of the development of digital twin technology in new type power systems. *Power Syst. Technol.* **2024**, 1–21. [CrossRef]
9. Redmond, J. Revit 3D Modeling Optimizes Substation Design. In Proceedings of the 2022 IEEE Rural Electric Power Conference (REPC), Savannah, GA, USA, 5–7 April 2022; pp. 84–87.
10. Bai, H.; Guo, K.; Chang, L. 3D Power grid modeling and verification method based on GIM technology and YOLOv3 deep network. *J. Shenyang Univ. Technol.* **2023**, *45.03*, 247–252.
11. Sun, K.; Jing, T.; An, X.; Hu, J. Research on Data Lightweight Method of GIM Model Based on BIMBase Technology. *Electr. Power Inf. Commun. Technol.* **2023**, *21*, 9–15.
12. Shi, Z.; Meng, C.; Zhang, S.; He, S.; Zhang, H. Research on construction design scheme of power transmission and transformation project based on power grid information model. *Manuf. Autom.* **2023**, *45*, 71–74.
13. Tao, L.; Zhu, J.; Cai, H. Classic machine learning for image recognition in wall column construction drawings. *J. Shanghai Univ. Sci. Ed.* **2021**, *27*, 940–949.
14. Xiao, Y.; He, Z.; Lin, S. Rapid visual positioning technology of sheet metal parts based on electronic drawing template. *Inf. Technol.* **2023**, *6*, 24–29.
15. Liu, L.; Zhang, Y. Simulation of Fuzzy Recognition of Vector Symbols Based on Adaptive Matching. *Comput. Simul.* **2021**, *38*, 401–404.
16. Zhou, C.; Xu, L.; Qiao, W. Feature Recognition and Matching Method of Shaft Parts Drawing. *Mach. Des. Res.* **2022**, *38*, 126–129.
17. Wang, K. *Research on Automatic Recognition Technology of Electrical Wiring Drawings*; Southeast University: Nanjing, China, 2022.
18. Ma, M.; Jia, L.; Su, L. Application of Engineering Drawing Image Recognition Technology in Digital Delivery. *Pet. Chem. Constr.* **2021**, *43*, 63–65.
19. Dong, Z.; Zhao, Y.; Tian, F. Character recognition and detection algorithm of power grid engineering drawings based on improved convolutional neural network. *Electron. Des. Eng.* **2023**, *31*, 27–31.
20. Yang, Q.; You, H.; Shi, H.; Yang, Y.; Kong, D. Secondary circuit intelligent verification system based on image deep learning. *Manuf. Autom.* **2023**, *45*, 56–58+62.

21. Uzair, W.; Chai, D.; Rassau, A. Automated Netlist Generation from Offline Hand-Drawn Circuit Diagrams. In Proceedings of the 2023 International Conference on Digital Image Computing: Techniques and Applications (DICTA), Port Macquarie, Australia, 28 November–1 December 2023; pp. 364–370.
22. Yu, W.; Zhang, P. Convolutional Neural Networks' Applications in Automatic Target Recognition for Synthetic Aperture Images. In Proceedings of the 2021 International Conference of Optical Imaging and Measurement (ICOIM), Xi'an, China, 27–29 August 2021; pp. 9–13.
23. Li, W.; Gao, L. Improved RetinaNet process flow detection algorithm. *J. Electron. Meas. Instrum.* **2023**, *37*, 104–112.

electronics

MDPI

Review

Reinforcement Learning Techniques in Optimizing Energy Systems

Stefan Stavrev [1,*] and Dimitar Ginchev [2]

[1] Department of Software Technologies, Faculty of Mathematics and Informatics, Plovdiv University "Paisii Hilendarski", 4000 Plovdiv, Bulgaria

[2] Department of Air Transport, Faculty of Transport, Technical University of Sofia, 1000 Sofia, Bulgaria; dimginchev@tu-sofia.bg

* Correspondence: stavrev@uni-plovdiv.bg; Tel.: +359-889-716-824

Abstract: Reinforcement learning (RL) techniques have emerged as powerful tools for optimizing energy systems, offering the potential to enhance efficiency, reliability, and sustainability. This review paper provides a comprehensive examination of the applications of RL in the field of energy system optimization, spanning various domains such as energy management, grid control, and renewable energy integration. Beginning with an overview of RL fundamentals, the paper explores recent advancements in RL algorithms and their adaptation to address the unique challenges of energy system optimization. Case studies and real-world applications demonstrate the efficacy of RL-based approaches in improving energy efficiency, reducing costs, and mitigating environmental impacts. Furthermore, the paper discusses future directions and challenges, including scalability, interpretability, and integration with domain knowledge. By synthesizing the latest research findings and identifying key areas for further investigation, this paper aims to inform and inspire future research endeavors in the intersection of reinforcement learning and energy system optimization.

Keywords: energy systems; reinforcement learning; optimization; deep learning

1. Introduction

The pursuit of energy efficiency embodies the strategic utilization of technology to minimize energy consumption while maintaining or enhancing the performance of systems across various domains, including industrial operations, power grids, civilian infrastructure, military applications, and Internet of Things (IoT) ecosystems. Achieving higher energy efficiency is paramount in the global endeavor towards sustainability, offering a multi-faceted spectrum of benefits such as significant cost reductions, diminished environmental footprints, and bolstered energy security. The automation of system operations and performance through cutting-edge artificial intelligence (AI) methodologies stands at the forefront of this quest, heralding a new era of efficiency and intelligence in energy management.

Reinforcement learning, a sophisticated branch of machine learning inspired by behavioral psychology, presents a paradigm where intelligent agents learn to make decisions autonomously to maximize cumulative rewards in novel and evolving environments. This methodology, particularly in its advanced form of deep reinforcement learning (DRL), which combines RL with the computational power of neural networks, has demonstrated remarkable proficiency in navigating complex challenges. Its applications span from mastering strategic games like chess and Go to advancing the fields of robotics and autonomous vehicular navigation, highlighting its versatility and potential.

In the realm of energy efficiency, the adaptive nature and online learning capabilities of DRL are drawing increasing interest for their ability to dynamically respond to the evolving demands of energy systems. Through varied neural network architectures, from the foundational multi-layer perceptrons to sophisticated recurrent networks like Long

Short-Term Memory (LSTM) or Gated Recurrent Units (GRUs), DRL offers a rich toolkit for modeling and optimizing energy systems under diverse and changing conditions.

As the global demand for energy surges amidst the urgency to mitigate environmental impacts and facilitate sustainable development, the complexity and unpredictability of modern energy systems have escalated. These systems, marked by variable demand, intermittent renewable sources, and the challenges of grid integration, call for innovative optimization strategies capable of navigating their inherent dynamics and uncertainties.

Reinforcement learning, with its ability to learn from direct interaction with the environment without relying on predefined models or assumptions, emerges as a potent solution to these challenges. Unlike conventional optimization techniques, RL's experiential learning approach equips it to adeptly manage the nonlinear dynamics and the unpredictability of contemporary energy systems.

This review critically assesses the efficiency of reinforcement learning in the optimization of energy systems, delving into RL's foundational principles, its relevance to energy optimization, and a comprehensive analysis of its application in this domain through the scholarly literature. This paper looks at different examples and evaluates different reinforcement learning algorithms in solving problems to highlight what RL does well and where it struggles when dealing with the complex issues of energy systems. Moreover, it ventures into the societal ramifications of deploying RL-driven optimization solutions and outlines prospects for future studies. In this review, we aim to add to the discussion about moving to cleaner energy sources and explore innovations in the optimization of energy systems.

2. Background and Motivation for Using RL Methods

2.1. Basic Formulation of Energy Efficiency

One of the base concepts in energy system optimization is the objective function. It seeks to either minimize costs or maximize efficiency, considering various operational and environmental factors. In the case of cost minimization, the formulation can be expressed as follows (1):

$$\min_x C(x) = \sum_{t=1}^{T} (C_t \cdot x_t + f(x_t)) \quad (1)$$

where:

- $C(x)$ is the total cost function;
- C_t represents cost coefficients at time t;
- x_t are the decision variables related to energy production or consumption at time t;
- $f(x_t)$ encapsulates other cost factors such as fuel costs and operational and maintenance costs.

Sometimes, there are capacity or operational constraints that need to be satisfied as follows (2):

$$a_t \leq x_t \leq b_t, \forall t \quad (2)$$

where a_t, b_t are lower and upper bounds for x_t. As for demand fulfillment, we use the following (3):

$$\sum_{i=1}^{n} x_{t,i} = D_t, \forall t \quad (3)$$

where D_t is the total demand at time t.

However, it is often the case that the optimization method needs to satisfy multiple constraints simultaneously. It is therefore difficult in practice to choose one of the conventional optimization techniques over the others.

2.2. Conventional Optimization Techniques

In energy system optimization, several conventional optimization methods are commonly used to address various operational and planning challenges. These methods are designed to improve efficiency, reliability, and cost-effectiveness in managing energy resources and demand.

Linear programming, for instance, is a widely used method in energy systems for optimizing a linear objective function, subject to linear equality and inequality constraints. It is particularly useful for tasks such as cost minimization and load dispatching where the relationships can be linearized. LP provides solutions that are globally optimal if the problem is convex. A similar technique is Integer Programming (IP). It extends linear programming by restricting some or all of the variables as integers. This is useful in energy system optimization for decisions that require discrete choices, like the number of generators to run or units of equipment to activate. A more advanced approach is Mixed-Integer Linear Programming (MILP)—it combines LP and IP to handle problems involving both continuous and discrete variables. MILP is extensively used in the planning and operation of power systems, including unit commitment and the scheduling of energy resources, where decisions about which power plants to run and their operating levels need to be made simultaneously. Quadratic Programming, on the other hand, is used when the objective function is quadratic, which is common in cost optimization problems involving power generation. It can optimize parabolic functions subject to linear constraints, applicable in the optimization of fuel consumption and emission levels. For problems that can be broken down into simpler subproblems and then solved recursively, dynamic programming is often used. For instance, it is used for solving multi-stage decision-making processes like hydrothermal scheduling, where the output from various power sources needs to be optimized over time. In nonlinear problems and constraints, there are techniques called Nonlinear Programming. Finally, when there are uncertainties in input data, such as future demand, fuel prices, or renewable output, stochastic optimization methods are employed. Techniques like Stochastic Programming can model these uncertainties as random variables to make more robust decisions under uncertainty.

These conventional methods have provided the backbone for decision-making in energy systems for decades, offering robust frameworks for optimizing the complex operations and planning tasks required in the energy sector.

2.3. Disadvantages of Conventional Optimization Methods

Conventional optimization methods typically rely on predefined models and assumptions that may not accurately capture the complexities and dynamics of real-world energy systems. These methods often struggle to adapt to changes in the environment, such as fluctuating demand, renewable energy integration, and unforeseen operational disruptions. In addition, many conventional methods are model-dependent, requiring a precise and comprehensive understanding of all system variables and interactions. In the context of energy systems, where variables and conditions can change unpredictably (e.g., weather impacts on renewable sources), maintaining up-to-date models can be both challenging and resource-intensive. Furthermore, scaling conventional optimization methods to large, complex systems such as national power grids can be computationally expensive and inefficient. These conventional methods often face difficulties in handling the high dimensionality and the multi-objective nature of modern energy systems without significant simplifications. Finally, energy systems are increasingly influenced by stochastic elements like renewable energy sources, which introduce variability and uncertainty. Conventional methods often require complex and computationally expensive stochastic optimization techniques to address these elements, which can still fall short in real-time or highly unpredictable contexts.

2.4. Motivation for RL-Based Methods

Reinforcement-learning-based methods offer several compelling advantages for optimizing energy systems, particularly due to their inherent flexibility and adaptability. Unlike conventional methods that require complete models of the environment, RL can derive optimal strategies directly through system interactions. This feature enables RL to continuously adapt to new data and changing conditions, which is essential in dynamic and complex energy systems where variables frequently change. Additionally, RL is uniquely suited to handle environments characterized by high uncertainty and variability. This capability is crucial for effectively integrating intermittent renewable energy sources such as wind and solar, which experience significant output fluctuations due to changing weather conditions.

Moreover, RL methods excel in making real-time decisions based on current state observations, providing significant operational benefits for tasks such as demand response and real-time grid balancing. This is a notable improvement over traditional optimization methods, which often require model reruns or recalculations that are not feasible on a minute-to-minute basis. Furthermore, RL can operate effectively with minimal information about the system's dynamics, an advantage in scenarios where complete data may not be available or practical to collect.

Lastly, RL facilitates the simultaneous optimization of multiple objectives, enabling the balancing of cost, reliability, and sustainability in energy management. This capacity for multi-objective optimization aligns well with the complex trade-offs required in modern energy systems, making RL an increasingly preferred approach in the field of energy system optimization. A visual comparison is structured in Table 1.

Table 1. A comparison between conventional and RL-based optimization methods.

Aspect	Traditional Optimization Methods	Reinforcement Learning (RL)
Flexibility	Constrained by the need for accurate models; struggle with adapting to changes in the environment such as fluctuating demand and renewable integration.	Highly adaptable to dynamic and complex environments. Capable of continuous learning and adjustment as system variables change.
Handling Uncertainty	Often require complex and resource-intensive stochastic optimization to address uncertainties like fluctuating fuel prices or renewable outputs.	Inherently designed to handle high uncertainty and variability, making it ideal for integrating intermittent renewable energy sources like wind and solar.
Decision-Making	Decision-making is based on reruns of models or recalculations, which may not be feasible in real-time scenarios.	Excels in making real-time decisions based on current-state observations, which provide operational benefits for tasks like demand response and grid balancing.
Information Requirements	Requires detailed, comprehensive models of all system variables and interactions, which can be challenging and resource-intensive in maintaining up-to-dateness.	Can operate effectively even with minimal information about the system's dynamics, which is an advantage when complete data may not be available.
Optimization Objectives	Typically focus on a single objective like cost minimization or load dispatching; handling multiple objectives can require significant simplifications.	Supports simultaneous optimization of multiple objectives, such as minimizing cost while maximizing reliability and sustainability, aligning well with the complex trade-offs required in modern energy systems.
Computational Efficiency	Scaling to large, complex systems such as national power grids can be computationally expensive and inefficient.	Although computationally intensive, RL's ability to learn and adapt can offset the computational demand through more targeted and efficient processing.
Suitability	Well suited for stable environments with well-understood dynamics where changes are gradual and predictable.	Best suited for environments where rapid adaptation is needed, as well as for managing systems with high levels of unpredictability and operational dynamics.

3. Reinforcement Learning

RL encompasses foundational concepts crucial to its operation. An agent, representing the decision-maker, is described as "an abstract entity (usually a program) that can make observations, takes actions, and receives rewards for the actions taken, and transitioning to new states based on actions taken. The overarching objective for the agent lies in learning a policy that dictates optimal actions in various states, with the aim of maximizing cumulative rewards over time [1]. Given a history of such interactions, the agent must make the next choice of action to maximize the long-term sum of rewards. To do this well, an agent may take suboptimal actions which allow it to gather the information necessary to later take optimal or near-optimal actions with respect to maximizing the long term sum of rewards" [2]. Software agents have the capability to act either by following hand-coded rules or by learning how to act through the utilization of machine learning algorithms. Reinforcement learning constitutes one such subarea of machine learning.

Formally, most reinforcement learning problems can be described through a Markov Decision Process (MDP). An MDP is delineated as the tuple $\{S, A, T, R\}$, where S denotes a set of states, A stands for a set of actions, T represents the transitional probability, and R denotes the reward function. Within MDP environments, a learning agent selects and executes action $a_t \in A$ at a current state $s \in S$ at time t. Upon transitioning to the state $s_{t+1} \in S$ at time $t+1$, the agent receives a reward r_t. The primary objective of the agent is to maximize the discounted sum of rewards from time t to infinity, referred to as the return R_t, which is defined as follows:

$$R_t = r_{t+1} + \gamma^1 r_{t+2} + \gamma^2 r_{t+3} + \ldots = \sum_{k=0}^{\infty} \gamma^k r_{t+k+1} \tag{4}$$

where γ is a discount factor, specifying the degree of importance of future rewards.

The agent chooses its actions according to a policy π, which is a mapping from states to actions. Each policy is associated with a state-value function $V^{\pi}(s)$, which predicts the expected return for state s, when following policy π:

$$V^{\pi}(s) = E[R_t | s_t = s] \tag{5}$$

where E [.] indicates the expected value. The optimal value of state s, $V^*(s)$, is defined as the maximum value over all possible policies:

$$V^*(s) = \max_{\pi} E\left[\sum_{t=0}^{\infty} \gamma^t R(s_t, a_t) | s_0 = s, a_t = \pi(s_t)\right] \tag{6}$$

Related to the state-value function is the action-value function $Q^{\pi}(s)$, which gives the expected return when taking action a in state s and following policy π thereafter:

$$Q^{\pi}(s, a) = E[R_t | s_t = s, a_t = a] \tag{7}$$

The optimal Q-value of state–action pair (s, a), is the maximum Q-value over all possible policies:

$$Q^*(s, a) = \max_{\pi} E\left[\sum_{t=0}^{\infty} \gamma^t R(s_t, a_t) | s_0 = s, a_t = a, a_{t>0=}\pi(s_t)\right] \tag{8}$$

An optimal policy $\pi^*(s)$ is a policy whose state-value function is equal to (6).

In refining the RL framework and its application, researchers have emphasized the importance of accurately modeling the environment's dynamics through MDPs and continually refining the estimation of value functions and policies based on the agent's experiences. This process enables RL agents to adapt to complex, dynamic environments effectively, paving the way for innovative solutions in various domains, including energy system optimization [1].

3.1. Model-Based Learning

Model-based learning, a pivotal subset of reinforcement learning strategies, emphasizes the construction and utilization of an environmental model to inform decision-making processes. This approach hinges on the agent's ability to estimate or learn a model that encapsulates the dynamics of the environment, specifically the transition probabilities between states and the outcomes associated with various actions. By using this model, the agent can engage in sophisticated planning and decision-making to optimize long-term rewards. This section delves into the intricacies of model-based learning, exploring its mechanisms, advantages, and the challenges it faces, particularly in complex domains like energy system optimization.

3.1.1. Estimation of Environmental Dynamics

At the heart of model-based learning lies the construction of a model that accurately represents the environment's dynamics. This model typically includes the following:

- Transition probabilities $T\ (s' \mid s, a)$ which predict the likelihood of transitioning from a current state s to a new state s' due to the given action a.
- Reward functions $R\ (s,\ a,\ s')$, which estimate the immediate reward received after transitioning from state s to state s' due to action a.

These components are derived from observed interactions within the environment, allowing the agent to forecast future states and rewards based on its actions. The fidelity of these estimates is crucial, as it directly affects the agent's ability to make informed decisions.

3.1.2. Planning and Decision-Making

With a model of the environment in place, the agent employs planning algorithms to navigate the decision space efficiently. Techniques such as dynamic programming, Dyna, and Prioritized Sweeping offer structured methods for iteratively improving policy decisions based on the model's predictions [1]. More sophisticated approaches like Monte Carlo Tree Search (MCTS) and rollout algorithms expand the agent's capability to explore and evaluate complex action sequences, leading to the formulation of optimal or near-optimal policies. These methods balance the exploration of uncharted actions with the exploitation of known strategies to maximize cumulative rewards.

3.1.3. Advantages of Model-Based Learning

The strategic advantage of model-based learning resides in its predictive capacity, which enables an agent to anticipate the consequences of actions without needing to physically execute them in the environment. This foresight allows for a more efficient use of available data, reducing the sample size required to achieve effective policies. Furthermore, by capturing the environment's dynamics, model-based methods can adapt to changes or uncertainties in the environment with greater agility, enhancing the agent's performance and robustness in dynamic settings.

3.1.4. Challenges and Considerations

Despite these advantages, model-based learning faces significant challenges, particularly in environments characterized by complexity and uncertainty, such as energy systems. The accuracy of the environmental model is paramount; however, capturing the intricate dynamics of complex systems can be exceedingly difficult. Errors in the model can lead to suboptimal decision-making, undermining the efficacy of the approach. Moreover, the memory and computational requirements for maintaining and updating the model can be substantial, particularly for large-state and action spaces, where the complexity of the model may grow quadratically with the size of the state space and linearly with the action space, noted as $O(\mid S \mid^2 \mid A \mid)$.

Recent advancements in model-based RL, including the integration of deep learning techniques, have shown promise in addressing some of these challenges. Algorithms like Deep Dyna-Q [3] and Model-Based Policy Optimization (MBPO) [4] incorporate neural networks to enhance the accuracy of environmental models and the efficiency of policy optimization, even in complex and high-dimensional spaces. These innovations have extended the applicability of model-based learning, opening new avenues for optimizing energy systems through more accurate and scalable modeling techniques.

3.2. Model-Free Learning

Model-free learning strategies represent a pivotal branch of reinforcement learning, being particularly effective when an explicit model of the environment is not available or is too complex to formulate. Unlike model-based methods that require an understanding of the environment's dynamics for planning and decision-making, model-free approaches learn optimal policies through direct interaction with the environment. In this learning paradigm, an agent updates state or state–action values based on observed samples. In that way, the need for a pre-learned model of the environment is not required. The agent relies instead on the accumulation of samples to guide its decision-making processes towards optimizing the cumulative rewards over time [1].

Central to model-free learning is the notion of learning through trial and error, where the agent iteratively refines its policy based on the feedback received from the environment in the form of rewards. This method enables the agent to adaptively navigate the decision space and converge towards an optimal or near-optimal policy, even in the face of uncertainty and complexity inherent in the environment. The ability to learn without a model is particularly advantageous in dynamic systems, such as sustainable energy and electric systems, where the state space can be vast or continuous, and the environment's dynamics are influenced by stochastic elements like renewable energy sources and variable consumer demand [5].

Prominent Algorithms in Model-Free Learning

A classic example of model-free learning algorithm is Q-learning. It learns by updating the value of state–action pairs using observed rewards and the estimated future value, without requiring a model of the environment's dynamics. The evolution of Q-learning into Deep Q-Networks (DQNs) employs deep neural networks to manage high-dimensional state spaces, thereby extending the applicability of Q-learning to more complex scenarios. Double Q-learning, introduced by van Hasselt [6], and further refined in the Double DQN (DDQN) framework [7], addresses the overestimation bias observed in traditional Q-learning by maintaining two separate estimators (Q-tables) and updating them alternately, enhancing the accuracy of value approximation. Another example is Policy Gradient Methods. They offer an alternative approach within model-free learning, optimizing policy parameters directly to maximize expected cumulative rewards. This category includes algorithms like Proximal Policy Optimization (PPO) and Trust Region Policy Optimization (TRPO), which have been instrumental in advancing the application of RL in continuous action spaces. These methods are particularly suited for optimizing the control and operation of energy systems, where actions can be continuous, and the objective is to enhance system efficiency and reliability [8]. Yet, another example is True Online Temporal-Difference Learning, as detailed by [9]. This method exemplifies the continuous refinement of model-free methods, offering a more sophisticated approach to updating value functions that combines the benefits of both TD (lambda) and Q-learning. This method represents a significant advancement in the efficiency and effectiveness of model-free learning algorithms, further broadening their potential application areas.

The application of model-free learning to energy systems is motivated by the need for adaptive solutions capable of managing the uncertainty and variability introduced by renewable energy sources and fluctuating demand. By employing algorithms like DQNs and PPO, RL can optimize energy consumption, improve demand response, and enhance the overall efficiency of energy systems without relying on precise models of system dynamics, thus overcoming the limitations of traditional optimization techniques [5]. Despite their effectiveness, model-free methods come with their computational and memory requirements, typically necessitating space proportional to the product of the number of states and actions, denoted as $O(|S||A|)$. However, advancements in computational resources and algorithmic efficiency have made these methods increasingly feasible for real-world applications, including those in sustainable energy and electric systems.

3.3. RL Relevance to Energy System Optimization

Reinforcement learning techniques have garnered considerable attention for their potential applicability to energy system optimization tasks. One area of interest lies in demand-side management, where RL algorithms can dynamically adjust energy consumption patterns in response to changing conditions, thereby enhancing overall system efficiency and reliability [10]. For instance, RL-based control strategies have been explored for load balancing in smart grids, optimizing the operation of distributed energy resources (DERs), and scheduling energy-intensive tasks in industrial facilities [11,12]. Moreover, RL has shown promise in addressing complex optimization problems in power generation and distribution. By learning optimal control policies from historical data and real-time feedback, RL algorithms can improve the dispatch of renewable energy sources, reduce transmission losses, and enhance grid stability [13]. Recent studies have investigated the integration of RL with advanced control techniques to optimize the operation of wind turbines, microgrids, and energy storage systems [13,14]. Furthermore, RL-based approaches have been applied to energy market optimization, where they can facilitate strategic decision-making and risk management for market participants. By learning from historical market data and simulating future scenarios, RL models can support energy traders in optimizing bidding strategies, portfolio management, and hedging against price volatility [15,16]. Research in this area has emphasized the need for RL algorithms capable of handling large-scale, uncertain environments and adapting to evolving market dynamics [15].

In addition to operational optimization, RL holds promise for addressing long-term planning and policy-making challenges in the energy sector. By modeling the interactions between different stakeholders, infrastructure investments, and regulatory frameworks, RL-based simulations can inform decision-makers about the potential impacts of alternative strategies on energy affordability, environmental sustainability, and social equity [10]. Future research in this domain is expected to focus on integrating RL with system dynamics models, multi-agent simulations, and optimization algorithms to support holistic energy planning and policy analysis [10,17].

Overall, the versatility and adaptability of RL make it a promising tool for addressing diverse optimization challenges in energy systems. By applying advances in algorithmic techniques, computational resources, and domain-specific knowledge, researchers can harness the full potential of RL to drive innovation and transformation in the energy sector.

4. Challenges in Energy System Optimization

Optimizing energy systems is a multifaceted endeavor critical for ensuring sustainable energy supply, reducing environmental impacts, and meeting growing global energy demands. However, this pursuit is fraught with challenges stemming from the inherent complexity, dynamics, and uncertainties characterizing energy systems. The complexity arises from the interplay of various factors, including fluctuating energy demand patterns, the integration of intermittent renewable energy sources, and the complexities of grid management [18]. The integration of renewable energy sources, such as solar and wind power, presents a particularly daunting challenge. These sources exhibit inherent intermittency and variability, making their integration into the grid a nontrivial task [19]. The unpredictable nature of renewable energy generation necessitates advanced forecasting techniques and robust management strategies to ensure grid stability and reliability. Furthermore, the growing decentralization of energy generation, coupled with the proliferation of distributed energy resources like rooftop solar panels and electric vehicles, adds layers of complexity to grid integration efforts [20]. In addition, grid integration issues extend beyond managing renewable energy variability to encompass the broader challenge of balancing energy supply and demand in real time while maintaining grid stability. The increasing complexity of the grid, coupled with the need to accommodate diverse energy resources and fluctuating demand patterns, underscores the importance of grid flexibility and resilience [20]. However, traditional optimization approaches, while useful in many contexts, often fall short in addressing the complexities and uncertainties inherent in modern energy systems. These approaches typically rely on simplified models and assumptions that may not capture the nuances of real-world energy dynamics [21]. As a result, they may struggle to adapt to dynamic changes in energy supply and demand, leading to suboptimal solutions.

In the face of these challenges, innovative approaches are needed to enhance energy system optimization. Reinforcement learning emerges as a promising solution for addressing the complexities inherent in sustainable energy and electric systems. As a versatile class of optimal control methods, experiences, simulations, or searches may use reinforcement learning to derive value estimates in highly dynamic, stochastic environments. Its interactive nature fosters robust learning capabilities and the ability to adapt without the need for explicit models of system dynamics. This property makes reinforcement learning particularly well suited for addressing the complex nonlinearities and uncertainties present in sustainable energy and electric systems.

5. Applications of Reinforcement Learning in Energy Systems

In this section, we outline the prominent applications of reinforcement learning techniques in energy systems, providing examples and insight from recent papers.

5.1. Demand Response Optimization

Demand response represents a pivotal strategy within modern energy systems and aims to adjust consumer power consumption to match supply availability, enhance grid stability, and optimize energy costs. The integration of reinforcement learning into demand response optimization processes has emerged as a transformative approach, using the capability of RL algorithms to dynamically adapt to the fluctuating nature of energy markets and grid conditions [22].

RL's core strength in demand response optimization lies in its ability to learn and adapt strategies based on real-time data and feedback loops. By continuously interacting with the energy system, RL agents develop strategies that encourage or discourage power usage during specific periods, effectively shifting demand to off-peak times or when renewable energy availability is high. This adaptive learning process is crucial for maintaining grid balance and optimizing energy costs in the face of renewable energy integration and varying demand patterns [23]. Several examples underscore the potential of RL in demand response optimization. For instance, a study by Zhang et al. [24] demonstrated how an RL-based system could effectively reduce peak demand and energy costs in a residential community by dynamically adjusting the operation of HVAC systems and electric vehicles in response to price signals. Similarly, research by Mocanu et al. [25] employed deep Q-networks to optimize the charging schedules of electric batteries, highlighting significant improvements in energy savings and peak shaving.

The application of RL in demand response optimization offers a promising avenue for enhancing the efficiency and sustainability of energy systems. Through its capacity for adaptive learning and dynamic decision-making, RL facilitates the development of sophisticated DR strategies that can respond effectively to the challenges posed by renewable integration, variable demand, and the evolving landscape of energy markets. As RL algorithms continue to advance, their role in demand response and broader energy system optimization is poised to expand, heralding a new era of intelligent energy management.

One of the primary challenges is the accurate modeling of consumer behaviors, which are influenced by a wide range of factors including personal preferences, habits, and responsiveness to DR signals. Traditional RL models may struggle to capture this complexity, leading to suboptimal DR strategies. A promising solution lies in the adoption of multi-agent reinforcement learning (MARL) frameworks, where each agent can represent an individual consumer or a specific group of devices within the energy system [19]. This granular approach allows for the modeling of diverse consumer behaviors and interactions within the system, enhancing the overall effectiveness of DR strategies. In addition, studies by [26] provide a robust framework for managing power distribution across networked microgrids efficiently and safely, ensuring that both local and global constraints are met. The later research presents a Supervised Multi-Agent Safe Policy Learning (SMAS-PL) method aimed at optimizing power management in networked microgrids with a focus on maintaining safe operational practices. It addresses the common challenges in reinforcement learning where black-box models may not adhere to operational constraints, potentially leading to unsafe grid conditions. Unlike conventional RL that might overlook crucial operational constraints, this method integrates constraints directly into the policy-learning process. It utilizes gradient information from these constraints to ensure that the policy decisions are both optimal and feasible under grid operational limits. A distributed consensus-based optimization algorithm is introduced for training policy functions across multiple agents. The approach significantly reduces the need for re-solving complex optimization problems and offers a scalable solution to real-time decision-making in power distribution.

The fluctuating nature of energy prices, driven by market dynamics and the variability of renewable energy production, poses another significant challenge. Accurate price prediction is crucial for effective DR, as it informs the decision-making process regarding when to encourage or discourage energy consumption. Advanced RL models that incorporate deep learning techniques, such as Deep Q-Networks (DQN), have shown promise in improving the accuracy of price predictions. These models can process high-dimensional data and learn complex patterns, enabling more precise forecasting of energy prices and better informed DR strategies [27]. Furthermore, another model-free methodology [28] explores the utilization of reinforcement learning framework for managing power in networked microgrids under incomplete information scenarios, making traditional model-based optimization challenging. This approach employs a distinctive bi-level hierarchical structure, unlike the typical single-agent, flat-structure setup in standard RL, and innovatively handles incomplete information through aggregated data and predictive modeling. Additionally, it incorporates advanced adaptive learning techniques with a forgetting factor, allowing it to adjust to changing system conditions in real time, a significant enhancement over simpler RL methods that cannot dynamically adapt without retraining. This adaptive capability makes the system robust to changes in system parameters and operational conditions. In addition, the RL approach respects the privacy of microgrid data by not requiring detailed user or operational data, aligning with concerns about data privacy and confidentiality in smart grids. Compared to traditional optimization methods, the RL approach shows better adaptability and faster computational times because it learns from past experiences and predicts optimal power distribution without detailed system models.

Maintaining user comfort while optimizing energy consumption is a critical concern in DR. Aggressive DR strategies may lead to discomfort or inconvenience, undermining user participation and satisfaction. To address this issue, RL models must be designed with mechanisms to balance energy savings against comfort criteria. This can be achieved by incorporating user feedback into the learning process, allowing the RL model to adjust its strategies based on user preferences and comfort levels. Furthermore, reward functions in RL algorithms can be carefully designed to penalize actions that significantly compromise user comfort, ensuring that the optimization process remains aligned with user satisfaction goals.

The integration of renewable energy sources introduces additional variability and uncertainty into the energy system. RL algorithms must be capable of adapting to rapid changes in energy availability, especially from sources like solar and wind power, which are highly dependent on environmental conditions. Techniques such as robust reinforcement learning and stochastic optimization models have been developed to enhance the resilience of RL-based DR strategies to the uncertainties associated with renewable energy [23].

Overall, despite the considerable challenges, ongoing advancements in algorithmic techniques and model architectures offer promising solutions in this energy domain.

Through the adoption of multi-agent systems, deep learning enhancements, user-centric models, and robust optimization techniques, RL can effectively address the complexities of demand response, paving the way for more efficient, reliable, and user-friendly energy management systems.

5.2. Renewable Energy Integration

The integration of renewable energy sources into existing power grids represents a crucial step towards achieving sustainability and reducing dependency on fossil fuels. However, the intermittent and unpredictable nature of renewable energy sources like wind and solar power poses significant challenges to energy grid stability and efficiency. Reinforcement learning offers a suite of methodologies for addressing these challenges, enabling more effective integration of renewable energies through adaptive and intelligent control systems.

Accurate forecasting of renewable energy production is important for effective grid integration. Deep learning techniques have shown significant promise in predicting energy output from renewable sources. By continuously learning from historical data and real-time environmental conditions, these algorithms adaptively improve their predictions, accounting for the variability inherent in renewable energy production, such as in the work of [24]. Furthermore, energy storage systems play a critical role in mitigating the intermittency of renewable energy sources. There are examples of RL algorithms used to optimize the charging and discharging cycles of these storage systems, ensuring that stored energy is available during periods of high demand or low renewable production. As we discussed, model-free RL methods are able to learn optimal storage management policies, thus helping to smooth out fluctuations into the grid [29].

The integration of renewables requires adaptive grid control mechanisms capable of managing the variability and uncertainty associated with these energy sources. RL algorithms offer a dynamic solution by learning to adjust grid operations in response to changing energy production and demand patterns. This includes optimizing the dispatch of renewable energy, managing load balancing, and ensuring grid stability. Multi-agent systems, where different agents represent various components of the energy system, enable a coordinated approach to grid control [27].

Another application of RL in renewable energy integration is demand-side management (DSM). By influencing energy consumption patterns on the demand side, RL algorithms can help match demand with the availability of renewable energy. This might involve shifting energy-intensive processes to times of high renewable production or incentivizing reduced consumption during shortages. RL-driven DSM strategies not only support the integration of renewables but also promote energy efficiency and conservation among consumers [19].

While RL offers powerful tools for renewable energy integration, challenges remain in terms of scalability, data quality, and model interpretability. Future research directions include the development of more sophisticated RL models that can handle complex, multi-dimensional energy systems, the integration of RL with other artificial intelligence techniques for enhanced prediction and optimization, and the exploration of ways to make RL models more transparent and interpretable to facilitate their adoption in energy system management.

5.3. Smart Grid Applications

Smart grid technologies aim to modernize traditional power systems by integrating advanced communication, control, and monitoring capabilities. The advent of smart grids heralds a significant leap toward enhancing the efficiency, reliability, and sustainability of power systems. Smart grid optimization encompasses a wide array of functionalities including but not limited to real-time demand response, distributed energy resource management, and advanced metering infrastructure. Reinforcement learning is a pivotal technology in this arena, offering dynamic and adaptive solutions to the multifaceted challenges faced by smart grids.

Smart grids facilitate a more interactive approach to demand response and load balancing, which is crucial for maintaining grid stability and efficiency. There are several examples in that area that excel in balancing energy supply and demand in real time. Through continuous interaction with the grid and analysis of consumption patterns, RL models can predict peak-load periods and adjust demand accordingly, either by directly controlling smart appliances or through pricing incentives to consumers [30]. The best DRL model, as identified by Gallego et al. [31], achieves a complete listing of optimal actions for the forthcoming hour 90% of the time. This level of precision underscores the potential of DRL in enhancing the flexibility of smart grids, providing a robust mechanism for adjusting grid operations in response to real-time conditions and forecasts. This predictive prowess is pivotal for maintaining operational efficiency and optimizing the dispatch of energy resources within the grid.

Furthermore, RL enables the dynamic allocation of energy resources to where they are most needed, ensuring optimal load distribution across the grid. The management of distributed energy resources, such as rooftop solar panels, wind turbines, and battery storage systems, is another critical aspect of smart grid optimization. RL algorithms are adept at optimizing the operation of DERs, enhancing grid resilience and facilitating the integration of renewable energy sources. By dynamically adjusting the dispatch of DERs based on current grid conditions and forecasted demand, RL contributes to a more flexible and responsive grid system [32]. Gallego et al. [31] illustrate the application of deep reinforcement learning techniques, specifically Deep Q-Networks (DQNs), to select optimal actions for managing grid components.

Maintaining optimal voltage and frequency levels is essential for grid stability and the efficient operation of electrical devices. RL algorithms, through their ability to learn and adapt from environmental feedback, can be effectively employed for real-time voltage and frequency regulation. By continuously monitoring grid conditions and adjusting control mechanisms, such as capacitor banks and voltage regulators, RL ensures that voltage and frequency remain within desired ranges, even under fluctuating demand and generation conditions [22].

Despite the promising applications of RL in smart grid optimization, several challenges remain, including the scalability of RL solutions, integration with existing grid infrastructure, and the protection of consumer privacy in data-driven applications. Addressing these challenges requires ongoing research and development, as well as collaboration between industry, academia, and regulatory bodies.

Future directions in smart grid optimization with RL include the exploration of more advanced RL techniques, such as deep reinforcement learning and multi-agent systems, to manage the increasing complexity of smart grids. In conclusion, RL offers a versatile and powerful toolset for optimizing smart grid operations across a range of dimensions. Through its adaptive and predictive capabilities, RL not only enhances grid efficiency and reliability but also plays a crucial role in the transition toward more sustainable and resilient energy systems.

5.4. Grid Management and Control

Grid management and control are essential for ensuring the stability, reliability, and efficiency of modern power systems. Reinforcement learning techniques offer valuable tools for optimizing grid operation, addressing challenges such as voltage control, reactive power management, and distribution system optimization.

One notable application of RL in grid management is voltage control, which involves regulating voltage levels within acceptable limits to ensure the safe and efficient operation of the grid. RL algorithms can optimize voltage control strategies by adjusting the set points of voltage regulators and reactive power devices in real time. For example, a study by [33] applied RL techniques to optimize voltage control in distribution networks, achieving improved voltage stability and reduced energy losses.

Another important aspect of grid management is reactive power management, which involves the control of reactive power flow to maintain system stability and voltage regulation. RL-based controllers can optimize reactive power dispatch strategies, minimizing system losses and improving voltage stability. For instance, a study by Wang et al. [34] developed an RL-based reactive power dispatch algorithm for power systems, achieving an improved voltage profile and reduced system losses. Furthermore, RL techniques can be applied to optimize distribution system operation, particularly in the context of integrating distributed energy resources such as solar panels, wind turbines, and energy storage systems. RL-based controllers can optimize DER dispatch strategies, maximizing renewable energy utilization and grid reliability. For example, a study by Kumar et al. [35] used RL techniques to optimize the operation of a microgrid with renewable energy sources, achieving improved grid stability and reduced energy costs. Moreover, RL algorithms can be applied to address challenges related to grid congestion and load balancing. By optimizing the scheduling of energy flows and grid assets, RL-based controllers can alleviate congestion and improve grid efficiency. For example, a study by [36] applied RL techniques to optimize energy scheduling in distribution networks, achieving reduced congestion and improved grid reliability.

5.5. Summary

The summarized RL techniques and their applications are presented in Table 2.

Table 2. Reinforcement learning applications in energy systems.

RL Method	Applicable Energy System Scenarios	Benefits	Challenges
Deep Learning Techniques	All energy systems, including microgrids, transmission, and distribution systems.	Enhance predictive accuracy for demand and supply variations; optimize operational efficiency.	Require extensive training data; computationally intensive; may overfit without proper tuning.
Deep Q-Networks (DQNs)	Smart grids, particularly in demand response and battery management.	Offer robust decision-making under uncertainty; effective in policy optimization for load balancing.	Prone to overestimation of Q-values; require large and diverse datasets to train effectively.
Multi-Agent RL (MARL)	Distributed systems including microgrids and decentralized smart grids.	Facilitates cooperative control and decentralized decision-making; improves resilience and flexibility.	Coordination complexity increases with number of agents; risk of conflicting objectives.
Policy Gradient Methods	Voltage and frequency regulation in smart grids.	Directly optimize policy; capable of handling continuous action spaces.	Suffer from high variance in gradient estimates; slow convergence in environments with high-dimensional action spaces.

The table provides a comprehensive comparison of various RL methods and their applications across different energy system scenarios, outlining both benefits and challenges associated with each method. Deep learning techniques are applied universally across energy systems, enhancing predictive accuracy and operational efficiency, but require extensive data and significant computational resources. Deep Q-Networks (DQNs) are particularly effective in smart grids for demand response and battery management, offering robust decision-making capabilities, though they are susceptible to the overestimation of Q-values. Multi-Agent RL (MARL) is ideal for distributed systems like microgrids, promoting cooperative control and decentralized decision-making, yet faces challenges with coordination complexity and potential objective conflicts. Lastly, Policy Gradient Methods are utilized in smart grids for voltage and frequency regulation due to their direct policy optimization, but their application is hindered by slow convergence and high variance in gradient estimates. The presented comparison underscores the suitability of each RL approach depending on the specific needs and constraints of the energy system scenario, highlighting the critical balance between their benefits and the inherent challenges.

6. Discussion

In recent years, the application of reinforcement learning techniques in optimizing energy systems has witnessed several notable trends and phenomena, driven by advancements in technology, shifts in energy policies, and emerging challenges in the energy sector.

One trend is the increasing integration of RL algorithms with advanced data analytics techniques, such as machine learning and deep learning [3,7,24,37]. This integration enables RL-based controllers to use large volumes of data to learn complex patterns and relationships in energy systems, leading to improved decision-making and optimization performance. Furthermore, the rise of edge computing and Internet of Things (IoT) devices has enabled RL algorithms to be deployed directly at the device level, allowing for real-time control and optimization of distributed energy resources and smart grid components.

Another trend is the growing emphasis on decentralized and distributed energy systems, driven by the proliferation of renewable energy sources, advancements in energy storage technologies, and evolving consumer preferences. RL techniques play a crucial role in optimizing the operation of distributed energy resources, microgrids, and virtual power plants, enabling greater grid flexibility, resilience, and sustainability. Furthermore, the emergence of peer-to-peer energy trading platforms and community-based energy initiatives presents new opportunities for RL-based optimization and coordination among energy prosumers.

Effective RL applications depend significantly on the quality, granularity, and timeliness of the data collected. Diverse data sources, from real-time sensor outputs in smart grids to historical energy consumption records, provide the necessary inputs for training and refining RL models. The integration of IoT devices [38] and smart meters has revolutionized data collection, enabling more precise and continuous streams of information. These technologies not only facilitate the accurate modeling of energy demand and supply dynamics [39] but also support the training of RL algorithms that can predict and adapt to complex energy patterns efficiently. Additionally, advanced data preprocessing techniques such as normalization, anomaly detection, and feature engineering are essential to prepare raw data for effective learning and performance optimization [40]. This comprehensive data infrastructure supports the adaptive and predictive capabilities of RL models, ultimately driving their success in optimizing energy systems.

Moreover, the increasing complexity and interconnectedness of modern energy systems pose significant challenges for traditional optimization methods, which often struggle to handle nonlinear dynamics, uncertainty, and stochastic environments. RL algorithms offer a promising alternative by providing adaptive, model-free optimization approaches that can learn and adapt to changing system conditions over time. Additionally, the application of RL techniques in multi-agent systems and game-theoretic frameworks opens up new avenues for addressing strategic interactions and market dynamics in energy systems.

One interesting phenomenon is the convergence of RL with other emerging technologies, such as blockchain and quantum computing, to address key challenges in energy system optimization. Blockchain technology offers decentralized and transparent mechanisms for peer-to-peer energy trading, while quantum computing promises exponential gains in computational power for solving complex optimization problems. By integrating RL with these technologies, researchers and practitioners can explore novel approaches for optimizing energy systems at scale, leveraging the strengths of each technology to address specific challenges and constraints.

Furthermore, the increasing focus on energy efficiency and sustainability has led to the development of novel RL-based approaches for optimizing energy consumption and reducing environmental impact. RL algorithms can learn adaptive control strategies for energy-intensive processes, such as industrial manufacturing and HVAC systems, to minimize energy waste and improve overall efficiency. Additionally, RL-based controllers can optimize energy consumption in smart buildings and homes, by using real-time data and user preferences to achieve significant energy savings without compromising comfort or functionality.

In addition to traditional RL algorithms, there is a growing interest in meta-learning and transfer learning techniques for energy system optimization. Meta-learning enables RL agents to learn how to learn, adapting quickly to new environments and tasks with limited data. Transfer learning allows RL models trained on one task or domain to be transferred and fine-tuned for related tasks or domains, accelerating the learning process and improving generalization performance. These approaches hold promise for addressing data scarcity and domain-specific challenges in energy system optimization, particularly in scenarios where labeled data or expert knowledge is limited.

Moreover, the democratization of RL tools and platforms has made them more accessible to researchers, engineers, and practitioners in the energy sector. Open source RL libraries, such as TensorFlow 2.16.1, PyTorch 2.2, and OpenAI Gym 0.26.2, provide user-friendly interfaces and pre-trained models that enable rapid prototyping and experimentation. Additionally, cloud-based RL platforms offer scalable computing resources and collaborative environments for developing and deploying RL-based solutions for energy system optimization. This democratization of RL technology is driving innovation and empowering stakeholders across the energy value chain to explore new opportunities for efficiency improvement and sustainability.

However, despite the significant progress and advancements in RL-based energy system optimization, several challenges and limitations remain. One major challenge is the scalability and computational complexity of RL algorithms, particularly in large-scale energy systems with millions of decision variables and uncertain dynamics. Addressing this challenge requires the development of scalable RL algorithms, distributed optimization techniques, and efficient approximation methods that can handle the complexity and heterogeneity of real-world energy systems. Another challenge is the interpretability and transparency of RL models, which are often viewed as black boxes due to their complex decision-making processes and nonlinear dynamics. Ensuring the accountability and trustworthiness of RL-based controllers is crucial for gaining acceptance and adoption in safety-critical applications, such as energy grid management and control. Developing explainable RL techniques and model validation frameworks is essential for providing insights into the decision-making process and fostering trust among stakeholders.

In summary, while RL holds great promise for optimizing energy systems and advancing sustainability goals, addressing the remaining challenges and limitations will require interdisciplinary collaboration, innovative research, and real-world experimentation. By harnessing the power of RL algorithms, energy stakeholders can unlock new opportunities for efficiency improvement, grid reliability, and environmental stewardship, paving the way for a more sustainable and resilient energy future.

7. Conclusions

The application of reinforcement learning in optimizing energy systems offers transformative potential, addressing key challenges within the sector such as efficiency, reliability, and sustainability. This research has demonstrated that RL's capability to adapt to dynamic environments and handle complex, multi-objective optimization tasks can significantly enhance how energy systems operate. Particularly, RL's proficiency in real-time decision-making and its robustness against uncertainties prove advantageous over traditional optimization methods. These attributes facilitate the integration of renewable energy sources, optimize demand response, and improve grid management, thereby supporting the transition to more sustainable energy systems. However, challenges such as scalability, computational demand, and the need for interpretable models remain and must be addressed through continued interdisciplinary research. Looking forward, the implementation of RL could reshape energy management practices, making them more adaptive, efficient, and aligned with global sustainability goals.

Author Contributions: Conceptualization, S.S.; literature search, S.S.; review and analysis, S.S. and D.G.; citations and references, D.G.; discussion, D.G. All authors have read and agreed to the published version of the manuscript.

Funding: This research was funded by the Research and Development Sector at the Technical University of Sofia.

Data Availability Statement: No new data were created or analyzed in this study. Data sharing is not applicable to this article.

Acknowledgments: This research is supported by the Aerospace Equipment and Technologies Laboratory at the Technical University of Sofia and the Human–Computer Interactions and Simulation Laboratory (HSL) at the University of Plovdiv "P. Hilendarski".

Conflicts of Interest: The authors declare no conflicts of interest.

References

1. Sutton, R.S.; Barto, A.G. *Reinforcement Learning: An Introduction*; MIT Press: Cambridge, MA, USA, 2018.
2. Langford, J. Efficient exploration in reinforcement learning. In *Encyclopedia of Machine Learning*; Sammut, C., Webb, G.I., Eds.; Springer: Boston, MA, USA, 2011; pp. 1–5. [CrossRef]
3. Liu, Y.; Swaminathan, A.; Liu, Z. Deep Dyna-Q: Integrating Planning for Task-Completion Dialogue Policy Learning. In Proceedings of the 57th Annual Meeting of the Association for Computational Linguistics, Florence, Italy, 28 July–2 August 2019. [CrossRef]
4. Janner, M.; Fu, J.; Zhang, M.; Levine, S. When to Trust Your Model: Model-Based Policy Optimization. *Adv. Neural Inf. Process. Syst.* **2019**, *32*, 12519–12530. [CrossRef]
5. Yang, T.; Zhao, L.; Li, W.; Zomaya, A.Y. Reinforcement learning in sustainable energy and electric systems: A survey. *Annu. Rev. Control* **2020**, *49*, 145–163. [CrossRef]
6. Van Hasselt, H. Double Q-learning. Advances in Neural Information Processing Systems 23. In Proceedings of the 24th Annual Conference on Neural Information Processing Systems, Vancouver, BC, Canada, 6–9 December 2010; Volume 2010, pp. 2613–2621.
7. Van Hasselt, H.; Guez, A.; Silver, D. Deep reinforcement learning with double Q-learning. In Proceedings of the Thirtieth AAAI Conference on Artificial Intelligence, Phoenix, AZ, USA, 12–17 February 2016; p. 30. [CrossRef]
8. Schulman, J.; Levine, S.; Abbeel, P.; Jordan, M.; Moritz, P. Trust region policy optimization. In Proceedings of the 32nd International Conference on Machine Learning, Lille, France, 6–11 July 2015; Volume 37, pp. 1889–1897.
9. Van Seijen, H.; Mahmood, A.R.; Pilarski, P.M.; Machado, M.C.; Sutton, R.S. True online temporal-difference learning. *J. Mach. Learn. Res.* **2016**, *17*, 1–40.
10. Iqbal, S.; Sarfraz, M.; Ayyub, M.; Tariq, M.; Chakrabortty, R.K. A comprehensive review on residential demand side management strategies in smart grid environment. *Sustainability* **2021**, *13*, 7170. [CrossRef]
11. Ali, K.H.; Sigalo, M.; Das, S.; Anderlini, E.; Tahir, A.A.; Abusara, M. Reinforcement Learning for Energy-Storage Systems in Grid-Connected Microgrids: An Investigation of Online vs. Offline Implementation. *Energies* **2021**, *14*, 5688. [CrossRef]
12. Paudel, A.; Hussain, S.A.; Sadiq, R.; Zareipour, H.; Hewage, K. Decentralized cooperative approach for electric vehicle charging. *J. Clean. Prod.* **2022**, *364*, 132590. [CrossRef]
13. Puech, A.; Read, J. An improved yaw control algorithm for wind turbines via reinforcement learning. In *Machine Learning and Knowledge Discovery in Databases. ECML PKDD 2022*; Amini, M.R., Canu, S., Fischer, A., Guns, T., Novak, P.K., Tsoumakas, G., Eds.; Lecture Notes in Computer Science; Springer: Cham, Switzerland, 2023; Volume 13717. [CrossRef]
14. Mocanu, E.; Mocanu, D.C.; Nguyen, P.H.; Liotta, A.; Webber, M.E.; Gibescu, M.; Slootweg, J.G. On-line building energy optimization using deep reinforcement learning. *IEEE Trans. Smart Grid* **2018**, *9*, 3254–3264. [CrossRef]
15. Zhang, Z.; Zhang, D.; Qiu, R.C. Deep reinforcement learning for power system applications: An overview. *Front. Inf. Technol. Electron. Eng.* **2019**, *20*, 1358–1372. [CrossRef]
16. Glavic, M. (Deep) Reinforcement learning for electric power system control and related problems: A short review and perspectives. *Annu. Rev. Control* **2019**, *48*, 22–35. [CrossRef]
17. Alabi, T.M.; Aghimien, E.I.; Agbajor, F.D.; Yang, Z.; Lu, L.; Adeoye, A.R.; Gopaluni, B. A review on the integrated optimization techniques and machine learning approaches for modeling, prediction, and decision making on integrated energy systems. *Renew. Energy* **2022**, *194*, 822–849. [CrossRef]
18. DeCarolis, J.; Daly, H.; Dodds, P.; Keppo, I.; Li, F.; McDowall, W.; Pye, S.; Strachan, N.; Trutnevyte, E.; Usher, W.; et al. Formalizing best practice for energy system optimization modelling. *Appl. Energy* **2017**, *194*, 184–198. [CrossRef]
19. Palensky, P.; Dietrich, D. Demand Side Management: Demand Response, Intelligent Energy Systems, and Smart Loads. *IEEE Trans. Ind. Inform.* **2011**, *7*, 381–388. [CrossRef]
20. Cicilio, P.; Glennon, D.; Mate, A.; Barnes, A.; Chalishazar, V.; Cotilla-Sanchez, E.; Vaagensmith, B.; Gentle, J.; Rieger, C.; Wies, R.; et al. Resilience in an evolving electrical grid. *Energies* **2021**, *14*, 694. [CrossRef]

21. Rehman, A.U.; Wadud, Z.; Elavarasan, R.M.; Hafeez, G.; Khan, I.; Shafiq, Z.; Alhelou, H.H. An optimal power usage scheduling in smart grid integrated with renewable energy sources for energy management. *IEEE Access* **2021**, *9*, 9448087. [CrossRef]
22. Vázquez-Canteli, J.R.; Nagy, Z. Reinforcement learning for demand response: A review of algorithms and modeling techniques. *Appl. Energy* **2019**, *235*, 1072–1089. [CrossRef]
23. Ruelens, F.; Claessens, B.J.; Vandael, S.; De Schutter, B.; Babuska, R.; Belmans, R. Residential demand response of thermostatically controlled loads using batch Reinforcement Learning. *IEEE Trans. Smart Grid* **2017**, *8*, 2149–2159. [CrossRef]
24. Zhang, C.; Wang, X.; Li, F.; He, Q.; Huang, M. Deep learning–based network application classification for SDN. *Trans. Emerg. Telecommun. Technol.* **2018**, *29*, e3302. [CrossRef]
25. Mocanu, D.C.; Mocanu, E.; Stone, P.; Nguyen, P.H.; Gibescu, M.; Liotta, A. Scalable training of artificial neural networks with adaptive sparse connectivity inspired by network science. *Nat. Commun.* **2018**, *9*, 2383. [CrossRef]
26. Zhang, Q.; Dehghanpour, K.; Wang, Z.; Qiu, F.; Zhao, D. Multi-Agent Safe Policy Learning for Power Management of Networked Microgrids. *IEEE Trans. Smart Grid* **2021**, *12*, 1048–1062. [CrossRef]
27. Francois-Lavet, V.; Henderson, P.; Islam, R.; Bellemare, M.G.; Pineau, J. An introduction to deep reinforcement learning. *Found. Trends Mach. Learn.* **2018**, *11*, 219–354. [CrossRef]
28. Zhang, Q.; Dehghanpour, K.; Wang, Z. A Learning-Based Power Management Method for Networked Microgrids under Incomplete Information. *IEEE Trans. Smart Grid* **2020**, *11*, 1193–1204. [CrossRef]
29. Deng, R.; Yang, Z.; Chow, M.-Y.; Chen, J. A Survey on Demand Response in Smart Grids: Mathematical Models and Approaches. *IEEE Trans. Ind. Inform.* **2019**, *11*, 570–582. [CrossRef]
30. Siano, P. Demand response and smart grids—A survey. *Renew. Sustain. Energy Rev.* **2014**, *30*, 461–478. [CrossRef]
31. Gallego, F.; Martín, C.; Díaz, M.; Garrido, D. Maintaining flexibility in smart grid consumption through deep learning and deep reinforcement learning. *Energy AI* **2023**, *13*, 100241. [CrossRef]
32. Dall'Anese, E.; Simonetto, A. Optimal Power Flow Pursuit. *IEEE Trans. Smart Grid* **2018**, *9*, 942–959. [CrossRef]
33. Meng, X.; Zhang, P.; Xu, Y.; Xie, H. Construction of decision tree based on C4.5 algorithm for online voltage stability assessment. *Int. J. Electr. Power Energy Syst.* **2020**, *117*, 105668. [CrossRef]
34. Wang, N.; Li, J.; Hu, W.; Zhang, B.; Huang, Q.; Chen, Z. Optimal reactive power dispatch of a full-scale converter based wind farm considering loss minimization. *Renew. Energy* **2019**, *136*, 317–328. [CrossRef]
35. Kumar, S.; Krishnasamy, V.; Kaur, R.; Kandasamy, N.K. Virtual energy storage-based energy management algorithm for optimally sized DC nanogrid. *IEEE Syst. J.* **2022**, *16*, 231–239. [CrossRef]
36. Jiang, X.; Wu, L. Residential power scheduling based on cost efficiency for demand response in smart grid. *IEEE Access* **2020**, *8*, 197379–197388. [CrossRef]
37. Christoff, N.; Bardarov, N.; Nikolova, D. Automatic Classification of Wood Species Using Deep Learning. In Proceedings of the 2022 International Conference on INnovations in Intelligent SysTems and Applications (INISTA), Biarritz, France, 8–12 August 2022; pp. 1–5. [CrossRef]
38. Al-Fuqaha, A.; Guizani, M.; Mohammadi, M.; Aledhari, M.; Ayyash, M. Internet of Things: A Survey on Enabling Technologies, Protocols, and Applications. IEEE Commun. *Surv. Tutor.* **2015**, *17*, 2347–2376. [CrossRef]
39. Pourbehzadi, M.; Niknam, T.; Kavousi-Fard, A.; Yilmaz, Y. IoT in Smart Grid: Energy Management Opportunities and Security Challenges. In *Internet of Things. A Confluence of Many Disciplines, IFIPIoT 2019*; Casaca, A., Katkoori, S., Ray, S., Strous, L., Eds.; Springer: Cham, Switzerland, 2020; Volume 574, pp. 236–249. [CrossRef]
40. Alasali, F.; Haben, S.; Foudeh, H.; Holderbaum, W. A Comparative Study of Optimal Energy Management Strategies for Energy Storage with Stochastic Loads. *Energies* **2020**, *13*, 2596. [CrossRef]

MDPI AG
Grosspeteranlage 5
4052 Basel
Switzerland
Tel.: +41 61 683 77 34

Electronics Editorial Office
E-mail: electronics@mdpi.com
www.mdpi.com/journal/electronics

www.ingramcontent.com/pod-product-compliance
Lightning Source LLC
Chambersburg PA
CBHW040839250926
51850CB00007BA/1357
9783725871827